CONVERSATIONS WITH CRONKITE

Conversations
with Cronkite

WALTER CRONKITE AND DON CARLETON

FOREWORD BY MORLEY SAFER

Dolph Briscoe Center for American History
The University of Texas at Austin
Austin, Texas

Library of Congress Control Number: 2010927869

Frontispiece: Cronkite with his trademark pipe, undated, Walter Cronkite Papers, Dolph Briscoe Center for American History, the University of Texas at Austin (DI_0546 the Cronkite Papers.

Contents

Foreword

WALTER CRONKITE WORE HIS MANTLE as the most trusted man in America exceedingly lightly. As honored as he was by the phrase, he never actually believed it. For the forty-five years that we were friends and colleagues, I cannot recall a single moment of the pomposity, arrogance, or self-importance that is the common curse of anchormen everywhere. If he even came close to uttering an oracular pronouncement, his wife, Betsy, would puncture him with a glance, or, if necessary, an acid-dipped aside.

Cronkite was no saint, however, and as you make your way through Don Carleton's warts-and-all *Conversations with Cronkite*, you will discover a man who could be as ornery and petty and vain as most of us, but also a man who by nature could be relied upon always to do the right thing.

He was a reporter's reporter, who could have been the model for Rudyard Kipling's poem "If."

> *If you can talk with crowds and keep your virtue,*
> *Or walk with kings—nor lose the common touch,*
> . . . .
> *If you can fill the unforgiving minute*
> *With sixty seconds' worth of distance run,*
> *Yours is the earth and everything that's in it.*

To say that Walter Cronkite enjoyed being Walter Cronkite would be an understatement. The kid from St. Joe, raised in Kansas City and Houston, never quite got over the fact that he had made it into the big leagues, into the wonderfully overstuffed candy store that is New York City.

Some years ago, my wife, Jane, and I were having dinner with Walter and Betsy shortly after they returned from a cruise of the Baltic. In retirement, Walter's love of the sea made the offer of first-class passage in exchange for a couple of lectures irresistible. But knowing how people mobbed him and how they wanted to have their photographs taken with him, I asked why he accepted so many of these cruise line offers. Before he could answer, Betsy interjected, rather wearily: "You don't understand, Morley: Walter loves people."

While I know that there were individual people—plenty of them—whom Walter found unlovable in the extreme, he had an abiding affection and respect and fascination for humanity as a whole. Indeed he may have "walked with kings," but he truly believed in the common man.

Some years after he left the *CBS Evening News*, Walter made what amounted to a political confession when he told an audience that he was, and always had been, a liberal. It caused something of a sensation at the time, given that, over the years, CBS News had been accused by various Neanderthals of the right as being a hotbed of liberal bias. The fact is, Walter was scrupulous in maintaining and defending the objectivity and independence of the broadcasts he oversaw. In short, he only rarely let his own opinion leach into his reporting, and the few times that he did, he made it clear that it was his opinion.

It must be said that this attempt to maintain objectivity was not exclusive to Cronkite. It was part of the ethos of CBS News that was established by the company's founder, William S. Paley. A few months before Paley died in 1990, I was summoned to his apartment on the Upper East Side of New York. He was seeking an interlocutor, someone to engage with him in a conversation that would become an oral history of CBS. I was, in effect, being auditioned for the role. Paley was most interested in talking about the business and entertainment successes of CBS back in the beginning, when radio was in its infancy, while I, for obvious reasons, wanted to question him about the beginnings of the news division. He finally, with some impatience, acceded with a few short sharp sentences: "Look, I want to make it clear that I didn't have that much interest in the news . . . I was investing my money in the entertainment business, a whole new form of entertainment, back in the thirties. And in any new business, you've got to establish trust, and the best way to do that was to offer the news in as fair a way as possible and keep it separate from the entertainment and money-making side. If they trust the news, they'll trust the network. So don't think I'm some kind of news hero like Murrow; it was just a smart business decision."

It may have been a smart business decision, but the fact is that Paley regarded the news division as a crown jewel, and even though his reporters sometimes embarrassed him (and more often infuriated him), one of his great pleasures was to hang out in the overseas bureaus and get filled in on the latest political gossip.

Thus Walter Cronkite was simply maintaining "the trust," which will be evident as you make your way through this oral history, these conversations with Cronkite.

In Don Carleton, Cronkite found the perfect interlocutor, meaning a good listener, a rare quality in a time of incessant blather and blog, in which everyone seems to be either ranting or relieving themselves of buckets of banalities—and nobody listens. Don became a probing yet companionable Boswell to Cronkite's Dr. Johnson, forcing him, through well-informed questions and observations, to separate reality from myth.

These conversations may also be an apposite epitaph for this age of journalistic anxiety, for in them you will, depending on your age, discover or rediscover a time when journalism, for all its faults, really counted. It may also help you understand how and why generations of young men and women simply fell in love with a job. And no one fell harder than Walter Cronkite.

MORLEY SAFER

support of the ... broadcast on the Discovery Channel in 1996. I was delighted to serve as a historical advisor to the series. After the series was broadcast, I placed the transcript of our interviews in the Walter Cronkite Papers at the Briscoe Center. At Walter's request, access to the transcript was restricted, mainly because ... knew that there was a significant amount of material that he ...

...ter's Life to keep it a reasonable ... point he might do another book, ... useful. Later, during one of ...cha's Vineyard, Walter told me ...

...xplained that he had signed the agreement several years ... another memoir. He asked me to ...and that Random House had been extremely patient with ... and correct some of the factual ...it was time to get to work. "The problem is that I have ...e to edit some of the material ...perspective on my own life," Walter said. "Not only ...be ...the things that I've done sort of ... ...rief ...a working ... ...cript, ...he quest... ... He ...ed back, ...hat our ...he woul... ...for me ...l gaze." ... ...g my ...o think a... ...n our ...the sense... ...y. ...nded him... ...whole se... ...l ...ed someone... ...y cente... ...a, and rec... ...ting a... ...book fro... ...Walter wa... ...l magazine... ...s career, ...He needed ... ...to those ... ...d, of cour... ...formation t... ...knowledge o... ...s papers, my ...an oral historian, and my professional interest ...he ...of journalism, he believed that I was well

...eat ...f ...a ...l ...th ...ies ...He ...roject, it was during our work sessions, especially when we ...sn't ...ere on his sailboat and at his house on Martha's Vineyard that ...atter for nearly two years before our

Introduction

MY RELATIONSHIP WITH WALTER CRONKITE began in 1988 in my capacity as director of the Center for American History (now the Dolph Briscoe Center for American History) at the University of Texas at Austin. As a historian interested in the relationship between politics and the news media, I was aware of the research value of the archival records and personal papers documenting the history of the reporting and editorial processes. I also knew that little was being done at the time to preserve these records and papers. To help fill this void in historical documentation, I decided to establish a news media history archive at the Center and ask Walter Cronkite to donate his papers as the founding collection. Cronkite was an obvious choice. Not only was he the most widely respected and influential broadcast journalist of his era, but he also attended the University of Texas. Happily, Walter accepted my invitation with enthusiasm. He loved the idea of an archive that would document the history of how news is gathered, produced, and disseminated.

For several months in 1988 and 1989, Walter and I worked closely as we assembled his papers and transferred them to Austin. During that period, we also became good friends. He flattered me by reading a book that I had written about the role newspapers had played in fomenting anticommunist hysteria during the post–World War II Red Scare. He also learned of my work as an oral historian with a specialty in twentieth-century U.S. history. Early one morning in November 1989, Walter called me at home. We were engaged in small talk when he said suddenly that he had a problem he wanted to discuss. Thinking he meant a problem with his papers, I began to describe the status of that project. He interrupted, however, and said, "No, no. That's fine. This isn't about archiving my papers. My problem is an agreement that I have with Random House to write my autobiography."

Walter explained that he had signed the agreement several years earlier, and that Random House had been extremely patient with him. But it was time to get to work. "The problem is that I have a limited perspective on my own life," Walter said. "Not only that, but the things that I've done sort of run together in my mind." As a working journalist, he had concentrated on breaking news and the quest for the next news scoop. "I've rarely, if ever, looked back," he said. "I've always gone on to the next thing." As he would later say to me more than once, "I'm not one to navel-gaze." The result was a kind of mental block when he tried to think about his past. He stressed that it wasn't a problem in the sense that he was losing his memory. Whenever someone reminded him about some past incident, it usually triggered a whole set of memories. "That's what I need," he said. "I need someone to trigger those memories, push me to clarify them, and record and transcribe my responses. I think I can write my book from that."

In addition, Walter was well aware of the extensive number of newspaper and magazine articles and books that discussed various aspects of his career, especially as the anchor of the *CBS Evening News*. He needed someone to research that material so he could respond to those publications' criticisms and claims about his career. And, of course, he needed someone to research his papers for information that he could use in his autobiography. Because of my knowledge of and easy access to his papers, my experience as an oral historian, and my professional interest in the history of journalism, he believed that I was well positioned to help him. "I know you are busy as hell," Walter said, "but would you consider working with me?" It took me about one-tenth of a second to say yes.

We agreed that I would do the research and conduct, transcribe, and edit the interviews. I also would advise him as he wrote his autobiography and, in his own words, "be a damn pest" in pushing him to get it written. But I would not be a coauthor, ghostwriter, or have credit in an "as told to" fashion. It was essential to him that he write every word of his book, and, in the end, that is exactly what he did. The tapes of our interviews and the raw transcript would become a part of his papers. I readily agreed to those ground rules.

Every three to four months, for a period stretching more than three years, Walter and I met for two or three days, sometimes longer, for me to interview him and to record the recollections of his extraordinary life and career. Those interviews were conducted in his office at CBS, his home in Manhattan, his summer residence on Martha's Vineyard, and in the British Virgin Islands on his sailboat, the *Wyntje*. My work sessions with Walter were squeezed in between his numerous speaking engagements, documentary projects, and sailing trips. Betsy Cronkite, his wife and essential partner in everything that he did, provided moral support for the project as well as a great deal of wry humor to lighten our workload. Betsy was herself the source of an unending stream of hilarious but insightful anecdotes. In hindsight, I regret that her comments and stories weren't recorded as well.

Although I had known Walter for nearly two years before our project, it was during our work sessions, especially when we were on his sailboat and at his house on Martha's Vineyard, that I got to know him more intimately. People we admire from a distance sometimes turn out to be less than admirable when they are seen "off camera" or in private. I'm happy to report that with Walter, the exact opposite was the case. The better I knew Walter, the more I liked and admired him. One of the most famous people in the United States at the height of his career, Walter was utterly free of the pretensions and affected self-importance that too often afflict the highly celebrated. He was an easy person to be around, always courteous and attentive to his guests, the perfect host. And he had a wonderful sense of humor. I haven't known anyone who enjoyed a good joke better than Walter Cronkite—the bawdier and more irreverent the better. Walter could engage in small talk, but he much preferred candid and lively conversations about substantive issues. He was one of the most curious individuals I have ever known. He had an almost insatiable hunger for knowledge, especially about how things worked and why. At one point during our work on his memoir, Walter told me that he would love to know what system shoe stores used to ensure that they had the correct sizes of shoes available for their customers. "Most of the shoe stores I've been in," Walter reflected, "aren't warehouses. They're relatively small. I'd like to know how they figured that one out."

At least with me, Walter's curiosity was focused on the world around him, not the world within him. During our conversations, he generally resisted my attempts to get him to be self-reflective. Walter made it clear that questions requiring personal introspection bored and annoyed him. That didn't keep me from asking him those questions, however, and he did answer a few. I'm not a psychologist, and I refuse to speculate much about the reasons why Walter resisted self-reflection, but I never believed that it was because he had something to hide, and I know that he was not a shallow thinker. I just think that he felt his inner life was no one's business. Frankly, I can't fault him for that. One point to this discussion about introspection, however, is that Walter not only tolerated my questions that annoyed him, he also appreciated them. Whenever we had a testy moment because of one of those questions, sooner or later he made it clear to me that he found the question to be useful and necessary, no matter how irritating, and that he didn't want me to be afraid to ask him anything. And that was the course I took.

Eventually, Walter and I produced more than sixty hours of recordings and more than a thousand pages of transcript, which served as the base source for Walter's autobiography, *A Reporter's Life*. Walter read every word of the raw transcript, and he made numerous factual corrections. And, per his request, I was a pest during a brief period when he had serious doubts about actually writing the book. After we had completed our recordings, several months passed without any sign that Walter was writing. My wife, Suzanne, and I joined Walter and Betsy for dinner in a small Italian restaurant on the Upper East Side of Manhattan. During our meal, I urged Walter to move forward. He listened patiently and then informed us that he had just about decided that the memoir wasn't worth the effort. "For Pete's sake, Don, I left the *Evening News* thirteen years ago," Walter argued. "That's a lifetime in television. Nobody remembers me or cares, for that matter. At my age, I need to enjoy my sailboat instead of sweating over a book about myself." I suspected that his complaint had more to do with his lack of interest in self-reflection than anything else.

As Walter finished his argument for no book, Betsy, with a straight face, said, "Walter, a couple of those people who don't remember you are here wanting autographs." Sure enough, a young couple from the Midwest was standing behind him, waiting for a polite moment to ask Walter for his autograph. As he always did, Walter greeted them with enthusiasm and duly signed a note card. I should add that other fans stopped us as we left the restaurant and while we were on the street waiting for a taxi. In the cab, Betsy said to her increasingly sheepish husband, "It's a good thing no one remembers you, Walter. We would never get home."

Walter, of course, did complete his book, and his children and his other friends and colleagues played a much more significant role in its completion than I. His longtime associate at CBS, Sandy Socolow, and his dear friends Joe and Shirley Wershba, who have their own notable place in news media history, were key to that process. Marlene Adler, who entered Walter's life in the early 1990s as his chief of staff, also played a key role. Published by Alfred Knopf in 1996, *A Reporter's Life* shot immediately to the top of the *New York Times* nonfiction bestseller list. It remains in print fourteen years later. So much for Walter's lament about being "forgotten."

The interviews Walter and I conducted were equally important in support of the eight-part television series *Cronkite Remembers*, broadcast on the Discovery Channel in 1996. I was delighted to serve as a historical advisor to the series. After the series was broadcast, I placed the transcript of our interviews in the Walter Cronkite Papers at the Briscoe Center. At Walter's request, access to the transcript was restricted, mainly because he knew that there was a significant amount of material that he had had to leave out of *A Reporter's Life* to keep it a reasonable length. He thought that at some point he might do another book, and the transcript might prove useful. Later, during one of my visits to his place on Martha's Vineyard, Walter told me that he wasn't going to write another memoir. He asked me to clean up the raw transcript and correct some of the factual errors. He also encouraged me to edit some of the material from the transcript and publish it to benefit the Briscoe Center's news media history program. We had done a few brief follow-up interviews that weren't in the original transcript, which provided additional material for this publication. He also suggested that the title should reflect the fact that our interviews really were discussions because of his need for me to talk to him about information that I had found during my research—a need that resulted in my talking much more in our interviews than is typical in a traditional oral history.

I agreed to edit and publish a book, but my professional responsibilities as the administrator of a major history center and my obligations to complete two books that I was writing at the time made it difficult. Time passed. And then Walter died on July 17, 2009. I attended his funeral at Saint Bartholomew's Episcopal Church in Manhattan and, two months later, CBS's impressive tribute to Walter at the Lincoln Center. It was at the latter event that I decided to put aside everything else and complete the book you now hold in your hands. Walter Cronkite played a significant role in my personal and professional life for two decades. And like millions of my fellow baby boomers, I "knew" television's Walter Cronkite for thirty-five years, several decades before I actually met him. So, among a number of other important reasons, publishing *Conversations with Cronkite* is an act of personal closure for me, giving me an opportunity to revisit the most exciting and satisfying four years of my professional life.

. . . . .

An explanation about how I edited *Conversations with Cronkite* is in order. I have moved and matched some portions of our conversations to fit within relevant topics. More importantly, I have included material that either was left out of *A Reporter's Life* entirely or was discussed more fully in our conversations than in that book. This book is not just a retread version of *A Reporter's Life*; it is a companion to that book. *A Reporter's Life* is Walter Cronkite's definitive memoir. There are a few stories in *Conversations* that are relatively close to the versions in *A Reporter's Life*, but I have included them for the sake of narrative flow or because I felt the full version of the story was livelier. I have also had to revise and edit some of my questions and comments to fit the rearranged order of discussion. Readers of *A Reporter's Life* will note that *Conversations* has minimal information about Walter Cronkite's family and his childhood in Kansas City and Houston. In addition, there are well-known episodes in his career that are missing entirely from this book, despite our having discussed them in detail during our working sessions. The reason for their absence is that *A Reporter's Life* includes all of our conversations about those subjects, and although they are not word for word, his comments in our interviews were very close to those he included in *A Reporter's Life*.

DON CARLETON

not many p...

canopies over most of the sidewalks where people sat in ch...
out in front of stores to get the little bit of air there was
under the shade. I remember that the Rice Hotel, which was the
big fancy new hotel when we arrived in town, had rocking chairs
out on the sidewalk. You know, Texas was not looked upon from
...side the state as a great place. The economic opportunities
...were just beginning to be apparent.
...the late twenties and early
...think, gave Houston its big boost
...e lost jobs in the east and north,
...tunity.

...e seems to be a small industry of television analysts
...examined and interpreted the meaning behind every move
...de.

...end in Houston?

...I think it's something I have to make quite a lot of
...k, Don, because to me it's so ridiculous. This is the
...of people who have to "find them...
...the fifth grade at Woodrow Wilson
...r people
...Junior
...I was a
...re I fel
...San
..., when I
...nd I tho
...ything, y
...other
...umstances
...hers. I
...osition a
...istory
...ght have a
...intere
...occurred

...'s just s
...St. Josep

...long. My fa... ...ed in Kansas City when Dad
...the war in 1918.

...1933?

...My
...idn't
...I
...d,
...ute,
...logy
...est

...e family move to Texas in February 1927?

...as

...act that Austin was the state capital was a plus. But more
...had a strong interest in politics, so the
...portant, I liked that the University of Texas had a daily

CHAPTER ONE

From St. Joe to Austin

DON CARLETON (DC): Okay, Walter, I have several notebooks filled with factual information that we can use as we talk, but I think it'll be critical that I ask you many more "why" than "what" questions. If you don't mind, I hope we get a chance to explore your private feelings about some key moments in your life and career. Finally, I have a large number of quotes about you from television critics, historians, and memoirists that I want you to react to, especially from some who have spent time analyzing and interpreting your career.

WALTER CRONKITE (WC): That's exactly how we should proceed. But you know, Don, I've never spent any time examining my navel. And I'm bored with people who do. I wasn't conscious through any part of my career, "This is a big break; this is going to change my persona; this is going to change the way people perceive of me." That was the furthest thing in the world from my thinking then or now, or at any time in between.

DC: There seems to be a small industry of television analysts who have examined and interpreted the meaning behind every move you've made.

WC: Yeah, I think it's something I have to make quite a lot of in the book, Don, because to me it's so ridiculous. This is the same cult of people who have to "find themselves" and are worried about other people finding themselves. I know where I've been. I knew where I was at nearly all times. The only time in my whole career where I felt I was at any kind of a possible watershed was in 1964, when I was fired from anchoring our convention coverage. And I thought that very possibly that was going to change everything, you know. But that was only because of the set of circumstances that clearly

Cronkite studying as a University of Texas student, ca. 1934–1935 (DI_05818).

dictated some examination of my career position at the moment. It wasn't anything that I was thinking might have an impact on my public persona. Those things never, never occurred to me. But go ahead and fire away.

DC: Well, let's just start from the beginning. I understand you were born in St. Joseph, Missouri, in 1916. How long did you live there?

WC: Not very long. My family settled in Kansas City when Dad came back from the war in 1918.

DC: Why did the family move to Texas in February 1927?

WC: Dad went to Houston to teach at Texas Dental College. That's now part of the University of Texas at Houston. I was eleven when we moved there. Actually, I was very disappointed when we first arrived. I'd read about Texas; I did my homework. I was always a researcher, and anything that interested me I'd go to the *World Book Encyclopedia* for information. Our family owned a set. I looked up everything about Texas. I knew about the ship channel and the cotton business in Houston. I expected to see an oceangoing ship when I got off the train right on Main Street. And, of course, that wasn't true. It was weeks before we ever got out to the ship channel for me to see a ship. And that was disappointing. As a Midwest boy, I'd never seen a ship or the ocean. I also thought Houston would be a Wild West town, but there were no cowboys. There was nobody on horseback. It was all very disappointing.

DC: Would you say that in those days Houston had more of a southern culture than a western one?

WC: It was a very southern town, a very lazy town. There were not many people on the streets at the heat of day. There were canopies over most of the sidewalks where people sat in chairs out in front of stores to get the little bit of air there was under the shade. I remember that the Rice Hotel, which was the big fancy new hotel when we arrived in town, had rocking chairs out on the sidewalk. You know, Texas was not looked upon from outside the state as a great place. The economic opportunities in both Dallas and Houston were just beginning to be apparent. The boom was just beginning in the late twenties and early thirties. The oil business, I think, gave Houston its big boost despite the Depression. People lost jobs in the East and North, and moved there seeking opportunity.

DC: What schools did you attend in Houston?

WC: Well, I started out in the fifth grade at Woodrow Wilson Elementary School. After that, I attended Sidney Lanier Junior High, and then I went on to San Jacinto High School.

DC: How would you rate the quality of your education at San Jacinto High School?

WC: In journalism, it was terrific, in every respect. In other things, it was spotty. I didn't have many inspiring teachers. I did have a good civics teacher, who included a lot of history, and I'm grateful for that because I think that sparked my interest in history and in politics. And one of my English teachers was very good. The others were very bad, or at least I didn't like them. I was a teacher's pet, I guess, in a way. I kind of conned my way through a lot of courses. Teachers seemed to like me, and I ingratiated myself to them. I never failed a course in high school, although I wasn't very good in several of them. When we got to chemistry and physics, I was not very good, but I was very good in arithmetic. When I got to mathematics, I began to lose interest in algebra and trigonometry. But I didn't see much value in those subjects. I was already career oriented. I wanted to be a journalist.

DC: How did you become interested in journalism at such a young age?

WC: I had a teacher at San Jacinto High School by the name of Fred Birney, who I credit with guiding me into the journalism profession. Birney also helped me to set some professional standards very early on that I have tried to follow ever since. Birney was a newspaperman. I think he worked for the *Houston Post*. He talked the public school administrators into letting him teach journalism part-time at all of the high schools in Houston. He just made a circuit. I met him in my junior year. Birney talked me into being the sports editor of the *Campus Cub*, our school newspaper. That was my introduction to newspaper work, and I was hooked from then on.

THE UNIVERSITY OF TEXAS

DC: Why did you decide to go to the University of Texas after graduating from San Jacinto High School in Houston in May 1933?

WC: Well, I could have gone to college back in Missouri. My grandfather had a dental practice there. But honestly, I didn't think I could hack that because of the distance from home. I had no interest in staying in Houston to attend Rice Institute, because in those days Rice was more of a science and technology school. My real motivation for going to Austin was my interest in journalism, and I thought highly of the University of Texas journalism program at the time. A couple of other things attracted me to UT. I had a strong interest in politics, so the fact that Austin was the state capital was a plus. But more importantly, I liked that the University of Texas had a daily student newspaper, the *Daily Texan*. So I just knew that I wanted to go to the University of Texas.

DC: Did your parents encourage you to go to college?

WC: Yes, that was just understood. After all, my father was a professional. But money was a problem for us. One thing that helped was that I got a job as the campus correspondent for the *Houston Post* right away. I used to have a brief story almost every day, sometimes two stories. It was a pretty good little stipend, just a few dollars a week, but a few dollars a week were important during the Depression. This was during the Depression, and money was hard to come by, even for a dentist, although that may be difficult to believe for anyone who visits a dentist regularly today. My father finally decided that we could scrape the money together for me to go.

DC: Let's talk about your time at the university. Had you ever been to Austin before you enrolled?

WC: No, I hadn't. I went to Austin to visit the campus a little bit before classes began to set up my *Houston Post* business and to be there for registration week. I also went to the *Daily Texan* office. Fred Birney told me about the *Texan* and how good it was. That first visit I met D. B. Hardeman, a very nice guy who was going to be the editor that year. After school started, D. B. kind of took me under his wing, and got me pledged to his fraternity, Chi Phi. I was a lifelong friend of D. B.'s. [*Hardeman died in 1981.*]

DC: Who were your friends at the university?

WC: I was lucky in that I made friends with a couple of students who sort of became mentors. One was D. B, who had an especially keen interest in politics and showed me around the legislature. I was in a leftist campus clique that D. B. Hardeman headed. But every time I turned around on campus, I seemed to meet somebody who was really knowledgeable and very interested in being helpful. Another student mentor was Stuart Long, a journalism major. Lady Bird Johnson was a year ahead of me in journalism school. This was before she married Lyndon Johnson, and she was known as Claudia Taylor. We weren't socially connected in any way, but I knew of her. She wrote for the *Texan* occasionally. My best friend was a guy named Vance Muse Jr., whose father was a famous lobbyist in Texas. Vance had also been a classmate of mine at San Jacinto High School. He wrote a column for the *Daily Texan*.

DC: Who on the faculty had the most influence on you?

WC: Well, that would have to be DeWitt Reddick. I took his second-year reporting class. He was a marvelous teacher, highly effective. Unfortunately, I didn't get the full benefit of all that he had to offer as a teacher because I left the university before graduating.

DC: Do you have memories of other professors?

WC: I took a physics course from Dr. [C. Paul] Boner during my freshman year. I didn't do well in that class. Actually, I believe that I flunked it. Many years later, when I was covering the race to the moon and I was explaining celestial physics to a palpitating public of millions of viewers, I would worry that if poor Dr. Boner was watching me explain physics, he might be having a stroke. For Pete's sake, I couldn't even figure out in his class how a pulley worked. I still can't [*laughs*]. I also had a professor named Robert Montgomery, who had a great bushy head of hair and wore glasses. My memory of him is looking very much like a Hearst cartoon version of a Bolshevik. Montgomery was under constant attack in the legislature. They were always raising the question of Montgomery teaching Marxism at the University of Texas. Well, few of them knew what Marxism was. But I suppose my economic ideas were formed a great deal by him. I didn't take J. Frank Dobie's famous course, "Life and Literature of the Southwest," but I dropped in on some of his lectures. I think D. B. Hardeman persuaded me to go with him to listen to Dobie, who was the most famous member of the faculty. Dobie used to have informal groups of students meet at his house, and I attended some of those gatherings, usually with Stuart Long. To us younger people with literary pretensions, Dobie was a hero.

DC: I understand that you also acted in the university's Curtain Club, the student theater group?

WC: Yeah, well, I don't know, I just thought it was a good idea at the time, but I don't know what inspired me to do that. I certainly didn't do much acting. Eli Wallach, who later became a famous movie and stage actor, was a graduate of my class at the Curtain Club. Eli and I have been good friends over the years. But of course there were a lot of other famous ones around. Zachary Scott, who also became a well-known movie actor. Elaine Anderson, who married Zachary, was in my class. Elaine became a stage manager in New York. She later became John Steinbeck's third wife. Elaine and I have also been friendly ever since college days. [*Elaine Anderson Scott Steinbeck died in 2003.*]

DC: Did you join the Curtain Club to improve your voice skills for radio?

WC: No, I was just having some fun with a lot of other students who knew how to have fun. The only play I can remember acting in was *The Ninth Guest*, which was something of a disaster because of a problem I had with my glasses falling off of my nose. I had no thought of being an actor or of being able to speak on the radio. I always was intrigued with radio, but I never really thought a lot about being a radio reporter. I remember when I was in Houston and still in high school, I became friendly with a guy named Kern Tipps at KTRH radio, who became a radio legend in Texas, especially for his work as a sports announcer for the football broadcasts that the Humble Oil Company sponsored. Anyway, Kern Tipps imitated Floyd Gibbons, who was famous nationally in those days as a radio announcer and movie newsreel narrator. He talked very rapidly. Kern pasted his script together in a scroll so he wouldn't waste any time turning pages. He had this long script on the floor, and as he stood at the microphone, he ran this script along his fingers. I went down to watch him broadcast two or three times. And I kind of had a hankering to do that sort of thing, but my main interest was in newspapers.

DC: But didn't you work on the radio when you were a student at UT?

WC: Yes, I worked for KNOW Radio, which had started out as KTUT. I did five minutes of sports a day. A guy named Harfield Weedin was the station manager. I got a job as a sports reporter for the station doing this five-minute thing, and they paid me about a dollar a day. My gosh, it was a primitive setup. We had no news wires, so I had no way to get the baseball scores. Our studio was in downtown Austin, so I would go down to the alley behind the Driskill Hotel on Sixth Street to a smoke shop that had an old Western Union baseball score ticker. It carried all the major league and minor league baseball scores. They were all daytime games then. But this smoke shop had a big blackboard, and the bartender would go and read the ticker whenever he had time. He would put the latest line score up on the blackboard, along with home runs and strikeouts and everything. Well, I'd go there to get this information for my radio program. I was so terrified that I was stealing this information that I wouldn't write it down. It was one of the best bits of journalistic training I ever got. I was afraid to write it down, so I memorized it. I would sit there and I'd get a 3.2 beer, which was illegal for me to have. I sat there and studied that blackboard, memorized all those damn games, finished the beer, and ran back up this alley to the radio studio before I forgot the scores. I wrote the scores down quickly and then went on the air. I did that for about a year and never got caught.

DC: You mentioned to me that while you were a student, you saw future Texas governor W. Lee O'Daniel in the days when he peddled flour on the radio.

WC: That's right. Oh gosh, the greatest fun I had at KNOW was when I filled in, on a few occasions, announcing W. Lee O'Daniel and His Light Crust Doughboys. They were regulars on the Texas Quality Network. They broadcast from our studios whenever they came to Austin. The Texas Quality Network needed a local announcer, so they gave me the job a couple of times. That was sensational fun. They would start playing and—over the music—I would announce: "W. Lee O'Daniel and His Light Crust Doughboys are on the air!!! LIVE!!!" [*laughs*] Oh, God, nobody would've thought in those days that O'Daniel would be a governor of Texas. That was just unthinkable to me. I mean, the man was vacuous. But that was an early example of my inability to make accurate political predictions. [*laughing*]

DC: I found a story in the *Daily Texan* in 1935 announcing a new program on KNOW every Tuesday and Friday afternoon at 5:15. It says that you would create and announce all programs. The ad states that you would "include the news behind the news, and the latest gossip gathered by a corps of operatives on the campus."

WC: [*laughing*] Oh God, that must have been a heck of a program. I don't even remember it very well, to tell you the truth. We tried several things like that from time to time; none of them lasted very long. Frankly, there wasn't a great demand for our programming. KNOW was always looking for program ideas, so it wasn't difficult to talk Harfield Weedin into putting us on the air and do anything we wanted. He didn't have a lot of options. It's interesting. Harfield Weedin was doing auditions for a full-time announcer for the station, so I auditioned and he turned me down. He said that I would never really make a radio announcer. It would be best that I forget about being a broadcaster. As it turned out, that same Harfield Weedin became the general manager of Lady Bird Johnson's KTBC radio station and later the West Coast head of CBS Radio.

DC: I found some notes in your papers stating that your radio experience in Austin gave you an opportunity to be a one-time announcer on a national radio network broadcast right after you left the university.

WC: Well, I forgot about that. My gosh, that's right. I did announce once, but only once, for famed big band leader Ben Bernie on a national network. I was down in Galveston covering Bernie at Sam Maceo's Hollywood Dinner Club for the *Houston Press*. The announcer was late showing up, and the network's program director asked me if I did radio work as well. Because I had done some radio at the university, I could truthfully say yes. Actually, I may have exaggerated a little and said, "Why, of course, I've done quite a lot." I announced the first three numbers of Ben Bernie's band on the air. Bernie was the guy who first recorded "Sweet Georgia Brown." By the way, nobody hired me as a result of this performance. I mean, lightning didn't strike exactly. But I loved announcing: "Good evening, everyone, from Sam Maceo's Hollywood-on-the-Beach in Galveston." Oh, that was great. Maceo's was a legendary gambling joint, very illegal of course, that attracted the most popular bands and singers of the day. A lot of the churchgoing Houston business elite could be found in the casino on Saturdays, gambling—discreetly of course.

DC: Did you have other jobs in Austin while you were at the university?

WC: Well, I was running around getting jobs wherever I could. The truth is, I didn't go to class very often, as my student records will show. Instead, I went around trying to make a little money here and there.

DC: I understand that Vann Kennedy, who owns a television station in Corpus Christi, gave you a job while you were a student at the university. [*Kennedy died in 2004.*]

WC: That's right. I got a job working with Vann, who had the International News Service (INS) Bureau and also was publishing his own little paper. Vann taught me a great deal. He's a man of such integrity. We've remained in touch all these years. Vann had a little tiny office up in the very top of the Capitol. For some reason or other, he wasn't given space in the pressroom. He had a lot of things going besides his INS job. My guess is, he was a stringer for INS and he was by himself, which was typical of INS. It was a very thinly staffed service. Vann hired me as his office boy, and I'd cover the Senate and the House committees. I stayed with Vann until I was offered a job with the Scripps-Howard bureau in the Capitol. Scripps-Howard had three newspapers in Texas—the *Houston Press*, the *El Paso Herald Post*, and the *Fort Worth Press*. I worked practically full-time as a correspondent covering the legislature and the governor's office.

DC: Why did you drop out of the university?

WC: Well, it just sort of happened. In the spring semester of 1935, I still was allegedly going to school, but if an important legislative committee hearing was being held during class, I'd just skip class. During the summer break, I worked at the *Houston Press*. I was moving along quite rapidly and was really doing very well there. When fall came, I just didn't go back to school. I'd had a kind of a tough time at the university. Studying was a problem, and I wasn't carrying my weight at school. I was very embarrassed by it. So I stayed and continued to work for the *Houston Press*.

But despite the experience of being a terrible student, I nonetheless learned a lot by simply being on that wonderful campus and being exposed to a lot of bright fellow students and brilliant teachers. I always was rather voluble and read very heavily and could be argumentative about my ideas of life and social structure and politics and economics. I was lucky enough to be in with people like D. B. Hardeman and Stuart Long, who were good students themselves, or at least they were very aware people. But the university experience was not a wasted one for me. Although there may be a lot of dropouts around the world who are just plain old goof-off dropouts, there must be others like myself who were readers, who were aware, conscious of affairs surrounding them, that are current with the mystery of the moment and interested in the past, who read and looked up things, who learned a lot, without the formality of the classroom. So my time at the university certainly was not wasted as far as I was concerned. Nevertheless, I still wish I had stayed with it and graduated. I'd like to have gone on and done a lot of scholarly things, as I look back on it, but that wasn't my thinking at the moment. The University of Texas was a very good school then, but it's a great one now. I'm really proud of my association with UT, and apparently it's proud of me. They've made me a Distinguished Alum, despite the fact that I didn't even graduate. [*laughing*]

was trying to get a job anywhere, but my goal w
a newspaper job. This was the only time I've been unemployed
in my whole life. since the time I was a junior in high school
re   ere was about three months where I didn't ha
errified. I begged a lot of free meals from
ds.

McCormick would call stuff in

reporter
station
s a rewr
details   iley was
e way it   r. Harry
tabloid   been a
ver got   im. We had
y on tha   we drank
o think
all of th
owever, t
s today.
formance
sources.   you
ng that,   beer
would cut   ur
bably not   'm
such major   stay
wer could   ry
have to b

o

did you lea

he summer o
grandparen
io station,

DC: We

true?

WC: No! Nobody was killed. It was a minor fire. The scaffolding
burned on this new city hall building. His wife lived in a

CHAPTER TWO

The Young Journalist

DC: You stayed in Houston to work for the *Press* in the fall of 1935. The *Houston Press* was always last in circulation, behind the *Houston Chronicle* and the *Houston Post*.

WC: That's right, which meant that we tended to focus on more sensational stories. I'm afraid that the professional standards weren't high at the *Press*. I'm very proud of journalism today because we have progressed a great deal in the years since I was a cub reporter. The practice before World War II on many newspapers was to publish stories that were largely fiction based on few key facts. That was the case with the police reporters particularly. On stories that didn't matter much to anybody except those who participated in them, the reporters would give a rewrite man on the desk only bare facts of the story. Rewrite guys were known to be pretty good novelists. They would make up a great human-interest story around a very few facts. When I was on rewrite, I wrote stories that were highly fanciful, really. And everybody else did. It was just part of the game.

Our chief crime reporter, Harry McCormick, would call stuff in from the police station, and he would give you a bare outline of the story. As a rewrite guy, it was expected that you would fill in a lot of details, conversations, and dialogues until you imagined the way it was. I wouldn't be sure that doesn't go on at some of the tabloid newspapers today. I read stuff in there that I doubt ever got said. Of course, newspapers in Houston had no monopoly on that behavior. It was the case everywhere. But I really do think there's a major effort by most newspapers today to get all of the facts and all sides of the story. I do deplore, however, the increasing use of the unnamed source in newspapers today. I think it detracts from the otherwise credible performance of the newspapers when they indulge in too many unnamed sources. The *New*

York Times has gotten too far along in doing that, for instance. If I were managing editor of the *Times*, I would cut back on that. If I managed that newspaper, I would probably not use an unnamed source ever, unless it was a story of such major importance in my community that the whistleblower could not be named and simply had to be protected. That would have to be very rare.

KCMO RADIO

DC: When did you leave Houston and move to Kansas City?

WC: In the summer of 1936, when I took my two-week vacation to visit my grandparents. When I got to Kansas City, I read that a new radio station, KCMO, had come into being. So I went to the station and asked if they needed someone to announce the news. They hired me at a salary considerably better than I was making at the *Houston Press*.

DC: KCMO had just gone on the air?

WC: Well, yes, as KCMO, but it had been on the air for a few years, operating under other call letters. Its broadcasting power was so low that you couldn't pick it up very far from the station. That didn't last long, however, because this little radio station in Kansas City was due to become a big station quickly because it was owned by allies of Thomas Pendergast, the city's political boss, whose protégé was Harry Truman. Truman had been elected to the U.S. Senate a couple of years earlier. KCMO's license was upgraded in 1936 to allow it to increase its broadcasting range considerably. I've never done research on this, but I always assumed that it was Senator Truman who got that approval for the station. Our program director was a former nightclub singer named Bob Simmons. The manager of the station, August Slicker, was an accountant who had been loaned to the station from the Crown Drug Company, which owned the station. Neither Slicker nor Simmons knew anything about broadcasting or journalism. Simmons and I had a big problem one time about reporting a fire at city hall, among other problems.

DC: What happened?

WC: One day, Simmons came to my desk and said, "Get on the air with a flash! The new city hall's on fire, and three firemen just jumped to their deaths!" I said, "No kidding, my gosh!" And I grabbed the telephone. He said, "What're you doing?" I said, "I'm checking on the story." He said, "You don't have to check on it; my wife called and told me." And I said, "I do too have to check on it." And he said, "Are you calling my wife a liar?" And I said, "No, I'm not calling your wife a liar, but I don't know the details." And he said, "I've told you the details. The new city hall building's on fire, and three firemen have jumped." I refused to go on the air with the story, so he went on the air and adlibbed a news bulletin.

DC: Well, was the fire story true?

WC: No! Nobody was killed. It was a minor fire. The scaffolding burned on this new city hall building. His wife lived in a cheap hotel across the street from this place, and she'd called, hysterical, telling him what was going on. None of it was true. That incident probably wasn't the only reason I was fired. They felt that I was getting a little big for my britches around there, perhaps. And I was fed up. This was just part of a long series of things that went on.

DC: So you were you fired from KCMO?

WC: Yeah, for insubordination and intolerance of their stupidity. I was there for a little more than one year. But I didn't like local radio. This was 1936, and we forget how recent radio was really. The 1924 election was the first one ever reported on radio. That's how new the business was.

DC: What did you do after you were fired?

WC: Oh boy, I was trying to get a job anywhere, but my goal was a newspaper job. This was the only time I've been unemployed in my whole life, since the time I was a junior in high school, really. I think there was about three months where I didn't have a job, and I was terrified. I begged a lot of free meals from relatives and friends.

DC: Were you living on your own at that time?

WC: I was in an apartment with another guy. Harry Bailey was his name. Harry worked at KCMO as a continuity writer. Harry was a funny guy, but he also was very strange. He had been a University of Missouri type, and I took a liking to him. We had adjoining desks. I was doing the news and sports, and we drank in the evenings together.

DC: Why do you say he was a strange guy?

WC: Well, I had been living at the YMCA, I think, and Harry was living in a hotel downtown. We made no money, you know. Those jobs didn't pay anything. So we were drinking beer at a bar, and I said, "You know Harry, why don't we pool our resources. I mean, you're living in this cheap hotel and I'm living at the Y. I've got to move out of there; I can't stay there very much longer. Why don't we get an apartment?" Harry said, "No, no, you don't want to live with me." And I said, "Why wouldn't I want to live with you?" I thought he was going to tell me some terrible sexual secret or something. And he said, "Well, you just wouldn't want to live with me, that's all." Well, he wouldn't tell me, and I kept nagging him about it. Finally he said, "All right. I'll tell you. I'd just burn the place down. Wherever we live, I'll burn it down. If I stay in this hotel long enough, I'm going to burn it down. I burned down my fraternity house at the university, I burned down a hotel in St. Louis, and I burned my father's house in Springfield." He said, "I drink and I get drunk, and I smoke in bed and I start fires, and you don't want to live with me." I said, "Harry, come on, you're making it up." "Yes, I do." But I talked him into taking an apartment. We weren't there a week until we had a fire. [*laughs*]

UNITED PRESS

DC: After you were unceremoniously asked to leave KCMO radio, where did you get your next job?

WC: I finally got a job with United Press in the summer of 1937. I was trying to get a job anywhere in the newspaper business, including the wire services.

DC: Didn't you meet Betsy Maxwell, your future wife, during this period?

WC: Well, I met Betsy when I was still at KCMO. She got a job as a writer of advertising copy after she graduated from the University of Missouri. I saw her come to work one day, and I was enamored when I saw this gorgeous girl coming down the hall of my office. I was stricken, absolutely stricken. But she worked in another part of the office. A couple of days passed. I hadn't arranged to meet her yet, and I was getting a little desperate. Finally, Bob Simmons came along and said, "Come on, Cronkite. We need a voice for a commercial." Commercials were all done locally then, even for national-brand products. We wrote the copy and did everything. Richard Hudnut, a cosmetics manufacturer, was one of the accounts.

Betsy had written a bit of copy for Richard Hudnut, and here she was, standing at the microphone to be the girl voice. I was to be the male voice. They handed me the copy, and we did the commercial with no rehearsal. The announcer, a guy named Moreland Murphy, said, "A street scene in Kansas City. A boy and a girl." And I said, "Hello, angel. What heaven did you drop from?" Betsy said. "I'm no angel." I said, "You look like an angel." Betsy responded, "That's because I use Richard Hudnut." Betsy didn't last long as an advertising writer. But we met over the microphone. This was the winter of 1936–1937.

DC: You knew Betsy for about four years before you were married?

WC: Before we married, yeah. I was out of town most of that time. But then I got the job with UP.

DC: Did UP send you back to Texas then?

WC: No, not immediately. I worked there on the desk at the Kansas City bureau, which at that time was one of the largest bureaus of the United Press, and it was where the wires "broke," as we called it. All the eastern wires came into Kansas City and stopped there. And everything had to be refiled for the West Coast. All the West Coast copy came in to be refiled for the East Coast. It was a very big bureau. Our job was to rewrite copy from one wire to prepare it for another wire, edit it, and so forth. It was good newspaper and press service training. We also reported news from that area, of course. We had this bank of teletype machines that were terribly noisy. God, it was like a boiler factory in there! There were always at least six of them running, relaying wires around the country, and we had six operators sitting there doing the typing on the machines. And we sat on the other side of the desk, editing these copies and shoving it to the editors for the various wires.

DC: I've found a photograph of you that was taken in 1938 during the time you were with UP in Kansas City. You are sitting at a desk, with two guys standing by, and there are Coke bottles with candles stuck into them, and you are talking on the telephone. What was that about?

WC: We had an electricity blackout in Kansas City, which in those days was rare. It was a big national story. In fact, that picture appeared in *Life* magazine. I was the overnight editor for Kansas City at that time, which was the toughest job in the bureau. We had our offices in the Kansas City Journal-Post Building. It was a union action. They pulled the main plug.

DC: Oh, it wasn't an accident?

WC: No. And it was really a terribly irresponsible thing to do. Of course, hospitals went with no light, the streetcars stopped in the street—it was in the middle of the night, around, if I remember, two o'clock in the morning or something. But we were here with this main relay station for United Press. Associated Press had the same setup in Kansas City. So both of the major news sources for the morning papers across America were knocked out. We had no electricity for our teletype machines.

The blackout happened while the army was conducting military maneuvers in Louisiana. It was the largest peacetime movement of the army in U.S. history. The First Army was designated the red army for the purpose of this exercise. The Third Army was designated the blue army. The UP reporters covering the maneuvers sent their reports to us by Western Union. I had to write the stories from their rather sketchy messages wired to me. They were in telegraph code, practically. But I could never keep straight in my mind which army was red and which was blue. It was confusing, so I had written on two big pieces of copy paper in big letters, "Red is First," and "Blue is Third." We had a lot of spindles that we filed copy on, so I put these pieces of paper on the spindles so that I could keep them sorted correctly. If you look closely at this picture, you can see these two signs sitting in front of me. Newspapermen all over America laughed at the picture when it was published in *Life* magazine, because everybody else had the same problem. *Life* didn't identify me, unfortunately, but it was my first national publicity.

DC: Weren't you also involved in a strike against UP during this period?

WC: Yeah, I was an early member of the Newspaper Guild back in Houston, Texas, a town where unions weren't exactly popular. Heywood Hale Broun started the American Newspaper Guild in New York, and I found the idea exceedingly appealing, so I joined in Houston. Later, United Press had a chapter of the guild in Kansas City, and I became active in that. About 1937, our negotiations with UP in New York for a new contract collapsed, so the guild called a strike meeting in Columbus, Ohio. I was a delegate from our chapter in Kansas City. Somehow, I got elected chairman of the meeting. The union organizer had come out from New York to lead us through the steps in voting for a strike against UP, which had never happened before. He assured us that he had promises from the International Telegraphers Union that they would observe our picket lines and not work if we struck. This was critical to any possible success. UP could continue its operations as long as those printers were working. We didn't have any strength without the ITU behind us, so on the basis of that promise, we voted to strike. I got back to Kansas City, and United Press buckled instantly.

After the strike was over, I went to the head of the Kansas City ITU unit. I think his name was Charlie. I said, "Charlie, you know we couldn't have brought this off if you guys hadn't supported us." And Charlie said "Well, where'd you get that idea?" I said, "That's what our guild organizers said." He said, "We haven't taken any action on this strike. As a matter of fact, there was sympathy not to support you. But listen, my sympathies were with you." By that time, the guild organizer was coming back to Kansas City to organize the *Kansas City Star*. I met him down at the President Hotel, and I confronted him. I said, "Did we misunderstand you?" He said, "Oh no, you didn't really misunderstand me. I had to tell you that, or you guys never would have ordered a strike. Boy, you just don't understand trade union organization." I blew my top. I called a guild chapter meeting and resigned. I told them, "I was forced to resign. I can't hold my head high after a situation like this. I'm out, finished, done with the guild, the whole thing."

DC: Do you think that, generally speaking, there's a need for unions?

WC: Oh absolutely, I believe in unions. One of the tragedies of our time is the collapse of the union movement. I was a member of the American Federation of Television and Radio Artists (AFTRA) union the entire time I was at CBS.

THE NEW LONDON DISASTER

DC: Now at some point, didn't UP send you back to Texas?

WC: I went to Dallas to let a guy get some vacation time in March 1937. I was there just two or three days when the schoolhouse at New London, Texas, blew up. That was a terrible tragedy that took several hundred lives. I had done fairly well as an editor in Kansas City, but the New London story was really my first big break as a reporter with United Press.

DC: Let's talk about that.

WC: The guy I relieved in Dallas handled the Texas state UP wire service. He gathered reports from all of our Texas bureaus. The wire from our Houston bureau closed at three o'clock, and there was no further communication with them until the night wire came up at about six o'clock. Roy Forrest was our bureau manager in Houston. On Friday afternoon, March 18, the oil reporter at the *Houston Press* got a call from a contact at Humble Oil, which owned most of the oil field around New London. This contact said, "We've got a terrible disaster. The school blew up, and there have been a lot of people killed." That oil writer called over to another reporter and said, "Hey, we've got this message that there's been a school explosion in New London." Roy Forrest heard that, so he sent an uppercase message out on the Texas state wire.

DC: What do you mean by "uppercase message"?

WC: Those were messages meant to be read only by the United Press person that the message was addressed to, but there wasn't any great mystery about them. The upper case of the shift key included numbers and various punctuation marks, so if you knew your uppercase code, you could easily read them. You got used to doing that as a United Press man. But that was my first year with the United Press, and I had not had that many uppercase messages to deal with. It took me a minute or two to figure the symbols and numbers out.

At any rate, I saw this message come in, addressed to the Dallas bureau: "DA: MAY HAVE BIG STORY, HOLD WIRE OPEN." It didn't say what the story was. Well, this was one minute before we closed the wire, so I told my operator that I was closing the wire anyway, that I would read it later. I told the operator to send a "Good Night" to Houston. The operator started typing "Good Night," and Roy Forrest down in Houston got on the wire and started ringing bells. He kept trying to interrupt the "Good Night" message. The operator said, "What the hell's going on here? Somebody's trying to interrupt my message." I told him to wait a minute. Roy then got through with his message: "URGENT! HOLD WIRE!" So we held the wire open, fortunately, and about five minutes later he sent the first bulletin that a school had exploded in New London and that an urgent request had gone out for medical help.

I called Bill Baldwin, our bureau manager in Dallas, and he said, "Stand by, I'll pick you up and we'll go down there." I was terribly anxious to go to New London. We didn't really know the dimensions of this tragedy quite yet, but we knew it was big. We realized the full immensity of the situation as we got to Tyler and saw this line of cars at the funeral home, which was right on the highway outside of Tyler. New London is south of Tyler in East Texas. Then we got to the disaster scene at about nine o'clock. Big searchlights that the oil companies had brought in from the oil fields lit the scene. We could see this collapsed structure and these hardened old oil field workers whose children were buried underneath the rubble. They were digging with their bloodied hands, pulling the pieces of stone away to try to get to their kids. It was a terrible scene.

DC: Were you and Baldwin the only reporters there at that point?

WC: A couple of *Houston Press* people beat us there, but Bill and I were the first wire service reporters on the scene. We were soon joined by some absolutely top-notch people from UP.

DC: Describe the scene at New London for me.

WC: Well, this was a three-story, consolidated high school building. Everything went wrong there that could go wrong. You wouldn't believe it. The school was heated by residue gas, which is highly volatile and odorless, and it's illegal to use. That's the gas you see burning as flares at oil fields and refineries. It's so volatile they can't work with it. It's illegal to use it for anything. But all through the oil fields in those days, people would illegally tap into this gas and use it to heat their homes. Well, they actually used this stuff to heat the consolidated school building. The pipes came into the ground floor of the building.

The gas escaped on this particular day from a broken pipe in the subbasement. You could not have built a more perfect bomb. In the shop on the ground floor, the shop teacher told a boy to turn off his band saw. A spark from the switch ignited the gas and blew up the building, with everybody in it. There were very few survivors. The explosion happened the closing minute of the school day. The PTA was meeting in the gymnasium in back, so the mothers were all there. I got our Acme photographer to take a picture that played all over the world. One of the walls still partially standing had a blackboard on it. The blackboard said, "Oil and Gas are East Texas' greatest blessings."

I got some very good lessons in emergency coverage at New London. I interviewed the school superintendent, who told me about the use of the gas, and I wrote two or three stories that got some notice. But we went sleepless, most of us. Bill Baldwin went back to Dallas the next day to run the bureau, and he returned the next day. I had no clothes or toothbrush or anything, but it didn't matter. I worked through Friday night, Saturday, and Saturday night.

DC: Did you go back to Dallas after that?

WC: I did, but UP immediately sent me to Austin for a special session of the Texas Legislature. I think the purpose of the session was to repeal horse race betting. I don't remember much about the session, really, but I do remember Coke Stevenson, who was Speaker of the Texas House. I thought Stevenson was something of a hillbilly, but

I was still impressed with his handling of the legislature. It struck me as rather lacka-daisical at the time, but I learned that was his style. I also remember that most of the members of the legislature were all kids who were not much older than I was, and I was only twenty-one.

FOOTBALL GAME ANNOUNCER

DC: Where did you go after the legislative session was over?

WC: I was in Austin for several months. UP decided to open a bureau in El Paso, so they asked me to go there. My gosh, that's a long drive from Austin to El Paso. I had to make the trip in a beaten-up old car. A few days after I arrived in El Paso, I got a call from a guy named Gayle Grubb at WKY in Oklahoma City. The people in radio who I associated with in those days all had names right out of a Charles Dickens novel. The commercial manager at WKY was a man named Matt Bonebreak, and Gayle Grubb was the general manager. Gayle was an old vaudevillian himself, I think. He wore loud checked suits and was a fast-talking character. He called, and he said, "This is Gayle Grubb, WKY." I didn't know what WKY was. He said, "How soon can you be in Okla-homa City? I want to talk to you about broadcasting football for us." And I said, "Wait a minute, I'm not looking for a job." I told him that I had only done re-creations of games based on wire reports. I had never done live football broadcasting. Grubb said, "Well, we want to audition you anyway. We want to find out if you're really our man."

So I asked Grubb how much they were paying. I think I was making $22.50 a week with UP. And he said, "We're talking $75 or $100 a week." I said, "Oh, well, maybe I can get a day off around here and come to Dallas." I was feeling very isolated out in El Paso, and I was worried about keeping my relationship with Betsy going. I couldn't get all the way to Oklahoma City, but I could take a train to Dallas. Grubb said, "Okay, but we have to do this right away. We've signed up the University of Oklahoma. We have an exclusive. Kellogg cereal's going to be the sponsor, and it's a big deal for us." I went to Dallas, and they put me in an empty studio and said, "Okay, do us a football game." So I had to do an imaginative football game. I did a few minutes, and they came out and said, "All right now, when can you leave UP?" I explained that I couldn't just quit UP like that. Grubb said, "Well, if you can't be on the scene in three weeks, we'll have to let it go." So I gave UP three weeks' notice.

I moved to Oklahoma and lived on campus at Norman that football season, and I did the football games. The first thing I did when I got there, I said, "Now look, I don't know how good I'm going to be at identifying the players on the field and all that." They said, "Well, how many spotters do you want?" WKY was a very rich NBC radio station, and they would have spent anything to get this done. They hired a couple of spotters to identify the players for me. There was a big buildup for the first game, over in Tulsa. Betsy came down from Kansas City, and all the Kellogg officials were in from Battle Creek and a New York ad agency, and they had a big party the night before the game. I got up to the booth, and my spotters were terrible. They didn't know anything.

I had not learned the names and numbers of the players, because I depended on these spotters. I knew something about the tactics of the two teams. I'd done that little research, but as far as the identity of players, which is the key to these things, I didn't know that. It was the worst balls-up you ever saw in your life. And all I could hear throughout the game was Gayle Grubb standing behind me, saying, "Jesus. Jesus! Jesus!" He invoked the Lord's name in every conceivable combination. "Jesus. Je-sus! Je-ie-sus!" It was awful. I knew that was the end of my career. I was so embarrassed—it was just awful. The engineers knew it, and everybody knew how terrible I was.

DC: That must have been a nerve-wracking experience.

WC: Well, it was, but I actually survived. To my surprise and relief, the station management just asked me to make some adjustments; otherwise they thought I was okay. But that experience did teach me a very valuable lesson for the future. If you're doing a live broadcast and you know that you will need to ad-lib, never depend upon anybody else to do any part of your work. You have got to be fully prepared to do it on your own. From there on out, right on through to my last days and today when I do a documentary, I try to know more about that subject than anybody else in the whole CBS operation knows about it. That drove my staff at CBS a little crazy when we were doing political conventions and election nights and the space launches, because I insisted on doing my own research. The research people were turning out these fact-filled books that were intended for the entire staff, which didn't satisfy me. I had to do it and know it myself. I never depended on the research book that CBS put out.

DC: Did CBS give you much help with research?

WC: At the beginning of my extemporaneous broadcasting for CBS, which was basically the 1952 political conventions, CBS turned out a very flimsy series of research sheets. Now they produce books of material, more than anybody can absorb. But even with those, I had to do it myself. I can't read something and get it. I've got to work with it. So I'd make my own book of anecdotal material that I might want to use and so forth, and I found that by doing that I implanted it in my mind in such a way I never had to refer to the book. I was prepared always to handle that on my own. And that came from the lesson I learned from the 1937 football season at the University of Oklahoma, at WKY.

DC: Now, you left WKY before the next football season to work for Braniff Airlines. How did that come about? That was a path away from journalism.

WC: Yes, it was. Well, working on radio didn't give me the satisfaction that print gave me, and I was not too happy there, actually. By the time the spring came, I got a job with Braniff, which was a struggling, fairly new airline at the time that began in Oklahoma. Braniff sent me to Kansas City to be the new station manager there. Which was a happy development because it got me back to Betsy, who I was still courting. This was the spring of 1938, and I was just twenty-two.

DC: How did the job at Braniff work out?

WC: Well, I had some fascinating experiences. But I also learned a lot about diplomacy and, I suppose, business courtesy, in a sense.

DC: Why did you leave Braniff?

WC: It was pretty much a low-pay business. I don't know how far I would have gone in it. I don't know that I'm a businessman, although I handled the office at Kansas City well, I think. I guess I had about a year with Braniff. But it was getting on to the late winter of 1939, and the war clouds were gathering over Europe, if you'll pardon the cliché. I decided I had to get back in the newspaper business, preferably at the UP. I loved the United Press, and I'd missed it ever since I left. So I went to the UP office and threw myself on their mercy. The management had not been happy about my leaving so precipitously a couple of years before. But they welcomed me back. And that was to be my home for the next ten years.

BACK TO UP

DC: It sounds as though World War II or not, you probably would have gone back to journalism.

WC: I undoubtedly would have. Back in Kansas City, I was running around with Betsy and all of her University of Missouri journalism friends and my buddies from my previous incarnation there. They were all in the newspaper business.

DC: I understand that you knew John Cameron Swayze when you both were still in Kansas City. Swayze, of course, became famous during the 1950s as one of the first news anchors for NBC television and as a pitchman in television commercials. I remember his commercials for Timex watches.

WC: I knew Swayze very well. After I left Braniff, I was the overnight editor at UP. Swayze was a columnist for the *Kansas City Journal-Post*, which had its newsroom across the head of the stairs from our UP newsroom. Swayze did a seven a.m. radio news program from that newsroom. Swayze frequently showed up about five minutes before his news program every morning. He'd dash up three flights of stairs, and he'd rush in to our office, breathless, and he'd grab these black flimsy copies of news stories that we had stuck on spindles during the night. Swayze would ask me "What're the big headlines?" I'd walk across the hall with him and brief him on all the headline stories. I'd say, "Well, President Roosevelt signed such-and-such a bill overnight," and this was happening and that was happening around the world, and so forth. He would sit down at his desk with these copies, and the broadcast light would come on. He'd say, "Good morning. John Cameron Swayze with the news from the *Kansas City Journal* city room. Today . . ." And he would just repeat word for word whatever headlines I had just told him. He had a terrific memory. Then he'd say, "Now we'll be back after a word from our sponsor." In the minute or minute and a half of the commercial, he'd get this copy in order and come back on the air and read it. [*laughs*] He was really very good at that. And, as you say, he went on of course from there to fame on the *NBC Nightly News*.

DC: Didn't Swayze have a reputation as kind of a flamboyant character and a lightweight?

WC: Swayze was ridiculed by newspeople in New York quite a lot, and around the country, as kind of a dandy and more show business than news. But Don, that was the image that everybody had of television newspeople in the early 1950s, including me, by the way. We're now talking about 1950 or so. I'd always defend Swayze because I knew that he was a good news broadcaster. He understood news and could handle it well, and he could write. He always wore a boutonniere and fancy clothes, and was a little bit of a dandy and a stylist. He loved to end his broadcasts with "Glad we could get together." He would also open his broadcast with "John Cameron Swayze, hopscotching the world for headlines." That kind of old radio-type stuff.

DC: During this time, in the late 1930s, did print journalists look at that as just "performing"?

WC: Oh, we looked at it as strictly show business, having nothing to do with the news business. There was an odd episode when Swayze was anchoring the NBC television news broadcast that did not do his reputation any good. When I covered the first open atomic bomb test at Yucca Flat, outside of Las Vegas, in 1953, CBS provided the pool camera feed, but we each had our own announcing staff. We had our anchor booths in trailers. Swayze was covering for NBC, and I was the anchor for CBS. The countdown for the explosion was stopped, and they announced there was going to be a delay. We didn't know why there was a delay, but we knew that bomb was all charged up out there on that tower and troops were in the trenches and all this. But we held the air for a short while, ad-libbing about the delay and not knowing quite what the cause was and having to fill up a minute or two. Finally, they announced the delay would be a half hour. At that time, both of the networks threw it back to the studios in New York.

About fifteen or twenty minutes later, they announced that they were going to resume the countdown in three minutes or something like that. So the NBC guy came running from the NBC trailer over to our trailer and said, "You have to tell the atomic people they can't go yet. We won't be ready to go for a half hour." Somebody said, "We can't tell them that. In a minute and a half, we're going on the air." And then the NBC guy said, "But Swayze's ad-libs haven't been written yet!" And that line unfortunately was spread throughout the news corps. Now I don't know whether it was true; it may have been a wisecracking NBC guy. It may not have been Swayze's fault at all. Unfortunately, it lives in legend today. But I went around saying, "Don't kid yourself about Swayze. He's a good newsman." I liked his news broadcasts. They were stylized, but he did a pretty good job of covering the world.

DC: He had a popular news broadcast. Wasn't it called the *Camel News Caravan*?

WC: Yeah, and it was more popular than Doug Edwards's CBS news broadcast. I think that Edwards overtook him, at one point, and I believe that's when NBC brought in Chet Huntley and David Brinkley to replace Swayze.

DC: You went back to UP in 1939, and you were still dating Betsy Maxwell. You and Betsy married on March 30, 1940.

WC: Yes, it'll be fifty years if we make another couple of weeks out of it.

DC: [*laughs*] What brought about the decision to marry?

WC: Well, as a matter of fact, I proposed marriage very soon after meeting her. We had decided two or three times to get married secretly. The way it usually went was that one of us would be gung-ho for this marriage idea and the other one would be dragging his or her feet. And then the reluctant one would become convinced that this was the proper course, and by the time that one of us had picked up the pro-marriage argument the other one of us became anti-marriage. [*laughs*] It took us four more years before we finally married. And she, I don't think, would ever have actually gone through with a sudden, unannounced, runaway-type marriage, because she was very fond of her family, in particular her father, who would've been very badly hurt by that kind of thing. So I don't think an elopement was ever in the cards, really. But we did then have a very formal wedding. She had a lovely gown that her mother helped make. The other major feature of the wedding was that she was around forty-five minutes late for the ceremony. And it's survived nonetheless for fifty years. [*This conversation occurred at the beginning of March 1990. They were married for sixty-five years. Betsy died on March 15, 2005.*]

DC: Let's talk about the months before your marriage, when you returned to the United Press and the war broke out in Europe. Where were you when Germany invaded Poland in 1939?

WC: I was on the overnight desk in Kansas City. Our night editor was John Hampton. There was no real clue that night of September 1, 1939, that Hitler was moving. There had been rumors for days about his building up troops on the border with Poland, and the Danzig crisis was very much in the news. There was a lot of fear that something was about to break, but it hadn't happened yet, and there was no reason to think it was going to happen that night. Hampton had left the office and was on his way down the hill to the bus stop when the flash came that Polish radio had declared that German troops had struck across the border. I immediately went to the window of our office and shouted out, "Hampton, Hampton! Hey, come back! There's a Polish radio report that the Germans have moved across the border!" John called back to me and he said, "Oh, those Poles are saying that every day. I'll be at home if you need me." And he walked on. John kicked himself around the block, for the rest of his life, I guess, for missing the excitement at the office that night.

course, I'm sure that had a lot to do with it, but you
ven today, I still have that first momentary feeling
why am I leaving home and wish I weren't going. That's
larly true when I sail a boat _____ _____ ____ing on a long
That first night at sea there ____ ____
f it's your own comrades at s____
____ness to the moment. That sta____
____th the Arkansas and maybe th____
____hat experience.

____ut your loneliness that firs____
____ly?

____It did. ____
Captain ____
____ no admi____
____ was a ____
____ how lu____
____as terri____
____own bath____
____kened ve____
____was our ____
____tside th____

WC: That's right. We were assigned to a service for a period of
time, maybe only for one operation. That relaxed considerably
as the war went on. In the early stages they thought that
each service should issue its own credentials, and there was
even talk of their having their own uniforms. ____
got to that, really ____

WC: ____ ____insignia
____hand-designed. ____ ____ ____ing the war, some of which were
Brooks Brothers. So I had an officer's uniform, which I bought at

____navy. He was a cool, clear-eyed man from New England. But
____teran of many years in
Bryant didn't know what to do with a news correspondent. There
were no written regulations for him to consult. The navy just

CHAPTER THREE

War Correspondent

DC: The United States was suddenly at war in December 1941 after the Japanese attack on Pearl Harbor. How did you become a war correspondent?

WC: Immediately after the attack on Pearl Harbor, UP called me to New York and put me on the foreign desk to prepare for going overseas. And almost immediately after that, I got credentials with the navy with an assignment to cover the North Atlantic convoys.

DC: Is that the way that the press basically operated during the war, Walter, in that correspondents were assigned to one service or another, and you had credentials from that service?

WC: That's right. We were assigned to a service for a period of time, maybe only for one operation. That relaxed considerably as the war went on. In the early stages, they thought that each service should issue its own credentials, and there was even talk of their having their own uniforms. But it never got to that, really. At the beginning, the navy issued its own credentials. And the navy had to provide you facilities aboard ship, and you were going to be with them for a long time.

One of the shocking things was that neither the army nor the navy had any ideas about what to do with a war correspondent, and they were really kind of ad-libbing as they went along and making it up. For instance, they didn't know what to do about a uniform. Finally, they decided they were going to give correspondents the simulated rank of field-grade officer, above major, rather than company-grade officer, below major. So we got a field-grade officer's uniform, which meant that we could eat at the superior officers' messes and get superior accommodations, which was very nice of them. They regretted that later and downgraded us when there were so many corre-

Cronkite at the press censorship office in London, ca. 1942–1944 (DI_05633).

spondents in the war. We had officers' uniforms but no insignia of rank or of branch of service. The only thing to distinguish us was a wide *C* made of green felt. That was the first correspondent insignia of several they developed during the war, some of which were hand-designed. So I had an officer's uniform, which I bought at Brooks Brothers.

COVERING NAVAL CONVOYS

DC: What was your first assignment with the navy?

WC: I was covering the navy headquarters in New York. I think it was at 90 Church Street. I let the navy know that I wanted to go on interesting convoys. And when one came up, sometime in July 1942, they let me know only that morning so I couldn't get out and spread the word. As a matter of fact, they really preferred that I go straight from 90 Church Street right to the convoy, but I convinced them of my trustworthiness to go home and get my bag. The night that I boarded, Betsy was in New York, and I went home and told her good-bye. The navy told me that I could only take a musette bag, one change of clothes, and my typewriter and carbon paper, and that was about it. I had to take a shore boat from one of the navy piers out to the battleship *Arkansas*, which was anchored in the lower bay near Staten Island. I went down to the dock where I was to meet the conducting officer who was going to take me out to the ship. It turned out that the captain of the *Arkansas* sent the ship's chaplain to meet me.

DC: Do you recall if there was any special reason why the ship's chaplain was sent to meet you?

WC: Well, I found out later, while we were at sea. The captain of the *Arkansas*, C. F. Bryant, was a veteran of many years in the navy. He was a cool, clear-eyed man from New England. But Bryant didn't know what to do with a news correspondent. There were no written regulations for him to consult. The navy just sent him a message that I was coming aboard and that I was not to have access to the radio facilities or be given naval secrets. Thankfully, the navy also told him that he was free to talk to me about anything within reasonable bounds and that he should be cooperative. He was told that I would write my stories after I got ashore. All he was obligated to do was transport me on his ship. So Captain Bryant decided that he needed someone on his staff to look after me. The only person on his staff who really had little to do was the chaplain, so that's who got the assignment.

DC: Was this the first time you had been on a ship the size of the *Arkansas*?

WC: I'd never been on a large ship in my life of any kind, much less a battleship. I remember that we got to the *Arkansas* just as it was getting dark. My God, it looked a mess.

Stuff was piled everywhere on deck, mainly crates and boxes that were stored inside the ship after we embarked. We sat there most of the night, with no way to get off. No one could tell me when we were leaving. But as soon as I boarded that ship, I was part of its operation and I could not have any contact ashore. Well, there was Betsy, right across there where those lights were coming up in Manhattan, and I here I was on this strange ship with these strange people, not one of whom I'd ever met before in my life. I don't think I'd ever been away from home in that circumstance. This was also my first trip overseas. I was twenty-four at that time, I guess, and I was damn homesick that night. I didn't really want to go on this journey very much, and I was very depressed. But I got over that very quickly.

DC: Don't you think that was just an understandable case of anxiety about shipping out across an ocean filled with German U-boats?

WC: Of course, I'm sure that had a lot to do with it, but you know, even today, I still have that first momentary feeling about why am I leaving home and wish I weren't going. That's particularly true when I sail a boat overnight, going on a long trip. That first night at sea there is a very deep loneliness. Even if it's your own comrades at sea, I feel that there's a loneliness to the moment. That started with my very first trip to sea with the *Arkansas*, and maybe that's what it is, a carryover from that experience.

DC: But your loneliness that first night on the *Arkansas* passed quickly?

WC: It did. I have to admit that one of the things that helped was Captain Bryant assigning me to the admiral's quarters. We had no admiral aboard, even though we were the convoy's flagship. That was a pretty luxurious way to go to war. I didn't realize just how luxurious it was until I was on other ships later on. I was terribly pleased to be in this great big bedroom. I had my own bath and all that. Very early the next morning, I was awakened very rudely by the worst noise I've heard in my life. It was our three-inch guns and .50-caliber guns going off, right outside this piece of metal that was the wall of my room. [*laughs*] We had just steamed out into the open ocean, and Captain Bryant had ordered gunnery drill.

DC: Do you recall the military units that were transported in the convoy?

WC: We carried most of the nucleus of the Eighth Air Force to the United Kingdom, and there were thousands of men on these ships. I didn't find out until after I got to London that this was mostly Eighth Air Force, and I couldn't put that in the story because of censorship. But it was obvious that we were carrying troops, because the convoy included thirteen of the biggest passenger ships in service. That first convoy was the biggest that had ever been mounted as far as tonnage or shipping and people involved. Our speed was up to twenty knots, which was a pretty fast convoy in those days. The *Arkansas* was the major escort vessel, and we were accompanied by the cruiser *Brooklyn* and five destroyers.

DC: Did U-boats attack the convoy?

WC: We had a couple of nights of alerts, but that's all. One of the interesting aspects of the voyage was that we had one of the first experimental radar sets placed on a U.S. ship. A young lieutenant was in charge of it. At that time, the radar was such a huge hunk of equipment that the navy had to build a special radar room aft of the flying bridge to house it. The room was kept absolutely pitch black, and nobody could go near it because radar was highly secret.

DC: Where did you land?

WC: In Scotland. We landed on the Clydeside, up at Glasgow.

DC: What did you do after you arrived?

WC: Well, I could not use the telephone. I was under the control of the navy, so I asked if I could go ashore and advise the London office that I was there. They said it was all right with them, but they didn't know if that would be all right with the Admiralty. Telephones had been taken off the docks at that time so you couldn't call about ship movements. So it was agreed that I'd better just go on to London. I was supposed to return to the U.S. on the *Arkansas*. I had only three days, and it's a long overnight trip from Scotland down to London. It was a very great thrill, getting on a British train, and a little bit frightening. I didn't know my way around, and I found the language peculiar. But I went down to the UP bureau on Bouverie Street just off Fleet Street, in the old News of the World Building, and met everybody.

The guys at the UP office told me to go over to the British Ministry of Information, where I sat down and wrote two or three stories about the convoy, which I had to file with the ministry because everything we wrote that was related to the war had to go through them first to be reviewed by the censors. But my story didn't clear for a couple of months, as a matter of fact, and by that time it was old stuff. They didn't want to tell the Germans they were moving troops in fast convoys. I don't think my stories were printed by very many papers, if any.

DC: Well, that raises a question about military censorship and being a reporter. How did you know what not to write about?

WC: Well, you didn't always know. That's why this Ministry of Information was set up. That permitted you to go and write the story as you would've written it, whether there's censorship or not. Then your story went in to the censors, and the censors killed it, cut it, or did whatever they needed to do to it. And then they sent it back out to you, whether you wanted to file it that way or not. Sometimes, if you didn't care how they censored it but just wanted it to move as quickly as possible, you could mark it "Read and File." This meant for them to censor it and then send it to your office in the censored form. It might not make much sense, but you would feel that your office would get enough of the story out of it.

DC: Would rewrite people come in at this point, once it got back to the United States?

WC: Yes, but in that case, you ran into another set of circumstances. We had voluntary censorship in the United States. So the rewrite people were on their honor to try to preserve anything censored in it, not to make up anything in there that they thought they had to fill in from some knowledge that they'd gotten from maybe a correspondent who had come home. In World War II, the press was almost 100 percent responsible, in the military censorship sense. We argued like fury with the censors; there were violent scenes going on all over the room as correspondents would argue with the censors about their stories. But you've got to be pretty smart yourself. I had to ask myself if the content of the story was something the Germans know or don't know. Like the movement or location of troops, that sort of thing.

But the real question was, can you say without doubt that the Germans have the information that you were writing about? And if they did, then you could argue with the censor, saying, "Come on, you know, what are you hiding? You're doing this for political reasons back home," or for some other reason you could charge them with. There were always fights about it. But it worked with considerable smoothness, despite that.

DC: I know you can get into trouble whenever you say "the press," as though everyone's the same, but do you think that your colleagues felt they had a mission to help win the war and that affected the way they reported the news?

WC: If you had charged the press with that, I'm sure that most correspondents would have denied it. But they did, as a matter of conscience. We understood the need to be in this war. I don't know of any correspondent overseas in World War II that was critical of our being involved in the war. They could be highly critical of the way the war was being conducted, but not in our commitment to be there, as with Vietnam later.

DC: So did you remain in London very long after that first convoy?

WC: No, I returned to the States, and I went immediately back to covering the navy's Church Street headquarters. I went on another convoy shortly after that and got to England just at the time of the disastrous Canadian raid on Dieppe, France, in August 1942. The UP kept me in London long enough that I missed my return convoy. So I just stayed there for maybe a month or so, and then I shipped out on a convoy going back. I did two convoys in all, but that second convoy was completely uneventful.

LANDINGS IN NORTH AFRICA

DC: How did you get involved in the North African landings in November 1942?

WC: I suspect that our bureau chief in London already had some inside knowledge of the African landings being planned. The military gave notices to the bureau chiefs for the big press services, AP, UP, INS, and maybe the *New York Times* and the *New York Herald Tribune*. The military would say, "You are going to need some people in place because we're going to have something going on. We're going to have a place for three correspondents from United Press. You had better have them on standby." They wouldn't say where. There was a lot of guessing, but very little speculation. Correspondents were very good about keeping secrets because their own lives were at stake. We didn't want the Germans to know we were coming and set a trap.

But returning to how I got involved in the North African story: I was sent back to the States in October and reported to 90 Church Street. Within a few days, I was told to report to Norfolk, the East Coast headquarters of the navy. When I did, I was told that "this will be a mission and you'll be gone for some time." Once I entered the base, I was not permitted to leave, which meant that something was going on. Then I was taken to amphibious headquarters, where I was told that we were going to make a landing on a foreign shore, but they didn't say where. I was told to report to the battleship *Texas* right away and that I'd be aboard the *Texas* until such time as the operation was completed.

They also requested that I take a pledge that I would remain with the navy, that I was not going to join the forces ashore. I could visit the forces ashore, but I couldn't stay with them if they stayed. The navy said, "We can't tell you whether this is hit-and-run or whether we're staying somewhere. But if the army stays, you can't stay; you've got to come back with the navy. The army has its own correspondents that it's assigning to land." However, the United Press had enough—I don't know—premonition, perhaps, is all, of what this was about, because already they'd had to send some guys down to the army units. So obviously we could tell there was going to be some kind of a landing. UP instructed me: "You're going to be assigned to the navy, but as soon as you land, go with the army. We don't really care about the navy's story. What we care about is what the army does."

When I arrived at Norfolk, I met the correspondent for INS. We weren't supposed to tell what ships we were getting on, but he couldn't resist telling me that he was going on the *Massachusetts*. I would have preferred to be on the *Massachusetts* because it was our newest battleship and it was a better story.

DC: When did you find out where you were going?

WC: We didn't know until we were at sea and then we found that we were on our way to the western side of North Africa. Our target was Port Lyautey, which was east of Casablanca in Morocco. Unfortunately the *Massachusetts* was going to Casablanca, so the guy from the INS was going to get all the good stories. [*laughs*] Admiral Monroe Kelly, who commanded the navy's entire attack group for the North African operation, which was called Operation Torch, was on board the *Texas*. Our captain was a guy named Roy B. Pfaff, who wasn't the regular captain of the *Texas*. The regular captain had, in a terrible scandal, committed suicide just before the mission. So the navy had to find a new captain in a hurry. The naval command finally had to go to the West Virginia arsenal to find a guy who had retired from the Yangtze and the Huangpu gunboat service in China a few years earlier.

DC: How did you report from the *Texas*?

WC: Well, they actually let us write news stories and communicate them from the ship. The navy gave us so many words a day on the radio, and we filed our stories in the navy code to Gibraltar, where they were vetted and then relayed on to London by the British. I filed thirteen stories in the two weeks that we were anchored offshore.

DC: What do you recall about the troop landing after you arrived off Port Lyautey?

WC: I remember that our landing was not a terribly successful one. There was stiff resistance for a couple of days. The French had blocked the port by sinking a lot of ships. The port was not large anyway, but it would've been big enough to run landing craft into, but we couldn't even do that. So they were trying to land supplies for the troops on the beach. The troops were still just on the beach and in the town of Port Lyautey. They weren't doing a heck of a lot better in Casablanca, but somewhat better. The other landings were around on the northern coast, although there was a further landing on the west coast of Morocco at Safi.

DC: Was that your first military action?

WC: Yeah, the first time I had heard any guns fired in anger. In my case, I was going to stay ashore, of course, violating my pledge to the navy, but keeping my pledge to UP, which was more important. Obviously, it was only a bureaucratic thing; the army was assigned a certain number of men and the navy was assigned a certain number. That kind of bureaucratic dictum was constantly violated. We didn't pay much heed to it if we could get around it.

I went ashore during the day to cover the fighting on the ground, and then I slept on the *Texas* at night. After a few days of that, I learned that the *Texas* was going to Casablanca. And I thought, well, what the devil, I'll go there, which is a better story. At that point, contact had not been made between the Port Lyautey landing party and the Casablanca landing party. You couldn't get from Port Lyautey to Casablanca on the ground, because the Vichy French still held the road. We started out to Casablanca, escorting two partially unloaded ships. That night, midway in the voyage, a German submarine got in among our little convoy—we were fairly close to shore—and this German submarine hit one of the ships. Or at least I think that's what happened. I never was sure of that, but we turned and started out to sea. The naval command decided to send the *Texas* back to the States in a convoy with several other ships. Instead of staying and reporting on the fighting on the land, I was on the *Texas* headed back home. I thought, oh boy, United Press was going to be sore at me for not staying onshore. But I knew I'd filed thirteen good stories, and I was happy about that.

I would just have to live with whatever bad reaction UP might have. Besides, I realized that there would be one good thing about it. I would be the first correspondent back from the North African landings. I would write the first story about the landings. That would be a great story. So that was my comfort.

On the return voyage, we ran into a terrible storm, and oh boy, it was a miserable trip. One interesting but anxious moment was when I was up on the bridge and we were getting green water up there. I forget now how high it was off the deck, about forty feet or so, which means that the waves were breaking that high. I was standing there on the bridge, on top of this tripod, with Admiral Kelly and Captain Pfaff. The ship would roll over in these waves, and then just sit there—trying to decide whether it'd roll all the way over or come back onto its bottom. It would roll, and it would sit there very gracefully for two or three rises in these waves, and then it would rise up and roll, and then sit. You never knew which way it was going to go.

Admiral Kelly said to Captain Pfaff, "Where is your list meter, Captain?" That's the meter that shows how much you're listing; it's just a simple instrument. Captain Pfaff, who didn't know the *Texas* as well as the previous captain, said to Executive Officer Hannigan, "Where is the list meter?" Hannigan said, "We don't have one, Captain." The admiral said, "Get one." So Hannigan said to some lieutenant, "Get me a protractor, a piece of string and a bolt or a nut." The guy came back very shortly and thumbtacked the protractor up on the bulkhead, ran the string down, and tied the bolt to the string. That was our list meter. It showed how many degrees we were listing. Here we were listing twenty-three degrees or some terrible amount, which is a long way for a boat to list. It was a horror to see how far we were listing. Admiral Kelly looked at this contraption, and he said, "Captain Pfaff, what's your maximum list under the present configuration of the *Texas*?" And Pfaff said to Hannigan, "Commander Hannigan, what's the maximum list of the *Texas* under your present configuration?" Hannigan replied, "Twenty-one degrees, Captain." Captain Pfaff then said, "Admiral, twenty-one degrees." [*laughs*] The darned thing was showing twenty-two or twenty-three degrees—in other words, it indicated that we were about to capsize. It was a very interesting moment, but we obviously survived the storm. My guess is that our string-and-protractor list meter was less than precise.

THE FIRST CORRESPONDENT BACK HOME

WC: As we steamed toward the States, I got Captain Pfaff and Admiral Kelly excited about the fact that I was going to be the first correspondent back home. They were suffering with me over the fact that I hadn't stayed ashore and the trouble I was in with the UP office. The admiral assured me that he would get me back to the States before any other correspondent. "We're going to make this old boy go, and we're going to get you back first," he said. "There's no problem; the rest of the correspondents are all back in North Africa." I told him that was a relief, because my chief competitor was on the battleship *Massachusetts* and I knew that it was a much faster ship than the *Texas*. Admiral Kelly said, "I know the *Massachusetts* is going around into the Mediterranean first before coming home."

One morning, Kelly called me up to his quarters, and he said, "Cronkite, I have some bad news for you. I intercepted a coded message. The *Massachusetts* is on the way back to Boston." And I said, "Oh, no," because she was three times as fast as we were. I said, "How long has she been under way? Where is she?" He said, "As nearly as I can make out, she's been under way for at least two or three days." Which meant that she was nearing Boston, and we were still a couple of days out of Norfolk. It looked like the INS correspondent was going to be the first one back, which was a very unhappy development for me. I went down to the wardroom with the navy pilots on the ship. Those old battleships had catapult aircraft, called Kingfishers, which were little pontoon airplanes that carried two men—a spotter and a pilot. They were catapulted off the ship on a rail. The plane fitted into a shell, and it was fired by a sixteen-inch gun. You were literally shot out of a cannon. And you went only twenty or thirty feet down this rail and dropped off the edge of the battleship. The pilot had this single engine, revving it up all it would go before the gun was fired. And as he got that engine roaring and the plane was pulling its chocks, trying to get away, the gun went off—wham!— and away he went, dropped right down to the water's edge practically, and now you're on your way. And then you were recovered by landing alongside the battleship, and they picked you up in a crane.

Well, they had two of these planes aboard, and navy pilots for each. One of the pilots said, "Listen, Walter. You ever thought about the possibility of talking the old man into letting me fly you back? We can gain a whole day on your competition." I said, "Never thought of it! Gosh. Boy, would you do that?" "Of course," he said, "I'd love it. I'd get back a day early myself." So I ran up to see Admiral Kelly. It didn't take any talking to him at all. He said, "Great idea. I've got dispatches I'd like to get back anyway. I was kind of thinking that." So they drew a circle on the map for the maximum gas supply they had available, and their probable gas consumption, and drew that circle out to where we were. We took off the minute we hit that circle. We flew to Norfolk, and we ran out of gas as we landed. The last few miles, the pilot was saying, "I don't know about this, I don't know about this." It was open cockpit, you know. I was up in the front seat and he was in the back. We landed in the water, and just as we neared the dock, we ran out of gas.

Anyway, I got to Norfolk. In those days, you couldn't telephone anyone from a military base, so rather than go off base to take time to call the office, I hopped a ride on a plane going to Floyd Bennett Field in Brooklyn. When we landed, I was told that I couldn't telephone from there either. There was a guy headed into New York, so I hitched a ride with him. As far as I knew, the last United Press had heard from me was when I filed my dispatches from the coast of North Africa. They were probably wondering where in the devil I was. It had been almost two weeks since I had filed the last dispatch.

I walked into the United Press office on the twelfth floor in the Daily News Building in New York, and the receptionist got all excited about my arrival. She said, "Walter, you're all right!" I thought she seemed awfully excited about the mere fact that I had come back to the office. When I walked into the newsroom, I saw Mert Akers, a real tough, old-fashioned city editor who had a heart as big as they came, but a tough exterior. Mert jumped up from his desk and came halfway across the room and grabbed me. He said "Walter! You're okay! You're okay!" and then he kind of pushed me from him and said, "Where in the hell have you been?"

DC: Hadn't the UP received your stories?

WC: No. It turned out that none of my dispatches from North Africa had gone through. I had disappeared the day that I went aboard the ship in Norfolk, and that's the last that anybody had heard from me for several weeks. Apparently, my dispatches never got past British naval communications at Gibraltar. I'm certain someone would have told me if they hadn't been able to send them from the *Texas*. The deal was that the British were relaying all press messages from Gibraltar to the proper offices in London. As a result, a lot of U.S. dispatches didn't get through.

DC: Why didn't the American messages get through?

WC: Because the British military gave priority to Reuters and to the British newspapers. Betsy was back in Kansas City, and she had made inquiries about whether they'd received any dispatches from me, because none had shown up in the *Kansas City Star*. Betsy was a little concerned, but not overwhelmed, because the UP told her there were communications problems.

DC: Were you able to do something with your missing stories once you got to the UP office?

WC: Yes. I explained to Akers that I'd filed thirteen stories. I had copies of them with me, so Akers told me to get a typewriter and write new stories. I took my thirteen pieces and put them into about three stories. After I did, Akers immediately put the stories on the wire with the editor's note "First correspondent back from North Africa." Nothing had appeared from the INS guy in Boston, so we assumed that I had beaten him. I found out later that the INS guy had arrived back in Boston before I arrived at Norfolk. Because I had told him I was staying in North Africa, he assumed I was still there and he had no reason to hurry. He took a couple of days home leave and was sitting out at his home outside Boston, where he lived, resting up and getting ready to write his dispatches when—wambo!—INS was on the phone, saying Cronkite's back and he's on the wire, the first man back from North Africa. [*laughs*]

DC: That was a great scoop, even if it was accidental.

WC: It was a great scoop. It was accidental except for the fact that we talked the navy into flying me back on that plane. That was enterprise journalism and the kind of thing you have to do to be a good journalist. A good journalist has to take advantage of every opportunity that comes around to get the scoop. It worked in that case, and it paid off. By the way, I got my first on-camera experience as a result of that. Paramount News asked me to do a piece for a newsreel. "First correspondent back from North Africa" kind of thing. I was filmed sitting next to my typewriter and in my war correspondent's clothes. Paramount tied it together with some of their film.

DC: They interviewed you on film?

WC: They didn't interview me. It was a very corny approach. I'm sitting at the typewriter, and I look up and I say, "I'm the first reporter back from North Africa, and the fight goes on there." Paramount followed that with some film of the North African campaign. I was deeply disappointed that my newsreel performance failed to attract any movie offers from Hollywood. [*laughs*] But it did impress my friends back in Houston and Kansas City.

8th Air Force ...
personal message from a friend. My calls were usually from a
guy named Hal Lyshon. Hal would just call and say, "Hey! We're
getting together a little poker game tonight, it's going be
up at my house. Come on over anytime you can get free—8:30 or
whatever time you can get free." And that was the signal, to
... the hell out to our previously designated air base, which
... Molesworth. Homer Bigart was also
... was a little tiny crossroads,
... he U.S. was only sending forty
... , and they were only going short
... rning how to do this really, and

I arrived in England, the U.S. Eighth Air Force was
...med. The Army Air Corps made it known that they would
...e correspondent from each of the major
...the New York

...ean th
...s?

...they m
...actua
...ews se
...Tribun
...also
...So UP n
...ress no
...nd Andy
...ne guy

...assigned

...rly days
...er bases
...y dozen
...ferred to
...om our offices in London, although we usually had a
...to cover. Raids were not a daily occurrence in

...carrier. We covered

...were critical to the story. The first
...hing you ever asked anybody was, "Where are you from?" That was
...e very first order of business. The UP was wild for a

CHAPTER FOUR

The Eighth Air Force

DC: Where did the United Press send you after you returned from North Africa?

WC: Back to London to cover the air war. We all knew the Army Air Corps was moving a lot of people over there. It was obvious that England was going to be the base for our coverage for a long time to come. I got an apartment with a Jim McGlincy, who became a close but very difficult friend. He was a beautiful Irish writer with the news in his head, but a drinker and a fighter. Jim was my roommate for most of my London days. We were in two different apartments. He went to the Continent and stayed before I did.

DC: You mentioned earlier that UP was sending you to England to cover the air war, which meant the Allied bombing campaign in western Europe. Let's talk about your work as a correspondent covering that part of the air war.

WC: When I arrived in England, the U.S. Eighth Air Force was being formed. The Army Air Corps made it known that they would accept one correspondent from each of the major news services and from the *New York Times* and the *New York Herald Tribune*.

DC: You mean they denied access to reporters from other newspapers?

WC: Well, they may have made this offer to all of the newspapers, actually, but the only ones that accepted were the three news services and the *New York Times* and the *New York Herald Tribune*. CBS Radio and the army newspaper, *Stars and Stripes*, also had correspondents attached to the Eighth Air Force. So UP nominated me to be its correspondent, and the Associated Press nominated a guy named Gladwin Hill. INS named Bill Wade, and Andy Rooney was the *Stars and Stripes* guy. The *Herald Tribune* guy was Homer Bigart, and the *Times* reporter was Bob Post.

United Press correspondent Cronkite with a bomber flight crew in World War II, ca. 1944 (DI_05808).

DC: Were you assigned to specific air bases?

WC: In the early days of the air war, there were only four American bomber bases in England, but that number grew very rapidly to many dozen, and they were all over England. That's why England was referred to as one big aircraft carrier. We covered the air war from our offices in London, although we usually had a delegated base to cover. Raids were not a daily occurrence in the early days. Weather conditions had to be almost perfect.

DC: How did you cover the air war? Did you fly on bombing missions?

WC: We would be in our office, and we'd get a phone call from Eighth Air Force public relations in London. It would always be a personal message from a friend. My calls were usually from a guy named Hal Leyshon. Hal would just call and say, "Hey! We're getting together a little poker game tonight; it's going be up at my house. Come on over anytime you can get free—8:30 or whatever time you can get free." And that was the signal to get the hell out to our previously designated air base, which for me was the 303rd Group at Molesworth. Homer Bigart was also assigned to Molesworth, which was a little, tiny crossroads, hardly a town even. At first, the U.S. was only sending forty or fifty planes over the target, and they were only going short distances. They were just learning how to do this really, and most of that time they had British fighter escorts. Bigart and I would grab our musette bags we always had ready and run down to Fleet Street and hail cabs. Usually, all the correspondents would collide on Fleet Street somewhere because we were all going to the same railway station. We'd catch the first train going to Bedford, a little industrial town north of London. All the bases were reachable from there. At Bedford, they'd have a jeep waiting for us with a driver to take us out to the air base, and we usually got there before the planes returned.

We very seldom interviewed the crews before they left on the mission. We waited for them to return and stood out there with the ground crews and the commanders counting the planes coming back. Some of the planes came back with their wings and rudders shot up. The pilot fired a red flare from the cockpit if he had wounded crew members aboard. The red flares would go up as they were landing, and the ambulances would go out and meet them as soon as they could come to a stop. We had to wait for the crews to be officially debriefed by A2 intelligence officers before we could interview them. We couldn't talk to the crews until they were out of debriefing, because sometimes they had to be warned about something that had happened on the raid that had to be kept a secret. When they came out, we'd interview them about the raid. We'd talk to them, go back to the Ministry of Information in London, and write our story.

DC: So what type of story would you be after?

WC: A personal, first-person story rather than the story of the raid, because the story of the raid would be very heavily censored. The army would give us a statement such as: "American Flying Fortresses and Liberators today were again over the submarine pens of Saint-Nazaire." In the early days, they didn't say how many planes were on the mission.

DC: They'd just give you a factual framework, and then you could personalize your story?

WC: Yeah, which was still highly censored, but we could talk about the experiences on a given airplane. If they were hit, somebody was wounded on the plane, or the pilot might have been hit and the copilot had to bring the plane back—stories of that kind. You know, personal heroism stories. And we could write something about the raid. I mean, we could talk about what they saw frequently. You know, the bombs dropping, the submarine pens blowing up, and things like that.

DC: So did UP particularly like stories with a lot of names of boys and hometowns?

WC: Oh, sure, hometowns were critical to the story. The first thing you ever asked anybody was "Where are you from?" That was the very first order of business. The UP was wild for a hometown story. And then almost every day you'd write the lead story and get some of the stuff that belonged, the description of the target, the description of the fighter opposition, the flak, and all that sort of thing, but then you would immediately get off to the sidebar stories. There was always a feature story or two or three out of the mission. And whether you got them was a question of grab bag luck.

DC: What would be a good example of something like that?

WC: Well, one of my more popular stories had the lead "This is a story of nine crying boys in a Flying Fortress." Their pilot had been hit and killed instantly by a 50 mm shell that burst in the cockpit and pierced his heart. The plane didn't suffer a lot of damage, but the captain was dead, and they had a tough and long fight. They had shot down several planes, but the copilot was brand new to the crew, and they didn't have much confidence in him. The plane came back, and it had to land at our field because it was so badly damaged that it couldn't make it to its own field. Therefore, I had the extra story of their being at a strange base. But my basic story was about the effect on the crew of the death of this one guy. You had stories about tremendous airmanship and bringing back planes on one engine. I remember one plane coming back with all of its ailerons shot off. With no stabilizer control, the plane drifted all over the sky. But they finally got the thing down to the ground. I had stories about crews that ditched into the ocean and were saved by the rescue service, sometimes under the guns of German gunboats.

DC: But you had to write all of those stories at the Ministry of Information?

WC: In the very early stages of the war, that was the way we had to do it. After it was determined that the Germans were taking a defensive posture and that there was no buildup of cross-channel invasion craft, they began to relax a little. As they did, they relaxed the communication facilities that we had. Public telephone boxes were put back on the street corners in England, and we were permitted at that point to write the stories at our office and transmit them by teletype to the Ministry of Information. The purpose of having to sit at the ministry and write our stories disappeared, although the ministry remained the pressroom for independent reporters who didn't have offices. But we worked out of the UP central office.

Then there came a day, later on in the war, when we were permitted for the first time to telephone our stories from the bases back to the bureaus. And boy, that was like the emancipation document had been signed. We could stay overnight at the base and mix with the guys and really get some stories and not have to ride those darn crowded trains. The first day—Homer Bigart was with me—we went up to Molesworth, got our stories, and went into the A2 office to write them. The A2 officer left his sergeant to clear the copy. Homer and I hammered away at our typewriter. We finished our stories about the same time. Homer was a marvelously funny guy. He had this terrible stutter, which interestingly enough got less and less with each Pulitzer he won. He won two Pulitzer Prizes for foreign correspondence, and with each one he got more confident and the stutter disappeared, but in those days it was still quite terrible.

Homer said as we finished, "You g-g-go-go-go ahead f-f-first, C-C-Cronkite, be-be-be-because you're-you're a-agency," meaning press service, as opposed to the single newspaper. It was very kind of him. A lot of guys would not have done that, but he knew that I was racing AP's Glad Hill. I submitted my copy to this sergeant, who looked at it and made a couple of changes, but nothing important. And then I had to telephone over a field phone, which is a line that they laid across the countryside. You had to hold a button down when you talked, and the button was kind of hard to hold, and your thumb got very tired if you were on the phone very long dictating.

The office in London had a terrible time hearing me. I was shouting. And you had to spell every proper name phonetically. I finally got it finished, and it was Homer's turn. The sergeant cleared his copy, and Homer went over to this phone. He looked at the sergeant and said, "S-S-Sergeant, woul-woul-would-would-would you—would you—would you mind r-r-reading this to my—to my office." The sergeant slouched up from his position, snatched the copy out of Homer's hand, picked up the receiver of the phone, and said, "Why can't you read it to 'em?" And Homer looked at him with great dignity and said, "Because, da-da-da-dammit, I'm d-deaf." Oh, gosh, those were good days.

DC: That's a great story. I know Homer Bigart is considered to be among the greatest war correspondents ever. He had a long career. Didn't he even cover some of the war in Vietnam?

WC: Yes, he did. Books could be written about Homer. In fact, I'm surprised somebody hasn't collected the stories about Homer, because every correspondent who ever worked with Homer had some. Homer was terribly handicapped at any news conference or at an ad hoc meeting with a news source. You know, a guy coming out of a courthouse or an officer at a briefing or something, where everybody gathers around and throws questions at this guy. Homer would have a question. He'd try to raise his finger and say, "G-g-general," by that time somebody else would have another question. It was a terrible handicap for him. Homer would eventually get so frustrated he'd throw both arms out to the people around him, pushing them back and saying, "Ju-just a m-m-m-minute!!!" Oh, gosh. [*laughs*] He was wonderful.

BOMBING MISSIONS

DC: When did you get to fly on a bombing mission?

WC: In February 1943. It wasn't allowed at first, but they decided eventually that if we got some training, we could qualify to fly with the bombers. So we went to combat crew replacement center 11, or CCRC11. CCRC11 conducted a one-week course, or maybe it was two. At any rate, the course taught us how to apply high-altitude first aid and how to parachute, as well as other skills for high-altitude survival. We also were taught how to operate a .50-caliber machine gun, the theory being that there really weren't any extra spaces on the bombers, which were B-17 Flying Fortresses and B-24 Liberators. If we were going to fly, then we were going to have to carry a load. Now, this was a violation of the Geneva conventions, which prohibited journalists from being combatants. But the Air Corps also figured that what the devil, if we parachuted out of an airplane, nobody knows whether you fired a gun when you were up there or not. We weren't carrying a gun on our person. So they taught us how to take apart a .50-caliber machine gun in the dark and that sort of thing, put it back together again, and how to fire it.

DC: What was the first mission?

WC: My first mission was the second bombing raid on Germany, which was in February. The first raid had been in January. The mission I flew on was a raid on Wilhelmshaven, a submarine base up north of Hamburg. It was selected because it was on the coast of Germany and we could fly over the North Sea and attack without flying over Germany itself too extensively. It was a pretty horrendous raid. Poor Bill Wade of INS didn't make it to the target. He was safe, but they aborted the flight. His aircraft had mechanical trouble, and they turned back over the channel. Homer Bigart and I flew from the same base at Molesworth, England. We had a choice to a degree. I had been covering the 303rd, and that's why I decided to fly with the 303rd. I knew them better than the others. It was the same way with the other guys. But the big headline in those days was "Fortresses Bomb Europe." Liberators were hardly ever named. So we all wanted to go in the Fortresses, because that was obviously a better headline.

DC: Do you remember much about that first raid?

WC: Oh, boy. Yes, I do. The RAF Spitfires escorted us out over the channel very close to the coast of Holland, about as far as they could go. At that time, the fighters were very limited in their range. The American fighters were even more limited then the RAF Spitfires. We went around the northern coast of Holland over the Frisian Islands. We flew at about seventeen thousand feet, which in those days was considered high altitude. I remember being able to see the Luftwaffe fighters taking off from their bases to attack us. I would say we were under attack for about two hours and forty-five minutes. When we got back to England, I was really almost up to my hips in shell casings around that gun. Not all of the correspondents had the experience of being given a gun. My crew put me on the third gun in the bombardier's compartment, which is a plastic nose out in front of the plane. The bombardier sat right in the nose, the navigator sat over to the left and they had three guns between the two of them. They gave me the starboard gun, on the right-hand side, and I flew up in the nose with them. Some of the guys flew standing between the pilot and copilot, which was a very cramped, awkward, and uncomfortable position. One guy on another plane rode back in the radio room in a little, tiny cubicle area. I can't imagine that he saw very much.

DC: But you had a ringside seat.

WC: I had a great seat, the best you could have. The nose of the Flying Fortress is Plexiglas. I fired at an awful lot of Focke-Wulfs and Messerschmitts that day. I don't think I hit any. I may have hit a Liberator or two—I hope not.

DC: Did you have to worry about flak?

WC: My gosh, we had an awful lot of bursting flak. Germany was very well defended. It was pretty terrifying. We had an added starter; the Liberators did not fly the same type of formations that the Fortresses did. They were not built to hold that steady of a course. They wandered a bit, so they couldn't hold a tight formation. Because of that, they always went alone on the targets outside of the B-17 formations. The whole idea of the Flying Fortress formation was that the guns surrounded the Flying Fortress and each Fortress interlaced with the guns of the neighboring Fortresses so you had a field of fire to protect from all areas. The Liberator didn't have that advantage, because of the nature of their flight characteristics. They were supposed to be over the target immediately after us, but they got there ahead of us for some reason or other, and they were up above us, dropping their bombs right through our formation.

DC: Did they hit any of the Fortresses?

WC: I don't think so. I mean, as far as I know. I'm quite sure that they didn't, but at that altitude, the relative speed of the bomb having just been dropped a couple of hundred feet above you coming through the visual effect is very slow. So there was this surreal thing of these bombs floating right past our window, and you could practically read on them "To hell with Hitler. Signed, Mabel Brookland."

DC: Did the mission lose very many bombers?

WC: Unfortunately, we did. Bob Post of the *New York Times* did not get back from that mission. Bob was in a Liberator that was shot down. They never knew what happened. There were reports that some parachutes were seen opening, but I don't know that any of the crew members were ever recovered. At least Bob wasn't. So Homer Bigart, Gladwin Hill, Andy Rooney, and I were the only ones that got over the target, I think.

DC: Do you recall much about the story you filed after you returned from the mission?

WC: Oh, I certainly do. When we got back, Homer Bigart and I were riding in the command car, which was a big open vehicle. It was cold as the devil that morning. We were driving back from Brampton Green, where we where going to be debriefed, and then go to London to write our stories. Homer said, "W-w-w-w-what's your l-l-lead?" I had been thinking about this, obviously, as he is thinking of it. I told Homer, "I think I'm going to say I've just returned from an assignment from hell, a hell at seventeen thousand feet. A hell of bursting flak and screaming fighter planes." And Homer said, "Y-y-y-y-you wouldn't." [*laughs*] But I did, and I swept the British papers with it. I was the first person to write like that. The editors loved it, and I got the banner line on every British newspaper. It was a great coup.

DC: Is that the piece that made that anthology of war stories that was published after the war?

WC: Yeah, but that book was badly done. I don't know where they got the version of my story they published. Somebody had edited the story before it ever got into that book. I'm very embarrassed by that very badly written piece. It was cut down and not good.

DC: When you were in the bomber flying over Germany, did you talk with the pilots?

WC: We chatted all of the time. When nothing's going on, I mean, on the way to the target, there is chatter on the intercom just within the planes. Communication between planes was very limited. The only advantage of having been up in the cockpit would have been able to hear some of that, which I couldn't hear. But on the plane over the target, then it's all business. There's silence among the crew on the bomb run. After that, it's all about sighting the planes coming in. You know, "Bandit at eleven o'clock and bandit at three o'clock. We have a bandit over here in the middle. You know, bing, bing, bing." And occasionally you could hear, "I think we got some hits back here, but nothing damaged. We're okay back here, go ahead." That's going on all of the time.

DC: Had you decided you'd just shoot at whatever you saw?

WC: Well, you're supposed to shoot at anything that seemed to be coming at you. And boy, they came at you. They would come right in and then peel off. I was always amazed that there weren't more midair collisions. But it was a very exciting bit, I'll tell you that.

DC: Did you say this was a submarine base that was being bombed?

WC: Yeah. Submarine pens. That's what they were going after mostly in those months. The Battle of the North Atlantic was very severe at that time. Submarines were a prime target.

DC: Did you lose many friends in action?

WC: Oh yeah, a lot of fine young guys that I knew. A lot of the guys that were my age, twenty-four and twenty-five, were already majors and colonels, but they were lost, too, because they went on raids. But the younger ones were the pilots.

WARTIME ENGLAND

DC: What was it like to be living in England at this time? Do you have any memories of wartime England that stand out in your memory?

WC: I have very brilliant memories. When I first got over there, the British had not yet been inundated by American troops, and there was a great open-arms welcome. The officers' club had a bulletin board filled with invitations to lunch and to dinner at people's homes around the bases and in London. I went out to one of those just as an experiment to see what it was like to go to a British home for a Sunday meal, and they still had enough food that they could share at that time. Later on, it became much more difficult to do that.

DC: Do you recall any of the times you had a meal with the locals?

WC: Well, I went to the home of some people named Howarth. He was a superintendent of some kind of a boys home. I don't quite remember whether it was an orphan boys home or bad boys home. But they had a very nice house. It was right on the outskirts of London. They served a joint, which was the big thing in England for the Sunday meal. They were able to get one, probably had to give up a lot of ration points. They had one for me, who they kept referring to as "our American visitor" throughout. I kept saying, "Please, call me Walter!" They had a fairly large dinner table, and I think there were four or five members in the household, including a not uncharming daughter. Which may have been their point, I don't know, although they didn't say they were planning on marrying her off soon.

DC: But my understanding is that the Americans soon wore out their welcome.

WC: Oh, that's right. The attitude of the British changed during the war. They got pretty damn tired of their island being weighted down by tens of thousands of these rather brash Americans as well as their own colonial troops. They got equally tired, probably, of the Australians and the New Zealanders. There were not as many of them there— they were down there busy defending their homeland—but there were some, as well as Poles and Hungarians. They had all of the refugees from Europe that had formed up into different armies. I think they got a little tired of that.

DC: I have read that you had quite a rivalry with the Associated Press's Gladwin Hill.

WC: Well, yes. Gladwin Hill and I were intense rivals in covering the air war. We remained at the head of our air war desks, which they later became. At one time, I had four other correspondents working for me, just covering the air war. That was the big story from Europe, of course, because we weren't on the Continent yet. The African story had phased out at about that point, and the big story was the air raids in Europe. Glad and I were writing the leads back in London, and we were directing staffs of people. As the air war built up, the military had a kind of a code system. They called raids a light raid, medium raid, heavy raid, and a very heavy raid. Those codes meant that the light raid, let's say, had up to 250 planes. That figure could be wrong. I'm just using that as an example. I think a heavy raid had 500–1,000 planes. A very heavy raid had more than 1,000 planes. Within the parameters of those definitions, we could use any number we wanted in our stories. We could say there were 780 or 820 planes or whatever number we wanted. So it became a highly skilled exercise in estimating what the size of the force really was.

We'd make our estimates, and the papers would either print the AP or UP stories, depending on who had the most planes, usually, unless we had some fact that the other didn't get. That was usually the criteria for the headline, and Glad and I were pretty close to it every time. I mean, it really got to be quite a science, estimating these numbers. I'd get my information, then I'd figure that there must've been about 875 planes over Dusseldorf or wherever. And then I would worry, "Gosh, I wonder what Glad is going to write." I didn't have time to think this over, because I was writing bulletins. "Bulletin! The United States Air Corps in large force attacked the industrial city of Dusseldorf today." I wanted that to go through, so I wouldn't speculate about the numbers in the first paragraph. So I would just write "in large force." The first paragraph of the bulletin would go out. In the second paragraph, though, I would add, "Experts estimated that 875 United States Flying Fortresses and B-24 Liberators were over the target." Glad was doing exactly the same thing at AP. We'd finish our stories and go down to the Bell Pub and get a gin and lime. I usually beat Glad to the pub. When Glad would come in, he would shout from the door, "How many did you say?" I'd say, "Eight seventy-five." He said, "No, you didn't. You wouldn't say 875." I said, "Eight seventy-five were over the target today." "Come on, Cronkite, what did you really say?" I said, "Eight seventy-five." "'Scuse me a minute," and he'd go to the telephone and call the office. [*laughs*] He would say, "Make it 880." He'd have more than I'd had. And whoever said more was going to get his story in the papers back home.

DC: Golly, Walter, I thought everything I read in the newspaper was exactly the truth. When I write my World War II bombing book, I'll be wary of the bomber estimates in those stories. [*laughs*]

WC: Well, my estimates were more accurate, of course. It's Glad's that you have to worry about. [*laughs*]

Your colleagues still didn't know where you had gone?

No, they had been looking all over town for me. They called
apartment, of course, as th...
e they thought I was, b...
o the office, they were...
rst question was where...
I told them the story,...
Everyone at UP would h...
ey agreed it was the th...
y been written and furt...
eared in a swarm of cop...
pondents on the ground.

l you...

hink...
f cou...
w exte...

you st...

l staye...
s foun...
orps g...
ineers...
ght on...

On the night of June 5, when all of the correspondents,
including my roommate, McGlincy, had been called out for
"maneuvers" yet again, I went to bed fairly early. At about
1:30 in the morning, I heard a rap on my apartment door. When I
opened the door, I found a good friend of mine, Hal Leyshon, a
newspaperman from New York who handled public relations for the
8th Air Force. Hal and I...

CERTIFICATE OF IDENTITY OF NONCOMBATANT
(Par. 76, 94, and 100, FM 27-10)

APO 887, 3 January 1944. (Place and date)

The bearer, WALTER LELAND CRONKITE whose signature appears
below, is hereby certified to be Acc News Correspond

IDENTIFYING INFORMATION

Age 29   Weight 170
Height 5 ft. 11½ in.
Color of hair Light Brown
Color of eyes Blue

FINGERPRINTS—RIGHT HAND, IF OBTAINABLE

THUMB

attached to the Army of the United States in the European
Theater of Operations (Defense Command) and, as such, in event of capture
by the enemy is entitled to be treated as a prisoner of war, and that (s)he
will be given the same treatment and afforded the same privileges as an
officer (enlisted man) in the Army of the United States of the grade of
Captain

By command or by order of Theater Commander

SEAL   ELMER F. FOEHLE 1st Lt AGD (Signature of issuing authority)
(Signature of holder)

HQ.SOS.—22-5-43/1½M/8879 (44/5 P227)

before. We put the names of all you guys in the Flying 69th in
a hat and your name was drawn." Hal had labeled a small group
of correspondents who covered the Eighth Air Force, including
Andy Rooney and Homer Bigart, the "Flying 69th," which was just
a joke. Hal said, "If you want to turn this assignment down you
can do so and I'll leave and that's the end of it except you're

gr...
The bombers were ordered to bring them back. We made the first
pass and then we went up and turned, went through the clouds
...some depth. So we couldn't drop the bombs anywhere.
...had landed already and they were on the
...where the troops might...t drop

CHAPTER FIVE

D-Day to the Battle of the Bulge

DC: I know, Walter, that you were involved in covering the Allied landings on the beaches of Normandy, France, on D-Day, June 6, 1944. Let's talk about that.

WC: As I said, I had been writing the leads in London, and the UP brass nominated me to write the lead story on D-Day, which was a great tribute. I wasn't assigned to troops. I was supposed to stay at my desk and pull together the reports from our correspondents on the beaches and write the story. I greeted that assignment with considerably mixed emotions. I wanted to be macho, and I thought I ought to be there on the ground. On the other hand, writing the lead story sounded like a pretty good assignment. While I was assigned to stay at my desk in London, our correspondents were assigned to various troop units, as the army dictated. To disguise the buildup of forces in preparation for the D-Day landing, army intelligence would frequently call all of the correspondents out to attend secret maneuvers. We didn't know whether the maneuvers portended an actual operation or were really maneuvers. So you never knew what was really happening. But everybody knew the landings were imminent any day now, but nobody knew precisely when.

On the night of June 5, when all of the correspondents, including my roommate, McGlincy, had been called out for "maneuvers" yet again, I went to bed fairly early. At about 1:30 in the morning, I heard a rap on my apartment door. When I opened the door, I found a good friend of mine, Hal Leyshon, a newspaperman from New York who handled public relations for the Eighth Air Force. Hal and I had palled around a little, played a little poker, went out on the town, and drank a bit. So having Hal show up at my apartment at 1:30 in the morning wasn't too surprising, except that he was in his uniform. When he came in, he asked if I was alone. He walked over to the living

Certificate of Identity of Noncombatant issued by the War Department to Cronkite on January 3, 1944, so that he could cover the European theater for United Press during World War II (DI_05802).

room and looked around. I said, "What in the devil are you doing, Hal?" And he said, "I just want to be sure that there is nobody here." Then he said, "Listen, I'm not going to tell you very much, but it's got to be secret. You can't tell anybody; you can't call your office or anything of the kind. You've got to pledge that." I said, "OK, whatever." And I began to get a feeling that it had something to do with D-Day.

Hal said, "We've got a new mission for the Eighth Air Force. And it's going to be highly dangerous, something we've never done before. We put the names of all you guys in the Flying Sixty-ninth in a hat, and your name was drawn." Hal had labeled a small group of correspondents who covered the Eighth Air Force, including Andy Rooney and Homer Bigart, the "Flying Sixty-ninth," which was just a joke. Hal said, "If you want to turn this assignment down, you can do so and I'll leave and that's the end of it, except you're not permitted to say anything about it for the time being. If you accept it, you'll come with me. You can't advise your office, but you'll be able to let them know within a reasonable amount of time. If you come with me, I promise you'll get a pretty good story, but it is highly dangerous." I said, "I'm in. I'm with you."

So I threw my clothes on and we got in the car—he had a military driver, so it was secure—and he said, "We got a very late request to take heavy bombers in at low altitude behind the beach. This is D-Day. It's on. One group of heavy bombers will go in over the beach, a mission they've never been trained for. The army wants some extra heavy bomb power in that particular area." And he added, "You have the greatest story of the war because you're going to get back before any other stories will be released. You will be back in your office ready when the story of D-Day starts hitting the wires. You will be able to write 'I've just returned from flying over the beaches.'" I thought, "Jesus Christ, that's the greatest."

This is now 2:30 or 3:00 in the morning of D-Day, and we were on the way up to the base. It turned out that they had selected the 303rd group. The same one I had flown with before and I'd been covering carefully, so I knew a lot of people. The mission was, indeed, a highly dangerous one because they were to go in at something between low and mid altitude. I forget what it was precisely, a thousand feet perhaps, something like that. They weren't trained to operate at that low of an altitude. Holding position at that altitude is very difficult, and with loaded bomb bays and with any flak, even small-arms fire at that height could be a problem. It was a dangerous mission, but flying over the beaches at that altitude would let me see an awful lot.

Well, unfortunately, after we took off and got over the assembled naval armada in the English Channel, the cloud cover was very heavy, although I did get a pretty good look at the armada down below. I didn't get a very good look at the beach. The beach was covered in fog, but I could see amphibious craft hitting the beach. I couldn't tell much about the men down there, it was too hazy for that, but it also was too cloudy to bomb. Normally in a bomb run, you have alternate targets or you jettison your bombs: you're over enemy territory, the hell with them, you just drop the bombs somewhere. But we didn't know where the troops might be. The airborne troops had landed already, and they were on the ground in some depth. So we couldn't drop the bombs anywhere. The bombers were ordered to bring them back. We made the first pass, and then we went up and turned, went through the clouds with all these bombs loaded in the bomb bays and armed, ready to blow up. Went up through the clouds and came around and made one more pass, and still we couldn't see. We went back to England, where the fog cover was almost total. They landed these airplanes with the bombs still loaded, which was an anxious moment. But there were no casualties or explosions. So, anyway, we got back to London. It turned out that communications worked far better than anybody anticipated, so that the first dispatches were already in the office by the time I arrived. I was the only correspondent to fly that day.

DC: Your colleagues still didn't know where you had gone?

WC: No, they had been looking all over town for me. They called the apartment, of course, as the alert went up. I don't know where they thought I was, but I can imagine. And by the time I got to the office, they were pretty upset about my being missing. The first question was, where were you shacked up last night? When I told them the story, they accepted the reason why I went. Everyone at UP would have done the same thing, of course, so they agreed it was the thing to do. But the lead story had already been written, and, furthermore, my own story virtually disappeared in a swarm of copy that flooded into the bureau from correspondents on the ground.

DC: Did you fly over Utah or Omaha beach?

WC: I think it was Omaha. We didn't know about those names, then, of course; all I knew was it was the beach. I didn't even know how extensive the landings were.

DC: Did you stay in London, or did you get to the beachhead?

WC: No, I stayed in London. I went to the beach the first time on D-Day plus four or five. It was fairly soon after the landing. The Air Corps gave me the opportunity to go with the Ninth Air Force engineers. They had put a landing mat down behind Omaha Beach, right on the beach, practically. They got some steel mats down for mostly liaison planes flying people in and out, that sort of thing. So they were able to take me over. The story was to be the Ninth Air Force story, of course, and we went over and covered that, but then stayed and augmented the beach coverage for a few days. Then London wanted me back because we had so many people over there.

DC: I know that you eventually wound up covering the ground forces in Europe. How long did you stay in London?

WC: Well, I was in London most of the time for that summer of the battle in Normandy in 1944. The UP assigned me to the airborne forces. I was given airborne training to a degree, but it wasn't very extensive. But our missions kept being cancelled, including one in which we were supposed to take part in the liberation of Paris. We actually boarded the planes, but the mission was called off. They set up several other missions, which I was nominated for, but they were all cancelled.

A BUZZ BOMB ATTACK

DC: Oh, before we talk about your experiences on the Continent, I want to ask you something else about this period while you were in London during the summer of 1944. The Germans began their V-1 missile attacks on the city that same summer. Did you have any experiences with those buzz bomb attacks?

WC: Yes, indeed. In fact, I had one experience that was too damn close. By that summer, the German V-1s were hitting London every night. I was actually bombed out of an apartment. I've forgotten the name of the building, but it was back on Buckingham Gate Road, which ran from Buckingham Palace around toward Parliament. I think it's gone now, but it had some old apartment buildings around a kind of a crescent there, and behind us was the battery guard barracks and so forth. McGlincy and I had a top-floor apartment there.

McGlincy was in France. I'd been over to France and come back, and the V-1s had started. At that time, we were told that we had around fifteen seconds to seek shelter after we heard the V-1's engines quit. But then it turned out that they were hitting without giving that cutoff engine warning. At any rate, there was an air raid one Sunday morning, and air raid sirens went off. I had just pressed the servant's button to ring for breakfast. We had this old retired guardsman, George, who was the building's butler. But George hadn't shown up yet when this air raid sounded. I went to look out of our window, and right below us was the roof of one of the grenadier guards barracks. They had sandbags and a couple of antiaircraft gun emplacements on the roof. I saw the guys running to the sandbag area and to their gun. That was no reason for alarm, particularly. But the engine was getting louder and louder. The gunners were looking up, and suddenly they began to fire, and then they ducked. At that moment, the engine cut out, and there wasn't any fifteeen seconds.

I turned and started running back toward the door to get out in the hall. I got about halfway across the bedroom when this thing hit. It landed on the guards' chapel in the middle of services on Sunday morning. It killed a lot of American and British senior officers and their wives. The Germans couldn't have hit a better target at that particular moment. The explosion shook our old brick building terribly. The doors into the hall were opaque glass. The door came off its hinges, blew inward, and the glass all shattered, of course, and the dust came out of the walls, which was inevitable in every bombing. The dust of centuries came out of these old buildings, almost a choking dust. And a couple of the windows blew out, of course, and a couple of pieces of furniture moved around the room a bit. It didn't knock me down, but it knocked me against the wall. I was all right, though. But there was the sound of all this tinkling glass all through the hallway.

I wasn't fully dressed yet, so I went to grab some clothes and get out of there in case of fire or building collapse. As I was dressing, I heard somebody coming down the hall, crunching down through this glass. There was a knock on the door frame, which was all that was left of my door. I went to where the door had been, and there was George, standing there, holding a towel over a cut on his head, and there was a lot of blood on the towel. You'll never guess what he said. His words were, in the middle of this disaster, "Did you ring, sir?" Carrying out his mission, by God, in the best British style.

DC: That's what the Germans didn't understand about the English.

WC: That's right, God love 'em. And I said, "George, for heaven's sakes, are you hurt?" He said, "I got a bit of a gash here, I think, sir." And I said, "I think we ought to see if there's anybody who needs help here." He said, "That's a terribly good idea, sir." And we went and knocked on a couple of doors, and nobody was home. I don't think anybody was hurt in our building. But the building was uninhabitable, so I had to move.

DC: My notes indicate that a V-1 hit Wellington Barracks chapel, killing 121 persons, on June 18, 1944. This must have been the attack you experienced.

WC: Oh, yeah. I think that's right.

DC: Was that your only close encounter with a buzz bomb?

WC: That was the closest. I frequently heard explosions caused by V-1 strikes, but they were much farther away, thankfully.

DC: Did you ever see the German rocket launch sites on the Continent?

WC: Yes, but it was before the Germans started their buzz bomb campaign. In the spring before D-Day, some guys I knew who flew medium bombers said, "Listen, we're going after some interesting targets these days, and they're pretty dangerous missions; we've lost two or three planes on them. They're low-level missions, high-precision bombing, and they're short runs over to the coast and back. Not much fighter danger, because we're flying too low, but a lot of flak problems. If you'd like to go, it's going to be very interesting for you." So I went, and we flew right into the coast of Belgium, and we bombed some funny-looking damn emplacements. I didn't know whether they were railways or big cement ramps. I took a look at them; they were some kind of fortification, I had decided, but I didn't know what they were. It turned out they were V-1 launching sites. And later on, I actually witnessed a V-2 rocket launched in Holland. This was after we'd made the airborne landing and were in the Netherlands.

DC: Let's go back to your experience in the Netherlands later, but how did you see this rocket launch?

WC: Well, the Netherlands is a very small country, of course, and when the visibility is good, you can see clear across the country. We were in the eastern side of the Netherlands; and we could see the Germans launching V-2s from a site outside The Hague. We could see their vapor contrails. We were among the first to see a V-2 launch, even at a hundred miles or so.

TURNING DOWN MURROW

DC: Before we talk about your experiences on the Continent, there are a couple of other things I want to talk to you about. While you were in London, Edward R. Murrow offered you a job with CBS.

WC: Well, I had met Ed on two or three occasions in London that winter. Sometime during the summer of 1943, Ed called me to have lunch. I understood him to say, "Meet me at the Saddle Club." He said, "Do you know where that is?" I didn't, but I wasn't going to admit it, so I said, "Of course." Ed was a bit of a presence back home, and I was rather pleased. I got in the cab on Fleet Street, and I told the guy I wanted to go to the Saddle Club. "Don't believe I know it, governor," he said. I said, "Everybody knows the Saddle Club. You must know where the Saddle Club is." "Sorry, governor, never heard of the Saddle Club." Well jeez, I had to get out and look it up in the phone book, but no Saddle Club was listed. So I called back to the UP office, and I got somebody on the phone, and I said, "Hey, where the hell is the Saddle Club?" They said, "The Saddle Club? Don't know the Saddle Club. What kind of place is it?" I said, "I don't know. I'm supposed to meet Ed Murrow there for lunch." They said, "Oh, you must mean the Saville Club." That's how much I knew about club life in England.

So anyway, I was a little late and embarrassed. In the course of lunch, Ed asked me if I would like to join CBS and go to Moscow or Kuibyshev, where the Russian government was at the time, to replace Bill Downs, CBS's man there. Murrow offered me $125 a week plus commercial fees. He said, "Almost every time you get on the air, and you'll be on the air a lot, you've got $25 or so for being on a commercial broadcast. It's not bad income." That was well over what I was making at United Press, which, I think, was about $57.50 a week. It also seemed prestigious. I did, however, have a lot of doubt about radio. I hadn't liked my experience in radio. I thought it was kind of a shlock business compared to print. But I still thought, well, $125 and a chance to go to Russia, I probably ought to take it. So I accepted it, and I was going to give United Press a couple of weeks' notice, which, frankly, wasn't adequate in wartime.

I went back and told Harrison Salisbury that I had this offer and that I had accepted. Salisbury said, "Oh my gosh, I've got a cable here. I've had it for three days and haven't had a chance to tell you yet, but we want to give you a big merit raise, the biggest they've ever given in the history of the UP London bureau. I'm going to raise you to

$75 a week." This was a $17.50 raise, which was unheard of in UP. I don't know to this day whether Salisbury was telling me the truth or whether he made it up or ad-libbed it. But Harrison said, "Hugh Baillie, the president of UP, has got such faith in you that he insists that you get this raise. Boy, with that kind of a vote of confidence, are you sure you want to leave UP?" Well, he drove a stake right in my heart, because I loved the UP, I really did. I said, "Well, gee, you know, I told Mr. Murrow that I would accept his offer, and I think I'm going to have to carry that out." Harrison said, "Well, you better think this over."

That night, Hugh Baillie managed to get this call through to me from New York. He gave me a sales pitch like I never heard in my life. Baillie said, "Walter, I'm going to raise you $20 a week just to show my good faith. You're going to be president of the United Press before you're very old." And I said, "Does that include the $17.50 that Salisbury just told me already?" There was kind of a long pause, and he said, "No, no, this is on top of that," which meant I was going up to $95 a week, a huge amount for United Press. So I said, "Well, let me think it over, but I'm quite sure, Mr. Baillie, with that kind of vote of confidence, I want to stay with United Press." So I told Murrow, and he didn't take it too kindly. He didn't say anything particularly, but his attitude was such that he indicated that he felt that I had used this as a bargaining tool with UP, which, of course, in effect I had. I hadn't meant to; it wasn't my intention when I accepted Ed's offer. But it worked out that way, and Ed had every right to feel that way about it. So I stayed with United Press.

DC: A. M. Sperber, in her biography of Murrow, says that he never forgave you for that rejection. Did she make too much of that incident?

WC: I don't think so. I think that's probably true.

DC: Do you think that it was always hanging over your relationship?

WC: I think so. I think he always did feel that, you know, that it showed a certain lack of character, or something of the kind.

DC: Do you think that he felt that his team, the so-called Murrow's Boys, were probably the cream of the crop and just . . . [*"Murrow's Boys" refers to a renowned group of CBS broadcast journalists who served as correspondents under Murrow's direction during World War II, including Charles Collingwood, Eric Servereid, Winston Burdett, and Richard C. Hottelet.*]

WC: Oh yes. I don't doubt that at all. If I had gone ahead, I would have been one of the Murrow's Boys, too, undoubtedly. But as it was, I was not only not a Murrow's Boy, but probably an anti–Murrow's Boy in Ed's mind. Let me mention something about CBS. Despite my turning down Ed's offer, CBS kept inviting me to do pieces on the air. They kind of used me as an air war correspondent, and I did two or three pieces on the night that they made that raid on Germany. And later, sometime in 1945, I was on

CBS's weekly roundup of war news. I did a piece for them. So I had a connection with CBS through that whole period.

DC: And you got to know some of Murrow's Boys?

WC: Yeah, I got to know them fairly well. They weren't as close as my writing buddies were, but I knew them all. I palled around with Bill Downs quite a lot. I knew most of the others through him. Charles Collingwood was probably the one I knew best out of that group. When I got to Moscow after the war, Dick Hottelet befriended us, and we were very close.

THE WAR ON THE GROUND

DC: Let's talk about your work as a correspondent reporting on the war on the ground. Why were you reassigned from covering the airborne troops?

WC: Well, I actually wasn't reassigned. I got on the Continent with the airborne. With Patton and everybody moving so fast across western France at that point, these airborne assignments kept getting cancelled. They set them up, and the ground force would get there before we could get there. But finally there was the mission that became Market-Garden. It was the big operation that turned the flanks of the Germans on the Meuse River. The British dropped across the Meuse, and we dropped on the other side of the river, thank goodness. The 101st dropped at the south end of the line at Eindhoven. I went in with the glider forces; I didn't parachute. When they assigned me to a glider, I almost refused the assignment because I had seen the gliders crashed all over Normandy. Gliders turned out to be a very poor way of moving troops. I do not recommend it as a way to go to war. If you ever have to go to war, don't go by glider.

DC: Where did your glider land?

WC: We were near the little town of Zon. That night another correspondent, Stanley Woodward of the *Herald Tribune*, and I found refuge in a house in the outskirts of the town. It was the home of a nice little Dutch couple. They were welcoming Americans, glad to see us. We wanted to move back into the town of Eindhoven, cross the Zon canal harbor. The objective of that particular group of the 101st that I was with was to grab the bridge at Zon, which is on the main highway from Belgium to Arnhem. The airborne was supposed to grab that bridge and hold it until the British arrived. Well, like all these other bridges, the only problem was that the Germans had blown it up as soon as we arrived in the area.

So now there was a canal that had to be crossed to get over into Eindhoven. The way Stanley and I got across was on some rafts made of oil drums that were towed across the canal. I guess it was the second night after we landed that I got to Eindhoven. It was where the British would come first, so I wanted to be there when the British arrived. They had to bridge the canal, so there was going to be a day or two of operations on the Eindhoven side. I got a room in the Orange Hotel, which was still operating right by the railway station. The British arrived the next day, but the bridging equipment hadn't gotten there yet.

The British did some strange things in the war, but they did seem incompetent from time to time. They brought all of this military equipment up to the bridge despite the fact that the bridge-building equipment had not arrived. So they had to clear the road to get the bridge equipment up. The road was totally choked right through the town of Eindhoven with armor, supplies, ammunition, and fuel—all the stuff needed to maintain an army. I was at the Orange Hotel in the late afternoon when rumors came that German tanks were on their way down the canal road to try to cut the road off at Eindhoven. Just as we got that information, the Luftwaffe came over and dropped a couple of bombs around the railroad tracks and right by the hotel. The British correspondents had caught up with us at this point. Bill Downs of CBS was also there. Bill and I were having a great time downstairs in the bar at the hotel when the bombs hit. Boom, boom, boom, boom! They fell right down the railway track and blew out the windows of the hotel.

Before the bombing started, we had poo-pooed this Tiger tank attack rumor as not likely. I think we had been briefed by some of the minor officers of the 101st. They said their patrols didn't indicate that kind of action was going on there. But with the bombing, we began to think maybe something was going on. They are softening us up. So Bill Downs and I hopped in the jeep and drove out across the main road to the 101st Airborne headquarters, which was in a school. It was just beginning to get dark.

Before we could get to the school, here came more Luftwaffe dive bombers. They went for the convoy, of course, because it was all jammed together on this narrow road at the canal. The Germans hit it, and my God, it was the worst holocaust. The ammunition and fuel trucks blew up right in the middle of Eindhoven. I was in Bill Downs's British jeep with a British driver when the bombs started falling. We pulled under some trees, right next to a little housing development. There were trees and a park and a big chain-link fence under the trees in the park area. We leaped that fence and got on the other side. For the first time, I used my trenching tool and tried to dig myself a foxhole real quick. It was ridiculous because the ground was too hard. It was getting dark, and all this flame and stuff was shooting up a couple blocks from us, and more bombs were falling.

At that time, the Germans were dropping a lot of antipersonnel weapons called butterfly bombs. They were little tiny mines, really, that had metal wings on them. They'd drop slowly, and they'd settle in the trees and bushes so that if you were trying to go through these areas, they would blow up. They were dangerous as hell, and the assumption was that they'd sowed the woods with them on these raids.

Well, I don't know how long the bombing lasted, maybe a half hour or something.

I started looking for Downs, but I couldn't find him. I was sure that the butterfly bombs were in the trees, and the trees had fallen because of bombing. I thought, well, Downs is gone, he must be dead, he's not calling for me. So after a short while of looking for him, I went back to the fence. How the hell we ever jumped that fence with a pack, I don't know; it was far too high for anybody to climb, and I thought I was trapped forever in there. I finally found a tree that had fallen. I climbed up the tree and over the fence, and I worked my way back to the jeep, which had been covered with dirt and dust and debris. It was still fairly intact, but it wouldn't run. So I went to the nearest air raid shelter, which was filled with crying and frightened Dutch children and old people and others. I asked if they'd seen an American correspondent. Nobody had. They were all clinging to me, asking me what was going on, and of course, I didn't have any idea.

I went to 101st Airborne headquarters, and they were pretty active, trying to figure out how many trucks were burning and that sort of thing. They thought the Germans were coming in, too, to follow up on the bombing. Indeed, one Tiger tank did come up the canal road and fired a few 88 rounds, but it was nothing serious. [*The main gun on a Tiger tank had a caliber of eighty-eight millimeters.*] I decided to hell with this; I'm going to go back to Brussels. There was no communication from out of there at all, and I now had a lot of stories accumulated. I went to Brussels to file my stories, and then I came back to Eindhoven a couple of days later.

I went to a little Dutch house that night on the outskirts of town and bedded down for the night with a Dutch family. The next morning, I hitchhiked my way back to Brussels, which is normally an hour-long trip, but it was about a four-hour trip because of the crowded roads and road damage. When I got down to Brussels, I was tired and ready for a bath. I walked into the Metropole Hotel in my filthy uniform, and I thought, well, I don't care how I look. I'm going to buy a bottle of champagne to take up to the room. I figured I'd have a bath and some champagne, and walked into the bar, and there is an immaculate, well-dressed Bill Downs, standing at the bar, knocking them down [*laughs*], and I was furious. I said, "You son of a bitch. For crying out loud, I spent my time wandering through that minefield calling your name, trying to find you, and here you just turn around and come to Brussels. And you don't look for me or anything." Bill said, "I looked for you, Walter. I left word for you around a couple places. I called your name a couple of times, and then I realized if the Germans had really infiltrated and I'm in this woods crying, 'Cronkite, Cronkite,' they're going to think I'm sick and they're going to take me to a hospital." [*laughs*] "Cronkite" sounds like a German word for "sick." I told him that was a very poor excuse.

DC: You said something earlier that made me wonder if you had any weapons on you when you landed in Holland.

WC: No, because of the Geneva conventions. A few correspondents did. They were macho characters most of them, Hemingway types. But that was very rare. I could never see a situation where I needed a weapon. Maybe in that woods in Eindhoven if one German had approached me, maybe I could have used a weapon. But most of the time, you had troops surrounding you or somewhere nearby. One weapon wouldn't have done you any good.

THE BRITISH FRONT

DC: So where did you go after you returned to Brussels after the Eindhoven incident?

WC: I rejoined the 101st Airborne and then went on up to Nijmegen. The British were going to drop alone at Nijmegen and then try to grab the bridges. I attended the briefing meeting, and I was rather appalled at the sketchy kind of briefing that they got, compared to the American briefings, which were very thorough. At the British briefing, there was an occasion where a small unit was supposed to cross a little, small bridge across a canal at Nijmegen, and when they were asked for questions by the lieutenant colonel who was doing the briefing, the sergeant said, "How are we supposed to do this job? What if they've blown the bridge?" The officer answered, "Can't you bloody well swim?" That was his answer.

DC: Well, that's a big help, isn't it?

WC: Yeah, that's a big help, isn't it? You know, you might think he'd say, "Well, there is another bridge up here; maybe that will be available," but "Can't you bloody well swim?"

DC: So you were back with the 101st Airborne. Any close calls or other memorable incidents?

WC: We had several, since we were fired at quite a lot. But on one, I took a jeep when we barely had a hold on the road between the 101st and the 82nd. My purpose was to drive up to check on the 82nd Airborne and spend the day with them. I stayed too long, and we were forced to drive back in the dark, which we didn't want to do. We were coming down the road when suddenly we heard tanks. Now, the American units in that sector didn't have any tanks. The British had tanks, so we thought maybe we were hearing the British coming down the road. But they weren't due that soon. We pulled over to the edge of the road under some trees. Just as we did, the first tank comes down the road, crumbling up the pavement as it went. We could hear them talking, and we realized they were all speaking in German. They were German tanks. We sat there frozen in the jeep. Five tanks went by, and they were talking and shouting orders back and forth, just as comfortable as they could be. They apparently never saw us. They went by, and then, of course, we had a horrible ride the rest of the way because we thought there might be another bunch coming at us.

DC: Okay, what did you do after you landed in Holland?

WC: I covered the war on the British front, which was Montgomery's Second Army. I also

covered Belgian politics, which were very fiery that winter. The Belgians brought
their exile government back from London with the liberation of Brussels, which was
in August 1944. The formerly exiled government called on everybody who had arms
to turn them in. But there were a number of communist-controlled resistance fighters who said the hell with that. So everybody was interested in how this was going to
come out. There were tanks in the streets of Brussels, and there were threats against
the government buildings. If there was any shooting, it was very minor. This went
on for a couple of months during that winter, so that was a story that I was covering
behind the front and also covering General Montgomery's war effort.

DC: So now you were also covering Montgomery's war. How did you feel about Montgomery?

WC: I thought about him like most American generals did. He really didn't deserve the
credit he got. Montgomery was a man who, according to, I think, most American
opinion and a lot of British opinion, rode on the back of other people's capabilities
and sometimes their actual accomplishments. That was particularly true in the desert
in North Africa, where he made his first reputation. He used the strategy that British general Harold Alexander developed to win. In Europe, Montgomery demanded
overwhelming forces on his side before he'd make a move. He sat on the Rhine intol-
erably long, really, and maybe could have turned that flank at the Meuse if he had been
willing to really take a gamble.

DC: Did you ever get a chance to interview him. I know you did years later, but during war?

WC: I attended many briefings and asked questions, along with other people, but I never
did a one-on-one interview.

THE BATTLE OF THE BULGE

DC: Weren't you also in the Battle of the Bulge?

WC: Well, I was back in Brussels the night that Field Marshal Von Runstedt started pounding through the Ardennes. I got a call from UP in Paris that something had happened,
they didn't know what. This was maybe two or three in the morning. They said that
something was going on in the Ardennes. They wanted me to check with Monty's
headquarters to find out what was happening. I had hardly hung up the phone when a
guy named John Fleischer, our correspondent with the First Army, came to my apartment and said, "This goddamn thing is real. We have a headlong retreat." The First
Army press camp had been overrun, and Fleischer had fled back with the troops. He
said, "I'm going to turn around and go right back out, but I wanted to tell you about
it, give you the facts, let you write something, get it on the line. Then I'm going to

drive right back to Namur. I just wanted to let you know, because communications are shot." So Fleischer turned around and went back. He was killed shortly after that. I filed Fleischer's story, and then I called Paris and said I was on the way to the front if there was any to be found.

DC: Was it difficult to get to the front?

WC: My gosh. The roads were packed with fleeing American forces. We had never had a military retreat like that. The American army had never run like that. And jeez, you couldn't go on the road. I used the side roads to get down as far as Namur. I ran into the military police right outside Namur, and they demanded a password. I didn't have any goddamn idea what the password was, so I talked my way through and finally got to Luxembourg City. The Germans were still in the woods, out in the Ardennes. The retreat was not quite as disorderly, in reality, as it had appeared to me. The troops just kept flowing back, and that was probably by instruction, I don't know. But the main forces that were still on the front had held and were in a fierce battle with the Germans. The situation wasn't as unhealthy as it looked in the back of the lines.

Anyway, I got all the way to Luxembourg and learned that General Patton's Third Army was being wheeled around from the south and was moving to this front. I was at the First Army front, and it had broken up completely. The Canadians and the British were on the north side of us, and they were turning some forces back down. But Patton, with his extraordinary ability, accomplished one of the greatest feats of modern war. He turned the entire Third Army around and brought them back up into Luxembourg and into that battle in about forty-eight hours. It was an incredible feat, absolutely dumbfounding. Patton's army was arriving or just about to arrive when I got to Luxembourg, so I joined the Third Army.

DC: That must have been a harrowing experience, being on that front.

WC: Well, Don, I have to confess that I was in the fur-lined foxhole of all time. This beautiful little principality of Luxembourg hadn't been touched by the war and wasn't about to be. It had very moderate damage during the Battle of the Bulge. So I was in this fairyland relatively untouched by the war. We made the Grand Cravat Hotel our press headquarters. The Cravat Hotel actually had hot running water and plenty of champagne in the bar. We got out of our warm beds and put on all our old clothes and got in those open jeeps and went out to battle, and came back to champagne and hot baths every night.

The Third Army press camp was actually in a schoolhouse down in Esch, which is a mean little coal-mining town just outside of Luxembourg City. The press there had the usual pitched bedrolls and cold water. But General Vandenburg's Air Corps headquarters and General Bradley's Second Army headquarters were back in Luxembourg City. Patton would also make Luxembourg City his headquarters. In fact, all three commands were housed in the Cravat Hotel. So I just checked into the Cravat, for heaven's sakes. To hell with the press's cold-water camp in Esch, which was not where the story was anyway.

DC: That certainly sounds like the most reasonable strategy to me. So how did you cover the actual front from the Hotel Cravat? Or did you just do stories from briefings made at the hotel?

WC: No, no. I slept at the hotel, but I went out in the field everyday. I got up in the morning very early. The army assigned me a jeep and a driver who would take me down to Esch. I got there in time for the briefing every morning. That was how all the armies worked. Sometimes you were actually out in the field with a division or you were out with a smaller unit, and then you just stayed with them and did whatever they did. But if you were covering the overall military front, you went to the briefing in the morning and the briefing officer told you what had happened overnight. Such stuff as what the patrols had discovered, where the forces were, where they expected action that day, and what our intentions were. They didn't give you so much information that if you were captured, you might give away any useful secrets. It was enough information to give you a sense of where to go that day if you wanted to get into any particular kind of action. Once you made up your mind, you told the press officer, "I want to go to such and such." He either said you could or you couldn't go.

DC: How was that decision made?

WC: Well, it often depended on whether they thought you needed an escort. If you had an escort, a lot of factors came into play. But usually you could go where you wanted to go and usually without an escort. And you always had your driver. There weren't enough vehicles, usually, for everybody to have their own jeep, so we had to double up. You had to choose somebody to go with you who wanted to go on the same mission. And then you went out to that place and got a story or didn't get a story. Then you came back maybe in time for the evening briefing or not, and that was it. I would file my story, and the censors took over and decided whether to pass it.

One day during this time, I had a different driver than normal. Patton would not let us have the windshields up on the jeeps, because if the windshield was up and the sun caught it, the reflection was like a searchlight to the enemy artillery spotters. The windchill factor must have been minus 100. God, it was cold. And we had to have the windshield down. We looked like Washington's army at Valley Forge. We had those khaki mufflers around our faces, and our eyes just barely showing, huddled under our coats. That was the way we drove up to this town. So the troops I was with entered a town, and we got into a firefight right away. It was very intense. My driver and I hopped out of our jeep and got in behind a doorway. The Germans were at one end of the main street, and the GIs were coming up the other side. It was a pretty good firefight. I looked up and saw a GI in the doorway, leaning out, taking a shot or two back behind the doorway. I knew this was a story. You know, "Brave little GI fighting his war in this doorway." So I yelled out, "What's your name, soldier?" "Colonel Jones." I said, "Where are you from? What outfit are you with?" He said, "Hell, Mr. Cronkite, I'm your driver." [*laughs*]

DC: Were there very many hairy situations like that in the Bulge?

WC: Oh, they are all hairy, you know. You had moments when you thought you got in a little deeper than you ought to have. Like that firefight, for example, things like that. I mean, there may have been some macho correspondents who were out looking to get into the action, but most of us wanted to get just near enough to the action to understand what was happening, get the stories from the guys who had done it, and then get the stories out. We frequently got mortared or had to endure some other fire. You couldn't avoid that. Sometimes you would be on the road and come under some artillery fire. And that would be goddamn uncomfortable. There was one episode, however, when I declined an invitation to go to a battle that would have given me a hell of a story. That was at Bastogne, where the Germans had the 101st Airborne surrounded. Since this was the outfit I'd been in with in Holland, I was particularly anxious to get the story of the army getting into Bastogne and relieving these guys. I went out and found an armored-division combat unit commanded by a guy named Creighton Abrams, who then went on to some fame in Vietnam. Creighton Abrams's armored outfit was spearheading the effort to get into Bastogne. Another correspondent and I went up there that day, and we got there just as a patrol came back from having gotten through to Bastogne. We got a report from them about what they'd seen. This was a great story, because there had been no news from out of Bastogne. We were getting kind of antsy to finish up and rush back to Luxembourg, where we could file this great story of the patrol getting into Bastogne, when a jeep came bouncing into the headquarters bearing Maxwell Taylor, who was the commander of the 101st Airborne. I had gotten to know him back in England.

    Taylor had been on leave at home when the Bastogne battle started. He flew back right away, and he rushed to the front still wearing his dress clothes. When he was told that a patrol had gotten through, he asked, "Can you take me back there?" And the patrol leader said, "Yes sir, we can take you back going the same way, if it's still open." And Taylor said, "Let's go." He turned to me and said, "Cronkite, are you coming?" Well, gee, what a terrible choice. It's the one time when I really chickened out. My rationale that I live with today was that I had this great story about the patrol getting through and I needed to file it. On the other hand, I had the possibility of being the first correspondent into Bastogne. But my story would be delayed by however long it took to get into Bastogne. That is, if we made it in at all. Now, I don't know whether it was cowardice or wisdom that directed me to go back to Luxembourg and file the story rather than go with Taylor into Bastogne. And, obviously, now I wish I'd gone, because it would make a better story. But at the time it seemed like the wise thing to do.

DC: That's a very understandable reaction.

WC: Yeah, Don, it's understandable, but that's not what you're there for as a correspondent. So obviously, I have some regrets about it.

"I'LL SHOW YOU HOW THIS WORKS"

WC: But this thing about my decision at Bastogne reminds me about something else that happened during the Battle of the Bulge. I had a thing about not getting killed on Christmas. So I decided that Christmas would be a great day to do a story about the artillery. There was something happening in the artillery called TOT, which I had not really received a full explanation of from anybody. I knew it was a devastating artillery tactic that they had developed. So I went to an artillery headquarters and almost got killed getting there. As we were driving down the road, there was a little hillock behind us, and suddenly three shots rang out, and they pinged on the dirt behind us. You know, we speeded up like hell, not knowing where they came from. This was quite a distance behind the front lines. It could have been a sniper, or it could have been a GI having fun, I don't know.

Anyway, I got to the artillery base. The general came out and was glad to have me there. They were going to entertain me for lunch and all this. He explained that TOT is "time on target" fire. It was made possible by a fairly new and very accurate barometric fuse, which made it possible to explode shells at various distances from the ground. They could load concrete-piercing and ground-piercing shells in one battery of guns. There were shells to explode on first contact, which would get the top floors of a building, and another battery would explode shells at fifty feet above, while another would explode a hundred feet above, with antipersonnel weapons. And it was almost like an atomic attack. It would just wipe out a huge area like that. It was a very devastating. Nobody had written about it yet. The general didn't know whether censorship would clear it or not, but he told me about it. He was talking about it in his headquarters room. There was a big map on the wall with notes all over it and little pins sticking in places. The general said, "Now, this is our sector right here. Go ahead and pick a target, and I'll show you how this works." So I just picked a little crossroads village without thinking much about it. He said, "Well, now, here's the way this works. I'll look up the coordinates for that village. I then call the telephone-operator sergeant like this." He picked up the phone and read the coordinates. He then said, "TOT, 13:20 hours," which just happened to be about three minutes from then. And the general said, "Now that's the way we do it. I give an order like that, and the sergeant plugs things in, based on these orders. And I can assure you that in three minutes, that town goes."

So I said, "Well, that's very interesting, General, that's fine." We went on talking about something else when suddenly "boom, boom, boom, boom, boom." The goddamn guns are going off all across the countryside. I said, "Gee, what's that?" He said, "Oh, that's our TOT at 13:20, right on the dot." And I said, "Not on that town?" He said, "Oh yeah. Boy, that town's not there now, I can tell you that." And I said, "But I thought you were just asking for a demonstration." "Well, yes, that's the demonstration. I was showing you how it works. It's really something." I said, "But gee, I didn't realize . . . but, my God, there could be innocent little . . ." He interrupted me and said "Oh, that's not an innocent town. You picked a good one," he said. "That's a five-road crossroads right there." He said, "We've been meaning to hit that for some time. I don't know if we got any traffic going through today, but . . ."

DC: That's the kind of thing you might find in a Kurt Vonnegut novel, where some poor soul gets wiped out just because somebody picked a random place on a map.

WC: Isn't that something? Yeah, Vonnegut's a friend. I should tell him that story. It would certainly reinforce his view of the world. [*Vonnegut died in 2007.*]

DC: Did you see a lot of human carnage when you were a reporter during the war?

WC: Yes, I did. I don't know that I saw as much as a lot of others did. It seemed to me that I was fortunate in kind of missing seeing a lot of that. But I did see a lot of soldiers killed in action.

DC: The reason I raise that point is that there have been a couple of books published recently that argue that because of the way wars have been covered in the past by the press, the inherent horror of war has usually been glossed over, often for reasons of maintaining morale back home.

WC: You know, there's another reason for that to happen. You can't write horror stories every day because nobody would read it, for one thing. It's repetitious. You have a war that's going on for five years with all the carnage, and that stuff was written about. Take the Japanese rape of China, for example. That horror was written in detail. You've got incidents such as the storm of German Stuka dive bombers and the horror they unleashed on Poland. That was written about extensively. The German aerial blitz on London was written about.

DC: Well, yes, but the examples you cite are about enemy atrocities, which both sides publicized extensively for propaganda reasons. You know, the *Why We Fight* thing. But there are some who argue that one of the side effects of the "gloss over" type of reporting about American casualties is that war has been glorified and romanticized. Or at least the wrong impression about its true severity has been made.

WC: Oh, I think that stuff can only be written by people who have not been through war themselves. I don't think anybody glossed over the horrors suffered by the American forces. The horrors the marines suffered on Iwo Jima come to mind immediately. I believe that story was disseminated back to the U.S. very quickly. And of course, there were stories of heroism and self-sacrifice in war. Those stories were deliberately written about. There is no doubt about that. These critics you cite are propagandists themselves, it seems to me. They would prefer that we wrote antiwar propaganda day in and day out. And the big reason not to do so is it doesn't sell. Nobody would read it. You can only read so much of that. And besides, it loses its impact with repetition. Who is going to read it every day?

DC: So what was your assignment after the Battle of the Bulge?

WC: I didn't do an awful lot of war coverage after the Battle of the Bulge. I covered the Canadians and the British up in the Netherlands and covered the political stuff in Brussels.

DC: Where were you when the Germans surrendered?

WC: I was in the Netherlands. The liberation of the western Netherlands had taken place a couple days before the general surrender, so I was filing the Netherlands liberation story, which got lost, of course, in the general jubilation over the end of the war in Europe. There were a number of great stories in the Netherlands, but I didn't get to print any of them because of the German surrender.

DC: Did you reopen the UP bureau in the Netherlands?

WC: Yeah, we didn't have a bureau in Luxembourg, and we didn't have one in Brussels either, for that matter, but I established bureaus in both places. In fact, we got our first wire into Brussels. Our teleprinter didn't work in the Netherlands. We didn't have any wire to connect it to in the Netherlands. But in Brussels during that winter, we got a bureau office, and we got the first direct wire from Paris. That wire gave us a big beat, but it also gave me a terrible experience. Very shortly after we got the wire in, the teletype was running, and there came a flash on the wire: "Americans drop new mystery bomb on Japan. Bomb said to have equivalent of ten thousand tons TNT." I told the staff, "Now wait a minute, wait a minute. That can't be. There isn't any bomb that has ten thousand tons of TNT. It's got to be a thousand tons of TNT," so I duly corrected it for the Belgian newspaper. And then I queried Paris and said this can't be. And by that time, the next thing on the wire was that the bomb was said to be an atomic bomb. It was the bomb we dropped on Hiroshima, of course.

DC: Did your false correction get in the papers?

WC: No, nobody put it in, thank God.

amusing. During the conduct of the trial, we did something
I thought was a little bit extralegal. We, of course, controlled
all of the German files. In order for a defendant's lawyer to
get a file, he had to specify the file. He couldn't do a discovery
procedure by simply going through the files, he had to ask for a
...ific document, which handicapped their search quite a bit,

...tes in his lavender notebook. This
t Goering had. Now I've got some
, but here is the essence of the
n the stand, Jackson said at one
933, you met with defendant Schacht
...uss the continuing financing of the

stands out in your memory about the trial?

the personalities stand out, in their own ways.
ring not just to the defendants but

as thinking that we were going to have to print
was putting in the record and let it out for the

id you spend much time in the courtroom?

, and it was conducted on the second floor.

CHAPTER SIX

Nuremberg

DC: The trial of the top surviving Nazi leaders on war-crimes charges began in Nuremberg, Germany, on November 20, 1945. You covered that trial for the United Press.

WC: Well, I wasn't there for the opening of the trial. I didn't get there until January. General Patton was fatally injured in an automobile wreck in early December and lingered for several days before he died. UP asked me to cover that story, which took most of December. I went to Patton's funeral in Luxembourg. As I think about it, it seems to me that I was at Nuremberg by Christmas. I might have my dates a little confused, but I wasn't there at the opening of the trial, which was the very dramatic part. I did get there in plenty of time, however, for the revelation of the documents and the horrors of Nazism, the showing of the films of the concentration camps.

DC: That reminds me of another question I was going to ask you earlier. Did you see any of the concentration camps?

WC: No, I never went to a camp. But we saw the films there at Nuremberg the first time.

DC: What stands out in your memory about the trial?

WC: Well, the personalities stand out, in their own ways. I'm referring not just to the defendants but also to other participants in the proceedings. I met the Jewish military doctor who was put in charge of Hermann Goering when he was captured. He later admitted that he tried to kill Goering by withdrawing him cold turkey from his heroin habit. But Goering tolerated an awful lot of heroin, apparently. Goering survived withdrawal and actually became remarkably healthy, considering his earlier lifestyle of drinking and dope and whatever. A guy named Colonel [Burton C.] Andrus headed

United Press correspondents Douglas Werner, Walter Cronkite, and Richard Clark reporting on the Nuremberg Trials, 1946 (DI_05805).

our security forces in Nuremberg. They did petty things that I suppose conquering jailers are likely to do. For instance, they gave Goering one of his pearl grey uniforms, stripped, of course, of all braid and ribbons and other decorations. They let him live in this uniform that was three and four times too big for him, throughout the trial. He was a vain man, and there he was not even tailored for the big occasion. But Goering was remarkably alert mentally and had a damn good mind. When he was put on the stand by Robert Jackson, the chief prosecutor, Goering read into the record of the trial a testament to Nazism. Jackson seemed unaware of what Goering was doing. But Goering obviously figured that one thing that we were going to have trouble censoring in the future was the trial proceedings at Nuremberg. It seemed obvious to me and to others that Goering was thinking that we were going to have to print that stuff he was putting in the record and let it out for the schools and everybody else. So for his three days on the stand, he told what mistakes the Nazis had made, which sounded like he was being very candid about Nazism, but in effect he was saying here is how you do this again. You avoid these mistakes, and you'll win the next time. It was so cleverly done that I don't think Justice Jackson even realized it was happening.

When Goering asked for a notebook during the trial, they gave him a lavender one. The jailers all thought that was very amusing. During the conduct of the trial, we did something that I thought was a little bit extralegal. We, of course, controlled all of the German files. In order for a defendant's lawyer to get a file, he had to specify the file. He couldn't do a discovery procedure by simply going through the files; he had to ask for a specific document, which handicapped their search quite a bit, I guess. But Goering made notes in his lavender notebook. This was the kind of sharp mind that Goering had. Now I've got some of these dates and names wrong, but here is the essence of the story. When Jackson got him on the stand, Jackson said at one point, "And on December 31, 1933, you met with defendant Schacht at the Dresdner Bank to discuss the continuing financing of the National Socialist Party." Goering shook his head and said, "No, that's not right." Jackson said, "What do you mean, that's not right? I've got the documentation here in my hand. It is a letter about the meeting you had." Goering said, "No, that's incorrect. If you would look at the letter more carefully, the meeting was held on December 27th; the letter was written on the 31st." Goering hadn't seen that letter in twelve years, but he had that kind of memory. He just infuriated Jackson time after time. He was so cool on the stand, and Jackson was perspiring. Jackson was not a very good cross-examiner. Tom Dodd was the strength of that defense team. Dodd was a very good, old district-attorney type. He understood criminal law, which Jackson had no experience in.

DC: And Jackson was on the U.S. Supreme Court by this time. He was Justice Jackson.

WC: Yes, and he helped draw up the bill of particulars for the whole Nuremberg trial.

DC: Did you have much of an impression of the president of the tribunal, British Lord Justice Lawrence?

WC: Oh, he was a splendid, terrific British jurist. The second British judge was Sir William Birkett, a redheaded, unprepossessing-looking guy. He was known as one of the great wits as well as one of the brilliant minds of the British judicial system. There was a great story that everybody told about him in a London trial in which he gave the convicted defendant the last word and the guy said, "As God is my judge, I'm innocent." And the justice said, "He isn't, I am, and you aren't." And the British prosecutor, G. D. Roberts, went on to become the home secretary in England. He was married to an Egyptian woman. They were a delightful couple. I got to know them quite well, and Betsy and I kept up with them for years after the trial.

DC: Do you recall much about General Rudenko, the chief Soviet prosecutor?

WC: Yeah, I do, but we didn't have any real contact. The Russians kept their distance. We did have the first opportunity to mix with the Russian journalists, however, at the press camp. The Russian reporters were in the press camp with us, and they were very friendly. There was a lot of social intercourse with the Russians in the press camp at Nuremberg.

DC: Did you cover the trial for UP by yourself or with a team?

WC: We had four or five people there.

DC: Who were some of the people you were working with at this time?

WC: A guy named Doug Werner and a very good journalist named Ann Stringer. She was a correspondent whose husband, Bill Stringer, was killed in the war. She came over and took his place in kind of a dramatic bit from Texas. The Stringers were Texans. I don't think they were Longhorns; I think they went somewhere else to school. [*Ann Stringer was a UT journalism graduate. She died in 1990.*] Bill signed on with Reuters when he was quite young. Reuters really raided the American newspaper market for cannon fodder for the invasion. Bill was killed shortly after the invasion. Ann got herself overseas as a correspondent and became a top-notch UP correspondent. She helped uncover some of the documents at Nuremberg that were most revealing.

DC: What was your focus at Nuremberg as a news story? Was there anything special you were trying to do in coverage?

WC: Well, the real skill was in getting tipped just to documents that were in the files before they were brought out in trial and to get access to them. Ann Stringer worked the prosecution staff pretty well for tips on these documents. As a result, we got a lot of damn good front-page stories revealing the depths of the depravity in Nazi Germany.

DC: I understand that the trial was in the Palace of Justice, a building in Nuremberg, and it was conducted on the second floor. Did you spend much time in the courtroom?

WC: Oh yeah, we spent a great deal of time at the trial. The trial had a U-shaped arrangement with the judges of the tribunal on one side, the defendants across from them, and the press and spectators at the bottom of the U. The defense tables were out in the middle, and the witness stand was down on one end. We sat in the two end seats of the press row, maybe twenty feet from Goering.

DC: Were you allowed to interview the defendants?

WC: Absolutely not. We were never permitted in the jail. We never could approach them, we couldn't write to them, and they couldn't write to us.

DC: How did you feel about that?

WC: Oh, I didn't chafe very much at the time, so I must not have felt very strong about it. I guess we just sort of assumed that was how it had to be. Probably today we'd put up more of a fight.

DC: What was your impression of the defendants other than Hermann Goering?

WC: That they were a pretty unimpressive lot except for Goering. Of course, they had the wind taken out of them and had fallen off their high perches. I really wanted to spit on them, to be honest. But poor Hans Fritzsche shouldn't have been there at all. He was a minor deputy to Joseph Goebbels in the radio department of the Propaganda Ministry. They had to have somebody from propaganda, and he was the only survivor. So he was a stand-in for Goebbels, who had committed suicide. But Fritzsche was acquitted.

DC: Walter, was there a feeling that it was a show trial? Did the press take it seriously in that respect?

WC: Oh, we debated that point every damn night. We'd get drunk around the bar and debate the value of the trial and whether there should be ex post facto justice. We discussed all of the arguments. I had my own idea that I promoted at every opportunity, but nobody listened very much. We all acknowledged that there couldn't be another world war because of atomic weapons. But my thought was that if you were going to set up any standards on which to organize world government, which is the only real hope of keeping eternal peace, you presumably would build it on much the basis that we've built our government. And that would be a three-legged stool: the legislative, executive, and judicial. You can't wait for World War III to establish precedent for the judicial system and for what is right and what is wrong in the conduct of war and conspiracy to wage war. So we had to establish the precedent then. Therefore, the only way to establish precedent was through a trial of those who we could consider to be guilty of breaking the future law of civilized existence. I felt that idea made the whole enterprise worthwhile. Jackson never quite got around to saying that was his think-ing, and Dodd didn't either, really. But that was because they were so loaded with legal theories that they had trouble articulating them for the average man, I think. I still think that this was the rationale that made the trial proper.

I think one of the real proofs that it might have been worthwhile is that the very same question of responsibility was raised in Vietnam. Do junior officers and enlisted men have to obey orders, or do they obey a higher law? That question was raised by one of the prosecutors at Nuremberg, and it should have been raised. But I think the issues that were raised in the trial at Nuremberg are profoundly important.

DC: What was the atmosphere like in the city of Nuremberg during the trial?

WC: That's a good question. Well, to tell you the truth, it was kind of strange. All sorts of strange and ironic things went on. For example, the United States permitted the Germans to use the great field outside of Nuremberg where Hitler had held the Nazi party rallies. This field had an elaborate stadium. On one side was Hitler's reviewing stand. At both ends of the reviewing stand were two great marble Wagnerian bowls. I guess that's the way to describe them. During the trial, the U.S. authorities allowed the Germans to have a big rally for peace at the stadium. A lot of the people in Nurem-berg went out to this thing. I was curious about this rally, but I also wanted to see the stadium where Hitler had paraded around. So I got there, and I noticed that children were climbing up on these big bowls. The first words spoken in that stadium over the public-address system after Hitler's war were "Will the children please come down from the sacrificial urns?" I was stunned by that—the "sacrificial urns"!

DC: Did you cover the Nuremberg trial until the end?

WC: Unfortunately, no. The UP asked me if I would accept an assignment to Moscow, which, of course, I was anxious to do. Henry Shapiro, our longtime chief correspon-dent in Moscow, left the United Press rather suddenly. So UP wanted to get some-body in there as early as possible. I was going to be a one-man bureau. At that time, it took about three months to get a visa to go to Moscow. It looked like the Nuremberg trial was wrapping up and that they would punish these guys. I had a pretty good idea about how long it would be between the sentencing and the executions, if that's what the sentences wound up as. I felt that would happen within three months easily. So UP applied to the Soviet embassy in London for a visa for me to go to Moscow. And for heaven sakes, the darn visa came through in two or three weeks. I had to go because the visa specified a date of entry. You had forty-eight hours or seventy-two hours or something like that to enter the country on that visa. Betsy and I had to re-equip to go to Moscow for two years. We had few clothes and no household provisions in Europe. So we had to leave Nuremberg instantly. Betsy was with me in Nuremberg by that time. We flew home and re-equipped and then went to Moscow.

was Moscow and Eisenhower's chief of staff, Bedell Smith, was replacing him as the new U.S. ambassador. During the war, the one person in the military that I thought was an awfully tough guy and very difficult to get along with was Bedell Smith. I almost told UP I wouldn't go, because I thought, if I've got the Russians on one side and Bedell S...

r, I'm

s. The

man. So

I got

Betsy and

e went to

ed about

: After getting this assignment, did you have any opportunity
prepare, or did you just sort of jump in?

: Well, I immediately bought a Russian language book to try
get some familiarity at least with the alphabet. And I got
ook on Russian history, whic...
n't kn...
lly th...
Moscow...
. emba...

: Did y...
sy woul...

: Becaus...
going...
guy had...
the em...
ssian ce...
letter t...
on it w...
me throu...
scow and...
epared fo...

g like that on

to the whole

banned from

tion. So I

lly understand

: You were only thirty years old when UP sent you and Betsy to
scow. Despite the difficult living conditions, you both must

ries were

heir intelligence, like the British, for instance?

WC: That was far more likely, I think. I just don't think that
the standards elsewhere are quite as strong as they are here.
But I tell you where the real area of danger is. It's with the

CHAPTER SEVEN

Moscow

DC: UP sent you to Moscow in 1946, which was an especially bleak period in the Soviet Union.

WC: It was indeed, and those conditions made it very difficult to do any real reporting. It was a completely closed society.

DC: After getting this assignment, did you have any opportunity to prepare, or did you just sort of jump in?

WC: Well, I immediately bought a Russian language book to try to get some familiarity at least with the alphabet. And I got a book on Russian history, which was very helpful, actually. I didn't know that much about Russian history at all. That was really the extent of my reading before I got there. After I got to Moscow, I did some study of U.S.–Soviet relations by using the U.S. embassy library.

DC: Did you have any sense beforehand of the difficulties you and Betsy would face living there?

WC: Because of reports I got from others, I knew how difficult it was going to be to work and to live in Moscow in those days. Our UP guy had sent out some advisories to me about the situation via the embassy, because you couldn't get it through censorship. Russian censorship was very tough in those days. If you sent out a letter that might suggest there were shortages in the Soviet Union, it wouldn't get past the censor. But they got messages to me through the embassy pouch about what I should bring to Moscow and the difficulties of living there and what we should be prepared for.

DC: You were only thirty years old when UP sent you and Betsy to Moscow. Despite

---

Cronkite in Moscow as United Press bureau chief, ca. 1946–1948 (DI_05638).

the difficult living conditions, you both must have seen that assignment as a great adventure.

WC: Yes, we definitely saw it as an adventure that we could share after being apart during most of the war. We were young, with no kids, so we were ready for an adventure. It was funny, but knowing how difficult it was going to be, I thought at least there would be one great thing about it. Our ambassador in Moscow was Averell Harriman, who I had known in London during the war, and I liked him immensely. I thought, oh boy, that's going to be great. Harriman's daughter [Kathleen] was also there, and she was a great young lady. In London during the war, everybody knew her and liked her. She was his official hostess in Moscow. So I thought this is going to really be great.

The day after I accepted my assignment to go to Moscow, I saw a story in the *Stars and Stripes* announcing that Harriman was leaving Moscow and Eisenhower's chief of staff, Bedell Smith, was replacing him as the new U.S. ambassador. During the war, the one person in the military that I thought was an awfully tough guy and very difficult to get along with was Bedell Smith. I almost told UP I wouldn't go, because I thought if I've got the Russians on one side and Bedell Smith on the other, I'm in trouble. Bedell Smith was very tough with the press. The generals didn't like him, because he was Ike's hatchet man. So I thought, oh, that's going to be impossible. But when I got there, Bedell Smith was cooperative and very helpful. Betsy and I became good friends with Bedell and his wife, Mary. We went to Spaso House, the U.S. ambassador's residence, and talked about the war a great deal. Smith opened up one room of Spaso House for a bunch of us from the embassy and elsewhere to set up a model train.

DC: Why do you think there was there such a difference in Smith's behavior from when he was on Eisenhower's staff?

WC: Well, I learned that Bedell Smith was a man who was totally dedicated to whatever job was assigned to him. He did everything up to the hilt. When he was the chief of staff, he protected the boss, and that was his job. When he was ambassador, he was ambassador. Smith later became deputy secretary of state. When we all came back to the country a couple of years later, we saw him often at his home on Foxhole Road in Washington. We had dinner there one night, but we waited a long time on Bedell, who finally sent a message we should go ahead and eat because he was delayed at the office. When he came in, we were halfway through the meal. It was just the three of us, and he came into the dining room. He said good evening to Betsy and me very pleasantly, and then said, "I'm afraid that I've got to go upstairs and continue to do some work." He said, " I won't be able to join you tonight. Sorry about that." It was the last time we ever saw Bedell Smith socially. It turned out that was the day he was named head of the CIA. He figured that with that job he shouldn't have newspapermen friends. We saw his wife quite a lot, but we never saw Bedell again. That was the kind of guy he was.

DC: But it sounds like Smith made your time in Moscow a little smoother.

WC: He certainly did. It could have been terrible with an ambassador who wasn't that way. We had no sources except the embassy, really. It was very hard to talk to Soviet citizens; they were all afraid to talk to us. There were constant warnings in the Soviet press against talking to foreigners. And I was unable to even meet with, much less interview, any government officials. I couldn't even see the Foreign Office spokesman, who should have been my liaison with the Soviet government. I think during my two years in Moscow, I saw him once. None of us were allowed anywhere near his office. We had to correspond by letter with Soviet officials if we wanted anything, even a plumber. If you needed a plumber, you had to send a letter to the ministry of, I don't know, for relations abroad or something like that. So to get any kind of help, you had to write a letter to this ministry. Maybe two weeks later they would write a letter back, saying, "You didn't specify really what you want the plumber to do." You had to tell them precisely. It was awful.

DC: In the meantime, no plumbing.

WC: Yeah. It was incredibly difficult.

DC: Speaking of the U.S. embassy and Bedell Smith, did the U.S. State Department or anyone else from the U.S. government contact you about the possibility of being a source for U.S. intelligence while you were in Moscow?

WC: No, I was never approached in any way. Never in my whole journalistic career was I ever approached to do anything like that.

DC: Did you have colleagues who were approached by the U.S. government?

WC: Not that I know of. We heard later about some correspondents who were asked to do special little things for the CIA. I don't know whether we had any correspondents who were full time CIA agents. I can imagine. It seemed perfectly logical to me, and not terribly sinful, that the CIA might have asked somebody for help. I can see that happening. And I can see an otherwise absolutely straightlaced correspondent who didn't believe in that kind of thing still doing some little thing like that on occasion. But I think it is terribly dangerous to the whole profession. It could easily end up in our being banned from countries and from important sources of information. So I disapprove of the practice, but I can pragmatically understand it happening.

DC: Do you think that nationals from other countries were working with their intelligence, like the British, for instance?

WC: That was far more likely, I think. I just don't think that the standards elsewhere are quite as strong as they are here. But I tell you where the real area of danger is. It's with the freelance types. Those who worked for established and reputable news organizations were very unlikely to be involved in spying. But boy, there are those people out there who probably are CIA plants in many cases, or they are with the secret services of other countries. They are planted as journalists who get press credentials to represent a magazine or a kind of offbeat newspaper or even an offbeat news service. There are some of those around. Some of them, I think, have been probably fronts for CIA-type activity. That sort of thing goes on; there is no question about it. Those are the really dangerous ones.

DC: Did any Soviet ever approach you for information while you were in Moscow?

WC: No, never. We did have one American correspondent who seemed to have particularly good sources of Soviet information. We all wondered how he got it. Not only did he have good sources, but also his housing was always a little better than anybody else's. His automobiles were imported a little easier than any others. There were a lot of things that made us wonder how he could possibly be getting all that. Was he really that much cleverer than we were? As a matter of fact, he's still there.

DC: Oh, he's still in Moscow?

WC: He's still there. He was there in 1946, and he'd been there during most of the war. He's been there fifty years.

DC: Can you tell me his name?

WC: Well, it's Ed Stevens, who was with the *Christian Science Monitor*. But he's not with the *Christian Science Monitor* any longer. But he's actually a good correspondent. He won the Pulitzer Prize after I left Moscow. [*Edmund Stevens died in Moscow on May 26, 1992.*]

DC: Who were some of the other U.S. correspondents in Moscow?

WC: There was a very small press colony of Americans, numbering perhaps a half dozen or so. We were the only Americans in Moscow in those two years that I know of, other than the embassy staff. There were no U.S. businesspeople or anything. American fur buyers came once or twice a year. And then once in a while there would be some kind of official visitation. FDR's son Elliot Roosevelt and his wife, Fay Emerson, came and made quite a stir. Eddy Gilmore was the AP guy. Dick Hottelet was there for CBS, and Robert Magidoff represented NBC. There was no one from ABC; they weren't in the ballgame then. Joe Newman represented the *Herald Tribune*, and Drew Middleton was there for the *New York Times*. And I've already mentioned Ed Stevens from the *Christian Science Monitor*. That was about it. The only guys who had Russian connections were Magidoff and Stevens. They had Russian wives. The AP guy lived with a Russian girlfriend who he married later on.

But mentioning Magidoff reminds me of something. During the time we were in Moscow, the anti-American campaign really began steaming up. The Russians kept their distance. We weren't invited to homes, and there was no real intercourse with them. But about a year after we arrived, it got even more intense, and they started really putting the clamps on. The newspapers were full of warnings to Soviet citizens to be careful about talking to foreigners, even in shops. It was claimed that we were very seductive and we would try to engage them in conversation.

About that time, an incident occurred that frightened us all quite a bit. A letter appeared in *Izvestia* denouncing NBC's Robert Magidoff as being a spy. Magidoff was Russian-born, but he was an American citizen. Magidoff's secretary, a girl named Cecelia Nelson, wrote the letter. She charged that he passed secret information out through the American embassy because he couldn't get it through the Russian censors. Nelson was one of the many unfortunate Finns who had immigrated to the United States during the post–World War I depression in Europe in the early twenties. They'd come to this country for work and were marvelous workers, mostly woodworkers of one kind or another. And then when we hit our Depression some years later, a lot of these Finns had become American citizens. But the Russians recruited them to come back and work in the Soviet Union, and a lot of them went because of the Depression. They were promised good jobs, multiyear contracts, and that sort of thing.

When they got to the Soviet Union, the Russians took their passports and said they would hold them until they were ready to go home. Well, the poor Finns gave up their passports, and the Russians held them, literally, as prisoners and never let them go home. At the end of the war, there was quite a scandal about the hundreds or thousands of U.S. citizens caught in the Soviet Union, most of whom were these Finns. Well, most of these Finns were now stateless. They had no legal way to live and were in terrible shape. We gave several of them jobs. I had one work for me as a maid. She was an older woman who was actually the aunt of this Nelson girl who worked for Magidoff. Nelson was a very attractive, nice young lady, and she spoke perfect English. She may have been born in the U.S. She was married to another young Finnish guy who was a very good musician.

The letter in *Izvestia* denouncing Magidoff was written under duress, quite clearly. The girl disappeared, of course. The day the letter appeared, she didn't show up for work, and she never was seen again. It was a terrible story. But that letter in *Izvestia* was a warning, of course, to all of us. The Soviets never charged Magidoff with anything, but he wanted to get out with that kind of pressure, and he did. They let him and his wife go to the U.S.

Because of this incident and the general atmosphere, Joe Newman and I felt that we needed some advice from Bedell Smith about the extent of danger to us. We were concerned that this was possibly the beginning of a series of moves against the press. We went to the embassy and asked Bedell, "What should we do when they knock on our door in the middle of the night?" He said, "They'll take you down to Lubyanka," which was the secret-police prison. And then he advised us to be "good soldiers." "Give them your name, rank, and serial number and that's all. Don't talk, and we'll make demands to see you. Then we'll make a complaint about your being held." He said, "That will be about it." We said, "Wait a minute, whoa, make a complaint? There has to be something more to it than that." He said, "Well, what would you suggest?" I said, "Well, I mean, gosh, you got to get us out." Bedell said, "Well now, let's just be reasonable, gentlemen. Do you really expect the United States to go to war to get a correspondent out of Lubyanka?" So in effect, we didn't get any advice at all from him.

DC: Were any other correspondents denounced?

WC: I don't recall that anyone else was denounced by name, but there were more pieces in the paper every day about the American spies in their midst and so forth. And the situation was tense. Betsy and I experienced an incident that got our attention. One day, Betsy and I came home to our apartment in this broken-down little building. The front door of our apartment was covered in a strange leather padding. It may have been a noise control thing at one time. But anyway, we came home, and there was a dollar sign chalked on our front door. It was kind of like a swastika on the door of a Jew in Germany. It was a warning to us. Although Betsy, as ever, God bless her, saw some humor even in that. We went inside our apartment, and I was muttering something to her about this being a warning. So Betsy said, "They must not know you work for the United Press, Walter, otherwise they would have painted a cent mark instead of dollar sign."

DC: Betsy does seem to have a knack for the quick and witty retort. [*laughing*]

WC: You don't know the half of it.

DC: Well, her remark reminds me that UP had a reputation of being extremely tightfisted financially. In fact, you've already made references to UP's stinginess in terms of salaries and pay raises. Did UP's tightfisted ways cause you any problems in Moscow? I ran across a story that UP told you to buy a bicycle instead of a car.

WC: Oh, I don't think so. I don't recall being told to buy a bicycle. Somebody might have suggested it, but they couldn't have been very serious. You couldn't get around Moscow on a bicycle.

DC: How did you get around Moscow? Were there taxis?

WC: Well, you had to have a car. There wasn't any public taxi transportation, and the streetcars were jammed. People hung on the outside of the streetcars and the few buses that ran. So you had to have a car. With a car, you had to have a chauffeur because you couldn't get a driver's license. That was the way they really kept tabs on the movements of all foreigners. We knew the chauffeurs all worked for the KGB. Probably like my secretary and everybody else. They probably weren't full-time spies, but they were called in for reports every once in a while. Anyway, the UP car was a very tired old automobile, and it was just barely running. But we made it through the couple years that I was there.

But I do have one outstanding example of UP's penuriousness. There were no foreign newspapers or that kind of thing, of course. The only way you could get any outside information was by radio tuned to the BBC world broadcast. We didn't have a radio in the bureau. Shapiro, I think, had taken the radio with him when he left Russia. So I requested that UP send me a radio, which, by the way, took some time because that was a very sensitive customs item as well. In fact, I had to get it sent through the embassy, as I recall. But I urgently requested the radio. UP told me, "We are sending a radio, but we need to know what disposition was made of the Atwater Kent number so-and-so and so-and-so, shipped to Eugene Lyons on September 26, 1927." I mean, my God, it was the most incredible thing you'd ever seen in inventory control. I answered back, "I have no damned idea!"

DC: I know Betsy was educated as a journalist at the University of Missouri. Did she work while she was in Moscow?

WC: Yeah, at the U.S. Information Agency. But the job was mainly about food. To live in the Soviet Union in anything like the style to which one was accustomed, you had to import food. We had ambassadorial privileges as correspondents, and were considered of ambassador rank, so we had the best food coupons. Still, you couldn't really feed a family of two and a maid on Soviet ration coupons. As civilians, we couldn't import food. The other embassies helped the one or two correspondents they might have had in the Soviet Union. The British had three or four. They offered them a ration of food from their embassies. But the United States Embassy wouldn't do that. The State Department wouldn't permit it. They said they couldn't afford to do it, that it would set a bad precedent. The only way we could get a ration was to have Betsy work there. She got this job at the USIA, which was just as well, because it gave her something interesting to do. She might have done it anyway. But the main purpose was to get this food ration. It was an incredibly difficult life. We were one of the only couples who had an apartment out in town. We had an apartment because of Eugene Lyons.

DC: You mean the famed journalist who was UP's correspondent in Moscow during the late 1920s and early 1930s?

WC: The same. Way back during Lenin's New Economic Policy, when they were building housing and getting people to dig up their cans of rubles they'd buried in the backyard and try and extract this stuff from the people, they started cooperative apartments. People brought their money out to buy these apartments, and then as soon as they had them all built, well, they seized them back from them. I don't know whether Lenin planned it that way or not, but it's the way it worked out. Well, Eugene Lyons convinced the tightwad head of UP, Roy Howard, to buy an apartment to use for an office. And when the Soviets seized it back, Roy Howard raised so much hell about losing his investment that the Russians said, "Oh, the hell with it." And they never sent a rent bill. I doubt that any of the tens of thousands of apartments built in Moscow during that period were ever given back except that one. That's the apartment we lived in. We never had a utility bill or a rent bill. Nothing. We lived there absolutely free. But the building was pretty much of a wreck, and in most buildings there was not enough heat. It was terribly cold in the winter. Fortunately, the flue of the building next to us was broken in the wall, apparently. It was clearly a fire hazard, but the wall heated our bedroom. It was the warmest room in Moscow, including the embassy, and we used to have parties in our bedroom. People would come over just to get warm. We'd sit around the bed and drink.

DC: Pretty bleak . . .

WC: Yeah. And working there was so difficult. We had no source of information. The Soviet newspapers were, of course, all propaganda. There was a service called the joint reading service that the embassies sponsored. It had a staff of translators that translated the entire edition of *Pravda* and other newspapers everyday. So we got translations of the newspapers. I also had our own translator in the office. I could read my nouns and verbs pretty well, but my verb endings weren't any good. So my crude knowledge of Russian really wasn't very valuable except I could tell the translator, "I want that piece translated right away."

REPORTING FROM MOSCOW

DC: How did you file stories?

WC: We had to use the Soviet state service. After you wrote your story, it had to be submitted by hand to the little office at the entrance on the side of the main post office downtown. You went in that little door, and there were two old ladies, babushkas, sitting there with their shawls and their heads wrapped, and their arthritic hands would enter your piece of copy, and then it went through a little slot, God knows where. We understood that sitting back there somewhere was a room full of censors, or some censors anyway.

DC: Did you have an opportunity to review a censored story or protest the way a story was censored before it was transmitted to UP?

WC: No. Before I got to Moscow, the correspondents had made a pact with the devil as far as I was concerned. They previously had a system in which the censored material was returned to them for review. If a correspondent still wanted to send the story after he reviewed the censored version, he could resubmit it and it was transmitted. Well, our correspondents decided this was too much delay. So they made this terrible arrangement, in my opinion, in which the copy was censored and then transmitted before they got the censored copy back. They picked up the copy later to see how it had been censored.

DC: So why was that a problem if the story was going to be censored anyway? Could you persuade the censors to revise their versions after you reviewed the copy?

WC: No, it's not that I felt the censors were open to a protest. I mean, the system would have been all right, perhaps, if you were diligent enough to get to that copy quickly enough and if they had permitted you to then send a correction and say kill the copy, but you couldn't. If you tried, in your next story, to refer back to the previous censored copy as being inaccurate, they just didn't let that go through. You couldn't kill the story. You couldn't add to the story. You couldn't do anything. So I thought it was a terrible arrangement, but that's what was going on in those days. You submitted your copy, and it went to the censors, and then at some point later you could pick it up and you could see where they had censored it. And it was often terrible. They would turn negatives into affirmatives, they would cut out the "nots," or something. It was just awful.

DC: What was the procedure back in the States when your story came over, because I'm assuming that your UP editors understood the problem.

WC: Well, that was the other half of the equation that was wrong. UP would take the story and make the best they could out of it. Drew Middleton and I begged our officers to slug the copy to indicate that it had been passed by Soviet censors, but they wouldn't play that game. I never understood why. They maintained that there were a lot of countries where they would have one kind of censorship or another, sometimes unofficially. And you couldn't say anything about it. That explanation never made much sense to me.

DC: So it was a little misleading when the public read news stories filed from Moscow.

WC: That's correct. And as usual, they were rewritten by the cable desk. So the stories were pretty well redundant, at least from the press services. Now the *New York Times* didn't do that as much as the *Herald Tribune*. Drew Middleton found a way to slip stories by the censors by making references to Alice in Wonderland and things of that kind. He created a kind of code. They wouldn't print the information he sent by code under his byline, but they would use it to write separate editorials.

DC: Did you ever try to communicate by code?

WC: Occasionally, if they felt the situation was dire enough and important enough, the embassy would let us send things through the diplomatic pouch. But they were very careful about it and very reluctant to use it at all. They would send a coded message if it was a matter of literally life and death. For example, when I became seriously ill one time with double pneumonia, they sent a message to the office because I kept getting these queries, "Where is your copy?" I couldn't let them know I was ill, because if you tried to send a message through the censor that you were ill, you knew they would censor that. "No one gets sick in the workers' paradise of the Soviet Union," you know, that sort of thinking, or they thought you might be implying that the Soviet authorities had done something to you.

DC: Were you hospitalized in Moscow when you had pneumonia?

WC: No. I resisted that. There just wasn't much sense of going to a Soviet hospital. The embassy did get some penicillin, which was very rare at that time. Penicillin in those days was put in a beeswax base. The beeswax was melted and it was injected with a huge hypodermic into your buttocks. The penicillin was in the beeswax so that it would be released slowly. They shot me in both buttocks with penicillin, and the beeswax took a long, long time to be absorbed in the body. It releases penicillin fairly soon, I guess, over a period of days, but the beeswax itself appeared as a big knot in both of my buttocks for a while. I remember when I sat down I kind of rolled around like one of those toys.

A TRIP DOWN THE VOLGA

DC: Were you able to travel to other Soviet cities?

WC: Actually, we had one great trip. Some friends of ours at the embassy said that they had six tickets on the first steamer of the navigational season down the Volga, and they were going to take this steamer all the way down to Stalingrad. They invited us to go with them, and we accepted eagerly, although I was a bit dubious about our chances of actually being allowed to leave Moscow. So with some trepidation we presented our tickets at the dock to go aboard. To my surprise, they let us go. They didn't ask to see our papers. We had this fascinating trip down the river about five days to Gorky, which is the town where the great Russian scientist and dissident just died. He was exiled there.

DC: Oh, you mean Andrei Sakharov?

WC: That's right. But Gorky really wasn't that bad of a town. I did a piece on the *Evening News* when he was exiled back in 1980, and I explained what Gorky was like. Boy, did I get a lot of complaints about that. But it used to be a lovely town. It's on the confluence of the Volga and some other river. Going to Stalingrad, you come down the Volga and make a turn there and join the other river going down to Stalingrad, out to sea. Part of Gorky is up on a high bluff, overlooking the fields around it. On that bluff is where there are lots of nice fancy hotels.

We had to change boats at Gorky. These were fairly good-sized river steamers and not in very good shape at that time. Public toilet facilities aboard were just ghastly. Betsy said she clinched for four days. We docked at Gorky and moved our baggage over to the next pier, where there were ships waiting to continue on. The authorities said, "Oh, we're terribly sorry, there is something wrong with your reservations. You don't have reservations on this ship." And we said, "Well, can we make reservations for the next one?" They said, "Oh, we're sorry, the ships are sold out for the entire navigational season." Well, we realized that we were in some trouble, so we said, "What can we do?" They said, "Well, we suggest you go up to the tourist hotel at the top of the hill." Now there was no tourist travel in the Soviet Union at that point of any kind, internal or external, so I had no idea what he meant by tourist hotel. So we lugged this luggage all the way up quite a long hill to this very nice building overlooking the countryside. We went in, and here was an empty hotel, which they had attempted to clean up before we arrived. They waved us over to the desk, and a woman said, "Welcome. We're so sorry, we didn't know you were coming. If you had only let us know you were coming, we could have prepared for your visit. But as it is, we managed to arrange some rooms for you. What are your travel intentions?" We said, "Well, we would like to get on the ship." She said, "Oh, that's sold out for the season. There is no way to get on the ship." We said, "Well then, we'd like to take the train to Stalingrad." "Oh, I'm terribly sorry," she said. "There are no reservations on the train for the next two months; it's a busy time of the year. But here are your tickets to fly back to Moscow. The plane leaves at six in the morning." When we arrived the next morning at the so-called airport, we saw that we were being flown in a military aircraft, an old DC-3. The airport was in an open field, which, incidentally, was the only place in Russia where I saw German prisoners of war at work.

DC: What were they doing?

WC: They were digging around the edges of the field. I couldn't tell why they were digging, but there were a lot of them.

DC: So what was the airplane like?

WC: It had a long bench along the side for seats. And it was carrying freight of some kind. So they flew us back to Moscow. We knew we were in serious, serious trouble. We had been caught leaving Moscow without permission. That sense of being in trouble intensified when we realized we weren't landing at the civilian airport—we were landing at the military airport. And we thought, oh boy, we're headed to Lubyanka Prison for certain. There was no terminal at this military airport, but there were a bunch of officers' areas and so forth. The plane took us right to the edge of the field, and the military stewardess got off, put the ladder up, helped us down, and put our baggage out. Then she said, "Thank you very much." She saluted, got back aboard, and left us there. Here we were out at the edge of the field. So we picked up our luggage and started back, expecting any minute for the military to come rushing in on trucks or something.

We walked back through the first gate we found, and we said to the soldier standing guard, "Good day." We walked through the gate, and then we said, "Wait a minute. What are we going to do now?" So one of our companions from the State Department spoke Russian. He went back and said, "Could we use your phone?" They allowed him to call the U.S. Embassy, and they sent a couple of cars to get us. We sat there on our luggage for about forty-five minutes waiting for the cars, and then they picked us up and we got home. The authorities never said a word to us about it. But when we got back to our apartment, we found it had been absolutely plundered. We had no clothes, nothing. My office files were still there, but they had gone through them. They had taken all of our clothes and all of our jewelry, such as there was. There was nothing except fraternity and sorority pens and that sort of thing. But clearly it was to teach us a lesson. You don't go off like that. And, you know, once you do something like that, you live in terror that it's over your head somehow.

DC: I found that you also left Moscow to do a Christmas story from the monastery at Zagorsk, which the Soviet government had recently reopened after it had been closed for several years.

WC: Yeah, we did get out to Zagorsk, but that's just outside of Moscow. It's just a day trip. Zagorsk is a wonderful old monastery town, very picturesque. Technically, it was outside of our range where we were allowed to go, but I got permission to visit there. That trip created a very difficult problem with Harrison Salisbury, who suggested that I do the story. Harrison had been the UP correspondent to Moscow at the time when travel was much freer and easier. He sent a message asking me to do the story, but because of censorship, I couldn't get word back to him that the Soviets wouldn't let me go. He kept sending me these messages: "When Zagorsk? When can I expect Zagorsk?" Finally, I persuaded the authorities to let Betsy and me go to Zagorsk. It was a nice story once I got there, but nothing earthshaking.

DC: What was the angle Salisbury was looking for? "Is there still religion in Russia?"

WC: Yes, I think so, and the isolated nature of religion.

DC: Did you cover any of those massive May Day parades in Red Square?

WC: Oh yeah, we did all the May Day parades. As I said, we were given ambassadorial rank and privileges, so we stood with the ambassador at the parade. We were in the stand just to the side of the main viewing place on Lenin's Tomb, so we had a side profile view of the members of the Politburo up on the stand. It was hard to get a view of Stalin, but you would get an occasional glimpse of him as he leaned forward to review the troops and so forth. We also viewed the October parade celebrating the revolution.

DC: When you were watching the military parade, did you pay attention to the type of hardware they had or anything like that?

WC: Oh, yes, we were comparing notes with the military attachés and ambassadors on anything new.

DC: Did you try to read the Politburo pecking order, such as who was closest to Stalin and that sort of thing?

WC: Well, the only way you had to know what was happening in the Soviet Union was the way they displayed the pictures. Who stood next to whom and whose pictures were displayed in the banners and so forth.

DC: Did you get a chance to meet Molotov or Stalin?

WC: Unfortunately, no, but we met most of the underling officials at diplomatic receptions. With this ambassadorial rank, we were invited to all the National Day receptions at the embassies, and there was one or two of those a week.

DC: Did Betsy stay in Moscow the entire time you were there?

WC: No, Betsy left Moscow after she became pregnant. Getting out was very difficult for her. Betsy went on the train from Moscow to Berlin with a young couple from the embassy. They got to Berlin just as the Russian blockade of the city began. So Betsy was stuck in Berlin for a few days until General Lucius Clay, who was the military governor of the U.S. occupation zone, put her on one of his planes flying out of Berlin to Frankfurt.

DC: Did you know that this was going on?

WC: No, I didn't know. And then after all that hardship, Betsy got on a third-class train from Frankfurt to Rome because she always wanted to go to Rome. Here she is, pregnant, trying to get back to America, and she takes this crazy side trip!

DC: How much longer did you stay in Moscow?

WC: I told UP that I wanted out at the end of my two years, which would be another couple of months after Betsy left. At one point during those last two months that I was there alone, I attended a party at one of the embassies, I don't recall which one. But at this party was a wild man named Arthur Yanson, who was the first secretary of the Dutch legation. Yanson had some special privilege to be able to drive his own car. Unfortunately, he drank quite a lot. But anyway, I accepted a ride home from Yanson after the party. Well, Arthur was pretty loaded, and we were going right through Arbat Square, and he hit some little old lady crossing the street. He was only going about one mile an hour. There wasn't that much traffic, and people didn't pay a lot of attention to lights and things. There were a lot of people walking across, and he just nudged this woman with his car. It wasn't anything serious. She wasn't hurt at all, I don't think. But the police, of course, were right there, and there was a big thing about getting Yanson's name for the police files. They finally let him go, but they got my name as well. And that's all the Soviets needed if they wanted an excuse to make a case against foreigners. I was terrified that when I got ready to apply for my exit visa, they were going to say, "You can't go. This case hasn't been settled." So I lived in real terror over the last month or so before I got my exit visa. That was the kind of life you lived in Moscow in those days.

CHAPTER EIGHT

Joining CBS

DC: Did you return to Kansas City after you left Moscow in 1948?

WC: I just went back there for home leave from the United Press. I was supposed to go back to Europe. The United Press had always assumed that I was going to be European news manager in London. That was a job I very much wanted. When I talked to Earl Johnson, who was managing editor of United Press, I asked him how much of a raise I would receive to take this new exalted post. His reply was, "You are already our highest-paid foreign correspondent, for heaven's sake, and we can't afford any more for the European news editor job." That's when I realized that I was never going to make enough money with UP to support a growing family.

DC: So what did you do? Did you take the London assignment anyway?

WC: No, I decided to leave UP. I took a job with a friend of mine, Karl Koerper, who was the operating head of KMBC radio in Kansas City. I went to Washington as chief national-capital correspondent for not just KMBC—they didn't feel they could afford me—but also for a syndicate of ten midwestern radio stations. Having tried radio before, I wasn't keen to do that, but our daughter Nancy had been born, and I didn't feel that I could be quite as footloose as I had been.

DC: So parenthood had a definite impact on your professional life at that point. Obviously, it does with everyone, but I mean in terms of your career decisions.

WC: I was thinking very much about that. Living conditions were not very good in Europe at that time, even in London. Certain baby foods, bananas, and things like that were not available in London even for a while. I was also thinking about the money. The

Cronkite on the air for CBS News, ca. 1950s (DI_05759).

new job in Washington doubled my UP salary, plus I had my expenses paid. They also provided me with a new office.

DC: Sperber says in her biography of Edward R. Murrow that you spoke on Murrow's CBS radio program the year that you returned from the Soviet Union, in 1948. According to Sperber, you told Murrow over the air that you had been "hog-tied" by Soviet censorship while in Moscow and that you had been worried that while you were in the Soviet Union that Americans weren't sufficiently worried about the dangers of Soviet aggression and so forth. But now, according to Sperber, you said that you were worried that "the pendulum has swung too far the other way. It does seem to me, Ed, that we Americans have gone hysterical over the Russian situation and over the prospects of war. Russia is simply not ready for a war right now. That is perfectly obvious to any one sitting in Moscow." Do you remember that?

WC: I don't remember the broadcast, strangely enough, although those sentiments certainly were what I was expressing generally. I do think it is probably right that they couldn't have conducted a war at that stage. They were flat on their backs economically. And while they were maintaining, obviously, a large military establishment, it would have been very hard to wage an offensive war.

DC: When you were on Murrow's program must have been the same time you were on the UP speaking tour. This would be prior to your new job in Washington. Was this speaking tour the first time you had made public appearances?

WC: Oh, these were the first public speeches I ever made. The first one wasn't very auspicious. I was persuaded to do it by a big banker in Kansas City. They had a meeting every summer of bankers in Kansas City. At the end of the meeting, they had a barbecue on the roof of the city bank building, and I was asked to speak there. These bankers were drinking heavily and eating barbecue. They had a barbershop quartet singing over the public-address system. They brought me up to the microphone, and of course, nobody knew me from Adam. I interrupted these guys in the middle of singing "Sweet Adeline" or something. The head banker said to the quartet, "All right, that's enough guys, get out." And then he said, "Well, fellows, tell you what we had planned to show you tonight. We had some film of that exciting Southern Cal–Notre Dame football game to show you. But instead, I've got a young man who just came back from Russia." These guys were about as ready to hear a speech about Russia as you could imagine. It was a very raucous group to which I spoke. It was rather discouraging, as an opening speech.

DC: Would you have stayed with UP if they had matched your new offer?

WC: Oh, I would have stayed in a minute.

DC: So you went on to Washington—this would be early in 1949. I guess you were in your early thirties by this time. Did you have any kind of professional game plan?

WC: No, I really didn't. I have never had one in my whole life. I was never goal oriented. I just took the next opportunity that came along. I've always thought that there is a tremendous amount of luck to life, and I've been very, very, lucky all along. But I don't ascribe success solely to that. I think you've got to be able to take those opportunities when they come. I know that's trite, but it's also true. And I was lucky enough to be prepared to succeed in each of these jobs as they came up.

DC: I understand that when you were in Washington working for these midwestern radio stations, your job was to cover subjects of interest to Kansas City and the larger Midwest, obviously.

WC: Yeah, I did two fifteen-minute commentaries a week for each state: one would be what was happening in Washington affecting that particular locality, and one regional, which would go to everybody. I represented five states: Missouri, Iowa, Nebraska, Kansas, and Oklahoma. The regional broadcast ended up mostly being national news. And I gave them daily reports depending upon their requirements for each station. What I was covering mostly was agriculture, some Commerce Department stuff, and a little military, but not a lot. I paid very close attention to their congressional representatives, naturally. Just about the time I started doing this, the Congress organized something called a joint recording facility that provided a studio for the members of Congress to make recordings that could be played on the radio stations back in their districts. I was able to use that facility to record my reports.

DC: No telephone hookup in those days?

WC: Well, we'd telephone the daily reports over a broadcast-quality wire we had into our office in the National Press building. I had one assistant who helped immensely, a brilliant young woman named Eileen Shanahan, who went on to become a *New York Times* reporter. I really knew nothing about doing that kind of radio report. I didn't know how to time a radio broadcast or how to produce at all. I just barged into it. As a matter of fact, I didn't think the timing was all that critical, and I got into a lot of trouble at first with the stations, running over a little bit here and there, running short, and things of that kind. I didn't learn enough about the absolute essence and importance of timing even then, and they let me get by with murder.

DC: When you were doing this work for the midwestern stations, of course, Harry Truman was president. I would suppose that your stations had an especially strong interest in Truman because he was from the Kansas City area.

WC: Yeah, but unfortunately very few stations used my reports properly. It was another one of my major disappointments with broadcasting, and I've had many through the years. Most of the news directors back at the local stations didn't know how to query me for information. Any good newspaper is always firing off queries to the Associated Press or United Press. Can you get this story or that story for us? I never got requests from most of the stations. Only one station really used it well, WMT in Cedar Rapids. And that was because of a news editor named Jim Borman, who was absolutely marvelous. He went on to WCCO in Minneapolis, probably the best news station in the country. Jim really used the bureau the way it should be; the rest of them, I never heard from. They bought a service and then forgot it. In some cases, I think, the news director also was on air. Some of them were jealous. They didn't want this extra voice in there.

DC: And in another sense, it may have reflected the very attitude that you were criticizing, that news really wasn't their primary business anyway.

WC: Yeah. It was a great experience for me, however. I really got into the depths of politics in Washington. It was really a lot of fun, because I made friends of every one of those congressmen from all five states. And I got in very deeply with the White House.

DC: Do you remember any particular congressman or senator?

WC: No, not offhand right now, but there weren't any of the particularly spectacular ones. I did, however, get in with the Texas delegation because my old college friend and *Daily Texan* mentor, D. B. Hardeman, was in Washington. I fell in with D. B. right away, and of course he was big with the Texas delegation, especially Speaker Sam Rayburn and Senator Tom Connally. D. B. introduced me to them.

DC: Did you get to attend any of Sam Rayburn's famous "board of education" meetings, where he would share some bourbon and water with colleagues and friends as they went over the day's happenings in the Congress?

WC: As a matter of fact, I went there several times. They were held in this small, out-of-the-way, and unadorned room in the Capitol itself. I sat there and listened to Sam Rayburn analyzing the day's events in the Capitol. He was the master of the House of Representatives. There was no doubt about that. That was really a remarkable learning experience. The other senator from Texas, Lyndon Johnson, attended those "board of education" meetings in a minor, kind of an apprentice role. He would sit or stand in the corner of the room being deferential to Rayburn and adding very little to the discussion.

JOINING CBS

DC: Okay, so you were with the Midwest radio syndicate for about eighteen months. And then CBS hired you in the summer of 1950. How did that happen?

WC: When the Korean War broke out in June 1950, I was reading all these dispatches from my old World War II buddies who were all rushing out to Korea to cover the new big war. I wanted to go, and here I was stuck with this local operation. So I sent a wire to

Wells Church, who was the CBS news manager in New York, saying if he needed an extra pair of hands in Korea, to let me know. I didn't hear from Church, but I got a call from Ed Murrow. Ed said that not many guys get a second chance, but would you like to join CBS and go to Korea? I said, you're darn right, yes. I never did know really whether he knew about the wire to Church or not, but he sounded like it was his idea. I told him that I had a contract with this syndicate of radio stations that I would have to get out of first. Ed said, "I gather all those stations are CBS affiliated. We could probably work out something where you could do special reports for them from Korea as well as do your CBS job." So, gee, I said that sounded like a way out. So I called KMBC in Kansas City and told them about Murrow's idea. They agreed that would be fine. It was okay with all the other stations as well. The deal was that when the war was over, they'd have an option to bring me back if they wanted to at that point. So Ed and I worked it out, and I signed on with CBS. I wanted to get out there as quickly as possible. So we closed up the midwestern broadcasting office.

DC: What did Betsy think about your going to Korea?

WC: Well, frankly, our family was growing, and the financial opportunity meant a lot. Betsy was pregnant with Kathy at this point. She was born three months after I signed with CBS. In addition, most of us thought the conflict in Korea was going to be very short term, so we didn't see it as something that would take me from home for a long time. She also understood that I was a little bored with the midwestern radio bit and that I wanted to be in the middle of a bigger, fast-breaking story.

DC: I know that you didn't make it to Korea, as it turned out. What happened?

WC: Boy, that's a long story. I got my shots and filed my paperwork at the Pentagon. And then CBS management decided that I needed to get some orientation about how to work at CBS. So they put me to work at CBS right away because they were very short-handed. They threw me right into doing broadcasts in Washington, filling in for some guys on vacation until I was ready to go to Korea. While I was doing that, I began to get a little nervous because it dragged on over a period of three weeks or so.

Meanwhile the Korean War was getting nastier, and it looked like it was going to be more of a drawn-out affair. And I didn't have quite the same eagerness about getting there before it was over. This was where this tremendous luck that I've enjoyed came into play. Right at that moment, the FCC decided to release a lot of long-pent-up applications for new television stations. CBS got a station in Washington called WOIC, which I thought were wonderful call letters. CBS, with this proud heritage in the news, wanted a showcase television news broadcast in Washington immediately. They didn't have anybody to put in, of course. There was no backlog of television newspeople anywhere to draw from, and there weren't any local stations to tap.

So CBS said, "Cronkite, you go to that new station and do a fifteen-minute evening news broadcast at six o'clock." The first thing they asked me to do was a Korean War briefing. Well, I'd been to enough military briefings, for heaven's sake, in my life. So I could do that blindfolded. And then CBS changed the call letters of the television station from WOIC to WTOP. CBS's radio station in Washington was WTOP, so they just took those call letters for the television operation as well. They asked me what I needed for graphic material to use on the air. I said, "Just give me a blackboard and draw an outline of Korea, mark the thirty-eighth parallel, and place Seoul, and that's all I need." So I went out and did this chalk talk on the air. Well, I did that about two or three nights, and it was all ad-lib. CBS said, "Listen, that's fine, now do the whole fifteen-minute news broadcast—continue the Korean briefing, but take over the whole news broadcast." I said sure, because this was all fun and experimental stuff. We were still trying to figure out how to do the news on television.

DC: When you say CBS asked you to do this, was that Sig Mickelson?

WC: No, it wasn't Mickelson. This was a guy named Ted Koop, who was head of the CBS Washington news bureau. So, I went on, and I did the fifteen-minute news broadcast. I ad-libbed the entire program. I never had a script for the news in Washington. My gosh, the next week they sold the program to a sponsor, Hechinger's Lumber. I remember the blurb: "Hechinger's, the world's most unusual lumberyard, home of Harry Homeowner." So I now had a little sign on the front of my news desk, "Hechinger's." That went on for another week or so, and then Esso said it wanted to sponsor the program. Esso had a news program on the radio all over the country, and they wanted to experiment with local television. They wanted to buy my six o'clock news program. Well, Hechinger's had it. We had a very smart manager at WTOP, and he talked Hechinger's into moving their sponsorship to eleven o'clock at night. He told them it had an even bigger audience, which was true. So Esso took the six o'clock program. Now I had two broadcasts a day. I was thinking that this was just for the week and next week. I'm just helping them get started.

This situation dragged on for a month or more. Finally, I went to CBS, and I said, "Wait a minute, I signed on as a war correspondent to Korea. I don't want to be stuck doing this television thing forever." They said, "Oh, no, you must be crazy. You've got two commercial broadcasts on the air. You really don't want to go to Korea." I replied that I did, in fact, want to go to Korea and that I had signed a contract to do that. CBS said, "Well, you need to reread your contract, because it doesn't say anything about going to Korea; it just says you're coming to work for CBS." I was so indignant I went up to New York to see Frank Stanton about it.

DC: Of course, Frank Stanton was president of CBS. Had you met Stanton by this time?

WC: No, no, I'd never met him. Stanton took a whimsical view of the whole thing. He said, "Well, maybe we can work out your going to Korea sometime, but why don't you go back down and do that local broadcast?" He gave me this big pitch about television being the future of broadcasting and that I would be making a big mistake to miss out on it.

DC: Did you find Stanton's argument persuasive?

WC: Well, there was an interesting twist to that. When I was still in Moscow, Bob Magidoff, who was with NBC, one day handed me a four- or five-page memo from a guy back at NBC headquarters in New York. This guy had been put in charge of something called television. This was back in '47 probably, and television didn't exist as far as we were concerned. Anyway, this guy outlined for the staff at NBC the great future of television. I thought the memo was fascinating, so I knocked off a letter to this guy at NBC. I have no memory of his name. I told him that I was fascinated with what he had written about the future of television at NBC. I told him that I would like to be a part of it and that I thought I could help NBC organize its television news operation. I had no thought of being on the air, necessarily, but I felt that I could organize the news operation. I wanted to be one of the pioneers in this field. I never got an answer from NBC. So here I am on television three years later, almost by accident. But anyway, Stanton convinced me that I should stay. I certainly was more open to the idea because of my exposure to the NBC report when I was in Moscow.

DC: This was your first meeting with Stanton. Do you remember anything about your impression of him?

WC: I remember that I was impressed, but he seemed to be rather stiff and formal. I didn't feel like I was cozying up to him exactly. He was very polite, very nice, but he clearly gave me as short shrift as possible. He had much more important things to do than talk to this pipsqueak from Washington. He paid me the usual compliments. He said, "Murrow says you're one of the top newspeople and you've got a great future. We're glad to have you on our staff." You know, that sort of thing. I guess maybe he'd seen some of my broadcasts.

DC: You hadn't met CBS founder and chairman William Paley by this time, had you?

WC: Actually, I had. I met Paley in London during the war. He palled around with a lot of top correspondents, of whom I wasn't one, but I hung around with them occasionally. I met Paley through them at some party or something.

DC: You mentioned that you worked in Washington without a script on the air. I guess those were the days when you and your colleagues were inventing the live news broadcast. There must have been a new challenge every day.

WC: It certainly seemed like it. When I went into television, nobody was theorizing about how you would present television, as far as I know. I certainly hadn't read anything, and I hadn't thought about it very much. But right from the beginning, I took the attitude that I was talking to one person when I was in front of the camera. In my head, I wasn't talking to thousands or millions; it was always on a one-on-one basis. And what do people want to know? Well, basically it's just like the managing editor of a newspaper walking into a cocktail party at night, and people say, "What happened today, Ed?" And you tell them. You don't have to give a lot of facts and figures. You just give them a good overall briefing of the day's events.

And that's what I did. I realized even then that you had to do a little more than that. You did have to give facts and figures and proper names. So I worked on the broadcast all day long and actually produced the broadcast as well. I had one director and one cameraman who worked with me. The cameraman also functioned as the art producer. If we had still pictures, he'd get those together as well. The three of us worked together all day long. I'd suggest local stories for the cameraman to go out and film. They would bring the film in and tell me what they had. I would look at the film in the lab and put everything together right there. Then toward midafternoon the director and I sat down and went over what I was going to do. I gave him a list of the stories in the order I would do them. I made notes all day on these stories, and that had the effect of planting in my mind what I wanted to say. I had a list of stories in the order I wanted to do them. That would remind me to get them all in. When there was a specific number or a proper name that I needed to remember, I put that alongside of a listed story. That's all—no script, just a list. I would just tell the news from that. With me, it was always in my head, and I was just able to rattle it off.

The director was also the person who punched all of the buttons. There was no union, so he and the cameraman filled several roles on the program. If we had a piece of film that we wanted to cue into, instead of my writing a detailed cue into that, the director knew what I was going to say in an approximate way. I had a big monitor over on the side of the set. The director would put "ten in the gate," as they called it. That's where the monitor would show the number 10 and then the numbers would count down to the film start. I could see that peripherally. When I got to a point where he thought I was about to go to the film, he would hit the button and the ten would start counting down. I could see it out of the corner of my eye, so I knew I had ten seconds to lead into a piece. It worked beautifully.

I had better vision in those days, of course, so I could see little tiny type. I wrote my list of stories on a slip of paper just as wide and as long as the Hechinger's or the Esso sign was on the edge of the desk. I pasted the list behind the sign on the desk, that way I could glance down and keep track of the items. That's the way we did the broadcast. Later on, when I went to New York to do the news broadcast for the first time, I announced that was the way I was going to do it, and my God, half a dozen people fainted when I said that. It turned out there was no way to do it in the New York studio because the facilities were so widely spread around the property. The film chain was in one room, and the still picture chain was in another room. The director was in yet another room, so they all had to have a copy of the script in order to know when to hit the film and still photos. I was disappointed that it didn't work out, because it's really the best way to do a news broadcast.

Which reminds me of another learning experience related to live broadcasting, but not on television. This was on radio. When I started out with CBS in 1950, they asked me to substitute one night for Eric Sevareid on his eleven o'clock at night radio broadcast. When I came into the studio, the producer asked me if I wanted a watch. I thought he was being snide about my being a freshman in this live-radio business. I thought he was talking about giving me a watch to retire. I said, "No, I don't want a watch; don't be ridiculous." Of course, that's the lingo for "Do you want me to slip you a one-minute time watch." Everybody operates that way. Here I'm saying I didn't want it. I was going to time the broadcast by the clock on the wall. The broadcast ran over, of course, and bells started ringing in central control at CBS in New York, Washington, and Philly. "What's he doing? My gosh, he's a minute over!" I threw the whole network into an absolute tizzy.

DC:　It's my understanding that Neil Strawser was your assistant in Washington during this period.

WC:　Yeah. I brought Strawser aboard as an assistant; that's right. When we went to the two-a-day broadcast, I needed some help in the early parts of the day, and we hired this young man. It was Strawser's first job. He went on to become a very good radio reporter. And then when I did the 1952 conventions, I told CBS that I wanted two assistants, one to keep track of communications and one to be an editorial assistant to read the news wires and call my attention to the material on the news wires and keep it separated. So I got Neil as my news assistant and a young woman out of New York as my communications assistant, Shirley Levine. Shirley went on to become one of the originators and producers of the College Bowl quiz contest program. It was either that or a program just like it.

DC:　At the Museum of Television and Radio Broadcasting, I viewed a kinescope of your broadcast from the White House in 1951 or 1952, when Harry Truman was president. This was when you were still working for CBS at WTOP.

WC:　Yeah, that was the first time live television had been broadcast from the White House, by the way.

DC:　Do you remember much about the background of that?

WC:　I imagine the networks had been after him to do it, but I had nothing to do with that. I think Truman wanted to show the renovations at the White House that had just been completed. I was advised that such a broadcast was going to be done on all of the networks operating at the time: NBC, ABC, and CBS. I don't recall if the DuMont network was involved. CBS nominated me to be one of the hosts. Each network had a host, and each of the hosts had a specific floor of the White House. We drew straws for the floors.

DC:　This was a tour of the White House?

WC: A tour of the White House hosted by President Truman with the network people being kind of escorts. I drew the basement. We shared the first floor somehow or other. It was a pretty good broadcast.

DC: Did you meet with Truman before the broadcast to plan the program?

WC: No, we did not sit down with Truman until the day of the broadcast. Each of us had a few minutes to talk about what we were going to ask him. He had been briefed, of course, by the White House staff and by the director. It was my first experience with a president in a non-news setting. I was impressed. Of course, we all knew that Truman was a cocky guy, but the major impression I came back with was how self-centered and egotistical he seemed to be. I had drilled myself silly over the history of every book-case, book, art piece, and everything else in the area that I was going to cover. The idea was that I would guide him with questions about these things. We walked into one room, for instance, and I said, "So this is where President Roosevelt did his famous fireside chats?" Truman said, "Yes, and this is where I've done all of my broadcasts. I sit right there in that chair, the microphones in front of me, and I do them." I got to another one, and I said, "And this is the mantel that Dolly Madison redesigned?" Truman said, "Bess has done a lot of the decoration in this particular room, and Bess has hung the pictures here beside them." Everything was about the Trumans.

I didn't know until later that all presidents are that way. They live in such a historical miasma that they are very anxious to separate themselves from the background and the history. They put themselves out in the foreground. Every one of them has been just the same in that regard. That's one reason why past presidents, like past executives at companies, are not very good advisors to their successors. We talk so much about using the wisdom of our former presidents, and I think we should, and we should find better ways of doing it. I've always thought they ought to have extra seats in the Senate, for instance. It would be a very good place for them. But as far as giving intimate advice to their successor, that doesn't work; the successor is always intent upon putting his personal stamp on history and on events. They aren't anxious to share it with their predecessor.

DC: I thought it was a very interesting broadcast in terms of how those things were done in the early days of television. I noted that you had to carry a huge microphone connected to a thick cable. Truman was very stilted, and everyone seemed to be feeling their way around.

WC: It was a very old-fashioned kind of broadcast. Of course, the technology was relatively primitive compared to what we have now.

DC: Did you cover other government stories as a reporter rather than as an anchor while you were at WTOP?

WC: Yes, in fact, that reminds me of an embarrassing incident. I covered Dean Acheson's briefing on the creation of the North Atlantic Treaty Organization. He was explaining what the terms of the alliance were and the matter of the NATO powers coming to the aid of another country that was attacked. I'd just come back from Moscow, and I had stopped in Czechoslovakia on the way back. I knew something about Communism and what was happening. So I asked Acheson what provision was made in the treaty for a government under threat from within. Acheson was a very arrogant man when he was in front of a group of reporters. I gather that in smaller groups he was quite the gentleman, but to the press he appeared arrogant. He really put me down with something like, "Well, I think if you read the treaty you would see that there is no such provision, nor should there be. A sovereign nation can go its own way." And I said, "But Mr. Secretary, I'd like to take a case such as Prague." He said, "We're not here to discuss Prague." Well, I was embarrassed because the older correspondents did not take that to be a serious question. As a new boy on the block at my first State Department briefing, I felt like I had stood up and asked a damned-fool question. But later on, some of the others came over to me and said, "That was a good question, but we didn't get an answer, did we?"

DC: Didn't you also cover General Douglas MacArthur's return to Washington in 1951 after President Truman fired him as commander of U.S. forces in Korea?

WC: Yes. I remember that quite well. It was a night arrival out at National Airport, and it was a big affair; there were a lot of people out there. The MacArthur-Truman feud had grown into a major national issue, and there were a lot of MacArthur supporters at the field. He still was a great hero in people's minds, so CBS covered it live. I was the anchor reporter, although I don't think we'd invented that title yet. The biggest problem I had was that my television monitor wasn't very good. I was in a location back from the actual microphone stand where MacArthur gave his remarks. I actually did the broadcast standing on top of a station wagon. Even so, it was hard for me to see through the crowd what was going on, and the monitor was no help. It was a very difficult broadcast to do for that reason, but it worked out all right. It actually won some praise, and I guess it furthered my career a little bit. It was the first of many such broadcasts I handled for the network.

DC: It's been noted that the MacArthur coverage demonstrated to the network your talent for ad-libbing and your ability to handle a fluid situation under difficult conditions. Was that one of the first live television broadcasts of an event like that?

WC: I hadn't thought of it, but as far as I know, it probably was. The conventions, of course, had been covered in 1948 in a very awkward way, with bulky equipment and a lot lighting that was very obnoxious to most people. But the MacArthur arrival was a different type of broadcast, and it was outdoors, which presented a completely different challenge.

that's what I would have done.

DC: A. M. Sperber's biography of Murrow is my source for that. She says that Murrow and Eric Sevareid and Charles Collingwood felt television was beneath them. Apparently Bob Trout had the ～ view. They all wanted to stay with radio.

, was the actuality broadcaster.
idn't need a script. Murrow,
wever, liked to have prepared
e of an ad-libber, but Murrow

ink it was for the 1952 convention that he came up with
te broadcast innovations, including the backpack set
eadphones for correspondents on the convention floor.

things through, they wanted to
on the air. That's not a bad

but it would be hard to credit th━
. I th━
. The ━
was Pa━
very i━
e good.━

ow and
lcasts.
some
ething as
ted to

y very w━
cks were━
ho was a━
big bac━
p aerial━
c and rus━
disks on━
st anybod━
hese stra━
headset.━

out the 19━
alled "Murrow's boys" appear on the television
id they stick to radio?

and
al
t━
t

microphone in or he tapped the wires. I think he either slipped
~oset up on an upper floor, and we put a reporter in there with
~ room outside.
meeting
He ran them into a broom

CHAPTER NINE

Fame Comes to the Anchorman

DC: The live broadcasts of the Democratic and Republican national conventions in 1952 were landmark events in your career. You were the sole anchor for the 1952 Republican Party convention. According to the sources I've seen, CBS News president Sig Mickelson tried to talk Edward R. Murrow into being the first anchor for the conventions. Do you recall that?

WC: No, but I have no reason to doubt it. That would have been the logical thing to do. If I were running the network, clearly that's what I would have done.

DC: A. M. Sperber's biography of Murrow is my source for that. She says that Murrow and Eric Sevareid and Charles Collingwood felt television was beneath them. Apparently, Bob Trout had the same view. They all wanted to stay with radio.

WC: Well, Bob Trout, of course, was the actuality broadcaster. He was a great ad-libber who didn't need a script. Murrow, Sevareid, and Collingwood, however, liked to have prepared material. Collingwood was more of an ad-libber, but Murrow and Sevareid wanted to think things through; they wanted to be prepared before they went on the air. That's not a bad trait. I wish more people would do that today. So Murrow and Sevareid were very reluctant to do extemporaneous broadcasts. They wouldn't mind doing a train wreck or a battle or some other sudden and unplanned event, but broadcasting something as complicated as politics and national affairs, they wanted to think it through.

DC: This was your national television debut, wasn't it?

WC: Well, not precisely, but it was certainly my biggest showcase at the time.

Cronkite, center, anchoring CBS's coverage of the 1952 Republican National Convention, the first of many he would cover during his career. CBS Photo Division, copy in Cronkite Papers (DI_02522).

DC: Wasn't this also Don Hewitt's break-in as a director?

WC: Well, Don Hewitt had been doing Doug Edwards's evening news since it began, which was, I think, 1948. He had four years under his belt and was already our top news director.

DC: I think it was for the 1952 convention that he came up with some remote-broadcast innovations, including the backpack set and the headphones for correspondents on the convention floor.

WC: Yeah, but it would be hard to credit those things to any individual. I think everybody was looking for mobility and flexibility. The producer for our coverage of the Republican convention was Paul Levitan. I could be wrong about that. But Paul was a very imaginative producer. He wasn't a Hewitt, but he was quite good. So I don't know who deserves credit for those innovations.

DC: Hewitt has been given credit for the backpack-and-headphone, mobile kind of interview setup.

WC: That may very well be. It sounds like Hewitt, certainly. Those backpacks were interesting. We had a guy named Don Hollenbeck, who was a fine broadcaster. Don was a floor man and had one of those big backpacks. These backpacks had a big aerial. It was a whip aerial, and when people brushed against it, we got a lot of static and rustle. To avoid that problem, they attached some plastic disks on the aerial that would keep them from rubbing against anybody. So now you had this backpack with this aerial with these strange plastic disks on them with a guy in his big bulky headset. He looked like a Martian in a bad science fiction movie.

DC: Talking about the 1952 convention, did Murrow and his team, the so-called Murrow's Boys, appear on the television broadcast, or did they stick to radio?

WC: It's interesting. For the first time, all of the radio people began to realize that television was a very big medium. There were more people watching television probably than listening to radio at that point. They were all beginning to want to make an appearance on television. So they had some spots during which they could analyze various developments and so forth. When they did that, they were impressed at the number of people that saw them and then recognized them on the street. Personal recognition was something that hadn't happened to them before. They all had their egos, and Eric Sevareid was especially impressed with this recognition thing.

DC: Do you remember much about what was going on at the 1952 Republican convention with Ohio senator Robert Taft still challenging Eisenhower's nomination?

WC: Oh, yeah, sure. The Taft and Eisenhower forces came into the convention almost equally balanced, but it wasn't any runaway for Eisenhower at that stage. The Taft forces challenged the credentials of the Eisenhower delegations from three southern states. Georgia was the one that became a test case. I think Texas was another one. But because Georgia was the first to be called up, it became the test. The Republicans fought this out in a credentials-committee meeting, which was closed to the press. The room in which the credentials committee was meeting had mirrored glass doors, so I announced on the air that this meeting was going on "behind the glass curtain." We stood outside that door and reported what we could find out from people coming and going.

This was fascinating stuff. Because the network's commercial time wasn't sold out, we had full play of the time. The Taft-Eisenhower credentials fight became quite an interesting story. If the Taft forces could throw out the big Eisenhower delegations and replace them with their own delegates, they could grab the nomination. Paul Levitan discovered that the wires from the public-address system in the committee meeting room ran out to a cloakroom outside. I think he either slipped a microphone in or he tapped the wires. He ran them into a broom closet up on an upper floor, and we put a reporter in there with headphones to listen to the whole thing. They brought notes to me about what was happening inside. I used this information, of course, on the air.

The Republicans went crazy trying to find how we were doing this. They finally traced the wires up to the broom closet and called the cops. As luck would have it, our correspondent had gone to lunch or some damn thing. Another correspondent from out of town happened to pass by the closet and saw our guy put some headsets down and leave. He went in to listen and was dumbfounded by what he heard. He was sitting there with the headsets on when the cops came. [laughing] They arrested this poor guy, and he's saying, "I don't know anything about this." One of our guys went down to the police station to get this guy out of jail.

DC: Talk about being in the wrong place at the wrong time.

WC: No kidding. I also remember New York governor Thomas Dewey, who supported Eisenhower, being down in one of the front rows at the 1952 convention. Everett Dirksen, a great orator, was at the podium making a speech in support of Taft. Dewey supported Eisenhower. Dirksen pointed his finger down at Tom Dewey and, referring to Dewey's unexpected loss to Truman in 1948, declared, "And he sits down there, the man who led us down the path of defeat." Later, I interviewed Dewey on the air. Dewey understood that on television it was effective to make a point by doing something that had a visual impact, unlike on the radio. But Dewey didn't understand that you had to warn the director about what graphic illustration you were going to use. At one point, he said something about the Democrats and the he pulled an egg out of his pocket and he threw it in the ashtray. Well, naturally, it broke and splattered. Quite pleased with himself, he proclaimed, "This is what the Democrats have done with their party, and they can't possibly put it back together again." It was a great visual gag, but he hadn't clued the director in, so no one saw it on air. The viewers only saw Dewey's face, his hand going up, and everybody looking down at something.

DC: Now, you were a newsman, and you had to maintain political neutrality in public. But what were your personal opinions politically during those days?

WC: Well, publicly, I didn't have any identification with one party or another. Personally, however, I had a liberal approach to issues. Actually, as personalities, I liked the old progressive Republicans the best. I enjoyed the free debate among the more liberal Democrats. But I liked individuals on both sides. I've never carried my political opinions into my personal relations. I found some of the old Republicans delightful people, and Dewey was one of them. I enjoyed Dewey's company. I saw quite a lot of him from time to time. I thought Dirksen was a fascinating guy.

DC: How did you feel about Eisenhower and Stevenson personally?

WC: My favorite was Adlai Stevenson. I didn't really appreciate Ike when he was president. But after he was out of office and I did the memoirs with him, I realized that he really was knowledgeable about so much that went on in his administration. But in 1952, I wasn't impressed with his capability to be president. I thought he'd gotten the nomination simply because of the hero worship of World War II, not by his ability to be president. Ike's association with a lot of the right-wing Republicans bothered me a great deal. On the other hand, we had this intellectual giant, Adlai Stevenson, who spoke so well, wrote so well, and thought so well, from my standpoint.

DC: How did you feel about Nixon at this early period?

WC: This was very early in Nixon's career. He was coming fresh into the vice presidency and off the House Un-American Activities Committee. That was one of the things I didn't like about Ike, his accepting Nixon as his candidate. It was a compromise to placate the right wing. I didn't like Nixon at all. I thought he was rather evil.

DC: The Republican convention in 1952 was also the convention where Senator Joe Mc-Carthy made quite a splash. Did you ever have any contact with him?

WC: Oh, well, yeah, I had a contact or two with him. Frankly, at that point, I couldn't believe that anybody was going to take McCarthy seriously. I thought he represented a kind of fringe fanaticism and a personal ambition that wouldn't be followed by anybody of import. A lot of the correspondents on the Hill rather liked him as a person. But that was largely before he went wild and crazy. They played poker with him, and he was one of the boys. Some of my colleagues told me at the convention that he was a good guy, but I couldn't see it.

DC: He had quite a reputation as a gregarious socializer, a cordial drinking companion.

WC: Yeah, the hair-down, tie-undone, relaxed, poker-playing-buddy kind of thing. As I say, he was rather popular in Washington with the press before he went crazy. I do think he went crazy, by the way. I had a scary encounter with him. I stayed in the Ambassador Hotel in New York when I went up on weekends to do *You Are There* and the Saturday and Sunday night news. I did the Sunday-night news special. It was at the height of the Army-McCarthy hearings in Washington. I got in the elevator one night quite late, and Mrs. McCarthy, a very attractive lady, and the senator were the only people in the elevator. He was very drunk, as he was pretty much of the time. I said hello to them when I got in the elevator, but I didn't make any conversation. I just faced the door. They got out first, and as the door was closing, I heard Mrs. McCarthy tell the senator, "I just want you to know, dear, *that's* Walter Cronkite." I went to bed with that comment ringing in my ears, thinking, am I next on his list?

DC: Nothing ever came of that?

WC: No, no.

DC: We were talking about Eisenhower and your own personal feelings about him. It was well known that Paley was a close buddy of Eisenhower's. Did CBS management ever hint or imply your coverage should favor Eisenhower?

WC: Absolutely not. You know, people find that very hard to believe. But it's absolutely true. In my forty years at CBS—well, let's say at least my twenty years on the *Evening News*—not once was I aware of any top-level-management attempt to direct our broadcast in favor of anyone. And that was also true of our commercial sponsors. Now, I know in the early days there were attempts by sponsors to influence programs in a political sense. Their contact was with the sales department at CBS, which, in the early days, tried to make overtures to us on that score, but they were rebuffed. The only time that I'm aware that we ever had that kind of problem, and I only really learned the details of it later, was in the Watergate situation.

DC: I want to talk about that in depth later, but naturally this question comes up in the abstract because newspaper publishers are known to dictate the political position of their newspapers. This well-known affinity that Paley had for Eisenhower would make an outsider wonder. But the fact that you felt no pressure during the Eisenhower campaigns, was that just Paley's way of doing things, or was someone else responsible for this insistence on objectivity?

WC: Well, yes, I think there were several people responsible for it. I think it was an ethic that grew from a lot of very good people at CBS having been at the right place at the right time. It began with Paul White, the basic founder of CBS News, and continued with Ed Klauber. Ed Murrow had an influence of course. But Frank Stanton and Paley both reinforced that ethic. Part of the reason was that Ed Murrow, Charlie Collingwood, and Eric Sevareid became very good friends of Paley's in London during the war. He admired them a great deal. Each in their own way educated him about the need for a factual, totally honest news department, uninfluenced by commercial and political biases.

DC: So that ethic of objectivity was formed during the heyday of radio, long before television?

WC: Oh yes. Absolutely. You know, Howard K. Smith left CBS over an argument about presenting his personal opinion on the air. Howard later tried to suggest it was because the opinion itself was counter to something that the network stood for, and I've forgotten what it was.

DC: Wasn't it over the Birmingham police department's brutal attacks on civil rights marchers in 1963?

WC: Oh, I guess it was, yeah. But what I heard at the time from Mickelson was it had nothing to do with the issue itself. It had to do only with the question of personal opinion. Howard had gone beyond what we considered an analyst should do. It comes down to the fact that there are basically three aspects of opinion broadcasting. One is the editorial, which is the strongest. That is when you go on the air and argue that this, whatever the issue, is the way things should be and this is what we say should be done about it. There's also the commentary, which is "this is the way things look to me." And finally, there's the analysis, which is "this is the way things are." The analysis breaks the issue down into its important parts without any suggestion of personal opinion or, certainly, of what should be done about the issue. Analysis was always considered to be what we did at CBS. I don't think we ever used the word commentary. But Howard wanted to step beyond that and do an editorial: "We've got to do something, and this is what should be done." That just wasn't the CBS style.

DC: Do you think that CBS management's keen awareness about the company's federal license played a role in that? The idea that using the public airwaves was a privilege, not a right, and that privilege could be taken away by the government as easily as it was given?

WC: I'm sure that would be one of the ways it would be sold on the higher level to Stanton and to Paley. It would be on those grounds, a concern about the broadcast license. Certainly, it was a matter of self-interest as well as public interest.

DC: Gary Gates says in his book *Air Time* that CBS's great success covering the 1952 Republican convention was a combination of Sig Mickelson's overall strategy, Don Hewitt's technical skill, and your on-the-air performance and ad-libbing skill. Do you think that's a fair characterization?

WC: Yes, but I'd also put Levitan in there. Paul died fairly early on. He was a feisty little guy without a lot of formal education. He is the guy who invented the name "anchorperson." It's sometimes credited to Mickelson, but I'm convinced that it was Paul Levitan who used the phrase first. As a matter of fact, people kept asking, what do you mean by an anchorperson? Paul said, well, it's the anchorman on the relay team, and that's where he got it.

DC: Going back to the 1952 convention, Gates says that you and Mickelson went for a walk along Michigan Avenue one morning and that Mickelson told you that you were a celebrity because of the great success you had anchoring the political convention. He suggested that you would be wise to get a manager and a new contract from CBS. Is that an accurate account?

WC: Yeah, that's true. This was after the Republican convention that summer of 1952, and we went for a walk at about two or three o'clock in the morning. It was after we left a party or something. Sig told me that I deserved more money. I think my base pay was $135 a week, but, of course, with commercial fees, considerably more than that. Sig, who was president of CBS News, said, "You know, I don't deal with that sort of thing. CBS has a business manager who will handle your salary. I think you need an agent." I said, "Oh, I don't need an agent. I'm a newsman. That agent stuff is for show business." Sig said, "Well, not in our business; you better get an agent." I told him that I didn't have the slightest idea about how to find an agent. Sig said, "Well, I'll give you the name of a mutual friend of ours who would know." I took Sig's advice and called this guy, who recommended Tom "Tuck" Stix, who became my agent. He was related to some big merchandising people in Cincinnati. His family was big in the Federated Department Stores chain. Tuck was a Yale Law type.

DC: Did he represent other broadcasting people?

WC: Yeah, he was a younger member of a firm of Stix and Gude, which included his uncle, also named Thomas L. Stix, and a guy named John Gude, who was a longtime CBS type. Thomas L. Stix was a literary book agent. Eleanor Roosevelt was one of their clients. They didn't have very many clients; it was kind of a small group.

DC: The incumbent president, Harry Truman, decided against running in 1952. The result was that the Democratic Party's convention, which was also in Chicago, was as torn by the battle for the nomination as was the Republican.

WC: Oh, very much so. Tennessee senator Estes Kefauver had been campaigning very hard in the primaries. You couldn't win the convention with primaries in those days, but Kefauver won a lot of pledged delegates. He was highly hopeful that he would get the nomination. Stevenson was a reluctant candidate, and he had not campaigned. He did not want the nomination, or at least he pretended he did not want it. It was only the people working for him that kept his name out in front of the convention. I think his name had been entered in some of the primaries, I remember, but he did not campaign. At the convention, he made a welcoming speech as governor of Illinois, which considerably enhanced his chances.

DC: The story is that he swept the convention with that speech, but that almost sounds too romantic.

WC: Well, actually, that was pretty much true. People didn't know Stevenson well, at the time. They had a chance finally to meet him and see him in action, and of course, he was around for receptions and so forth as well, but he made this fine welcoming speech. It was a literate, cultured speech that deeply impressed most of the delegates.

DC: Were there any incidents at that convention that stand out in your mind nearly forty years later?

WC: Well, I think it was that convention in which Kefauver did the unseemly thing of appearing on the convention floor before the nomination speeches. That was a real no-no in those days, and it still sort of is today. But Stevenson escorted his ninety-two-year-old father to a box seat, and of course, that started a stampede of his followers, which a lot of the old political leaders considered very unfortunate. Sam Rayburn, who was the powerful leader of the Democrats in the House of Representatives, was clearly not a Stevenson man, but he wasn't too keen on Kefauver either. Rayburn was the convention chairman, and he tried to hammer the convention back to order. Stevenson was standing there beaming in the box with his father. It was quite an interesting little sidelight.

DC: You interviewed Adlai Stevenson in North Carolina. I believe it was at his sister's place. Is there anything about that interview that you remember?

WC: Well, I remember I was very much impressed with Stevenson. I remember that I thought it was a great interview. I mean, great from his standpoint.

DC: What personal qualities about Stevenson do you remember from your own observation?

WC: There was something about Stevenson that would have made him a terrible president. One of the things that made him a warm and thoughtful person was that he saw everybody's viewpoint. He could understand the opponents as well as the proponents of anything. And he vacillated terribly in making up his mind on issues. Anybody who sees both sides and examines them with the intellect that he did is that way. Indecision was his hallmark, almost, and he was not a good executive. I don't remember his record in Illinois, but I just had a feeling he would not have made it as president of the United States. Which is too bad because he was so bright and he had so good a heart.

DC: Was he a good interview?

WC: Yes, he was. He was not didactic, and he was not doctrinaire. And he did not suffer fools gladly. If he thought a question was beneath him, or the level of the conversation, he'd let you know it. He'd give a very short, curt answer to a question he thought was beneath him. He wasn't impolite, but it bordered on that.

DC: You also anchored the election-night coverage in November 1952. This was the election-night broadcast when CBS featured its new Remington Rand Univac, which was a very early type of computer.

WC: Oh, gosh, I remember that Univac. We went to Philadelphia to see that thing, which occupied a warehouse. It had bulbs flashing off and on and whirring wheels and things. It was a real Doctor Frankenstein–laboratory kind of a place. But instead of Doctor Frankenstein, this place had a guy named Doctor Eckert. We kept referring to it as the electronic brain, and Eckert and his companion, who actually invented it, kept saying that it wasn't an electronic brain. We hoped that we could use Univac to call the election before all of the votes had been counted and beat NBC to the punch. The idea was that Univac would be loaded with a lot of baseline data, and then, as the vote returns came in, we would feed them into the Univac's base data. We believed that information would allow the machine to read the voting trends. CBS really built up the publicity about this thing. We planned to do our regular coverage without depending on the machine. The Univac was really a sideshow, a kind of gimmick, although we were assured that it might be accurate.

The way it worked was that CBS transmitted the voting results from our election studio down to Philadelphia by teletype line. The Univac people then fed back to us their information. Charles Collingwood gave reports on the air about Univac's predictions. Collingwood was in our studio, and he stood in front of a phony thing that was supposed to be the Univac. I think the thing in the studio had some flashing lights and fake meters and dials, but it was just a set. The actual information came to us from Philadelphia on the teletype. So Charles was actually reading the teletype information. Well, the first information that we got from Philadelphia was that the odds were 100 to 1 in favor of Eisenhower. This was about 8:15 in the evening. Off camera, Sig Mickelson said, "Oh my gosh, we can't go on the air with that, for heaven's sake."

Sig called Dr. Eckert, who confirmed that the machine was reporting those odds. So Collingwood and Mickelson finally decided against broadcasting that information. It just seemed so improbable. Eckert called back a little later and reported that he had adjusted the Univac and the odds were now in favor of Eisenhower by 2 to 1 or 3 to 1. So we broadcast those odds, and we were the first to predict Eisenhower's election. The interesting thing is that the Univac had it right the first time at 100 to 1. It was just a sideshow, but it was the first use of computers for election projections.

DC: Do you remember whose idea that was to bring in a computer?

WC: It could very well have been Paul Levitan, which was kind of the thing Levitan might have thought of. It also may have been Don Hewett.

DC: You mentioned Charles Collingwood. Did Ed Murrow have a role the night of the election?

WC: Yes. We used Murrow for analysis. By that time, Ed wanted to do television quite a lot. Interestingly enough, the old Murrow boys had a meeting to which I was not invited. They met with Murrow, wanting to know what the future of television was, what the future of radio was, and what their future was. I found out later that Eric Sevareid, who was one of the handsomest guys who ever came down the pike, complained at this meeting with Murrow that he and the rest of the old radio guys were all going to be out of a job. He declared that it was only "these pretty boys" who were going to get on the air in the future. That was funny because God couldn't have picked a handsomer group than Charles Collingwood, Ed Murrow, and Sevareid.

DC: But they were definitely warming to television.

WC: Oh God, yes. The 1952 convention was really a major turning point. People flocked to the stores to buy their first television sets after that. Murrow's guys knew that.

DC: I guess those 1952 conventions were the last of the old-time political conventions.

WC: Oh, they were. As a matter of fact, one reason the 1952 conventions were so much more interesting than the conventions that followed was the fact that the political parties did not realize what an impact television would have on the process. They conducted their business as they always had. But that was the end of the pre-television-age conventions; from there on out, they started sweeping the real business under the carpet, trying to put on a show. They've perfected the show now to the degree that nobody's going to cover it fully anymore. It's now covered in a very limited way because no business is done at the convention of any importance.

: And you were doing the weekend news at the same time in New
ork?

C: Yeah, I began doing the Sunday night news then.

C: So, y... do You are There, then you'd do the news that
night an...

WC: Right
Washingto

DC: Sinc

WC: Yeah
live. We
first sho
newsroom
and then
you are

DC: Were

WC: Oh,
the main
I was ri
placed t
stage th

k. In fact,
s a Texas
the Alamo.

y the last

eved to ha

e wall.
tting the
So, he
the
laying
p. The
le

ve
n-
h

evision, but they
because they couldn't work during

DC: So-called fronts?

WC: Fronts, yeah. Charlie Russell, who was our producer,

CHAPTER TEN

You Are There

DC: According to my notes, Walter, you began your work on the very famous television series *You Are There* in February 1953. How did you get involved in *You Are There*? I understand that originally it was a radio program.

WC: That's right. It was called *CBS Was There*. Well, I was simply invited to be the anchorperson. It was based on the idea of CBS newspeople being able to cover reconstructions of historical events. They finally decided to try to see if they could make it work on television. And when they did, they invited me to be the anchorperson on it. That's all I had to do with it. It was really kind of an acting role: the script was written every week, and I could change it if I insisted, but that was kind of hard to do.

DC: Was this a news-division program?

WC: No, the entertainment division of CBS put it on. It was a production of CBS News when it was on the radio, however. One of the things that annoys me a little bit today is that when some people talk about doing reenactments of the news on news programs, they are inclined to point back at *You Are There*. They say, well, Walter Cronkite and the CBS News department did that years ago and called it *You Are There*. Well, that's not true; it was not the news department. As a matter of fact, the news department really didn't like the program. They loaned CBS newspeople to the program with some reluctance. But we all enjoyed doing it.

DC: So in 1953, when you begin *You Are There*, you're commuting from Washington to New York to do it—is that right?

WC: Yeah, I commuted on weekends. I came in on Saturday morning. They blocked the

The highly popular You Are There *television series, with Cronkite as anchor, ca. 1950s. The show featured episodes on, clockwise from left, the Civil War, Joan of Arc, the American Revolution, and other historical events (DI_05801).*

show, as they called it, on Saturdays. That's the day they put chalk marks on the floor so the director and the cameramen could plot the actors' moves. I went up and just had a script reading on Saturday; there really wasn't much to that. Then on Sunday, we worked all day, from dawn until the show went on the air live at six thirty. For the first time, the actors were on the set, and midday they started rehearsing. We worked all through the day, rehearsing. At five thirty, we did a dress rehearsal, and then we did the show at six thirty.

DC: And you were doing the weekend news at the same time in New York?

WC: Yeah, I began doing the Sunday night news then.

DC: So you'd do *You Are There*, then you'd do the news that night and go back Monday morning to Washington?

WC: Right. I was still doing the news five days a week in Washington on WTOP.

DC: Since *You Are There* was live, I'm sure it was frantic.

WC: Yeah, it was live, and it had all of the thrills of being live. We did the crash of the *Hindenburg* zeppelin for our first show. When we went on the air, I acted like I was in the newsroom. I set up the show, gave a historical background to it, and then I said, "And all things are as they were then, except you are there." That was how the show opened.

DC: Were you in a separate studio for the opening?

WC: Oh, no. This fake newsroom where I sat was in a corner of the main studio where everything else on the show was going on. I was right next to everything. During the *Hindenburg* show, they placed the captain's deck right by my desk. When they wanted to stage the fire that destroyed the *Hindenburg*, they set off these smoke pots, and the guy who played the captain of the *Hindenburg* stood there doing his scene as the smoke poured out. That was the great climax of the show. The camera cut back to me to do my closing statement, and I was smothered in smoke. Hell, I could hardly breathe. I was choking to death on this smoke, trying to deliver these final lines through this cloud of smoke. I couldn't even see the camera. It was a poor moment in my career.

DC: As a kid, I watched *You Are There* every week. In fact, that show is my first memory of you. And, of course, as a Texas kid, I was especially interested in the show you did on the Alamo.

WC: Oh, my gosh, the Alamo show. Who was supposedly the last survivor? Was it James Bowie?

DC: Well, we don't really know, but Crockett is believed to have been.

WC: Crockett, oh yeah. Well, on the show, the actor who played Crockett was firing his musket through a peephole in the wall. The closing scene was supposed to have a cannonball hitting the wall, and then the wall was to crumble in and bury him. So he fires a shot and says his last line, and then—wham!—you see the cannonball hit, but the wall didn't crumble. The actor playing Crockett spoke his last line, and he doesn't know what to do. The wall's not falling. Finally, you saw on camera a broom handle reach forward and push the wall down.

DC: That's a great example of the perils of doing a play on live television. I know I saw that program, but honestly, as a seven-year-old, I probably thought the broom was part of the show. With this show being on the weekends in New York and broadcast live, CBS probably had a pretty good pool of actors from Broadway to draw from.

WC: Oh, absolutely the best. That was exactly the case. All of the actors in New York wanted to try television, but they didn't have the opportunity because they couldn't work during weeknights if they were in a Broadway show. Our show was perfect for them. They could do a reading on Saturday morning with the director and do the chalk blocking, and then they could do their matinee in the afternoon, and then the Saturday night show. They were free all day on Sunday. Paul Newman and Joanne Woodward were young, just starting out then. They worked on the show. We also had Ed Begley and E. G. Marshall. In fact, E. G. Marshall was one of the stock players for the program. We called them the Sidney Lumet stock players. Sidney Lumet was our director, and Johnny Frankenheimer was his assistant. Both of them went on to great fame as movie directors. Kim Stanley was also one of our actors. She played Saint Joan of Arc. They were all good. It was a great opportunity for me to work with so many talented people.

THE BLACKLIST

DC: *You Are There* went on the air in early 1953. This was at the height of the Red Scare in this country. I've heard that *You Are There* hired writers who were on the networks' blacklist, which listed individuals who were alleged, usually without substantive proof, to have communist sympathies or had been members of the Communist Party.

WC: That's right. We had several blacklisted writers who worked under phony names and used friends who weren't on the blacklist to act like they were the writers. They would deliver and get paid for the script that the blacklisted writer actually wrote.

DC: So-called fronts?

WC: Fronts, yeah. Charlie Russell, who was our producer, and Sidney Lumet arranged to get scripts written by these blacklisted writers from Hollywood. In fact, that's one of the reasons the show was so good, because the blacklist included many outstanding writers.

DC: Russell and Lumet did this knowingly?

WC: Oh yeah, very knowingly. And as a matter of fact, one of the executives of CBS, the deputy program director or something, got suspicious at one point. He demanded to have lunch with one of the guys who were fronting for blacklisted writers. Russell managed to keep them apart for several months, but finally, this executive insisted that he was going to meet this man. He told Russell that he liked the guy's writing and wanted to talk to him about doing some other work for us. Charlie Russell finally briefed the guy whose name they were using and tried to brief him enough to be convincing, because he was really no writer. Anyway, they finally arranged this lunch. Russell insisted on attending the lunch, and apparently Russell adroitly interrupted the conversation every time it got around to really pinning this guy down about his writing. And they got away with it.

DC: Was this widely done, do you think, in the live-television industry at the time?

WC: I suspect that it was. I wasn't aware of it because I wasn't in the entertainment part of the business except for this one program. But my guess is that yes, some of the directors and producers did it as much as possible. Of course, it took some courage to do that. If you got caught, you'd be in just as serious trouble as the individual that got blacklisted in the first place, probably more so. So it took a lot of courage. They wouldn't let me know about this practice of using fronts. They kept me innocent, but I suspected something. Some of these fronts used names, such as "Leslie Slope," that didn't seem real to me, plus we never met these guys. It seemed odd to me that they were never around the broadcast. One of the front guys got delusions of grandeur and began to believe he really was writing this stuff. He would come to the broadcasts and want to make revisions to a script that he hadn't actually written. He gave Lumet and Russell a hell of a time. He was trying to prove to himself that he was not just a phony. But I finally found out what Russell and Lumet were doing, when the series ended. I admired Charlie Russell and Sidney Lumet for doing it.

DC: I understand that because of the use of these blacklisted writers, Lumet and Russell, in league with the writers, often put a pro-civil-liberties slant to the content of the programs.

WC: Well, there was a very definite tinge of that in the broadcasts. But they had to do a lot of fighting to get some of that stuff in.

DC: Did you have any problems with the sponsors?

WC: Our sponsors were America's Electric Light and Power Companies. That was one sponsor. And then I guess Prudential Insurance was the other sponsor at that time. They were both quite conservative, certainly the power and light companies were.

We would hear a complaint from them every once in a while. They thought the script showed leftist tendencies occasionally. But it never got to be a major problem.

DC: There was one famous show that I remember. I think that E. G. Marshall was in it, on the death of Socrates.

WC: Oh, yes, that was a great show.

DC: And it had an anti-McCarthyism message, if I recall, safely buried in Greek history.

WC: It certainly did. It was very well done.

DC: *You Are There* does get invoked occasionally as an example of a news docudrama.

WC: Well, CBS did it themselves. It made me very unhappy with the Connie Chung Saturday night program that started out right away with doing docudrama-type stuff and reconstructions of news events. I was very much opposed to it. I think the CBS public relations people planted this whole idea that Walter Cronkite did that in *You Are There*. It wasn't the same thing at all. We weren't doing current events. There is no way that what we were doing on *You Are There* could be confused in the public eye with a real event, for Pete's sake. Nobody thought that television cameras were at the death of Socrates or Antony's meeting with Cleopatra or Solomon's decision. It was perfectly clear that these were historical reconstructions, not the current news.

DC: Why are you opposed to docudramas, Walter?

WC: Because they are confusing. The public has great difficulty separating the docudrama as presented by dramatists from the facts as presented by journalists, and I don't think that's fair. I think you ought to say that this is a drama or this is a documentary and present it as such. You can take all kinds of liberties once you put that docudrama label on something; whether that's a representation of fact that actually took place or not, I have no way of knowing. They're telling me it's based on fact, but how much is fact and how much is fiction? I have no way of knowing.

DC: So there's a real credibility problem.

WC: A serious credibility problem.

DC: I've heard that the device known as the teleprompter was first used on the *You Are There* show.

WC: I think so. It was the first time I ever saw a teleprompter. But that reminds me of a problem we had with some of these Broadway actors. One of the issues we had when the program was being planned was, what do you do with the correspondents? If they are in ancient Greece, they can't be wearing a modern suit and tie. You have to put them in costume. Put one of our correspondents in a flowing robe for the Solomon decision, and, you know, that's going to be ridiculous. So they came up with this interesting idea that the correspondent would always be off camera and never be seen by the viewer. This meant that the subject of the interview was talking to the camera as if the camera was the correspondent. The camera would come right in and shoot a close-up, and the actors were supposed to address it like they were talking to another person.

Well, that threw a lot of these stage actors into a slow spiral of sudden death. They just couldn't handle talking to that camera. A lot of them goofed up their lines. So they devised this teleprompter from which they could read their lines as they spoke them. Well, at first, unfortunately, the teleprompter wasn't through the lens. So they had to play the camera a little off to the side or underneath or below.

DC: It was like that for a long time, wasn't it? Because I can remember you could clearly see that people were looking above the camera to read.

WC: Yeah, but a lot of what really happened with the professional actors was that they had the prompter, which was usually above the camera, I guess, for them, depending on if the cameras were low or high, above or below. But once they knew it was there, and knew they had that prop, they didn't need it. It was just the psychological prop of knowing it was there.

DC: You were talking about the sponsor being rather conservative, and we were talking about the subject content being on the liberal side of the political spectrum. I have heard that the program had a lot of difficulty over a show about the Civil War and the Underground Railroad.

WC: Yeah, we had a great script on the Civil War, but the sponsors didn't want us to do a Civil War show. They were afraid it would offend the South. We had trouble with a lot of broadcasts, actually. It seems to me that there was a constant battle with the sponsors. That's not so unusual as an entertainment program, you understand. This wasn't a news project. If it had been news, it would have been a vastly different story.

DC: They wanted to be very selective about history.

WC: Oh, very. The sponsors wanted absolutely noncontroversial subjects.

DC: Well, given the fact that it was 1953 and 1954 and the Red Scare was in full bloom, that's an understandable feeling. Let's talk about the Red Scare atmosphere during this period. Did it affect you in terms of worrying about saying something on the air or being interpreted in such a way that somebody might want to put you on a blacklist?

WC: I think we all worried about it in the sense that we knew that that was a danger kind of thing. There was a little paranoia there, I think, on the part of all of us. I think we thought about it all the time, really. But I think that most of us were pretty courageous in the sense that we went ahead and did what we felt we had to do. It kind of felt a little bit like sailing in a thunderstorm, you know. You're out there in the ocean, you've got to sail along; although you know that that mast is a lightning rod, you can't do much about it. I think that's kind of the position we were all in.

DC: Was there much pressure on you, Walter, to speak out against the blacklist or McCarthy or anything?

WC: No, I don't think so. We were left pretty much alone in that situation, and after all, I wasn't as prominent a personality during the McCarthy period as I was later. I didn't even have a daily broadcast. I was doing *You Are There, The Twentieth Century*, conventions, elections, and those kinds of things. But I didn't have a daily broadcast.

DC: Of course, you might have been exposed because of what was going on in the *You Are There* situation, using the blacklisted writers.

WC: Well, that's true.

DC: Because, you know, needless to say, in those days it took a lot less than that to get in trouble.

WC: I think that's why Lumet and Russell protected me from it. They never let me know anything about it. They were protecting me in case anything came up. I could take a lie detector test and prove I didn't know a darn thing.

DC: What about CBS correspondent Don Hollenbeck's suicide? He committed suicide on June 22, 1954. Some people have blamed his death on McCarthyism and the Red Scare.

WC: Well, I think the suicide was a result of just a lot of things that preyed upon Don. He just didn't like the world he found himself in, the one that was developing after World War II. He was under considerable pressure from this very ambitious columnist in New York, Jack O'Brian, who wrote a television column for the Hearst newspaper, the *New York Journal-American*. He was always on Hollenbeck as a communist, just out after him. It was vicious stuff. It wore Don down quite a lot. It bothered Don to know that there were people like O'Brian in the world. He couldn't stand to think that people were like that. But there were a lot of things that bothered Don. For example, the new architecture on Park Avenue bothered the hell out of him. There was never a day he didn't comment about how awful it was to tear down the old mansion-type buildings to construct these boxlike concrete-and-glass skyscrapers. The increasingly bad traffic in Manhattan aggravated him immensely. I don't think he liked anything that was going on. Don also had domestic problems. He was fed up with his family, and he was lonely. I really don't think there was any one thing that you can say led him to suicide.

DC: Maybe this O'Brian stuff was sort of the last straw?

WC: I don't know if it was the last straw; it was certainly a heavy burden. He didn't like it.

DC: Hollenbeck was doing the local news at eleven o'clock?

WC: No, he was doing the Sunday news special, and he was appearing on *You Are There*. He was doing some radio as well.

JOHN HENRY FAULK

DC: Now, this is the time when CBS broadcasting personality John Henry Faulk was accused of being a communist. Do you remember the first time you met John Henry Faulk?

WC: I really don't know; I'm not sure when it was.

DC: When do you first remember John Henry?

WC: Well, I met him one Sunday up at a place on Hastings on Hudson. I think it was John Henry's house. And we got to know each other pretty well. Occasionally, we would have a lunch or see somebody and see each other around various functions. And then John took to fighting the blacklist. He and Charles Collingwood were putting a slate of candidates together to take control of the local New York chapter of AFTRA [American Federation of Television and Radio Artists] away from a group led by Bud Collyer, who was a popular game-show host. He was the host of *Beat the Clock* and *To Tell the Truth*.

Bud Collyer was a very conservative guy politically, and he was going along with the blacklisting business. Collingwood ran for the presidency against Collyer. I helped him in a very minor way. I wouldn't say that I was one of the leaders of the group by any means, but I certainly helped. I didn't shy away from it. It was kind of a courageous thing for people to do in those days, certainly for John Henry Faulk and Charles Collingwood. Well, they ran, and I think they got elected.

DC: Yes, they beat Collyer's group. Orson Bean also ran on the slate with John Henry and Charles Collingwood.

WC: That was the first time that the tide showed any sign of being turned against the blacklisters. It gave everyone considerable hope. That message was heard around the country.

DC: As you know, CBS fired John Henry Faulk not long after the AFTRA election victory. He made the charge that CBS fired him because the blacklisters demanded it. CBS denied that charge and claimed that he was let go because his program had such low ratings. Now, I know you weren't privy to management decisions, but what was your reaction to that?

WC: Well, to be honest, I think we all sort of had some doubts about what the real truth of that situation was. I don't think it was an open-and-shut case to any of us. Frankly,

John's show, which was local, was not that successful. It wasn't particularly appealing to New Yorkers because it was a hillbilly-type program.

DC: The program was called *Johnny's Back Porch.*

WC: Yeah, something like that. And so that allegation that CBS fired him because of pressure from the blacklisters kind of rolled off our backs a little bit. But the fact that he was fired was less important than the fact that he couldn't get another job. Nearly everyone in the television and radio business gets fired at some point if your ratings aren't good, but that doesn't usually keep you from getting work. John Henry couldn't get another job. I think he proved in court that he was on the blacklist. And fighting against the blacklist like he did took courage. John Henry was a feisty guy and was willing to take them on. Nobody else fought back.

DC: He won his case in court and proved that the television and radio industry had participated in a political blacklist system.

WC: Oh, of course. He hired Louis Nizer and beat the blacklist in court. He really broke it up. Everyone in the industry owed him one for that.

NEWS AS ENTERTAINMENT

DC: Well, getting back to *You Are There*, I noticed that CBS eventually quit broadcasting the program live. The show started being filmed in Hollywood in April 1955.

WC: Well, at first we went over to the old Edison studio in the Bronx and filmed them there for almost a year, I think, before we moved to Hollywood. Unfortunately, when we went to Hollywood, we lost a lot of integrity. Sidney Lumet and Charlie Russell and the whole New York gang were fairly faithful to the facts on the broadcast. They tried to have every word spoken by the principals actually come from historical writings and letters. That wasn't possible in many cases, but they did it as often as possible. Costume research and set research was very authentic. And, of course, we did some things that were fictional in the first place. We did Shakespeare's version of the assassination of Julius Caesar, for example. In Hollywood, that dedication to accuracy faded pretty fast. The scripts were just hacked out with little concern about accuracy.

DC: Is that when William Dozier took over the program?

WC: No, William Dozier was there from the beginning. In fact, Dozier was the guy who wanted to meet the blacklisted writer. I think Dozier had executive-producer credit or something.

DC: So did you have to fly out to Hollywood to do the filming?

WC: Yes. I went out to Hollywood two or three times a year and did several of the shows. But I only filmed my part. It was not as much fun because I missed seeing the productions. I just was doing the openings and closings. But it was kind of fun working in Hollywood, which I had never done before. We filmed on the old Hal Roach lot, and that was very interesting. I enjoyed it immensely. Just the mere matter of driving into a movie lot and giving your name and having the attendants practically salute and bow and say, "Yes sir, your parking space is waiting for you. Just a minute, here is a guide who will take you there in a motor scooter and direct you to your parking place, and here's your dressing room," and all that. It was pretty heady stuff for a young newspaperman.

DC: How long did you go out to Hollywood to film the program?

WC: Just a couple of years.

DC: Did Lumet continue the show out on the coast?

WC: No, I think he went straight into the movies.

DC: Gary Paul Gates said that *You Are There* was to you what *Person to Person* was to Edward R. Murrow. Quote: "It was a show that greatly increased [Cronkite's] popularity but did little to enhance his reputation as a journalist." Gates described the program as being "shoddy," that it was a "showbiz exploitation of both history and journalism." Then he went on to say, almost in the next sentence, that it won a Peabody Award in 1956.

WC: Well, it was far from shoddy. That it enhanced my public recognition, no doubt about that. I don't suppose it enhanced my reputation as a journalist, but I don't think, on the other hand, that it detracted from it either. As far as it being a showbiz exploitation, I think that kind of has to lie there for what it is. It's one man's opinion. It certainly was a mixture of journalism and history, and that was its intent. It was the whole raison d'etre of the program. It was not exploitation. Anything you put on the air, I suppose, is exploitation. I suppose the evening news broadcast is exploitation—exploitation of the day's events. People didn't do all those things just to be on the evening news, or most of them didn't, and therefore we are taking a set of events that occurred for some other reason and exploiting them by making a news broadcast out of it and selling the airtime. I don't think that's very sensible critique of the program. You know, we tried to bring it back at one time as a children's program on Saturday morning. That was done by the news department, and it was a disaster. The news department isn't capable of doing it. It's a dramatic program, an entertainment show.

DC: Was this in the early seventies?

WC: Yeah, I think it was. It had one basic fault which made it not work. On Saturday mornings, programs are cut up by so many commercials that you only have about three and a half minutes for a segment between commercials. You can't develop a character and all that in three and a half minutes, between these interruptions. So the program was doomed from the start. But if it hadn't been, it would have failed anyway because it was produced by Bud Benjamin, my dear friend, and directed by a very fine documentary producer, Vernon Diamond. Neither of them knew absolute beans about producing a dramatic show.

DC: Who took the Cronkite role?

WC: I did. I was delighted to have it come back. I was worried about the news department producing it from the very beginning. I was very concerned about that and argued against it, in a small way. It was set in concrete by the time I got into it all, but I didn't understand how badly the problem with the commercials would hurt us.

DC: What do you think about Gates's comparison of you with Murrow?

WC: I think there is some truth to it. There is quite a difference, however, in that Murrow helped to create *Person to Person* as a purely moneymaking venture. He was being told that he needed to own his own program. He couldn't own anything in the news division, so he and his partners, producers John Aaron and Jesse Zousmer, developed *Person to Person* as a commercial venture in the entertainment division. And, indeed, they all made a great deal of money on it. But Ed never had any real interest in the show. I think he hated it from the beginning. If you look back at some of the shows, you can tell that Ed's paying no attention whatsoever to the answers to his questions. The questions had been given to these celebrities in advance, and he's just going through this routine.

You know, talking to you about Ed Murrow, and the fact is that he wasn't quite as pure as he was made out to be. None of us are. A couple of years ago, I passed by a barbershop on Second or Third Avenue, and in the barbershop was a fly-bitten, double-truck ad in an old *Life* magazine, and it was Ed Murrow endorsing Colombian coffee. The ad had him sitting in his control booth with a cup, and it said, "I never go on the air without a cup of fine Colombian coffee."

this is a good

Sperber, in her biography of Murrow, quote: "Cronkite stayed
outside the Murrow circle, a sense of rivalry discernable
between the two men despite their disparate power positions."
She writes about a dinner party in Bethesda, Maryland, at the
home of Bill and Roz Downs. Allegedly, you and Murrow took
ling pistols down from the mantle and shot at each other. Roz
her husband and say, "I think they're

s was a very dear friend of mine, but Roz is a marvelous   hat. I remember the party very
nner. I don't know, it's perfectly possible that night   y such dueling pistol situation
and I had some words, maybe, a disagreement. It could   ly it happened, and if it happened
n about anything, it was a free-wing party. And Ed, as   ous. I'm not aware of any rivalry.
usual, as he got a little more loaded with the booze

party,
nal sword
elevision
member any
unlikely
t handle
p a dueli
ircumstanc
it's unlike
emonstrativ
Now Betsy
d I had a v
inker. I'll never forget the kitchen discussion in
"Cronkite, you better ease up, you're pressing
I don't know what year that was. Does Sperber

JC: I suppose that was true since nearly everybody else was in
he Murrow clique.

CHAPTER ELEVEN

"Good Night and Good Luck": Edward R. Murrow

DC: We were just discussing the *Person to Person* show. I think this is a good time to talk about Ed Murrow. According to Sperber, in her biography of Murrow, quote: "Cronkite stayed outside the Murrow circle, a sense of rivalry discernable between the two men, despite their disparate power positions." She writes about a dinner party in Bethesda, Maryland, at the home of Bill and Roz Downs. Allegedly, you and Murrow took dueling pistols down from the mantel and pretended to shoot at each other. Roz Downs was seen to turn to her husband and say, "I think they're serious."

WC: I don't remember any of that. I remember the party very well, but I don't remember any such dueling-pistol situation at all. I doubt very seriously it happened, and if it happened, it was not in any sense serious. I'm not aware of any rivalry. I would be flattered to think that Murrow thought there was any rivalry between us. I would be absolutely shocked and amazed that he felt such a thing. I certainly never felt that. Edward R. Murrow was the king, for heaven's sake. I wasn't even a pretender. I think his thoughts of me may have been much different. It may have been the other side of the coin of what I thought of him. I looked up to him, but I think he may very well have kind of looked down at me. I think he saw me as kind of a fairly successful practitioner of a new technique but without a lot of the background that he felt he had, probably. But I really don't know what Murrow thought. There was never any great friendliness toward me. There was never any companionship, as I gather there were between Murrow and some of his other people. But our collegial relationship was absolutely clean and pure as far as I know. I don't know of his ever attempting to undercut me. I couldn't have made an attempt to undercut him.

Roz Downs was a very dear friend of mine, but Roz is a marvelous tale spinner.

Cronkite and Edward R. Murrow in the CBS News booth during the 1960 presidential conventions (DI_05796).

I don't know; it's perfectly possible that night that Ed and I had some words, maybe, a disagreement. It could have been about anything; it was a free-wing party. And Ed, as was his usual, as he got a little more loaded with the booze, mumbled a bit. He chain-smoked, and he would sit with his collar undone, his sleeves rolled up half-way to the elbow, and leaning on his knees, muttering his deep thoughts to the floor. Those thoughts were usually his commentary on the evening or on whatever was going on. He did these Hamlet-like performances. I'm a more ebullient type, more active, hyperthyroid.

So at this party, we could very well have crossed some conversational swords at one time or another, about almost anything: television, radio, events of the day, McCarthy. But I do not remember any duel, and I don't remember any pistols. It's highly unlikely in my case because I'm scared to death of guns. I don't handle them if I can avoid it. I can't imagine my picking up a dueling pistol and waving it around under any pretext or circumstance. I'm just confident that that didn't happen. And it's unlike Ed Murrow. I've never heard of Murrow being that demonstrative about anything. So I just don't think it happened. Now, Betsy and I were the last to leave the party. Bill Downs and I had a very serious discussion. Downs was a pretty good drinker. I'll never forget the kitchen discussion in which he said, "Cronkite, you better ease up. You're pressing too hard." Now I don't know what year that was. Does Sperber mention a year for that whole thing?

DC: Actually, she doesn't.

WC: Well, I would guess, this was maybe 1954 or something like that, probably. I'm not sure, but Downs and I had been very close friends for a long time. He'd worked with United Press with me when I was in Kansas City, and we were together in London when he was with CBS. It was Downs who I was going to replace in Moscow when Murrow invited me to join CBS the first time. At any rate, we were good friends. Downs said, "You're pressing too hard." I said, "What do you mean by that?" He said, "Well, you're coming on hard. You're trying to climb the ladder at CBS. It's obvious." And I took some offense at that comment. I started talking to Downs about jealousy and about listening to people who didn't get jobs and so forth. As I talked to him, I was punching him in the clavicle with my index finger. The next morning, Downs called me, and he said, "What did you do to me last night?" I said, "What do you mean, what did I do to you?" He said, "I can't breathe. My left lung has collapsed." It hadn't really, of course. Apparently, I had punched him so hard in making my point, he had black and blue marks all over his chest. It was an interesting night, but it was a fun night as I remember it. But I certainly don't remember that thing with Ed Murrow.

DC: Here's a quote from David Halberstam from his book *The Powers That Be*: "Cronkite in 1952 was perhaps the one rising star within the company who was outside the Murrow clique."

WC: I suppose that was true, since nearly everybody else was in the Murrow clique.

DC: Talking about Murrow, this is a quote from Gates. He tells a story about you at some party, and you were doing an imitation of Jesus on the cross. Gates says that you were lifting your head, and you, as Jesus, said: "Good evening, Mr. Murrow." This was your joke about Jesus appearing in *Person to Person* because Murrow was so important. Does that sound familiar?

WC: That's perfectly possible. I extemporized at parties a great deal. I don't remember all of them, but I enjoy a good joke.

RIVALRY WITH MURROW

DC: Why has this Murrow-Cronkite thing become so big? It seems to be popping out in a lot of books. It's almost symptomatic of something, it seems to me, because people keep trying to set you and Murrow up as rivals, and, you know, you were telling me earlier that you couldn't see how there could possibly be a rivalry because of your relative positions, reputation-wise and fame-wise.

WC: I can't believe Murrow saw it that way either. I haven't thought about this until just this moment—this is off the top of my head. But I would suppose all of this stuff in these books is trying to reconstruct history in the light of subsequent events. We have these rivalries we now know about in the television business that have become far more intense as more and more people jockey for fewer and fewer jobs. That wasn't the case in my career. I fell into my job. There weren't any competitors for it. If there had been, I probably wouldn't have had it. And if Murrow had wanted it, I'm sure he would have got it, if he wanted to be the anchorperson of *CBS Evening News*. He never wanted that kind of a job; it wasn't cerebral enough for him. He wasn't that interested in the daily flow of news. But we know now about the desperate scramble for the top jobs at the network news organizations. I think these writers are trying to take the situation as it exists today and say that must have happened with Murrow and Cronkite. I think the interesting thing is that they haven't been able to come up with anything. This so-called rivalry just didn't exist. I never heard anybody say, "Hey, you better watch out. Murrow is after you." I think some of my friends in the Murrow group would have told me. Collingwood would have most particularly; and Sevareid certainly would have. We were close when they were working for CBS and I was at UP in London. We stayed close after I came over to CBS. Bill Downs would have told me in a minute.

DC: So what did you think of Murrow's famous Chicago speech that criticized the direction in which television seemed to be going to him? It got him in trouble with Bill Paley.

WC: I applauded it wildly, like all of us did in the news department. I admired his courage for saying it. I said, oh boy, there's our leader. Glad it was done. I was obviously sorry it got him in trouble with Paley, but I didn't consider that entirely unexpected.

COVERING CONVENTIONS

DC: Take a look at this photograph of you and Murrow. It was taken in 1956, and you are sitting behind an anchor desk. Murrow is sitting on top of the desk, looking at you, and the two of you are smiling. It's jumping ahead a little bit from where we are now, but since we were talking about Edward R. Murrow, I just thought we'd look at it.

WC: I don't remember that particular set. You know, during these conventions or during any special event, CBS paraded everybody through the anchor booth, and hundreds of pictures were taken like this. But it was totally meaningless except to show the character in Murrow's face and the blandness in mine.

DC: Sometimes a photograph can unlock a memory. I didn't know if that reminded you of anything.

WC: Well, actually, that photograph does remind me of a situation that I had forgotten about. At the 1956 convention, NBC brought in the Huntley-Brinkley team for the first time. The overnight ratings indicated they were doing very well. The local Chicago papers were making a big deal of CBS's slipping ratings. Don Hewitt always had a certain penchant for publicity and for dropping little stories, endearing him to the columnists. I'm sure it was Don who dropped a story that they were considering bringing Murrow in as a coanchor for the convention coverage, which may have been happening—I don't know. I didn't know about it, and I don't think Murrow knew about it. But whoever planted the story also said that I was opposed to Murrow coming in.

And then there was a story that I refused to be a coanchor with Murrow. The front page of the *Chicago Sun-Times* was "Murrow-Cronkite Feud," or something of the kind. I got the *Sun-Times* in my room at the Ambassador East Hotel, where both Murrow and I were staying. I had just never heard of any of this before. I had certainly never told CBS that I didn't want Murrow in the anchor booth with me. I possibly would have if they'd ever brought it up, but just because I believed in a single anchor, not because of Murrow. I was sure that Murrow didn't want to do that. It wasn't the sort of thing that he would want to do.

Anyway, after I saw the story in the *Sun-Times* that morning, I called Murrow. I woke him up. I said, "Ed, have you seen this morning's *Sun-Times*? He said, kind of grumpily, "No." I said, "After you get it, call me. I think we have to talk." A very few minutes later, he called back and said, "What in the hell is all this crap about?" And I said, "Well, do you know anything about it? Because I know nothing." Ed said, "Nothing, never heard anything. I don't want to be in that damn anchor booth. You do that job superbly well. I don't do that kind of thing well, and I don't like doing it. I wouldn't do it if they asked me, you know." And I said, "You know, I think, Ed, that we ought to try to put this down as quickly as possible. I'm sure we're going to be called today by every columnist in town." We both had our phones blocked to that sort of thing. I said, "They are going to be calling CBS public relations, all the columnists, all the newspapers are going to want to talk to us. I suggest we don't talk to anybody. I've got a different plan. Why don't you and I take the number one table at the restaurant downstairs, here today, for lunch, and let's the two of us go and knock back a couple of martinis and laugh it up at lunch and have a good old time. We'll sit around and talk about World War II." Ed said, "Great idea. I've got a lunch appointment, but I'll cancel." So that's what we did. We sat just in front of God and everybody. That was the place for the columnists to get a story. We sat there having a marvelous lunch. Every columnist in town came by and said, "What, are you trying to settle a feud?" We said, "What feud? We're having a great time." That quelled the damn story pretty quickly. But the story was planted, there was no question about it.

DC: Did you suspect Don Hewitt?

WC: Yes, I did. I faced him with it and he said, "Oh no, no."

DC: You anchored the presidential election returns in 1956 as you had in 1952, and Sevareid was the CBS analyst. According to Sperber, Murrow was assigned to cover the East Coast voting returns for that election. He was standing over on the side, and, I'm quoting Sperber again, "This was perceived by many to be a severe punishment for Murrow's Chicago speech attacking television news." According to Sperber, Mickelson told Howard K. Smith that he would be anchoring instead of you, because of your sore throat. They phoned you to tell you to take it easy, but fifteen minutes later, according to Howard K. Smith, you were in the studio. So Smith implied that you came out of a sickbed to return to work because Smith was going to replace you.

WC: Well, I had a sore throat all right, and I was doing a lot of spraying and so forth. Sandy Socolow, my closest coworker for all these years, maintains that I had psychosomatic colds before the big events. I never felt any nervousness at all unless I or somebody else was unprepared, then I'd be nervous. But I think I did get a psychosomatic sore throat and cold, sometimes to the point I couldn't really talk at all until the broadcast started, and then it disappeared. This episode in 1956 was one of my early experiences with that. I don't remember any Howard K. Smith involvement. Certainly, it wouldn't have been, as Sperber suggested, a threat that somebody else was going to do it. I knew somebody else would have to do it if I weren't able to do it. Who it was wouldn't have mattered to me.

DC: What about Murrow being resentful about his assignment?

WC: Well, you know, I don't remember Murrow being on the East Coast board. He must have been—Sperber couldn't have made that kind of mistake—but I swear I don't remember. If it happened, and it must have, that indicates how unimportant all this would have seemed to me. I never saw that dark, ugly hand of conspiratorial connivance in people's assignments.

DC: Later, in 1960, you and Murrow were the coanchors for the Democratic convention in Los Angeles, when John Kennedy won the presidential nomination. Or at least you were coanchors for part of the coverage. Both of the 1960 political conventions were ratings disasters for CBS. Huntley and Brinkley ran off with the ratings. According to several sources, during the middle of the Democratic convention, Don Hewitt supposedly suggested to Sig Mickelson that Murrow be brought into the booth to coanchor with you. This apparently was done without consulting you. Hewitt was later quoted as saying: "Boy, was that a disaster. I mean, if there were two chemistries, two personalities, that didn't blend, it was Murrow and Cronkite." Murrow was supposed to sit by himself in a corner of your booth, and the camera was supposed to cut to him for commentary. Murrow refused to do that and insisted on being moved next to you on camera. You apparently learned of this new arrangement when you walked into the booth and found technicians carrying wires out to make room for Murrow. Fred Friendly has written that, quote: "Both men were against this arrangement. Ed was not a facile ad-libber and Walter liked to work alone. They lacked personal rapport. On the air, there was a lack of ease between the two correspondents." This was during the 1960 Democratic convention.

WC: I don't know about Murrow refusing to sit in the corner because I didn't know about this until I found them tearing the desk apart. The problem was that I had a chain of information. I had these two people sitting on either side. I had this critical flow of information suddenly cut off. Now I had somebody sitting there between the person that is supposed to be slipping me information and myself. They did this without ever consulting me. I was furious. Who's supposed to do what? What's Murrow supposed to do? I don't think they said anything about him doing analysis. They just said that he was supposed to help me. They just wanted Murrow on camera to cash in on Murrow's popularity. As far as the chemistry between us, I don't know. I think that Murrow and I might have had chemistry that worked under different circumstances, but the arrangement at the convention in 1960 was not one to create great chemistry.

DC: After all these years, what's your view of Edward R. Murrow's place in the history of broadcasting?

WC: His place in broadcasting history obviously is assured, and it's an important place. The interesting thing about Murrow is that he came to broadcast journalism without any background in journalism whatsoever. He came to CBS with the idea of recruiting speakers and organizing panel discussions and that sort of thing. He decided to go to

England to do that. He was there at the time that the war started and became a news broadcaster because he was the only person there. CBS didn't have any foreign correspondents at that point, so he recruited a staff, and they turned out to be excellent. He had considerable guidance, undoubtedly, from the CBS News management in New York, including Wells Church, Paul White, and Ed Klauber. But he had to wing it a great deal. And between Klauber and, I guess, Ed's natural inclinations, they built an ethic that stands today for integrity in broadcast journalism. This insistence on news integrity was mostly Ed's work. He just felt it, understood it, and communicated it to others at CBS.

Radio broadcasting news was a pretty shlock thing before World War II and not very highly thought of. A lot of the commentators were more show business than they were newspeople. Local stations operated with very little wire-service input. A lot of local stations were directed by former vaudeville hoofers and singers with no journalistic background or ethic at all. It was really World War II and Ed Murrow that put radio news on the map. So Murrow's contribution was immense. When he came home to America, he insisted on maintaining those same high standards. He had the support of Frank Stanton and Bill Paley in doing that, quite clearly. His standards for recruiting correspondents were high. He put together a group of correspondents that brought credit to CBS and to broadcast journalism. He himself was a superb radio broadcaster and became quite effective in television as well. He was a thoughtful, serious man. Personally, I felt he was kind of overserious at times. He didn't seem to have a great sense of humor or any desire to have one.

DC: What do you think his shortcomings were as a newsman, as a broadcaster?

WC: Well, I don't really know of any shortcomings. I'm a daily-news man. I like gathering the news, putting it in together in an orderly fashion, and then putting some meaning behind it in relation to other stories. He was much more of an editorialist, the thoughtful essayist type. But that's not a shortcoming. We just were different.

radio, and we just took the radio show. Maybe we ought to sue ~~you~~ ~~It's been on CBS~~
you." Boy, he was furious. Since I was fairly new in televisio~~n~~
and show business and that kind of thing, I was really worried
about it. I reported the incident immediately to CBS, and they
dusted it off quickly. The very next Sunday after I had the
brush ~~with~~ ~~interviewed~~ Oklahoma Sen. Bob Kerr. I
~~cast~~ and said, "Thank you Senator Kerr for
~~eet~~ the Press." I didn't hear myself say
~~room~~ heard me say it. As I came out of
~~r,~~ Larry Beckerman, said, "What did you
~~u~~ do?" And I said, "What are you talking
~~d,~~ "You signed off Meet the Press." I

first discussion program that went on the network
~~Cap~~itol Cloakroom, which was on CBS Radio for years.
~~so far~~ as I know, the first of the radio discussion
~~wa~~s a political figure answered questions from a group
~~journalist~~s. That was the format of Capitol Cloakroom. It

~~resuming~~
~~e~~ ~~fore~~~~n~~ ~~or of~~
~~t a~~
~~the show~~ ~~owns~~
~~rew the~~ ~~onths—~~
~~th CBS~~
~~ay that~~ ~~ld~~
~~happened~~ ~~ut?"~~
today. ~~w~~
~~h.~~ I'm no~~C."~~
~~did the f~~ ~~t.~~
~~k that we~~
~~o do it.~~

~~was live,~~

~~problem we~~
~~They were~~
~~to act. S~~
~~r on telev~~
~~at with the~~
~~fundamentals.~~ I gave them suggestions like sitting on
~~e~~ of the chair to avoid slouching back into it, and

the

~~he~~ tower and
~~atever~~ had to be fixed, right
~~with~~ this armed nuclear bomb sitting there.
~~y~~, we had to wait for an hour or two in the trenches for
~~the~~ thing to go off.

CHAPTER TWELVE

CBS News's Utility Man

DC: I understand that during your years in Washington in the early 1950s you anchored some news discussion programs.

WC: Well, the first discussion program that went on the network was called *Capitol Cloakroom*, which was on CBS Radio for years. It was, as far as I know, the first of the radio discussion programs where a political figure answered questions from a group of correspondents. That was the format of *Capitol Cloakroom*. It was a longtime forerunner to *Meet the Press* on television.

DC: Is that the show that you have been quoted as saying that you just "threw the meat on the table" and let them go after it?

WC: Did I say that once? I don't remember that. But that was about what happened. That program became *Face the Nation*, which is still on today. As a matter of fact, I believe I initiated the program. I'm not absolutely sure of that today, but I believe I did the first one of those. They told me in the middle of the week that we were going to do this program on Sunday, and I agreed to do it.

DC: This was live, of course. Did everything go well?

WC: One problem we had on that program was getting the guests to talk. They were a little afraid of the medium; they didn't know how to act. So CBS conducted some free workshops about how to appear on television. We set up a session with a makeup girl, and I sat with them and showed them how to sit and some of the simple fundamentals. I gave them suggestions like sitting on the edge of the chair to avoid slouching back into it, and not putting their weight on their arms on the table to avoid hunching

Cronkite reporting from Rome for Eyewitness, *a pioneering news program considered a forerunner of 60 Minutes (DI_05817).*

their shoulders, and how to look at the camera. I told them to just view the camera as another person in the group.

Right after our first broadcast, I saw Larry Spivack, who had started *Meet the Press* on NBC television before we went on the air with our *Capitol Cloakroom*. He was furious. Larry was a very small man and a very cocky and tough one, and he attacked me like a bantam rooster. He was really coming at me, feathers flying, and saying, "I'm suing CBS. You've stolen my idea. How dare you go on the air with a broadcast like that?" I said, "Well, what the heck, Larry. It's been on CBS Radio, and we just took the radio show. Maybe we ought to sue you." Boy, he was furious. Since I was fairly new in television and show business and that kind of thing, I was really worried about it. I reported the incident immediately to CBS, and they dusted it off quickly. The very next Sunday after I had the brush with Spivack, we interviewed Oklahoma senator Bob Kerr. I was closing the broadcast and said, "Thank you, Senator Kerr, for appearing with us on *Meet the Press*." I didn't hear myself say it, and nobody in the room heard me say it. As I came out of the studio, our director, Larry Beckerman, said, "What did you say? My God, what did you do?" And I said, "What are you talking about Larry?" And he said, "You signed off *Meet the Press*." I said, "Oh, Larry, come on." I walked out of the room, assuming it was a joke of some kind. I walked toward the front door of the studio building, and the receptionist said, "You've got a phone call from Bill Downs." I picked up the phone, and Downs said, "Well,"—I'd only been with CBS at that time a few months—Downs said, "Well, that was one of the shortest careers with CBS of anybody I've known. Did you make any arrangements to hold onto your job at UP?" And I said, "What are you talking about?" And he said, "You signed off *Meet the Press*. I don't see how you expect to say at CBS. Maybe you can you get a job at NBC." It was terrible. But it got very little notice, oddly enough. Probably a sign that nobody was watching.

NUCLEAR BOMB TEST IN YUCCA FLAT

DC: In March 1953, you covered the first atomic bomb test in Nevada open to the news media. That must have been a memorable assignment.

WC: I'd say it was. None of us had ever seen an actual atomic explosion, and it was a very big deal. For some time, the press had been urging the atomic energy people to let us see a bomb test. They finally decided to do so at the Nevada Test Site at Yucca Flat, which is about seventy miles outside of Las Vegas. The big problem we faced was getting a television signal out of that remote location. A brilliant engineer who worked for, I think, KTLA in Los Angeles kind of jerry-rigged some type of transmission relay. The televised part of the press coverage was a pool effort. We broadcast from the top of a mountain and relayed it back from there down to the station in Los Angeles and on to the network. I covered the test for CBS, and John Cameron Swayze did it for NBC. It was kind of a long, drawn-out affair. They had to have just exactly the right weather conditions to do the test. We sat around Las Vegas for several days, waiting for the signal to go to the test site.

We finally boarded the buses at one o'clock in the morning or something for a long two- or three-hour ride out into the desert. The first time we went out, the test was scrubbed, and we had to turn around and ride all the way back. A couple of days later we went out again, and it was delayed. But it was a dramatic episode. There was something wrong on the tower, and the bomb was armed. A team fixed whatever had to be fixed, right there at ground zero with this armed nuclear bomb sitting there. Meanwhile, we had to wait for an hour or two in the trenches for the thing to go off.

DC: You were actually in trenches?

WC: They put us in trenches at the time of the actual blast, yeah.

DC: The idea was to have this on live television?

WC: Yeah, it was on live television. I'm assuming that none of us were exposed to radio-activity. These are the same tests where the troops were even further forward than we were. Some of the soldiers in the front-row trenches have since had problems with leukemia and other radiation-related conditions. There weren't any concerns at the time about it. Radiation was known to be dangerous, but nobody knew the precise nature of it.

DC: Do you remember much about the explosion? I assume that would be a memorable experience.

WC: Oh, quite vividly. We were advised to turn our backs before the explosion. We heard the countdown over the PA system, and we turned our backs. We wore heavy dark glasses. After the blast, we were supposed to count to five or something before looking around.

DC: Did you have any anxiety, or did you just totally trust the military on this?

WC: We pretty much trusted them. They had conducted several of these tests already. But I guess there was some anxiety, sure.

DC: Did you have a microphone?

WC: Yeah, we were broadcasting live. I turned my back, and even with my eyes shut, there was a terrible light. The light came first, of course, and then the sound, which wasn't all that terrifying. There was a little heat, not a blast. It didn't hurt, but you felt it. I turned around, and I could still see the big fireball. My gosh, it was something.

DC: Was it what you'd expected?

WC: We'd seen a lot of photographs of tests before this, so it looked about the way I expected it to. There weren't any major surprises that I remember.

IT'S NEWS TO ME

DC: I understand that you were the host of a program during the midfifties called *It's News to Me.*

WC: Oh, yeah. There was a period of time when CBS was fairly lax about our doing entertainment programs. I experimented with everything. My attitude was, "What the hell, I'm in New York for the first time." Producers Mark Goodson and Bill Todman were the kings of the game shows in those days, as they continued to be for many years. They asked if I would be a panelist on a game show called *It's News to Me.* That program ran for several weeks. They brought in people who had participated in news events. They brought in artifacts from news events. They did dramatic reconstructions from news events. They did songs that parodied news events. And the panel had to guess the news event that that these things represented. It was purely a game show, but educational and very well done.

I did that for a while, and then I did one other Goodson-Todman game show called *Two for the Money.* Herb Shriner, a homespun comedian from Indiana, was the host of that show. I've kind of forgotten, but it had an expert named Gross, who, I believe, was a dean out at Rutgers University. It was one of the hardest jobs I ever had. I was barely up to it. It was a show that had a set of questions, and panelists who were from the audience answered these questions. It had a kind of educational bent to it.

DC: What do you mean by an "educational bent"?

WC: Well, it featured serious questions about history and world events and general knowledge. I sat as a monitor, and I had to say whether the answers that were given by the panelists were right or not. There was a specific correct answer, which was on the cards I had in front of me, but there were shadings that could be accepted as correct or not. This Rutgers dean was terribly good at being a monitor, but he became ill and couldn't do it for a while, so they brought me in to be the monitor. It was a terrifying job, you know. I had to be right on all of those things, and I didn't necessarily know some of them. The dean had an encyclopedic knowledge of science and arts and was terrific.

DC: Why were you selected to replace the university dean?

WC: To be honest, I really have no idea. I guess I projected some high level of intelligence in some way. I don't know, but I can tell you that I was a poor substitute for the dean. That was a difficult show for me.

DC: A story in the *New York Times*, dated December 10, 1956, reported that you had asked CBS News for permission to host a new quiz show called *Nothing but the Truth*, but that CBS News had denied you permission to host it. CBS subsequently ruled that its news personnel could no longer work in the entertainment division.

WC: I don't recall the specifics, but I don't doubt that it happened like that. At one point, CBS called a halt to any outside appearance of its newspeople other than a news-produced broadcast. That included narration of industrial films, which a lot of us were doing at the time. I wasn't upset about CBS's decision. In fact, I think that I agreed that it was a good idea. I remember vaguely this business of asking permission to do the show you mentioned, but I was in some doubts myself that I should do it, from the very beginning.

DC: Why did you have doubts?

WC: I always felt a little uncomfortable with entertainment programming. Now that I think about it, I may have incited the ruling. There was a little bit of a ham in me, and I'm fairly good at that kind of thing. I don't think that most of my colleagues were. Most of my colleagues were much purer, perhaps, in their reportorial kind of devotion. But at the time, I was willing to experiment in different television shows. It was fun, you know. I'm more inclined, probably, to slip over and do an entertainment-type program today than my colleagues are, at this late juncture, simply because it's kind of fun.

DC: It's hard to envision Eric Sevareid doing a game show, just simply because his personality would not seem to lend itself well to that kind of thing.

WC: That's true, or almost any of those people of that era, such as Don Hollenbeck or Ned Calmer. It just wasn't their style.

LOGISTICAL PROBLEMS

DC: In the late 1950s, you also broadcast a midafternoon news program as well as your Sunday-night news special.

WC: That's right. The midafternoon news was only five minutes in length. I did that and the Sunday night news from about 1956 right up until I took over the *Evening News*.

DC: From reading Leslie Midgley's book, *How Many Words Do You Want?* it seems that CBS News had a severe logistical problem in the 1950s with its broadcasting, because its facilities were scattered around Manhattan.

WC: Oh, God, there were severe problems. The news broadcast was done from an old concert hall, Lederkranz Hall, which was up at Fifty-eighth Street, between Park and

Lexington. But they put the show together in the Grand Central Terminal building, which is where the newsroom was located. It was really kind of a loft space up there. That's where they edited the film for the news show. Then they had to run to the freight elevator with the film cans and the scripts and go downstairs. They ran out on Forty-fifth Street, hailing cabs at rush hour. It was crazy. They had a hell of a time getting it to the broadcast studio on Fifty-eighth Street. They would pile out of the cab and run in to Lederkranz Hall on the ground floor. Don Hewitt and Doug Edwards would rush into the studio, and the film projectionist would run the film for them to review. They'd get set up, the makeup person was there, and Doug sat there and did the news. They barely got on the air, day after day.

There were days when Alice Weel, who was the assistant producer and writer, took the film up there by flagging down any passing car that would stop. Once, Doug Edwards and Don Hewitt had to climb on the back of a motorcycle. There were many nights when they damn near didn't make it to the studio in time. There were some nights when the film didn't make it and Doug made it. Some nights the film was there and Doug wasn't there. I don't know why the company didn't hire a chauffeured car to do that. It was just dumb and crazy.

CBS finally set up a studio in the Grand Central Terminal building, but then we had to walk across from the fifth floor, across a catwalk that was high above Grand Central. It was safe enough, but you could look right down five floors, down to the people catching trains and all that. You went across the catwalk and then down two flights of stairs into the control room and the studio, and that's where my one o'clock news broadcast originated. That was the five-minute news show you mentioned. One day my director, a guy named Walters, who was General Vernon Walters's brother, and Sandy Socolow and I started down for the studio, and we got to that catwalk, and I glanced down at the railway clock down there, and it was one minute after one. We'd started with ten minutes to spare. "My God," I said, "it's one o'clock!" We ran down to the studio, and I went on the air so breathless that the whole three and a half minutes we had left, I was [pants] not really able to [pants again] talk. Well, it was just awful [laughs]. When we came out of the studio after that broadcast, the assistant manager of news said, "Come to my office and explain yourselves." The network had been dark for a minute and a half. Our clock had been wrong in the newsroom. It was just an electric wall clock. After that, we got Western Union clocks.

THE MORNING SHOW

DC: In 1954, CBS moved you from Washington to New York to host a new daily morning program to compete with NBC's *Today* show, hosted at that time by Dave Garroway. Why were you selected to do the morning show?

WC: Well, I don't know. Mickelson selected me. The Garroway show had been on for one year, exactly. And I guess that full year CBS had been looking at a possible show for the morning. Sometime during that year, they decided to go with a similar morning show, and there was an internecine fight at CBS as to whether it should be done by the news or the entertainment divisions. That fight has never really been settled to this day. There is always a scramble for those two hours in the morning. They decided the show would go to the news department, so Mickelson nominated me to be the host.

DC: If the news division was producing the show, was there a problem with its correspondents doing commercials? I reviewed some kinescopes and noticed that you had to do commercials.

WC: It was an issue, but the news division finally accepted the idea. On the *Today* show, Dave Garroway was doing his commercials a la Arthur Godfrey, which was a very freewheeling kind of commercial. They gave him the story line of the commercial, and then he ad-libbed around it, making it a personal experience. The sponsors wanted something like that for our show. CBS thought I was the guy to do it because of my ad-libbing skills. Well, I was naive enough to want to try it. I didn't think I was affecting my journalistic status one way or the other. It looked like there was some good money available for doing it and that it was going to be an interesting show to do, with a lot of ad-libbing and a lot of freewheeling conversation. So I agreed to do it, and that required my move to New York, quite obviously. Since I was already in New York on weekends, and now I was going to be there five days a week, clearly it dictated that I move to New York.

DC: How did Betsy react to this news?

WC: It was fine with her. We had two small daughters then, and we didn't look too much in favor of moving to New York, but it was another exciting assignment. I camped out in New York for two or three months until I found an apartment. Betsy and the kids moved up in the early summer of that year. Betsy and I found a nice apartment on Eighty-first and East End Avenue on the eleventh floor, with a balcony overlooking the East River, which was delightful. In 1957, when Chip was born, we needed more space. That's when we found the brownstone we live in now on Eighty-fourth Street.

DC: And your son Chip is Walter Cronkite III?

WC: We named him Walter Leland Cronkite III, thinking it would help get him into Princeton. But [*laughing*] we never got a chance to try it because he didn't want to go to Princeton.

DC: At this time in your career, when your children were still kids, was it hard for you to take time off from work?

WC: Well, I didn't have as much time with them as I would have liked, although I tried to be careful to preserve the weekends as much as I could. I suppose before the *Evening News*, I spent more time with the kids than most fathers probably do today, but the *Evening News* restricted my hours. I went in at nine thirty in the morning and got home at eight or eight thirty at night. Chip was pretty close to going to bed at that time, and I didn't see as much of him as I would have liked in those early days.

DC: Okay, so let's talk about your stint on *The Morning Show*.

WC: Paul Levitan was the executive producer, and it was an interesting program. As I've said before, Paul wasn't terribly well educated, but he was a very adroit producer. We had a big board, covered the whole side of a room, and we were on the air for three hours with this thing, and we had these elements for each half hour; one element was an interview each half hour. And every morning after the broadcast at ten thirty, the system producers, Levitan, and I sat around this long table and discussed program ideas. When these ideas were approved, they were placed on three-by-five cards in the proper slot on this big board with the time when they were booked.

DC: After all these years, how would you evaluate *The Morning Show* when you were the host?

WC: I think it was far more lively and interesting than the *Today* show. Every half hour, we had a remote go somewhere where people were doing something interesting that morning. We went on the air locally in New York for the first hour from seven to eight, and then the eight-to-nine section was broadcast across the country. From nine to ten, we repeated our seven-to-eight program for the West Coast. It was very difficult to get guests to stay around for two hours and then redo the same interview. The third hour was always just a little bit of a letdown. We had already done the show, and then we had to do it over again. But we had good remotes almost every day. We introduced water skis for the first time on the *The Morning Show*, for example. We showed a guy in the Hudson River, at seven o'clock in the morning, riding water skis. Then he came in the second hour and did an interview in the show.

DC: Let's talk some about the show. How was it structured?

WC: We had the Baird marionettes on every half hour with a number. The Bairds were very socially conscious and got a lot of surreptitious political digs in during their part. And then I did an interview in the studio. We also had a weather spot with a weather girl. Charles Collingwood did the news spot. It was a fight from the very beginning because the entertainment side was sniping at us the whole time about the show. They were jealous. They wanted the three hours of programming themselves, and they finally got it. Our ratings didn't take off right away, although the ratings were higher than any rating they've ever had on *The Morning Show* since. But that didn't satisfy CBS management because we weren't quite up to Garroway's ratings on NBC. I was on the show three months or something when the program department sold Mickelson on the idea that I should have a gag writer. I said, "Come on, that's ridiculous. If you want a vaudeville comedian, get one. There are a lot of guys out there that tell written gag jokes." I told them that I would comment on the news and make my little jokes while doing that. But that wasn't good enough for CBS, apparently. So I went along like that for a while. Then CBS brought in a couple of producers from the entertainment division to help Levitan get entertainment value into the show. Well, of course, these guys edged Levitan out right away, and then the whole show went over to the entertainment division.

DC: I've got a photograph here of you with Clare Booth Luce, sitting behind a desk. This may have been from *The Morning Show*.

WC: I look sleepy enough to have been on *The Morning Show*. I'm smoking a cigarette, which makes me think it was *The Morning Show*, since that was one of our sponsors. Cigarettes were one of our sponsors.

DC: Oh, were you supposed to smoke a cigarette?

WC: Unfortunately, yes. I had to smoke, and I don't smoke cigarettes. After a few times of trying it, they realized it was pretty obvious that I didn't smoke, so they agreed not to try that any more.

DC: I understand that Jack Paar replaced you on *The Morning Show*.

WC: That's right. Jack Paar was on the show for I don't know how many months. I was on five months, and I was just delighted to get off of it. *The Morning Show* was a terrible job because of the early-morning hours. The problem is that by noontime, you've been up eight, nine, ten hours or something. After Jack Paar, they brought in Will Rogers Jr. At one point they brought in Dick Van Dyke, who was a young comedian they found down in a local station in North Carolina. They asked if I would go back on the show as the newsman. We had a great new president of television at that time, Lou Cowan. A delightful man who got into trouble because of the *$64,000 Question* quiz show scandal, which I don't think was really his fault. But anyway, he begged and pleaded with me to come back. So I went on with Van Dyke. I did the show, I don't know, three weeks, a month, or something, but that's all. Dick Van Dyke didn't last long, and I returned to news duties after he was fired.

right. NBC has ...
using the navy's film archive. It told the navy's World War II
story and everybody watched it. As you know, I had covered the
air force during the war, so that was my beat. Sometime in 1953
or 1954, I went to CBS's documentary unit, which was very small.
I suggested that we ought to do something on the air force.
... was one of those natural program ideas after a show like
... successful. There was a guy in the
... in the air force during the war
... we'd do it and so forth. We asked
and I didn't like them. We had an awful time because ... heir film archive to do the program.
associate producer with me and we were producing the ... jealous of Victory at Sea. They
sending these films back. I heard that Ski would blow ... ar, so after we made our proposal,
ack in New York when he'd get this film and ... ble their
t that he'd writt... ce Base
cables ... o the
back an... they
m was th... osed to
me we ha... dcast on
programm... years
ilable f...

at CBS g...
n sponsor...
doing You... ned Per
and dropp... s until
. We did ...
"You are...
hat. We w...
The prob...
a much liv...
You are The...
r next yea...

... there
... over
s able to get the program on the air in time to ... nd
actual obligations with the air force? ... ree-
... us.
... aid,

... orce press and I wasn't even invited. ... hing
hese were the guys I had flown with during the war, for pete's ... shows at
ke. I knew them all intimately and it was a major insult. I

CHAPTER THIRTEEN

Air Power, The Twentieth Century, and Eyewitness

DC: Let's talk about the weekly documentary program you were on during the mid-1950s, called *Air Power*. How did that get started?

WC: *Air Power* was a very interesting television story in its own right. NBC had done a magnificent series called *Victory at Sea*, using the navy's film archive. It told the navy's World War II story, and everybody watched it. As you know, I had covered the air force during the war, so that was my beat. Sometime in 1953 or 1954, I went to CBS's documentary unit, which was very small. I suggested that we ought to do something on the air force. It was one of those natural program ideas after a show like *Victory at Sea* had been so successful. There was a guy in the documentary unit who had been in the air force during the war, and he did the outline of how we'd do it and so forth. We asked the air force for access to their film archive to do the program. Well, the air force was very jealous of *Victory at Sea*. They wanted to do something similar, so after we made our proposal, they passed the word around that they would make available their voluminous archival film at the Wright-Patterson Air Force Base in Dayton, Ohio. They would open those and other files to the network that made the most interesting proposal on how they would use them. They put it for bid, and we won. We proposed to do a series of twenty-six half-hour programs to be broadcast on prime time no later than fall 1956. We spent about two years developing the show.

DC: Who did you work with at CBS on this documentary?

WC: For some damn reason, CBS gave the show to a guy named Perry Wolff. He went by the name "Ski" Wolff. He was with CBS until very recently. They assigned the show to him for development and to me to narrate. Well, I was very much interested. I knew

---

Cronkite in Antarctica, filming a story for The Twentieth Century. *Photo from CBS promotional publication, copy in Cronkite Papers* (DI_05807).

this story better than anybody, at least the European-theater story. I went overseas and did a lot of production over there, a lot of filming. I had trouble with Ski Wolff because he had an overwhelming ego. He wrote the script for me, directing what I was going to do on these old air bases where I had been. A lot of the scripts weren't accurate, and I didn't like them. We had an awful time because I had an associate producer with me and we were producing the spots and sending these films back. I heard that Ski would blow his top back in New York when he'd get this film and it wasn't the script that he'd written. He'd get on the phone and send wires and cables asking why we couldn't use the script he wrote. We argued back and forth. But we completed the filming. Now the problem was that between the time we had bid for the show and the time we had completed filming, television had grown so rapidly in programming that there was no decent prime time on the air available for this show.

So somebody at CBS got the bright idea of talking to Prudential, who was then sponsoring *You Are There*. They sold Prudential on the idea of doing *You Are There* for one season as *You Are There at the Birth of Air Power*. We took that time period and their sponsorship and dropped the old *You Are There* format for twenty-six programs. We did programs like *You Are There at the Raid on Nuremberg*, *You Are There at the Battle of Britain*, and things like that. We went on the air under a little tiny *You Are There* credit. The problem was the ratings went up and Prudential said this is a much livelier-type programming than *You Are There*. Maybe *You Are There* has run its course. What do you have to offer us for next year, instead of *You Are There*? That's what eventually gave birth to the *Twentieth Century* documentary series.

DC: But CBS was able to get the program on the air in time to meet its contractual obligations with the air force?

WC: That's right, because we just took a time slot that we already controlled.

DC: How did you and Ski Wolff get along after you returned from Europe?

WC: Wolff was so infuriated over these scripts that he spread the word around CBS to Sig Mickelson and everybody who would listen to him that my producer, a good man who had the reputation of being a playboy, and I were playing around Europe, having fun and giving improper attention to *Air Power*. He told people that I always looked tired and worn out and that I had obviously been up all night drinking. He claimed that he couldn't reach us when he needed to reach us. He never said anything about the script problem. When I got back from Europe, I found these stories had been spread around. Well, we had worked our tails to the bone. We really labored on this project. There wasn't any truth to Wolff's claims at all. In fact, he flew over with his wife a couple times on big boondoggles in Paris and Rome and didn't do anything for the show. He had two- or three-day vacations with his wife. So this started a feud between us.

I did the narrations and finished the program out. The next thing I heard, CBS was going to preview the first two or three shows at a big party for the air force press, and

I wasn't even invited. These were the guys I had flown with during the war, for Pete's sake. I knew them all intimately, and it was a major insult. I mentioned it to Mickelson, and he said, "Well, of course you're invited. We want you to say a few words, obviously. That's terrible that you didn't get your invitation. I'll talk to Ski about it." Well, I don't know if they talked to Ski about it, but I went to the party. I hadn't seen the film in its final form myself. I had seen the final cuts, but not with all the titles and everything. Wolfe presided, and he never called on me to speak. They showed the film. In the opening credits, I was never mentioned. In the last credit, it rolled through with producer, director, cameramen, etc., etc., then, finally, "Words Spoken by Walter Cronkite"!

DC: I bet that was a shock.

WC: Yeah, well, that was changed, I can tell you. So I never spoke to Wolff again. I never have.

DC: He stayed with CBS for how long?

WC: He stayed with CBS until just this last year [1990]. He did produce some superb broadcasts. I think in those thirty years he probably produced a half dozen shows. He would take years to do them. I thought a lot of them were boondoggles, but I have to admit that a lot of it was artistic work. He actually did some magnificent stuff. The next time that I was asked to do a show with Wolff was a few years later. This was before I was on the *Evening News*. They wanted to put on a women's show in the middle of the afternoon. Well, it wasn't just a women's show; it appealed primarily to women, but it was also a highly educational news program. It had daily news and features, and it was going to be quite a production. They had some big advertisers lined up to do it. I was in Chicago when a CBS vice president called me and outlined this program. I didn't have my own show at that time, and it really sounded like a terrific opportunity. I said, "I'm for it, yeah, count me in." He said, "Well, then when you get back to New York, we'll all sit down with the producer, Ski Wolff." I said, "Whoops, hold it. I will not work with Ski Wolff." He said, "Oh, you got to be kidding." I said, "No way you can get me to work with Ski Wolff." He said, "Oh my gracious, well, let me see what we can do with this thing." The show never got on the air.

DC: Was this Mickelson you were talking to?

WC: No, this wasn't Mickelson; this was somebody in sales. The show never got on the air. There were a couple of other times after that when they wanted Ski to produce something they wanted me to do.

BUD BENJAMIN

DC: When did [Burton] Bud Benjamin come into the picture as a producer?

WC: I don't believe Bud was with CBS until *Twentieth Century*. I think they brought him aboard *Twentieth Century* with Ike Klinerman, who had produced *Victory at Sea*. CBS brought them aboard as a team. I had known him, but just barely.

DC: Well, let's talk about Bud Benjamin. Beginning with the *Twentieth Century* program, you and Bud Benjamin worked a great deal together as a team. According to Gates, the Murrow-Friendly team collaborated on nearly every phase of the production, but the *Twentieth Century* unit was much more contained and compartmentalized.

WC: Well, there wasn't a lot of collaboration in the *Twentieth Century* unit. Bud Benjamin looked on me at the beginning, I think, as a narrator. And I had the proper perspective on him too, which was that he was producer. My job was to come in on the given assignment day and read through the script and then record it. I wasn't seen on *Twentieth Century*; there wasn't any open and close with me. I was just a narrator. On all of Bud's productions, he had a very strong sense of identity and his own idea of how the production was going to go. He brought people in to do those parts of it that he wanted them to do. But as we began to work together more, I criticized some of the scripts, especially stories that I had had some association with. So we began collaborating to a degree. Now, I imagine that Murrow perhaps played a bigger role in his work with Fred Friendly—I don't know. But Bud had outside writers, historians, and others doing these scripts. I would second-guess them some, and Bud was always very tolerant of that. We would sit down and talk it through and sometimes make corrections, or he would go back to the writer and tell the writer what I had said. I went back to the files and checked things out, so there was that input from me, but it wasn't substantial. I don't deserve any credit for *Twentieth Century*; that was a Bud Benjamin and Ike Klinerman production.

DC: What about program ideas? Were they all Benjamin's?

WC: Nearly all of them were. I don't know that I ever suggested a program. It wasn't hard to think them up. They really just took the film they found in the archives and put them on the air. The film dictated the programs. Ike Klinerman was a great film detective. He was unbelievable in digging up footage in places. Oh, gosh, he was superb in Europe. He even found wing-camera pictures that had been taken home by Luftwaffe pilots. He looked up the records of Luftwaffe pilots and traced them to little towns and said, "Hey, did you save any of your wing-camera pictures?" And it turned out that a lot of them had. He also found that the American pilots had stolen these films themselves. The pilots had squirreled them away, and he found a lot of those. In Denmark, he uncovered a secret film that the Danish underground had made and were still keeping secret, which was a terrific whole half hour we did on that one set of films. It was great stuff. Ike was superb. He and Benjamin made a marvelous team.

DC: It was an outstanding documentary series.

WC: *Twentieth Century* goes on today as a videotape cassette series that CBS has released. They reedited and renarrated the shows. A funny thing: I always announced at the commercial break during the program that "*The Twentieth Century* will continue after this word from Prudential Insurance Company of America." Once when the series was still being broadcast, the University of Minnesota school newspaper printed a little box on the front page where they printed irony stories. The headline on one was "Thank Goodness. Walter Cronkite says that every Sunday on CBS the twentieth century will continue after this word from Prudential Insurance Company of America."

DC: I've heard that *Twentieth Century* was very popular in Europe.

WC: It was tremendously popular in Europe because they had never seen any of this wartime footage, except the propaganda footage that their own governments wanted to show them. They had never seen any of the war from the American side. *You Are There* was popular over there too.

DC: What was Benjamin's background?

WC: University of Michigan, journalism. After Michigan, I think he immediately joined a subsidiary of the Scripps-Howard organization. He joined the coast guard in World War II and was on coast guard ships in the Atlantic, mostly. He got into documentary filmmaking fairly early on.

EYEWITNESS TO HISTORY

DC: Beginning in 1959, you became one of the main correspondents for *Eyewitness*, a Friday night prime-time news program that soon found you scurrying all over the world to report on the week's "cover story." In his history of CBS News, Gary Gates called this program the most advanced TV news show of its time.

WC: There's no doubt about it. It finally did what television should be able to do but hadn't been doing yet. At that time, any hour-long production took a week to produce as a major documentary. Some of us believed that we could do better than that. We could take that week's big story, and we'll put it together on that Friday. We'll guess in advance what we think the big story will be, and we'll shoot a lot of footage. One thing that the program required was a big budget so that we could go out around the world and prepare a program. But if another story broke, we could throw it all out the window and just say that's too bad. Here's this other story, and we'd mount an instant special on Friday night.

DC: Did you very often have to throw out a program because of breaking news?

WC: Not often, but it happened most notably to me and Sandy Socolow when we were doing a story on the trial of the Nazi SS colonel Adolf Eichmann, which was to begin in Tel Aviv in April 1961. We went to Germany to trace Eichmann's SS career, and then to Argentina to trace his years in hiding there, and to Israel to work on his kidnapping by the Israeli secret police. A lot of effort went into the story. Socolow and I flew to Israel to cover the first day of the trial.

Socolow's wife was Nancy Krulewitch, who was the daughter of the first Jewish American Marine Corps general. General Krulewitch was a major secret hero of the Palestinian war in gaining independence for Israel. The United States loaned him to the Jewish movement, which wasn't a state yet, and then he secretly directed a lot of their military operations in Israel. He was much decorated by the Israelis later. Because of that, Soc had a lot of connections to people we needed to help us. The most notable one, the one who impressed me most, was Teddy Kollek, who later became the mayor of Jerusalem.

DC: What was your impression of Eichmann?

WC: Eichmann was such an evil-looking little man, kind of a weasel-like little figure. Of course, I remember the tight security, the glass box in which they were going to have him in the courtroom. That impressed us. But we shot our film and then left Tel Aviv early on Friday morning. Because of the time difference, we were scheduled to arrive back in time for the show that night. Sandy and I wrote my part of the script on the plane so that we would have it ready when we got there. When our plane stopped in Rome, we got off the plane to stretch our legs, and we saw the Rome newspapers with big headlines. We didn't have to read Italian well to know what they said, "Man Circles the Earth." Yuri Gagarin, the Soviet cosmonaut, had made the first manned orbital flight. Sandy and I immediately called New York and said that we assumed our show was dead. They said, "Absolutely, Gagarin is the show now. We'll have the script ready when you get here." We got back on the plane, tore up our script, and put our typewriters away. None of that Eichmann footage was used. Some may have been used as background later on, but basically it was lost copy. And that's the way the *Eyewitness* show worked, which was wonderful. It was always up-to-date, really terribly well done. I was very proud of the program.

DC: Did you take part in the development of *Eyewitness* as a program?

WC: Yes, I did. I talked a great deal about how this is the way we should be doing a show. And Les Midgley got very excited about doing it, and he pressed for it.

DC: *Eyewitness* became a regularly scheduled weekly show in September 1960, featuring Charles Kuralt as anchor, but the program actually began in early 1959, but not as a weekly show. It was more like a special, but it was broadcast frequently.

WC: I thought when it started, it was immediately a weekly show.

DC: According to my documentation, it became a weekly show in September of 1960. You were the anchor for that 1959 period, when it was not quite a weekly thing. In his book, Gary Gates claims that Kuralt "was the apple of Sig Mickelson's eye" and that he thought that Kuralt was destined to be the next Edward R. Murrow. Mickelson persuaded Les Midgley to make Kuralt the headliner of *Eyewitness* when it went weekly in that fall of 1960. According to Gates, "This decision did not sit well with Walter Cronkite. Cronkite thought that the role . . . should be his." Midgley, in his book, says that "Walter was too busy with *Twentieth Century* and the election coverage to handle a weekly program like *Eyewitness*." Another source says that CBS president Jim Aubrey didn't care for Kuralt and he had you replace him in January 1961.

WC: You know, not that I knew anything about the Aubrey thing—that comes to me as a surprise—but that does remind me a little bit now of the sequence of events. I guess we did do *Eyewitness* as a sporadic thing, and then it did go weekly, and it was Kuralt who did it first as a regular weekly program. It was allegedly because I was too busy to do a weekly show. I never knew anything about this back fighting going on. I stayed clear of all that.

Maybe I was like the cartoon character Mr. Magoo, kind of going through CBS without seeing the chaos around me. A lot of things may have been happening right behind me that I just didn't know. I never looked back. But I really stayed entirely clear of the politics of whatever was happening. Some people thought, and I think probably think to this day, it was because of disinterest. It wasn't that; it was just basically a feeling that it was CBS's candy shop and it was their job to make those decisions. I concentrated on whatever program I was doing.

DC: You mean the office politics and the fighting between Mickelson and Aubrey?

WC: Yeah. I do know that I was awfully busy with the 1960 election. I couldn't have done a weekly show at that time. In 1961, they asked me to come back on *Eyewitness*, and I felt badly for Kuralt. But they put me back and I took it. Charles was very good, as he still is today. He's terrific. [*Kuralt died on July 4, 1997.*]

WC: Oh, no. These interviews changed my opinion totally on
Eisenhower the president and politician. I had accepted the
general Washington press corps view that Eisenhower was a
lightweight as a president who operated on the old military
staff basis and was not closely acquainted with most of the
░░░tails of the government he led, or even the decisions he
░░░░░░░░░░░░░░░░░░░░░░░░░░░░░░░░░░░░░ ░░s that decisions were largely made
░░░░░░░░░░░░░░░░░░░░░░░░░░░░░░░░░░ when I did these series of

overed Dwight Eisenhower when he was the Allied
░░ in Europe in World War II and at the 1952 Republican
░. Let's talk about your coverage after that. We talked ░░░ews, we advised Ike of the broad
░░░░░ about the 1956 Republican conventi░░░ ░░░░░░░░ discuss the next morning, such as
░░ck to ░░'s all we
░░ in San░░on, John

░░ to meet ░░░░░░ally with the White House press
░░ relatively tiny before television. When
░░ in, presidential meetings with the press

░░░░░░░░░░░░░░░ ░░ course, seen a lot of Eisenhower in
░░ presidential campaigns, the White House news conferences,
░░ in Europe, and that sort of thing. But I really did not know

CHAPTER FOURTEEN

Ike

DC: You covered Dwight Eisenhower when he was the Allied commander in Europe in World War II and at the 1952 Republican convention. Let's talk about your coverage after that. We talked a little about the 1956 Republican convention earlier, but let's go back to that. What are your memories of the Republican convention in San Francisco in 1956?

WC: There had been some talk of dumping Nixon as vice president to Eisenhower, and it had been pretty well quashed before they ever got to the convention floor. There was still some talk around the hotels, but nothing developed. The Eisenhower administration moved in and quashed any little fires that began in that regard. It was a terrible convention. It was a coronation. Nothing took place at the whole convention that was likely to get the full attention of the press. It was totally a show for television. The political conventions had changed forever.

DC: You have seen some dramatic changes in the way presidential administrations have dealt with the press and the way the press has covered the presidency, as well as changes in presidential press conferences.

WC: Yeah, it has changed dramatically with television. The presidents used to meet informally with the White House press corps, which was relatively tiny before television. When television came in, presidential meetings with the press became far more formalized affairs. Beginning with Eisenhower, the White House became this major source of information, and there were a lot more correspondents. They had to expand the pressroom, shut the press off from the general reception area, and make accommodations for television. The news conferences became much more formal. I'm not sug-

---

Cronkite and former president Dwight D. Eisenhower at St. Laurent Cemetery, Normandy, France, for the CBS News special D-Day Plus 20, *1964 (DI-05798).*

gesting that television created the formal presidential news conference, but television made it even more formal and made it a big public show.

DC: Eisenhower was really the first president to have the big press conferences on television. He held them in an auditorium. Those were the news conferences when Eisenhower spoke in rambling, run-together sentences filled with non sequiturs.

WC: That's right. I had forgotten. You know, someone wrote a story recently claiming that Ike did that broken-syntax thing deliberately, as a kind of obfuscation strategy. I find it hard to believe. But I will say that when I did the memoir with him, he was much clearer than he was in those public appearances.

THE TELEVISION MEMOIR WITH EISENHOWER

DC: Speaking of the memoir, I note that you did three one-hour interviews with Eisenhower at his home in Gettysburg, Pennsylvania, in 1961. The program was entitled *Eisenhower on the Presidency*, and Fred Friendly was the producer.

WC: Actually, they were edited out of thirteen hours of tape. We taped five days, two to three hours a day, in the mornings, when he was fresh. The production crew and I spent the entire week in Gettysburg.

DC: Is this when you really got to know Eisenhower?

WC: Yes, it was. I had, of course, seen a lot of Eisenhower in the presidential campaigns, the White House news conferences, and in Europe, and that sort of thing. But I really did not know him, and he certainly didn't know me. I was just another face in the press crowd.

DC: How did you find him on a personal level?

WC: Oh, I found Ike quite interesting. I'm not sure that I want to use the word "delightful." I'm not sure "delightful" is really the word for him. He was a fascinating man, naturally, of course, having been president of the United States, fascinating in that particular way at any rate. He showed flashes of humor every once in a while. He had a good sense of humor, as a matter of fact, for a joke or a witty remark. He was intolerant of inefficiencies that he felt impinged upon his routine. If you were late or things were delayed or there were technical failures in the equipment that delayed us, he would become quite angry, although "angry" may be too strong. He became obviously displeased. But he was very free and friendly, talkative at most moments. When he tired, he became withdrawn, but when he was fresh and up, why, he liked to chat and talk about things. He dropped a lot of little anecdotes from time to time, things that weren't on camera.

DC: Do you recall if he had a list of subjects that would be covered ahead of time in preparation for the interview?

WC: Oh, no. These interviews changed my opinion totally on Eisenhower the president and politician. I had accepted the general Washington-press-corps view that Eisenhower was a lightweight as a president who operated on the old military staff basis and was not closely acquainted with most of the details of the government he led or even the decisions he made. The prevailing view was that decisions were largely made by others. I changed that view when I did this series of interviews at Gettysburg.

The evening before the interviews, we advised Ike of the broad subject matter that we would discuss the next morning, such as the Middle East, taxes, and those sorts of topics. That's all we gave him in advance. The questions were up to me. His son, John Eisenhower, was his chief researcher. We would sit there in the late afternoon and tell John, and the president if he was up and wanted to, what areas we would be discussing that next day. Now, that didn't give them much time to prepare. I'm sure that Dwight David Eisenhower didn't give up his western books at night to read tomes of research material. They may have suggested some obvious questions that I would be asking, but I was asking a lot of questions other than, I hope, the obvious ones.

I had a sheaf of notes on my lap as we sat at his desk at his farm. He had no notes, not a single one. And yet his recall of details of many rather obscure decisions was vast. It became quite evident that he did know what had been going on. He knew why decisions were made and what the anticipated effect was of them. He easily remembered his reaction to what happened later in those decisions. It was really impressive. We told him all along, "Anytime you want to stop on this, we can stop and go back and cover that if you don't feel you've done well. We'll ask the same question, but we are not going to knock out questions except on matters of national security." When you deal with a former president, you've got to maintain a caveat that if they themselves feel they have given an answer that spills over into a national security question, you've got to let them redo it. With Lyndon Johnson, when we talk about him, it became an issue in his memoir. But with Ike it never was. He never requested an opportunity to go back over anything. There never was really any need to go back, because he was quite smooth. The only time he flubbed it was the very last question. I asked him, "What, from a practical standpoint, having been the president of the United States, really are the powers of the United States president?" And he just went blank. Couldn't think of anything. And asked to think about that for a while and redo it.

D-DAY PLUS 20

DC: Let's talk about the trip to Normandy with Eisenhower in August 1963. You were anchoring the *CBS Evening News* by this time. I understand that you and Betsy went

over with William Paley; Dwight Eisenhower and his wife, Mamie; Fred Friendly;
and Paley's close friend Walter Thayer. The purpose was to tape a program about the
D-Day landings that would be broadcast on June 6, 1964, the twentieth anniversary of
the landings. How did that program come about?

WC: I think that was Fred Friendly's idea, originally. I was asked to telephone Eisenhower
and talk to him about doing it. Because of my interviews with him in Gettysburg, our
association was well established. My call was almost pro forma, because I think Fred
had really laid the groundwork very well, and Ike was very pleased with the memoirs.

DC: Had you gotten to know Paley very well by this time?

WC: Oh, pretty well, I'd say. I wasn't a Paley intimate at all, but I'd see him around.

DC: Was he there at the shooting?

WC: Oh, yeah. But it didn't affect me. I don't know whether it affected Fred or not. Paley
wasn't there all of the time. For instance, in Normandy, I know that he and Thayer cut
out for a gourmet trip down to Paris and back, and for a couple of days they were gone.
But I don't think it affected us. You would think it might have, but it didn't.

DC: It wasn't usual to have Bill Paley standing around while you worked.

WC: It certainly wasn't. Although he was in the control room on big events quite a lot.
He came to the conventions, and he was there on election nights. It wasn't unusual
for him to be around. He never stood in the background of the news broadcast or
anything like that. Paley, being a very sophisticated man, understood what his presence meant. He probably avoided being right on the scene when we were shooting. He
wasn't pacing around the background with a director's megaphone or anything.

DC: You've been quoted as saying that you enjoyed that assignment as much as anything
you've ever done. Any special memories of that experience?

WC: Oh, they're all special from that trip. One strong memory was the airplane trip back to
London from Normandy. The airplane developed some engine trouble, and we were
in some jeopardy. The pilot sent out an alert that we were having trouble. As I recall, an
escort plane came out to accompany us in. It was terribly disconcerting at the moment,
something the pilot was concerned about. In the middle of the crisis, I remember
thinking about the small print in which my name would appear with Dwight Eisenhower, Bill Paley, and all these people in the news about the crash. [*laughs*]

Perhaps the outstanding memory of the trip was when we were on Normandy
Beach and Fred Friendly had this picture concept. He decided that I would drive Ike
along the beach and he would talk about the beach as we drove. As we were about to
get into the jeep, I said to Fred, "You know, this is wrong. Ike's showing me the beach,
and he ought to be driving." Fred said, "Of course, that's right." He turned to the gen-

eral, and he said, "General, you drive, don't you?" Eisenhower said, "Of course I drive." Fred said, "Well, let's have you drive the jeep then." So Ike got in the driver's seat, and I got in the other seat. Betsy and Mamie were sitting up on a little bluff, watching the shoot. Mamie turned to Betsy and asked, "Betsy, is Ike going to drive?" Betsy said, "It certainly looks that way." Mamie said, "My dear, your husband's never been in greater danger. Ike hasn't driven in thirty years." Well, it turned out he couldn't drive very well. The jeep was a standard shift, and it bucked and it jumped. So I finally got it in gear for him and told him, "Now just press on the accelerator with your foot and go kind of slowly." Somehow, we got down the beach, but you can tell when you look at the program that the jeep was bucking and skidding a little bit and Ike was fighting the steering wheel.

DC: Had Eisenhower gone over Omaha Beach that closely since D-Day?

WC: No. It was interesting: throughout that trip, he kept being amazed because it was the first time he'd ever really seen the battlefield properly. Every other time, it had been a formal state occasion. De Gaulle had been with him once, and there had been military bands and huge crowds. They couldn't see anything. This time he could really look around. He was terribly impressed with everything he saw. It was like he was seeing it for the first time, and actually, he *was* seeing it for the very first time. When he saw Omaha Beach shortly after D-Day, of course, the battle was raging, and every other time had been ceremonial. Now he was able to see it as a civilian, really. He was the old soldier returning to the scene. Ike stood in a German bunker, looking out to the English Channel through a gun slit, and he said he couldn't imagine what those Germans thought that morning, looking out there at the Allied armada. He was really dumbfounded by the sheer cliff at Pointe du Hoc. He said to me, "How could we ever have ordered those soldiers to climb this thing?"

And then, of course, he had that extraordinary ad-lib closing. We told Ike that we were going to walk up the cemetery to the wall right by the beach, and he and I were going to sit there. I was going to ask him what he thought of as he visited this site. We told him that just a few minutes before we started the walk. Well, Ike ad-libbed a heartbreaking tribute to the American fighting man. They had just invented the gyroscopic mount for a camera on a helicopter. Up to then, the problem of shooting from a helicopter was the vibration. The gyroscope allowed us to get a nice, steady shot. And Fred Friendly, God bless him, had hired this helicopter. He had the helicopter pull back from the beach, and here you were, a close-up of Ike as he finished talking, and the helicopter pulled back to reveal the row after row after row of crosses marking the graves of our soldiers. It was very dramatic stuff.

DC: What a great opportunity, to be standing out with Eisenhower on that beach. I don't know if you've had an opportunity to see the biography of Eisenhower by Stephen Ambrose, but he writes about this episode with you and Eisenhower. He said that

Eisenhower entertained your group in the evenings at the dining table with stories about Patton in particular. As a result of this trip and the memoir program, Ambrose says that you and Eisenhower "became confidants."

WC: No, that's not so. I'd have been proud to be an Eisenhower confidant, and it would have been very enlightening, I'm sure, but it didn't happen. I know we were friendly. For example, after this trip to Normandy, he heard, somehow or other, that we were taking the family to Scotland on a tour. He called me and said, "Walter, I want you to use my castle." Well, after the war, the people of Scotland gave him this castle. Actually, it turned out that they hadn't. That's the way the press played it. He was given lifetime use of the private quarters of a National Trust castle that people tour. So naturally, I told Ike that we'd love to stay there. We had a wonderful time. When I got home, I called Ike on the phone to thank him. Ike had a funny telephone habit. I think it came from long years of military experience. He never said hello or goodbye on the phone. He picked up the phone and started a conversation. Obviously, an aide was supposed to say hello, and then Ike started the conversation. When he finished the conversation, he just hung up, which I didn't really know at that time. I knew about the not saying hello. But the hanging up, I wasn't aware of. I called him to thank him for the castle. I told Ike what a wonderful time we had, and he said, "How was the fishing?" I said, "Oh, well, to tell you the truth, Mr. President, I actually didn't go fishing." "Didn't go fishing?" I could tell that I was in serious trouble, so I said, "But, you know, after we left the castle, we stayed at Gleneagles," the famous golf course in Edinburgh. Ike said, "Oh, no kidding. Which course did you play?" I said, "Well, to tell you the truth, Mr. President, I didn't get a chance to play." Clunk went the telephone. [*laughs*] For Ike, there wasn't any more to talk about. I hadn't fished. I hadn't played golf. What the hell was there to talk about?

DC: Well, according to Ambrose, once again—in fact, there's a photograph of you and Eisenhower in his book—he said the two of you discussed possible Republican Party candidates for the 1964 presidential election while you were doing the D-Day program.

WC: If so, it was certainly cocktail-party conversation, with others present. It wasn't a serious discussion. Ike wasn't taking any notes; let's put it that way. Now, I wouldn't be surprised if he and Paley talked about it a great deal. Paley was very active in the Republican Party ranks at that time.

IKE AND MONTY

DC: A couple of years after the trip to Normandy, you were with Eisenhower for another special CBS program observing a World War II anniversary. This was on May 8, 1965, the twentieth anniversary of Germany's surrender. You hosted a program with Ike and British general Bernard Montgomery, who was in London but on the air via the *Early Bird* satellite.

WC: That's right. We brought Eisenhower and Montgomery together for the first time in any kind of public display. I believe, although I could be very wrong about this, that it was also their first private meeting since the war. The broadcast was memorable for the fact that Eisenhower and Montgomery hated each other, of course, absolutely despised each other, couldn't stand the sight of each other. As we opened this thing, Ike said something like, "Hello, Monty." And Monty launched right into, "Oh, hello, Ike, my fellow soldier in arms who led us all to victory. I'll never forget our going arm in arm . . ." And while Monty was carrying on, Ike muttered to me, "Son of a bitch." And we were on a live mike on the air. Thank God, Monty was going on at such a rate and with such atmospherics that nobody heard Ike. He had great trouble with Monty, whose generalship in the war was in considerable question.

IKE, GOLDWATER, AND THE 1964 REPUBLICAN CONVENTION

DC: On June 2, 1964, William F. Buckley's *National Review* reported that sometime during May 1964, you telephoned former president Eisenhower at his Gettysburg residence and asked him to speak out against Senator Goldwater's "extremism," and that Ike refused. However, a few days later, Eisenhower visited with Pennsylvania governor William Scranton at Gettysburg, and Scranton took their discussion as an endorsement from Eisenhower to run against Goldwater. Now, what the *Review* was implying was that you had intervened in the primary campaign against Goldwater through your connection with Eisenhower.

WC: I know very well Scranton's version of the Gettysburg meeting with Eisenhower and the repercussions therefrom. I don't think I made any such call to Eisenhower. It doesn't sound like me. I can't imagine my doing so. I certainly don't remember it. That just doesn't make any sense to me.

DC: From your knowledge of the man, would that be the kind of call that you would expect Eisenhower to welcome?

WC: Oh, he would certainly listen; welcome, I don't know. It would depend on what else he had to do that day, what you interrupted by talking to him about that.

DC: But you would have felt comfortable calling him?

WC: I would have felt comfortable . . . Well, I don't know. I don't know that I would, to tell you the truth. That's pretty high-powered stuff, and I didn't play those games. I don't recall ever talking to leaders of our government about what they should or shouldn't do. I see that as arrogance far beyond anything that a newsman ought to be doing. If I had been in conversation with Eisenhower about something else, if he'd called me to talk about some aspect of politics or something, or if I'd been at Gettysburg and he was talking about it, I'm perfectly capable of making a remark like that; that's possible. I could have said it to Eisenhower at some point, but certainly not as a major effort to get him to change his mind. And not as part of anybody's campaign.

DC: Is that an accurate description of your feelings about Goldwater?

WC: Oh, no doubt about that. I was privately enthusiastic about Scranton's campaign.

DC: Do you think that Eisenhower had any problems with Goldwater as a candidate?

WC: I think he probably did. Matter of fact, that story of what happened there with Scranton's visit, that was on the eve of the Republican Governors' Conference in Cleveland. Scranton was hoping for Ike's endorsement before going to that meeting. Those Republican governors' meetings that precede the national political conventions are terribly important. They set a pattern as to who is supporting whom and how they're going to go about it. And that year, Scranton was hoping for the Eisenhower endorsement, and he went down there and thought he had it. The story leaked—whether Scranton accidentally leaked it or how, I don't know, but it leaked—and it was in the paper the next morning, which was the day before the convention, I believe. But this story appeared in the paper as an "informed sources" type report that Scranton had got Eisenhower's endorsement in a meeting at Gettysburg.

I was in the lobby of the hotel in Cleveland when Scranton arrived. Scranton saw me and said hello, and I said hello and walked with him to the elevator and up to the room. We went into the room, and an aide called Scranton into the bedroom. Scranton told me later that Eisenhower was on the phone. He said, "Where did you get the idea I'd endorse you? I'm not endorsing you." What happened was that one of Eisenhower's principal friends and backers was a Cleveland industrialist named Eaton. He was also a big Goldwater backer. Ike was going to come to this meeting in Cleveland, I think, and he was going to stay with Eaton.

DC: Well, that took a lot of air out of the "Stop Goldwater" movement.

WC: Oh, it did indeed. It shot down Scranton at the governors' conference.

DC: At the Republican convention in 1964, Eisenhower gave a speech that referred to "sensation-seeking columnists and commentators who couldn't care less about the welfare of the Republican Party." That initiated a convention-floor demonstration against the television correspondents at the convention.

WC: That's right. The demonstrations were quite severe. They were looking up at the booths and shaking their fists at us. I went to the St. Francis Hotel to Ike's suite. He welcomed me open-armed and said, "Good to see you." I think I made this up, but I swear I seem to remember him saying, "You guys are doing a great job." It was something like that, which threw me. I'd just come to ask him about this statement he had made. Eisenhower had stood there on the platform after he said that, looking absolutely baffled. I don't think he'd ever read that line before, and he had no idea what he'd just read. Then this whole protest started. When I was in his hotel room, I was going to beat around the bush and finally get to this thing. But Ike said something right away, "You're doing a great job." I said, "Well, that's why I came. You made this statement." He said, "What did I say?" And I told him. And he said, "Well, well, well. We worry, of course, about you boys." He said something like that. But clearly this statement attacking the press was not from a conviction deep within his heart. It wasn't the kind of thing I think he would have said on his own. Ike himself was always very well liked by the press and always had a good relationship with the press.

DC: Do you think this was something that the Goldwater campaign placed in his speech?

WC: Oh, sure. They probably wrote the speech. It was much more the "queen's speech to Parliament" sort of thing than it was a reflection of Eisenhower's real convictions about the press.

aley for one reason or another, not to appoint me. I don'
know why. In person, Capote seemed perfectly friendly to me.
may have been that he just didn't like my approach to things.
don't know much more than that. Capote had a lot of influence o
Bill Paley's wife, Babe, at one time, and I felt that maybe it
was that row——   h he put pressure on Paley. If that's wha
                                 hat to be a fact. It was also reported
a bolt out of the blue. I gather that there had   in my removal as anchor for the 1964
ights that somewhere down the line they might be   's pure grapevine stuff, you know, just
g Edwards. But I wasn't aware of any imminent   about the Mickelson-Paley roles in
o reason to think that I was in line for it. No   hat doesn't ring true to me. Mickelson
d been made to me. There wasn't even any water   y close friend. He was before

ecided on Cronkite that March of 1962, although as
man learned years later, Paley's friend Truman Capote   etition was
Cronkite's screen presence and urged Paley not to use   ratings. What

he air. I

                                                            terrible on
                                    weening ambition to get to

CHAPTER FIFTEEN

CBS Evening News

DC: Let's talk about when you became the anchor of the *CBS Evening News* in April 1962. I understand that you heard through the corporate grapevine that Douglas Edwards was going to be replaced as anchor, a position he had held for about fifteen years. How did that all come about?

WC: It came as a bolt out of the blue. I gather that there had been some thoughts that somewhere down the line they might be replacing Doug Edwards. But I wasn't aware of any imminent move. I had no reason to think that I was in line for it. No suggestion had been made to me. There wasn't even any water-cooler gossip. Dick Salant called me into his office and said that I was taking over the *Evening News* the following Monday. I was shocked, and I went to see Doug Edwards right away. It was as much a surprise to him as it was to me. I must say, in a business not noted for this sort of thing, he was absolutely the most gracious gentleman after this terrible blow to him. Doug said, "I know that you didn't have anything to do with this, and I know you weren't angling for it in any way, and I appreciate that."

DC: Was that a decision that Paley himself would have made?

WC: I don't know that he made it, but I'm sure he cleared it.

DC: Sally Bedell Smith has written, in a biography of Paley, that it was Paley who chose you and that he had suggested that you should replace Edwards as early as 1960. Smith claims that Sig Mickelson disagreed, so it was not done. After Dick Salant replaced Mickelson as president of CBS News, according to Smith: "Paley decided on Cronkite that March of 1962, although as the newsman learned years later, Paley's friend

Cronkite consulting with his staff in the CBS newsroom, ca. 1960s. New York Times *photo, copy in Cronkite Papers (DI_05800).*

Truman Capote disliked Cronkite's screen presence and urged Paley not to use him."
Now, she cites you as the source for that.

WC: I heard that two or three times. Apparently, at various critical times in my career at
CBS, Capote was putting pressure on Paley, for one reason or another, not to appoint
me. I don't know why. In person, Capote seemed perfectly friendly to me. It may have
been that he just didn't like my approach to things. I don't know much more than that.
Capote had a lot of influence on Bill Paley's wife, Babe, at one time, and I felt that maybe
it was that route by which he put pressure on Paley—if that's what he did. I don't know
that to be a fact. It was also reported that Capote had a hand in my removal as anchor
for the 1964 convention coverage. It's pure grapevine stuff, you know, just rumor. I also
don't know about the Mickelson-Paley roles in putting me on the air. That doesn't ring
true to me. Mickelson seemed always to be a very close friend. He was before that time,
and he has been since that time. [*Mickelson died in 2000.*] I never thought that Paley was
that strong for me in those days. He became much more friendly and close later on,
but not before 1964, and certainly not in the 1962 period, when I got the anchor job. I
scarcely knew him then. That doesn't mean Paley wasn't watching me on the air, obviously. It seems strange to me that Mickelson would have resisted Paley. Now, Mickelson may have resisted letting Edwards go. I can understand maybe saying, "Give Doug
a better chance," or something. Mickelson may have given Doug a personal promise
that nothing would happen for another year, and he felt obligated to support him.

DC: On the other hand, Barbara Matusow claims that Sig Mickelson had wanted you to be
the news anchor as early as 1954. But according to her, you were not popular with the
so-called Murrow Crowd. She claims that they regarded you simply as an announcer,
that they couldn't understand your fixation on breaking news, and that you were also
different from many of them in that you enjoyed meeting people and socializing and
interacting, while many of them were almost antisocial in many respects.

WC: I think it's wrong if she said that they looked on me as just an announcer. I'm confident
that wasn't so, because I knew so many of those fellows in the field in war and in London. They knew damn well that I was anything but just an announcer. That's one of
the reasons I feel Matusow's book leaves a false impression in many areas. There's just
no way Murrow's group could have thought that.

DC: It's been in print, so we might as well deal with it here. The charge has been that Doug
Edwards had a drinking problem.

WC: Well, I think that's so. I think Doug was doing a lot of drinking in those days. I think
that was some of the problem. Doug was certainly closer to being just an announcer
than anybody we had on the news staff. He'd sort of come in to it that way, and was
never thought of particularly as a newsman. I think that's where Matusow may have
gotten her stories mixed up about their thinking of me as an announcer.

DC: What was your personal reaction to the news that you were replacing Edwards?

WC: Well, I was very excited about the opportunity to take it over. It's a big job. Obviously, everybody in our business would like to have it. It did come as a total surprise. I didn't know whether I was on the path to do that or not. Obviously, however, I was getting all these choice special assignments. There was a certain logic to my being Edwards's successor whenever they did make the move, but I did not contemplate it, nor think about it, nor did I have any plans of what I'd do if I got it; none of that sort of thing ever crossed my mind. I always lived in broadcasting day to day with the idea I was going to be fired the next day. Never did think I was that particularly good at it. I used to see kinescopes and tapes and think I was terrible on the air. I never had any really over- weening ambition to get to be the anchor. I always assumed that the day would come when I'd flunk out in broadcasting and I'd go back to the United Press, where I would have been quite happy.

RICHARD SALANT

DC: Richard Salant replaced Sig Mickelson in 1961. What was the reaction to that change?

WC: There was a lot of unease in the news department, because he was a lawyer from top management who had no news experience. We were terribly fearful of what that portended for the news department. It looked to us as if it were a power grab from the president's floor at CBS. What else would you think? We didn't know the fellow. He was in the system for Frank Stanton, the president of the company. We thought, "What the devil, is Frank Stanton taking over the news department?" I don't think, really, at that early stage, Frank had established his reputation as a defender of the independence of the news department and the freedom of speech and press. So there was a great deal of concern.

DC: We were talking about Doug Edwards's problems. He was also being beaten by NBC's Huntley and Brinkley in the ratings, wasn't he?

WC: Well, that's true, of course, obviously. They never change a man who's leading in the ratings.

DC: When you took over the *Evening News*, your competition was NBC's Huntley and Brinkley. They had the highest ratings. What was your game plan?

WC: I didn't have any game plan at all. My idea was to do the best that I could and do it as close as possible to my style. Don Hewitt, who was the director, is a very strong person in his own right, quite obviously, and he had no particular intentions of changing the broadcast simply because the anchor had changed. I don't recall that we did anything necessarily differently. There's not a lot you can do in fifteen minutes. A fifteen-minute broadcast is very short. Huntley-Brinkley's lead was a very thin one. It was well within the statistical margin of error most of the time, really.

The thing that was important about the Huntley-Brinkley lead is that NBC's very alert, strong public relations and press department sold the idea that they were just dominant in the news. Every ratings period, they took out an ad, "The Most Watched News Team on the Air." NBC kept pumping this up in the press releases and everywhere else. It was almost part of their name: "Huntley-Brinkley, the world's most watched news team." That claim was vastly overdrawn in relation to the actual rating difference between NBC and CBS, which was, most of the time, within one point. There was never any wide gap in there that I remember for either Doug or for me. It may have been wider for me, after I took over, than it was for Doug. Now, in special-events coverage, when their team started covering conventions, I think that was a wider gap between us.

DC: What about the title of managing editor that you assumed? Edwards did not have that title.

WC: One of the things that I wanted when I took over was to be the ultimate judge of the news content of the broadcast. I wasn't in a position to make demands at that point. It was just how I wanted to work. There was no opposition to that at all. Well, that made quite a difference to Don Hewitt's modus operandi, because he had been completely running the show. I gather that Doug was quite passive about what went into the broadcast. I wanted to work differently than that. It's coming to me through a rather thick miasma there, but there was a suggestion that I ought to have a title of some kind, and I think I suggested "managing editor." It was new in broadcasting. There were a lot of complaints from the newspaper business about it. There were a few snide newspaper columns about how dare a newsman on the air call himself a managing editor. Some journalist felt that was strictly a newspaper phrase and that it should be limited to print. Which I always thought was ridiculous. The title is as meaningful in broadcasting as it is in print.

DC: I've heard that a few days after you became the anchor, Andy Rooney, your old friend from World War II days, gave you some advice?

WC: Oh, Andy came into the broadcast room right after I'd finished a broadcast, and he said, "What are you trying to sell me? You broadcast like a pitchman. You're trying too hard. You're shouting at me. Calm down." Which was damn good advice. He was absolutely right. He helped me a great deal with that one candid comment.

DC: What was Rooney's position at this time?

WC: Oh, Andy was a gadabout writer with CBS. He wasn't on the air with anything at the time. He was just writing for different people. He wrote for Arthur Godfrey and later for Harry Reasoner.

"AND THAT'S THE WAY IT IS"

DC: When I reviewed tapes of your news broadcasts when the program was only fifteen minutes long, I noted that you ended every one of them with "And that's the way it is." Apparently, you began using that very early on.

WC: Well, Don, that just baffles the devil out of me. I would have sworn I debuted that closing when we went to a thirty-minute broadcast. That's how my memory is running these days.

DC: Well, I think that is natural, given how incredibly eventful your career has been. It was nearly thirty years ago.

WC: I don't think that's so natural. The story as I seem to remember it is different. When we decided to expand the *Evening News* from fifteen minutes to thirty minutes, I thought we would have time for a little vignette at the end of the show. That would make it appropriate for me to work in a closing line that I could use when we came out of these vignettes. But maybe it was for the fifteen-minute news. I remember talking with Betty Furness about that line. Betsy and I were seeing quite a lot of her socially in those days. She's godmother to our child Chip. But I remember talking over this line with her very specifically as to whether it would be a good idea or not. I trusted her judgment quite well.

DC: Why did you come up with "And that's the way it is"?

WC: I've always been intrigued with irony of fate-type news stories. They usually appeared as little two-paragraph boxes in the newspapers. I thought that it'd be nice to end a broadcast with one of those stories. I could use a phrase that could be used under any circumstances, no matter what the previous story had been about. I wanted a phrase that could be said with a tinge of sadness. Or it could be said with a tinge of irony. Or it could have a tone of sarcasm or disbelief. You can say, "And that's the way it is" to almost any thing, depending on the tone you use: "And that's the way it is" or "And THAT's the way it is" or "And that's the way it is?" [*speaking with different inflections*]

I had learned the value of a catch line, which is a show-business thing. It isn't news business, although newspapers do it too, of course, with the makeup of the front page and boxes and things of that kind. The *New York Times*, for example, uses "All the news that's fit to print." I'd learned the value of a catch line when I did *You Are There*. The end of the broadcast was a very stereotype ending: "What sort of day was it? A day like all days, filled with those events that alter and illuminate our times, and you were there."

DC: I still remember that line, word for word, after all of these years.

WC: Well, schoolkids did remember that line. I have people quote it to me today on the street, all these years later. Well, obviously, there's some value in impressing people's memories that deeply. So I was looking for some little catch line like that for the *Evening News*. And this was very deliberate. I mean, it just didn't come to me. I went out and I tested a few catch lines with friends. And, of course, I finally came up with "And that's the way it is."

DC: Maybe you tested "And that's the way it is" on the last few of your fifteen-minute broadcasts, and maybe that's the source of the confusion about when you began it.

WC: It's possible. But I certainly never thought, in the fifteen-minute broadcast, we were going to have time for those "irony of fate" stories. It's conceivable that I went into the fifteen-minute broadcast thinking I was going to have time for those pieces.

DC: Because the news segment was really only about, what, eleven minutes with commercials?

WC: Yeah, I guess so. I don't know exactly how long, but it wasn't very much time. Of course, we didn't have a lot to work with, either. We didn't have tape and satellites. Everything was by film coming in from around the world.

DC: And about this time you had very few correspondents, too. You really didn't have that big staff.

WC: Well, nothing like the staff that grew thereafter. But I must say that we had more correspondents who had something to say, who weren't just camera firemen. We had thoughtful correspondents. The old Murrow team was still together in all the capitals of the world, including Sevareid, Collingwood, Winston Burdett, and Dick Hottelet. Every capital of any size was staffed: Rome, London, Paris, Bonn, and Moscow.

DC: I want to ask you one more question about your sign-off, "And that's the way it is." Dick Salant was quoted as saying once that "If I were a tyrannical boss, I would forbid Walter to end the evening news that way." He added that he felt it was a grossly misleading implication that all the news had been reported.

WC: I think he's absolutely right. Salant and I had this discussion after I started using the closing. I didn't clear it with CBS in any way. I started using it, and he said, "This presupposes that everything we said is right, that that's the whole picture of the day's news. I don't really think you ought to be doing that." I think he was correct. But the thing had already caught on. It really was just rolling. So I got to kind of a point of being stubborn about it and said, "Well, I like it." Salant said, "Well, it's up to you." He let it go. It has been much criticized by serious television critics because of the argument that it was presumptive that everything we said was correct. Which was wrong. I shouldn't have said that. And particularly when we got into controversial subjects like the Vietnam War. In fact, there's a *New Yorker* cartoon with a guy coming half out of his chair and shouting at his television, saying, "That's NOT the way it is!"

DC: [*laughs*] That's a famous cartoon.

WC: But, you know, whenever Eric Sevaried was doing his two-minute commentary and it went to the end of the broadcast, I had to drop "And that's the way it is." He was doing a commentary that I would be putting a stamp of approval on if I said, "And that's the way it is." We dropped it two or three times before Eric caught on. Eric called and said, "I noticed after my commentary, you don't say 'And that's the way it is.' Don't you approve?" And I couldn't tell with Eric whether he was serious about it or not at the moment, but I don't think he was terribly serious. But he did bring up the matter.

DC: You spoke earlier about the logistical hassles caused by the studio's location in the Grand Central Terminal building. Did the *Evening News* move to a new studio after you became the anchor in April 1962?

WC: Well, it was in that same studio until we expanded to the half-hour broadcast. We moved over to the Graybar Building in 1963. For a while, we had to go down fifteen floors in the elevator in the Graybar Building to the main lobby of the Grand Central Terminal right at rush hour. We were running through all these people, going between one set of elevators and another set of elevators to get up to our studios in the Grand Central Terminal building itself. That went on for quite a while, until the half-hour program was imminent. At that point, I said, "Look, this is impossible. I do not want to do a half-hour broadcast when I'm going to be that far removed from the newsroom. I'm depending on people telephoning news bulletins down from the newsroom to the studio if anything happens. I have no control over the broadcast, and we can't have that. We've got to broadcast from the newsroom." I prevailed in that, and we set up the broadcast studio right there in the news studio in the Graybar Building.

DC: Hewitt built a combination newsroom and studio?

WC: Yeah, that's right. They wheeled the cameras in from the studio down below.

DC: You could always see some of the staff working while you were talking on the air. That's a common practice today.

WC: It's funny, Don, but there was objection to that from an artistic standpoint. It was felt that those people were distracting in the background. There was constant pressure to keep them off camera. I said, "Well, if you can figure a way to keep them off camera, it's all right with me, but the studio stays in the newsroom. I'm not going to move. The newscast has to be done from my desk." I organized my desk as a newsroom desk. It was a U-shaped desk, and the writers sat around the desk. I sat in the middle as the managing editor. They used that until they built the new studio for Dan Rather.

But this discussion reminds me that one of the reasons we were ahead of the other networks with the news that President Kennedy had been shot was that the wire-service printers were right there in the studio with us. In fact, I was standing there at the printer when the first bulletin came over the wire. That episode taught us another lesson. It took ten minutes or so to get a camera into the studio and warmed up after the news of Kennedy's shooting came through. Meanwhile, we were only doing audio with a slide of the CBS logo on screen. So thereafter we had what was called a "flash" studio that had a camera always warmed up, even though it cost us some money wearing out the tube. All they had to do was turn the switch, and you were on the air.

THE *EVENING NEWS* EXPANDS TO THIRTY MINUTES

DC: Let's talk about the CBS decision to expand the *Evening News* to thirty minutes.

WC: What brought that about was an absolute act of bravery and courage on the part of Dick Salant. We had been talking for a long time, going back before I took over the anchor job, of the need for a half-hour news broadcast. The local affiliates resisted it, just as they still resist an hour broadcast. Most of them said they wouldn't carry the *Evening News* if we went to thirty minutes, because news was a loss leader at that time. The half hour would have cost them almost twice as much, as a loss. Finally, after battling the affiliates for a couple of years, Salant was able to convince Stanton and Paley to do it. Salant didn't believe they would drop the program. Sure enough, we went to a half hour, and they all took it. NBC went the next week to a half hour, and ABC trailed along months later. But, frankly, the affiliates had no place to go. There wasn't anything for them to do except stick with us, so they did. And it was a success.

DC: Let's go back now to the expansion of the *Evening News* to thirty minutes, which occurred the month after your trip to Normandy with Eisenhower. Some observers have noted that it was more technologically feasible for you to have a thirty-minute program at this time because of the development of satellites and videotape. There was actually a concern that you weren't going to have enough news to put on for thirty minutes and that's one of the reasons why CBS added four new bureaus domestically.

WC: Yeah, that's all accurate, but I don't think we had satellite at that point, did we?

DC: Maybe it was the knowledge that *Telstar* was soon going to be coming online.

WC: Possibly we had *Telstar*, but after all, don't forget that *Telstar* had very limited use. They had only two land stations. I think maybe they only had one in Land's End or somewhere in England. But I don't think we had a French station yet.

DC: I think the point here about the technological developments, particularly with *Telstar* and videotape, was that apparently CBS News realized that it could actually compete with the newspapers in terms of timeliness. Nineteen sixty-three was a watershed year for television news, not to mention the country, but also for television-news programming. I think it was in 1963, Walter, that, for the first time, most Americans reported that they depended more on news from TV than from newspapers. Gary Paul Gates has argued that it was the expansion to the thirty-minute format that boosted television over the newspapers.

WC: Well I think the longer broadcast certainly called a lot more attention to the *Evening News*. We were able to do a much brighter, deeper, more thoughtful job. But don't forget that two months after the advent of the half-hour news came the assassination of John Kennedy. And that brought an awful lot of attention to television.

CHANGES AT CBS

DC: Let's talk about 1964, which was a rather troublesome year for Walter Cronkite.

WC: [*laughs*] Well, it turned out to be.

DC: In fact, it didn't really start out that well, because Richard Salant was removed as president of CBS News in March 1964 and replaced by Fred Friendly. According to some observers, Salant was removed because the *CBS Evening News*'s ratings continued to fall behind NBC's Huntley and Brinkley program.

WC: I was disappointed, because I liked Dick Salant a great deal. I didn't dislike Fred Friendly by any means. I felt that he was kind of a self-promoter, and I was somewhat concerned about his appointment. It was a wait-and-see situation when he came over to CBS News. My emotions were almost solely concerned with Dick Salant having to leave.

DC: Did you see any changes immediately when Friendly came in?

WC: Well, I don't remember any turmoil at the *Evening News* with his coming in. I think he was perhaps biding his time there. It seemed to me we went along on a pretty even footing.

DC: So he wasn't the kind of guy who came in and just started moving the furniture around?

WC: Well, he didn't on the *Evening News*. But that's exactly what happened with our convention coverage. I think Paley put Friendly in to get us in a better position for the conventions. He didn't want to lose the convention ratings to NBC again.

1964 REPUBLICAN CONVENTION

DC: Let's talk about the 1964 Republican National Convention.

WC: Well, our coverage of the 1964 Republican convention was a disaster. And it was a management disaster. I contributed to the disaster because I was not prepared for what Friendly did to me in the anchor room, and I was mad about it throughout. I was not getting the information I needed for my coverage. Friendly had just taken over, and they changed the entire way that we covered the convention. They changed the anchor desk. They changed everything. I didn't have the facilities to work with.

DC: As you know, there has been a lot written about it. According to Bill Leonard's memoirs, he and Robert Wussler called themselves the CAFOC, or Care and Feeding of Cronkite Club. He says the trick was to get you to do what they wanted you to do and keep you happy at the same time. Bill Leonard claims that you resisted all the changes that they tried to make in the booth. He also says that Fred Friendly suggested that Eric Sevareid be placed in the booth with you to serve as a commentator, sort of like David Brinkley. But, and this is Leonard again, quote: "Walter exploded." They were still able to get Sevareid on, but they had to keep him at a physical distance from you. Bill Leonard claims that Don Hewitt would direct you to go to the correspondents on the convention floor for coverage, but that you would ignore his instructions.

Leonard believes that the off-camera bad feelings came across very strongly on the air to the viewers. He blames himself for the problem and says it was his inexperience as a supervisor and that he should not have commanded you to do things. Sally Smith claims that the "CBS convention coverage was simply awful, and everyone was at fault. Cronkite talked to much, Friendly and Leonard directed the coverage badly, and while Cronkite was slow and windy, Huntley and Brinkley sparkled."

WC: Yeah. Well, now I'll tell you my version of what happened at that convention. After Friendly took over in March, he immediately consulted with me about the convention coverage. We had developed our coverage since 1952 into a rather interesting form in which I had two assistants: one for news flow and one for communications. We worked this system out by trial and error over time. When I explained the system to Friendly, he said, "Well, do you need all those people around? They get in the way of the picture." I said, "The picture be damned. What we're trying to do is provide solid information. And yes, we need them."

They expected me to listen to the control room and to talk to the camera at the same time. Well, I couldn't do that. The broadcast control room was always frantic. Their interruptions were just ghastly. The only person in the entire CBS operation who knew what was going on in the convention consistently as a running story was the anchorperson. The people in the control room didn't know what was going on at the convention at all. As an anchor, it was my responsibility to keep the story flowing.

But the control room would direct me to go to a correspondent because he had a New York delegate who had something to say about New York's upcoming vote on the credentials or something. Yet I had just told the television audience that we would now listen to the speaker at the podium because he had something important to say. So the guy on the podium had just started talking, and now they want me to go remote to a correspondent. The control room hadn't heard what I had said to the audience. They don't know what the guy at the podium is going to say. All they know is that a correspondent had said that he had an interesting delegate to interview and he wanted the airtime. And I'm the one who has to say, "I'll get to that. Just tell him to hold on." That was one of the things that gave me a reputation of being a microphone hog. I wouldn't go to people instantly, because I was creating a running story and trying to fit things into their proper place. I know that was annoying to the correspondent standing there with somebody he wanted to put on the air. They wanted airtime themselves, and they thought they had a good story, and a lot of times they didn't. But they thought they did, and that's all right. Really, that's just eager reporting, and that's fine.

After I explained the system to Friendly, he said, "Gee, I don't like that. We can't really see you without getting those other two people in the camera shot. People will wonder what they're doing there." I said, "Well, Fred, if you're asking me, yes, it's essential that they be there." He replied, "Well, why couldn't one person handle that?" I said, "Maybe. That would take a pretty exceptional person to handle it alone." Nothing more was said. I thought we had agreed that we were going to stick with what we had.

I arrived in San Francisco for the convention two or three days in advance, and Friendly met me at the airport. He said, "I want to ride into town with you. I want to talk to you. I've got some great ideas for the convention." Friendly always, you know, had these great ideas. He suggested that we stop by the Cow Palace, where the convention was being held, to look at the CBS booth.

We got out there, and the whole set was different. Nothing we had planned at all. He had an anchor desk that had me isolated. He had what he said was a guest spot near me, but it was clearly more than a guest spot. It was for a dual anchor. No question about that. And he had decided that I would have one assistant. He had hired a person I didn't even know who had been Huntley and Brinkley's assistant on the other conventions. He placed her across the room, about ten feet away, next to the camera, and she's supposed to communicate with me. She's off camera entirely. I looked at this new set, and I said, "Fred, what have you done? This is the very thing I said we couldn't do. How am I going to get my news copy?" He said, " Every time you're off camera, she'll hand it to you." I said, "Fred, I can't communicate with her. I've lost control completely." Which is what he wanted, of course.

Fred said, "Well, you know, Walter, what I'm really hoping for is maybe Eric Sevareid contributing a little more than he has been willing to contribute before. If I can give him a place at the desk, I'm sure he'd be willing to do that. I think you agree he's a big asset." I certainly did agree that Sevareid was a big asset, but not enough to justify destroying my whole setup.

Now, I had resisted having a dual anchor from the very first in 1952. Because, to my mind, if you've got the dual anchor, you've got that same situation of losing control of the story. You don't know what your dual anchor is going to do that will throw off the whole pace. I think if you look at the transcripts or look back at what Huntley-Brinkley did, you will see that's true. They had an entertainment show, but we were delivering one hell of a lot more information. Now, their show was far more entertaining. I would agree with that quickly, but it was not as informative as ours. Huntley-Brinkley was not as much of the civics lesson that we thought the conventions were for—those first few conventions, anyway.

So here I am at San Francisco with Fred having changed everything. And I said, "Fred, this will not work. I don't know how we're going to do this. Can't we go back?" Fred said, "Well, it's too late now. I ordered this. I thought you'd like it." He acted like he was very disappointed. Making the situation worse, Fred and Bill Leonard were just incredibly disorganized. They'd have one idea one minute and another one the next. My assistant across the room was of no help whatsoever. She would hold up a little sign: "Go to Pierpoint." They wouldn't even tell me where Pierpoint was. I would say, "Please, for God's sake, tell me what he's going to talk about for a lead-in." You've got to have something to lead in with. That was crazy, so I would just ignore the sign. During the break, Leonard kept coming in and saying, "We told you to go to Pierpoint. Why aren't you going to Pierpoint?" [*shouting*] I'd say "Please, please, please." He said, "Well, you have to go to Pierpoint right now."

DC: And then the camera would come back on, and here you were, angry at Leonard.

WC: Yeah, and I'm having to say, "We're going to Bob Pierpoint." And that's the way I did it. No explanation. I was annoyed. Let them worry about the lead-in. But it was awful. And I imagine that's what happened when they replaced me with Bob Trout and Roger Mudd in Atlantic City. Or Mudd-Trout, as the team was called. My guess is that's why their reporting was so bad. And then Friendly kept trying to bring Sevareid in. He was just as uncomfortable as I was. Eric likes to think in seclusion and write an ordered piece. That's what he's sensational at. He is a damned good extemporaneous essayist. He's awfully good at it, but he's not comfortable with it. Anyway, the coverage was in shambles.

DC: Just as an item here, not that you particularly want to be reminded of it, but NBC's rating for the Republican convention was 55 percent in 1964, and CBS got a 30 percent rating.

WC: Well, I'm surprised we got that high.

DC: I thought that was an interesting comment you made, Walter, that you feel that Huntley and Brinkley provided more entertainment than information and that's why that combination worked as smoothly as it did.

WC: Well, yeah. I'm not saying they didn't provide information. I think that our information flow was a little more serious.

DC: But you feel they were more focused on entertainment than on information?

WC: Yeah, because of Brinkley's acerbic wit, primarily. In everything Brinkley covers, really, his attitude is "Well, you know, this really isn't that important." It's kind of a sideshow of human behavior for him, like "And what are we all doing here anyway?"

DC: What other general memories do you still have of the 1964 Republican convention?

WC: Well, I remember that the Goldwater people demanded that I be moved from my suite at the Mark Hopkins Hotel because I was right under Goldwater's suite. They thought that I had taken this room in the hotel in order to eavesdrop on him, to tap his wires and all that sort of thing. The Mark Hopkins management didn't respond to that.

There was one unfortunate kind of episode. My daughter Nancy, who was sixteen at the time, was for Lyndon Johnson. I agreed to take her to the convention with me, but on a pledge that she wouldn't get involved in politics out there. She'd just be an observer. She agreed as to how that was a proper request on my part. The first day she was at the convention, she got a job at the Scranton campaign headquarters, downstairs in the hotel. I told her, "That's perfectly all right. You're certainly entitled to work for anybody you want to, but stay out of the press. Just don't get involved in any major public demonstrations of any kind." So the next day, I was down in the barbershop getting a haircut. There was a guy having a shave next to me, lying back with the hot towels on his face. The barber started talking to me: "Mr. Cronkite," this, and "Mr. Cronkite" that. And the guy next to me takes the towel off his face. He comes up in his chair, and he says, "Well, Walter, good to see you. By God, that's a cute little girl you've got here, that little daughter of yours." It was Walter Winchell. I said, "What do you know about my daughter?" He said, "Oh, I'm leading my column with her today. God, she's a cute kid." I said, "Where did you see her, Walter?" He said, "Well, when Senator Goldwater arrived at the hotel here last night, he had his supporters all out there in front of the hotel, and he got up on the steps and greeted them and made a little speech. She was right down in the front row there with a big Scranton sign, pushing it up in his face the whole time." I thought, oh, God . . . But it was the lead item in his nationally syndicated column.

DC: Did you get any flak from that?

WC: No. Actually, I didn't hear a darn thing, but I can tell you the CBS publicity people were absolutely frantic about it. But nobody else paid any attention to the story. Nancy got herself arrested later on at an anti-Goldwater demonstration out at the Cow Palace, but they didn't actually book them, thank God. They just took them all.

BARRY GOLDWATER

DC: Did you know Barry Goldwater by the time he ran for president in 1964?

WC: Yes, I knew him, and I liked him. Not nearly as much as I got to liking him later, however. I just abhorred his politics. But we had something in common in our interest in the air force and the air war. So we talked about that and avoided politics. I got to know him a lot better long after that race.

DC: How do you read Goldwater as a person?

WC: I think he's a fiercely independent soul and a rugged individualist in the best of the western tradition and of the military tradition. They come together very conveniently in the persona of Barry Goldwater and make him the man he is. It was a handy trait for the Republicans to try to exploit back in 1964, until they realized that his rugged individualism extended even to being critical of the right-wing itself from time to time. When they realized that, he became something of a maverick. Which is where he belongs. He was much more of an emotional than a thinking man. I don't think that Barry probably sits around worrying about the philosophical aspects of any question or even the sociological aspects of it. His politics come out of the heart rather than the mind.

DC: So you don't really see Goldwater as an ideologue in the classic sense? He is more of an emotional than an intellectual ideologue?

WC: That's exactly it. [*Goldwater died in 1998.*]

BEING REPLACED

DC: After the Republican convention, Sally Smith says, in her biography of Paley, that at a meeting in New York, Paley asked Bill Leonard and Fred Friendly, "What the hell happened to Walter?" Leonard explained that they tried to get you to go to the floor more often, as we mentioned earlier, but that you had "resisted." Paley said, "You mean he would get what amounted to an order, and he wouldn't obey it? Who can replace Walter right now? We can't have people who won't take orders. And anyway, it's not working." And then Smith goes on to say that "Paley wanted to get rid of Cronkite" and that he felt the world had moved on and "Walter was old hat." According to Smith, Paley suggested that Roger Mudd and Bob Trout should replace you. How did you find out about this decision?

WC: As a matter of fact, I didn't return to New York. I had my whole family out there, and we took the period between the two conventions to drive down the West Coast to

Disneyland. I didn't know anything about the meeting Paley had with Friendly. To Fred Friendly's credit, because this isn't the way it's normally done in our business, he telephoned me and said he'd like to come out and see me. I said "Well, sure, I'll be back to New York in a week." Fred said, "Well, this is something that won't wait. It's a fairly serious matter, and I would like to come out and see you right away." I don't think I asked him what it was about. I think I suspected and just didn't ask.

Fred came out to Los Angeles, and we had a meeting at the hotel at Disneyland. It was really a surreal moment. All this stuff is going on in the background, people wearing Mickey Mouse and Donald Duck suits and dancing around, and Fred's telling me that I was being fired. I must say for Fred, he did not say that Paley had ordered it. He simply said that the decision had been made. He said I was going to be replaced for the Democratic convention. He said, "Now, we want you to continue with the *Evening News*. You're not being relieved from that. We expect you to continue. You're very happy there." But I really doubted that. I thought, well, whomever does well at the convention will just move in to the *Evening News*. So I really believed that my CBS career was ending.

We finished the two or three days we had at Disneyland. We drove to San Diego, and then we were flying home from there. By the time I got to San Diego, the press had the story. I had a little news conference in San Diego, and I said that I couldn't find any complaint for their action. I said that I admired Fred Friendly for coming out and telling me. I admitted that the convention coverage was a shambles and that I shared some of the blame for it. As far as their firing me, that was their privilege. It's their candy store. That phrase got a lot of quotes in the newspapers. In other words, I didn't fight back. Which helped my situation a lot, I think.

DC: Bill Leonard says in his memoir, quote: "In the way that Walter took the demotion, he turned my worst moment into his finest. Cronkite came out of the affair a bigger man than before." In its story about the incident, *Newsweek* stated, quote: "Perhaps the real significance of the Cronkite demotion is that CBS News has become an offshoot of show business." Do you think that was a fair statement?

WC: I do think CBS was trying to duplicate the Huntley-Brinkley format, which, as I've said, had an entertainment value to it. So in that sense, I suppose you'd have to say that they were yielding to that pressure. But I certainly don't think they had an intention of subjugating news values to entertainment values in the broadcasts.

DC: Fred Friendly says in his book that this whole episode was "his worst blunder" as president of CBS News. Now, you said that you thought your career at CBS was over when Fred Friendly gave you the bad news.

WC: I'm not sure that I thought so as he recited the situation, but I certainly did as I thought through it immediately thereafter. But, Don, I always thought that there would be a day when I'd go back to the United Press. It just seemed inevitable to me that my career in radio and television broadcasting wouldn't last. I considered every day that Betsy and I lived on CBS's elaborate wage that this was not permanent and that we'd be going back to UP at some point.

DC: After you were replaced as the Democratic Party convention anchor, you did the *Evening News* every day from the convention site in Atlantic City anyway.

WC: That was rather interesting. While we were in San Francisco, they had moved the CBS News headquarters from the Grand Central Terminal building to 524 West Fifty-seventh Street. The old Cow Barn, as we call it. It had been the Sheffield dairy. It was their horse barn from where they delivered milk. That was the building CBS converted for its broadcast center. But at any rate, we moved, and actually that little episode of me being demoted got me a better office than I would have had otherwise. They assigned me a little office down a corridor somewhere. Don Hewitt looked at the plans and said, "I'm not going to have Walter put in that pigeonhole office." So he had a whole corner of the newsroom built for me, with glass looking out. Which is what I'd had in the other place. Hewitt himself ordered up this change and ordered up some fancier furniture and some bookcases. He really provided me a very fancy office. He wasn't going to have me come back from the 1964 convention defeat into a cubbyhole somewhere. It was very nice of him. I appreciated it very much.

DC: Who made the decision to have the *Evening News* broadcast from Atlantic City?

WC: Oh, I did. Everybody assumed that I wouldn't want to be there at all. I said, "Heck, no. I definitely want to be there. I want to be at that convention." Everybody tried to talk me out of it, but I said, "No. I've covered conventions, and now I'm the anchorman on *CBS Evening News*. I ought to be there." Of course, it created all kinds of furor, which the public relations people hated. The first time I appeared on the convention floor, a whole bunch of newspeople came rushing over. They turned on their lights, of course, wanting to do an interview. Well, that attracted more of them, like flies. I got a huge crowd of people, lights and excitement all over the floor. And I was told that up in the CBS booth, Mudd and Trout said, "Well, there's something very interesting happening on the floor of the convention. We're going to go down there now." And they went down to a correspondent, who said, "Why, well, it's, uh, yes, there's some little news conference going on." They explained it away quickly. That was a wonderful episode.

DC: That leads us into the actual election itself. Was there ever any question about your serving as anchor for election night in 1964?

WC: There must have been, because the assumption would be that Mudd and Trout were going to do the election.

DC: Mudd and Trout were a disaster in the convention ratings. Not only that, but according to various sources, Paley was deluged with mail complaining about your removal from the convention coverage. Apparently, he even complained to several of his friends that he never dreamed there would be such a clamor and that he told Friendly that he was quite willing to restore you to your usual position.

WC: I don't remember when the decision was made; it was probably made pretty quickly to dampen any further speculation.

MANAGEMENT CHANGES

DC: Ernie Leiser replaced Don Hewitt in December 1964 as executive producer of the *Evening News*. Gates, in his history of CBS News, describes Leiser as a person who ruled the news set by fear. He said that, nonetheless, he had a reputation for fairness and he inspired respect. Gates also says that "Ernie Leiser deserves much of the credit" for the significant improvements in the *Evening News* by 1965.

WC: I certainly think Ernie Leiser deserves a lot of credit. We became a more solid news organization under him than we were under Hewitt.

DC: Did Leiser manage by fear?

WC: Well, Ernie's a fierce guy. He is just as bighearted as the next guy—bigger, perhaps, than many—and he was absolutely fair. But he was a big and bluff growler, and he didn't pull any punches. He was the old "city editor with horns" kind of guy. And people of this current generation, like Gary Gates, aren't used to that. All young journalists today have to be stroked, for heaven's sake. It's ridiculous. I'm with Ernie Leiser. I'm not quick with a compliment. People have to go beyond what is expected of them to get a compliment from me. Doing what is expected of them doesn't necessarily inspire any great appreciation from me. That's what they're paid to do. [*Ernie Leiser died in 2002.*]

DC: In 1966, Fred Friendly resigned in protest over the network's decision not to televise George Kennan's testimony at Senator Fulbright's hearing on the Vietnam War. Were you involved in that affair?

WC: No. I was involved only in that I was one of those pressing to get it on the air. I thought we ought to be covering that thing. I so expressed myself to Friendly, and he agreed. He said, "We're going to go on. Don't worry. We'll get on." And then we didn't get the airtime.

DC: Did you know he was going to resign? Did he tell anyone?

WC: No, I didn't know about that ahead of time.

DC: Gary Gates claims that "Most of Friendly's colleagues were delighted to see him leave.

Especially Paley and Stanton." Gates says that Friendly's resignation had more to do with his being upset with having to report to Jack Schneider, the new president of the broadcast group, than any principle involved.

WC: Oh, I think that's true. I think that Fred was upset about not getting Kennan's testimony on the air, but it was just the straw that broke the camel's back. It was a matter of having to go through Schneider. He was fighting for the good of the news department. The news department should have reported directly to Stanton. It did at one time. They moved news one step down the chain of command, and he was right to oppose that.

DC: Was there a problem with Schneider himself?

WC: No. I would say that Schneider was darn good. Schneider had a good sense of news, and he had a strong sense of the total network problem, the costs of preempting scheduled programming, and so forth. It was his job to balance those things and make those decisions. I don't know whether this has been said publicly or not, but Jack was a good friend of mine, and he has said to me that very possibly, if Fred hadn't have pushed so hard, so adamantly, and even angrily, he might have put Kennan's testimony on the air. Jack got to the point where he almost couldn't put Kennan on and retain his dignity.

DC: Compare and contrast Schneider with Jim Aubrey, who was president of the CBS network during the early 1960s.

WC: No comparison of the two people. Aubrey was purely, totally, completely show business, with all the lack of ethics that that implies. There is no comparison.

DC: Richard Salant came back and replaced Friendly. Gates claims that you and Eric Sevareid went to Stanton and Schneider, urging them to give the job back to Salant.

WC: That's true. But we did it separately, not together. I thought that we'd gone through a period of turmoil and that Salant was the guy who could best pull us back out of that. Interestingly enough, even though Salant had no news background, he had more professional journalistic ethics than any man I've ever known. He just seemed to seize upon the ethical aspects of journalism. He lived by those rules.

DC: Most of the critics who have looked at this period at CBS say that Salant's second term gave CBS News a long period of stability. But some of Salant's critics claim that he was an absentee manager, that he delegated too much, that he gave Bill Leonard and Gordon Manning too much authority.

WC: I don't think that's a just criticism whatsoever. He gave them just the right amount of authority. That probably comes from some sour-grapes people who Gordon and Bill Leonard crossed and who Salant wouldn't hear their appeals.

DC: You do enter into a period of stability during these years. For instance, it's been pointed out that Bill Paley withdrew from active management of CBS about this time and let Frank Stanton and Jack Schneider run things.

WC: Well, you see, that was also a great boon to the news department because Stanton had total faith in Salant. But I don't think Salant was very appreciative of Schneider, particularly. Schneider represented show business to him, and he also chafed at the chain of command. When he was in the first time, he reported directly to Stanton. He came back the second time, and he had to go through Schneider.

DC: I would think that was an uncomfortable situation for Schneider, since Stanton and Salant were close.

WC: It was, because Salant could pick up the phone and actually talk to Frank Stanton any time he wanted to.

DC: Matusow quotes you in her book as saying, "I never believed my success would last as long as it did." And then she goes on to say that you were careful not to make undue demands on the company. She says that you were a master at survival tactics.

WC: Well, I don't know about demands on the company. I didn't see that there were any demands that were necessary, most of the time. I had an agent handling the actual negotiations for money. It always seemed fair compensation to me, if not even more than I could imagine, most of the time. That's what agents are for anyway. Tuck Stix did very well as far as I was concerned, and the company did well by me. I rarely had any demands to make.

COVERING POPULAR CULTURE

DC: Let's talk about some significant news subjects that critics claim you ignored or perhaps even ridiculed. Some media critics have stated that the *CBS Evening News* largely missed two of the most important stories of the 1960s and 1970s, and those were the women's movement and the revolution in popular culture, especially in music. In an interview in the *Washington Post* in October 1976, Frank Mankiewicz claimed that the *Evening News* played a negative role in early reporting of the women's movement. He specifically claimed that your news program emphasized the radical side of the movement almost exclusively: "It was calculated to create scorn for the movement, and the sight of Cronkite smiling condescendingly as the film ended as we came back to the anchor desk said a lot to the viewing public." Did you ever run across that?

WC: Never did run across it. I didn't know that criticism existed, even. I don't know how I'd respond to it. Goodness knows, I would be hard put to deny that categorically because, looking back on it, I think that was probably what my reaction was at that time. I don't remember any insidious campaign that we did. I thought the militant side of the feminist campaign was pretty silly. And I still do, although I admit that some of the silly things they did paid off in the long run, such as "Ms." My God, the first suggestion of calling women "Ms." was met with derision from most of us. And that old argument about "his" and "hers" and the male gender of many common nouns, that caused a great deal of levity. But that might have been the attitude of us male chauvinists on the *Evening News*. I think it highly possible. If so, it's something that I regret, obviously.

DC: You admitted later to *Rolling Stone* magazine that you failed to understand the news significance of the so-called Woodstock generation. That's somewhat ironic because your daughter Kathy actually went to the Woodstock concert in 1969.

WC: She was at Woodstock, yeah. Well, I was paying a lot of attention because I had two daughters who were part of that generation. I was very much concerned about it. I just didn't have any appreciation for it. I didn't like their music. I didn't like their attitude. I didn't like their dress code. I certainly saw Woodstock as newsworthy after it happened. I don't think any of us knew what it was going to be when it started. But yeah, we were forced to pay attention to it. I don't know that I really recognized it as a social revolution at the beginning. I didn't realize how far it was going to go as a permanent change of our entire moral structure, family structure, and all that stuff. I didn't realize that at all.

DC: Some television columnists have claimed that you really resented it when popular culture intruded on the news broadcasts. An example of the way you would rebel is when John Merriman wrote a story about the draft problems of Muhammed Ali, and . . . .

WC: I wanted to call him Cassius Clay?

DC: Yes, although he had changed his name to Muhammed Ali.

WC: His legal name was Cassius Clay. You can't just go around changing your name any time you want to be somebody else. That was just dumb. We had a knock-down, drag-out battle about it at the *Evening News*.

DC: There was another story, just along those lines, while we're on that subject, I think it was when Elvis Presley died, in 1977.

WC: Oh yes. I was on summer vacation in Maine, and I was checking in every day to see what was going on. They reported that Elvis Presley died, and they were going to lead the show. I said, "Leading with Elvis Presley? My God, a rock singer, that belongs in about fifteen seconds at the end of the broadcast." I forget what it was, but there was a pretty good story that day of far more significance, I thought. But I was wrong about that. It's certainly true that I probably have a stodgy approach to the news in the sense that it's the big movements of history that intrigue me, far more than things like that. But the staff did what I said. They buried it—buried may be an unfortunate phrase for it—they put the story elsewhere, they didn't lead with it. You probably didn't pick this up, but we did a brief segment about the popularity of the Beatles in England before they made their first appearance in the U.S. I should get some credit for not being totally out of it, after all.

DC: Okay, I'll do that! [*laughing*]

DC: One important mass movement of the times that you didn't miss was the environmental movement. I'm thinking specifically of your identification with the first Earth Day, April 22, 1970.

WC: We were ahead on that. I think I take more pride in that than in anything else we have done the whole time we were on the air. We were the first out of the block on the environment. A producer we had, Ron Bonn, first brought the matter to my attention. We'd both just been reading Rachel Carson's *Silent Spring*, and we had some concern. He knew that I had concern about these things. We'd done a piece or two on it. He suggested we do an ongoing series under a logo of some kind and that we name it something and do it regularly from time to time. We named it "Can the World be Saved?" Ron produced it. We started doing those pieces in 1969, I believe it was. We got a lot of attention and won some awards. By the time 1970 rolled around, *Time* magazine was calling it the decade of the environment. I really think that we did it, Ron Bonn particularly.

DC: Matusow says that the series "almost certainly helped create the climate for passage of the environmental legislation of the seventies, in particular the Environmental Protection Agency." The organizers of Earth Day also said publicly that you played a key role in raising public consciousness about Earth Day as an event. You also plugged Earth Day a great deal in your radio commentaries.

WC: That's right. I'm willing to take that credit.

DC: Now, you mentioned earlier about being on vacation when we were talking about Elvis Presley. You worked out a contract in 1973 that gave you three months off each summer. How did that come about?

WC: It came about because I was getting rather tired of the heavy pressure. It wasn't doing the *Evening News*. If it was just doing the *Evening News*, that would have been fine. But, boy, I was doing a lot of specials, and publicity appearances and speeches for CBS, and a lot of affiliate appearances. The routine was just terribly wearing, and I wanted some time off. And my contract was up, and they were offering me a big increase in salary. If I had played my cards right, I could have been the first million-dollar newsperson.

But I said no, I don't want that, I'd rather have time off. So I negotiated for the three months off instead of a raise. So I got a little bit of a raise, the same for nine months' work instead of for twelve months.

DC: Was it harder for them to deal with your getting time off than giving you more money?

WC: Yeah, actually it was much harder. It was really quite a concession on their part. I didn't expect to get it. I was surprised. Of course, I don't think my agent, Tom Stix, was too pleased with it either. It was very hard for him to get 10 percent of three months off. Johnny Carson and I used to joke about who could get the most time off. Every time I'd get a new contract, I'd send him a telegram and tell him that I'd passed him. I now had three months off. When he got his next contract, he'd send me a wire saying he was now getting three nights off a week.

DC: Eric Sevareid retired in 1977 or 1976. Bill Moyers moved from PBS to CBS and took Sevareid's place as a commentator.

WC: Well, not on a regular basis, no. I think that was perhaps the intention eventually, but it didn't start out that way.

DC: In his book *The Powers That Be*, David Halberstam talks about the difficulties that Bill Moyers had in fitting in at CBS. It was not a good fit, it seems.

WC: I'm not an authority on this by any means. I suspect it was a matter of just getting enough airtime. Bill had a lot of ideas. After all, a lot of them were very good, as we've seen on PBS. And he wanted to develop them, and just couldn't get on the air. CBS wasn't willing to give up that much time for that kind of serious programming. It was simple as that.

DC: He had *CBS Reports* for a while, didn't he?

WC: Yeah, but, see, that wasn't getting on the air very often either. This was in the twilight time of the documentary. The network documentary was dying out already at that point.

DC: Was there ever an attempt to find another Sevareid replacement?

WC: No, there was not. You know, in all honesty, it was a bit of relief for those of us in the *Evening News* broadcast. It meant we did not have to make room for someone three times a week or whatever it was. I had always enjoyed Sevareid. I always thought he was great, and I thought that he added a great deal to the broadcast. But I also felt that we should have had the right to say that we had more than we could handle on a particular day and we can't shoehorn Sevareid in. And that was very difficult to do. You know, occasionally we did that, but you can't do it very often to Sevareid or to anybody else.

DC: Sevareid did his part of the broadcast from Washington?

WC: Yeah. He'd frequently call me up and say, "I'm thinking about so-and-so. How does that sound to you?" Eric and I were very friendly. And occasionally, I'd call up and suggest a piece to him. Sometimes he'd make something out of it, sometimes not.

and governmental ...

Robert F. Kennedy. I know you reported on JFK's failed bid in
1956 for the Democratic nomination for the vice presidency. But
your coverage really picked up in 1960 when JFK campaigned for
the Democratic Party's presidential nomination.

... That's right. My first in-depth exposure to John Kennedy
... before I became anchor of the
... at CBS News could get the four
... to do that. You can forget it." And I said, "Well, if ... tial candidates on our thirteen-
... President Nixon, you'd almost have to do it then, ... sponsored by Westinghouse. My
... you?" And he looked at me rather coldly and said ... with the presidential and vice
... going to get him ...

... go first. And we did it just as I'd planned.
... from opposite sides of the room, with no other

... As I remember it was live. I'm not sure about that. At any
... I was out in the truck, and our producer, Warren Abrams,

CHAPTER SIXTEEN

JFK

DC: Your career at CBS intersected frequently with the political and governmental activities of John F. Kennedy and his brother Robert F. Kennedy. I know you reported on JFK's failed bid in 1956 for the Democratic nomination for the vice presidency. But your coverage really picked up in 1960 when JFK campaigned for the Democratic Party's presidential nomination.

WC: That's right. My first in-depth exposure to John Kennedy came during the 1960 campaign, before I became anchor of the *Evening News*. I had an idea that CBS News could get the four presidential and vice presidential candidates on our thirteen-week "Pick the Winner" series, sponsored by Westinghouse. My idea was that we would begin with the presidential and vice presidential candidates, and then we'd go to their campaign managers and various people important to both campaigns. Now, this shows you how much television has changed, but I came up with the radical idea that during these interviews, I would ask questions deliberately aimed at bringing out their personalities—or that was the idea. Because up to that time, we'd been talking almost entirely about issues. That seems so strange today because we've gotten so far away from talking about issues. The concentration today is far too much about personalities. So I guess I have to admit to some complicity in helping that unfortunate development. But I wanted to find out what makes these people tick. My plan was that we would not provide advance information that would help the candidates prepare. They would not know what we were going to ask in any way or form; the only thing they would know is that we were going to enter the room from opposite sides, on camera, and meet, say hello, sit down, and I'd start asking them questions.

Cronkite interviewing President John F. Kennedy in Hyannis Port, Massachusetts, for the inaugural thirty-minute telecast of the CBS Evening News, *September 2, 1963 (DI_05792).*

DC: So they would just do this cold, without a preliminary discussion with you.

WC: Just cold. My CBS colleagues said, "It's never going to happen." So I was thinking to myself, the one person of the four who was most likely to say yes would be John Kennedy, the young senator from Massachusetts, who most needed the publicity. I also felt that he would be more comfortable with the press than the others. So I went to see Kennedy in his Senate office, and he said, "You must think I'm crazy. I'm not going to do that. You can forget it." And I said, "Well, if I got Vice President Nixon, you'd almost have to do it then, wouldn't you?" And he looked at me rather coldly and said, "You're not going to get him. That's not my problem." So I left Kennedy's office, and I went downtown to Nixon's headquarters at Sixteenth and K. I explained the idea to Nixon, and he said, "Sure, I think that's fine. That's a great idea. I'd be glad to participate." My gosh, I was dumbfounded. I got in the cab and started back up Capitol Hill to see Kennedy again. Halfway up the hill, I suddenly realized that I had another big problem: who was going to go first? Whoever went first would have the big advantage of seeing how this program was handled. I thought I'd better get that settled. I turned the cab around and went back down to see Nixon. He said, "I don't care. I'll be glad to go first if it's any problem." Incredible. So I went to see Kennedy, who was furious, really. He restrained his fury, but his eyes were cold as could be. He said, "I suppose if you've got Nixon, we'll have to do something. You talk to my campaign manager." But he agreed to do it. So then I had to get them to get their running mates to do it. Lyndon Johnson was reluctant, I gathered. Henry Cabot Lodge wasn't too crazy about it either, but they both agreed.

DC: Did Nixon go first?

WC: Nixon did go first. And we did it just as I'd planned. We walked in from opposite sides of the room, with no other discussion between our staffs at all, except technical details like getting the cameras into his office. We walked in, we sat down, and my first question to him was, "Mr. Vice President, you're a skilled politician. You certainly can't have missed what people say about you. Many of them say 'I don't know what it is about the man, I just don't like him.' What do you think it is they don't like about you?" Well, Nixon, on that question and throughout the interview, acted as if it were all on teleprompter. I never saw anybody as quick and as smooth as he was on those things. He said, "Well, I think it's three things, Mr. Cronkite. I think the first is my physiognomy. I have a rather heavy beard and a dark complexion, and between those things, I just can't shave closely enough. I always look a little blue in the face, like I have little growth of beard, and that's unfortunate. The second thing is those campaigns for election to the U.S. Senate against Helen Douglas and for the Congress against Jerry Voorhis, which I would probably do a little differently. I wouldn't take back any of the charges I made, because I think they were perfectly justified, but I would handle it a little differently with the experience I have now. And third is my leadership on the

House Un-American Activities Committee. I'm not one bit ashamed of that, but that created a body of propaganda..." and so forth, da-ding, da-ding, da-ding. And he went on right like that all through the whole broadcast, which had a lot of other pretty good zingers in it. My last question was, "Mr. Vice President, of all of the possibly qualified people, why do you think you are best suited to be president of the United States?" He answered right away with a really smooth and impressive answer that I've forgotten.

The next week, we did Kennedy from his home in Georgetown, and he was a reluctant guest. I can't remember the first question, but it wasn't as hard as the one I asked Nixon. But the last question was the same: "Why do you think you should be the president of the United States?" Well, Kennedy blew it completely. You know when Teddy Kennedy had that interview with Roger Mudd a few years ago [1979], I was reminded of it so much, because it was just like Jack's interview with me. He wasn't prepared, hadn't thought it through. In this case, his advisors should have told Kennedy, "He's going to have to ask you that question." But he didn't have an answer. He said, "Well, ...uh...I think, well, I believe, I, well...uh...uh...You could probably say it's a sense of history. Uh...that's what it is. I've got a sense of history." He was really grasping. When it was over, we thanked him, and he was kind of mean about it. He gave me a rather perfunctory good-bye. I went out to look at the tape in the truck that was parked out in front. We were not able to broadcast it live, because of certain other considerations. The main consideration being that Kennedy was going to do another program with Charles Collingwood immediately afterward. So we had to accommodate Kennedy by not doing ours live.

DC: But Nixon's was done live?

WC: As I remember, it was live. I'm not sure about that. At any rate, I was out in the truck, and our producer, Warren Abrams, came rushing in and said, "We've got to do the program over." I said, "What's the matter with it? It's all right in here. I'm looking at it." And he said, "Well, the senator says we have to do it over." I said, "But we don't do it over again. That's part of the deal." He said, "Kennedy insists. He won't let it be shown this way." I said, "Well, what right does he have?" "Well, I don't know, but his complaint is that we had him sitting in a big soft sofa, and he didn't look right." I said, "Oh, come on. We know better than that; it's because he blew that last question. Where is he?" "Up in his bedroom." And I said, "Well, I've got to go talk to him." So I went up, and he was lying on one of the twin beds, and Ted Sorenson, who was one of his advisors and speechwriters, was lying on the other. They had their shoes off and their ties undone. There was this big Harvard banner up on the wall, and football pictures; it looked like a college dorm room. They were lying there dangling their feet, and Kennedy said, "Tell me when you're ready." And I said, "Senator, I don't think we ought to do this again." And he said, " I've already discussed it with your producer. We're going to do it." I said, "But you know, we're going to have to carry a disclaimer. We're going to have to say that Nixon's was unrehearsed, but that you requested to do yours over, and it was." He said, "I can live with that." I said, "I don't think you understand the impact of that disclaimer. It's going to make you look like you really weren't willing to fight on the same playing ground as Nixon. I don't think it's going to make you look very good." He said, "I'm not concerned about that." I argued a little bit longer but got nowhere. I said, "All right, Senator, we'll do it over, but I've got to tell you, I think it's the lousiest bit of sportsmanship I ever saw in my life." That got him where nothing else would. I turned to walk out, and he said, "Wait a minute. Let it run."

DC: Were you able to interview Lyndon Johnson and Henry Cabot Lodge?

WC: Yes. We caught Lodge at the Saint Francis Hotel in San Francisco. Except for a delay caused by a power failure, our interview went well. I interviewed Johnson in Austin, but I didn't get anywhere with him. He was barely polite. He didn't want to do it. Kennedy ordered him to do it. I thought that Lyndon Johnson was very cagey, politically. I didn't get much out of him. He ducked the personal questions.

DC: I think it's interesting that you had more luck with Nixon in terms of cooperation and giving you information. That clashes with the public images of Kennedy and Nixon.

WC: Oh, I know, absolutely. Kennedy was pretty good on issues, but he was not very good on the personal questions, which was the purpose of the broadcast, to bring out his personality. We had to do nine other broadcasts on the campaign, so I talked to a lot of their advisors and other top political figures. It was very interesting and good stuff. All of them were good.

DC: Did you have any contact with Bobby Kennedy during the 1960 campaign?

WC: Yes, I did. My first real encounter with Bobby was in the Wisconsin primary of 1960, which was the first major test of the Catholic vote and the anti-Catholic vote. Wisconsin has some perfect sample precincts of all Catholics, all Protestants, half Protestants, half Catholics, and so forth. The ethnic voting and religious differentiation was just beautiful for polling purposes. Everybody was making note of this, of course, because Jack Kennedy was a Catholic. Up to that point, the Catholic issue had not been faced at all by the candidate himself. The night of the Wisconsin primary, as the returns were coming in indicating he was going to win and we were making these comparisons for these districts, we got him on the air. We were the first to have him on our primary broadcast at eleven o'clock. I was interviewing him, going along at a fairly decent pace, and then I got to the Catholic issue. I said, "Now, we've been analyzing these Catholic precincts, and they're showing heavy Catholic favoritism toward you." He tightened up visibly. He said, "I don't think this affects the race at all; it's not an important issue. You're creating an issue here at CBS by mentioning this at all." He just cut me off. I couldn't get anywhere with that line of questioning. I kept trying, but he got tighter and tighter. As he got up angrily, I felt, to leave, Bobby stormed into the control room and said, "YOU VIOLATED YOUR AGREEMENT! You weren't going to ask any question about the Catholic issue!" I'd never heard that. Don Hewitt had talked Bobby Kennedy into getting his brother for our election coverage that night. I could never be sure what Don had promised people just to get them on the air. Well, Bobby was terribly upset about it. After that, I didn't see that much of Bobby. I don't remember when I saw him another time in the course of that 1960 campaign. I did see him a couple of times when he was attorney general. We made joint appearances at some events, but nothing very intimate. But I should add that later on during the 1960 campaign, Jack Kennedy appeared in Frank Stanton's office and, in an unbelievable display of arrogant threats, told him that he didn't like my coverage. He cited the primary in Wisconsin and said, "I must remind you, Dr. Stanton, that when I'm elected president, I will be naming the members of the Federal Communications Commission." I never heard of anybody quite making that open of a threat. The Kennedys were a very aggressive and really a self-centered kind of a group in that fashion.

DC: While it doesn't forgive Nixon's presidential behavior later on, doesn't that sort of give credit to Nixon's argument that he didn't do anything to manipulate the network news that his predecessors hadn't done?

WC: No, Nixon was far worse in terms of the tactics he used. This was a single episode for Kennedy. I don't remember that Kennedy ever did anything else.

DC: Do you have any other outstanding memories of the 1960 presidential campaign?

WC: Well, right at the beginning of the campaign, there was one thing that impressed me a lot. I went to the very first meeting at which Hubert Humphrey and Jack Kennedy appeared on the same platform. That was the New Mexico state Democratic convention, which was in a small meeting hall. Kennedy spoke to the group and laid an egg. It was awful, just a stumbling and meandering, unfocused kind of a speech, without any inspiration. Hubert Humphrey came out, and, my gosh, he had them standing on their chairs, cheering. I had a look at this first confrontation between these two men and thought that Kennedy didn't have the chance of a snowball in hell. He was a real neophyte as far as appealing to the party leadership. He was an upstart, of course, you realize. I mean, among the party hierarchy, he was an interloper, moving in with all of his money and trying to make something out of the primaries that before had been fairly unimportant in deciding the candidate. Humphrey was a man of the party, and the party leaders all took some umbrage at this young upstart and his money. And then, of course, Kennedy bought the West Virginia primary, which was the key toward the end.

DC: When you say bought the primary, what do you mean?

WC: Kennedy paid off the voters, in effect. They really just poured a lot of money in there, and Humphrey had nothing to match it. I mean, it was very blatant. It was a great tragedy, in my mind. At that moment, I think, privately, I was for Humphrey. In fact, I was up in Humphrey's hotel room when the West Virginia returns came in that night. I remember having a tear in my eye, talking to Humphrey personally, telling him that I was sorry that he lost the election. Everybody pretty well knew that West Virginia was going to be the deciding primary.

DC: The inauguration of John F. Kennedy in January 1961 was one of the most celebrated presidential ceremonies in recent history. You anchored the event for CBS. Do any special memories stand out after all of these years?

WC: There was a blizzard in Washington the night before the inaugural. It disrupted everything. People didn't arrive on time. Airplanes couldn't get into the airport. The traffic was terrible. Betsy sat eight hours, trying to get from National Airport to the hotel. We had laid cable all down Pennsylvania Avenue for the parade. Water got into the cables, so our guys were pulling cables all night. But the inauguration was very special. Everyone felt Kennedy's speech signaled a new departure, a spirited young approach to government. Robert Frost being on the stand seemed to set a tone for a new administration that would have a focus on the arts and literature. The inaugural parties were more glamorous than any of us remembered any of them having been, despite the weather. And everyone was entranced with the Kennedy family trooping around from inaugural ball to inaugural ball. We were struck by the obvious verve with which they tackled this social chore.

THE LABOR DAY INTERVIEW, SEPTEMBER 2, 1963

DC: I want to discuss that famous program on September 2, 1963, when you interviewed John Kennedy, which served as the debut show of the thirty-minute format for the *Evening News*. It turned out to be an important interview.

WC: It was a major event. Yeah, I flew up to Hyannis in a charter, and I stayed at the motel at Hyannis where the press stayed. We had a bit of a flap the day before the interview because Kennedy's press secretary, Pierre Salinger, leaked a story that the president would make an important comment on Vietnam. I was upset because it implied that I was serving as a press conduit for the administration. Salinger and I exchanged some heated words about that. But, obviously, the president was going to say whatever he wanted to say during the interview, whether or not I asked him. So at one point, Kennedy said, referring to the Vietnamese government, "In the final analysis, it's their war. They are the ones who have to win it or lose it." Then he added a comment about the South Vietnamese leadership. A couple of days after this, Diem, the president of South Vietnam, was assassinated. There was speculation at the time that Kennedy had used the broadcast to send the message telling Diem to get out or that he'd be removed.

Now, after the interview, I got on the phone and called Don Hewitt. They were sending the tape down by landline, and I said, "You know, the president planted that Vietnam thing with us. I don't think we ought to use it." Hewitt said, "Well, it's pretty good stuff." I said, "Use your own judgment, but I'm sore about it." But we put it on the air. It's generally accepted now that he sent a message to Saigon: "Diem get out or be removed." And that triggered, I assume, a CIA assassination plot. Years later, trying to rewrite history, Salinger wrote a piece for the *New York Times Magazine* in which he said that we had planted this story on Kennedy and had then so edited it as to make it appear that he was sending a message. We didn't edit the damn thing at all. He made a statement, and we left it intact.

DC: Yeah, what Salinger alleged was that Kennedy had praised Diem after he made that statement but that CBS edited that part out. Salinger also makes that claim in his memoir, *With Kennedy*. He calls CBS's version, quote: "A partial distortion of JFK's opinion of President Ngo Diem. Only the unfavorable presidential remarks remained, and JFK's praise of Diem had been deleted."

WC: Well, the record shows that we broadcast it intact.

DC: There's a book called *Making News* by Martin Mayer. His story is that Don Hewitt was getting married, and that his bride was a friend of Kennedy's. The story is that Kennedy asked them to the White House for a drink before they got married. He supposedly asked Hewitt's bride, Frankie, what she wanted for a wedding present. She asked him if he would do an interview on your program because it was expanding to thirty minutes and it would be on a Labor Day Monday. Hewitt had worried that you would have trouble getting an audience because of Labor Day.

WC: Well, that's perfectly probable. Don, being Don, was terribly proud of the fact that he claimed Frankie was one of the president's girlfriends. He exulted in this. I think this was one of her appeals to him, probably.

DC: Had you heard that story before?

WC: I hadn't heard it before. But as I say, it makes all the sense in the world.

DC: Mayer criticizes the interview and calls it a pseudo-event staged to make the *Evening News* look important.

WC: Oh, for heaven's sake.

DC: He says, "In retrospect, it is proof that even pseudo events eventually make history, because . . ." and then he goes into the Diem overthrow.

WC: How does he figure pseudo-event? I don't understand that.

DC: He refers to events staged for television. He calls them "pseudo events."

WC: How in hell do you do an interview with the president of the United States without staging it? Staging it in the sense you've got to put him down in a chair and put the interviewer down in a chair and have cameras there. Is that staging an event? That's some of that drivel that people write about television, I think. They have no sense of proportion or balance.

THE ASSASSINATION OF JOHN F. KENNEDY

DC: Well, let's go to 1963 and discuss your coverage of the assassination of President Kennedy and the impact the event had on television news.

WC: We had been in the new broadcast newsroom on the twenty-ninth floor of the Graybar Building for not quite three months. It was a very handy arrangement. The news printers were in the back of the room, right beyond the news desk. I was actually at my desk having lunch. I was in my shirtsleeves, tie undone. It was lunch hour, so most of the staff was gone. I very seldom went out for lunch. Suddenly, the five bells rang on the wire printer, signaling that a bulletin was coming in. UP's Merriman Smith sent the first bulletin that shots had been heard as the president's motorcade passed through the streets of downtown Dallas. I immediately shouted out to everybody, "Got a shooting in Dallas!" And then the next bulletin came through almost instantly and said the president's motorcade had broken off from the parade route and was on the way to a hospital. It was all within a minute or so. I said, "Let's get on the air. Let's get on the air." We didn't have a camera warmed up, so I ran over to a radio booth next door, and that's when they put the "CBS News Bulletin" slide on the air: "We interrupt this program." I went on the air with the bulletin, but it was a voice over the CBS slide. By that time, we had a little more information, and we stayed on the air for a brief period of time.

DC: But the slide is still up all this time.

WC: This is just a slide, "CBS News Bulletin." Now we knew they'd arrived at Parkland Hospital. The president appeared to be wounded. I believe that material went on the audio only. And then the camera finally became available. So I moved to my news desk, and from there on out, we were on camera all day. It was another hour or so before we got the information from Dallas that the president was dead. First of all, there was an unofficial report that he might be, and then the official report. Eddie Barker of KRLD, the news director of our Dallas affiliate, did some superb reporting with his staff. Dan Rather was also there. He was doing a hell of a job. [*Rather was at the Dallas Market Hall, waiting for JFK to arrive. CBS correspondent Robert Pierpoint was at Parkland Hospital.*] This was Rather's next big moment after Hurricane Carla. Because of Barker and Rather, we were on top of the story throughout. We had the story of the policeman's murder—J. D. Tippit, I guess it was. And then we reported the capture of Lee Harvey Oswald in the theater and Johnson taking the oath of office in Air Force One with Judge Sarah Hughes. It's funny how, if you cover enough news over a long period of time, how the stories all interrelate somehow or other. I had covered the confirmation fight in the Texas state legislature when Sarah Hughes was nominated by Governor Jimmy Allred and they weren't going to confirm a woman judge.

DC: So Sarah Hughes was a name that was well known to you, sitting up here in New York.

WC: Well known to me, yeah. Suddenly, Sarah Hughes is in the news. Hughes's confirmation fight was a big deal in Texas at the time. Anyway, the critical moment came when we had to announce the death of the president, and I had some problem with that. I choked up a bit at the moment I had to announce the death. We knew it was coming, but still it was hard to say. I was just desperately filling in at the moment.

DC: You took your glasses off and looked up at the clock. Was that a way to keep from looking at the camera?

WC: I think that's probably so. I know it wasn't conscious.

DC: One of the most famous moments in the history of television.

WC: Yeah. A terrible moment. But I was on the air until about six thirty that evening, when they said that Charles Collingwood would relieve me for a while. So I got up from the desk, and for the first time, I realized that I was in my shirtsleeves. Frank Stanton had issued an edict: "No man is ever supposed to appear in shirtsleeves at CBS News." Here I was on all afternoon without a coat. I was too busy doing other things to worry about that. My sleeves were rolled up, hair tousled, wearing my glasses, the whole thing. I was really just a disreputable character there on the air as far as my appearance went.

DC: How long were you off the air?

WC: Only about an hour or so. I don't remember for sure.

DC: Did you stay on coverage off and on that whole weekend?

WC: Oh, yeah. Right on through the funeral. One of the great misfortunes at CBS was we were off the air when Ruby shot Oswald. I watched it on one of the competing networks. We got on the air pretty quickly thereafter, but we missed the drama of that moment.

DC: Talking about the Kennedy assassination coverage, Martin Mayer raises the question about why television news kept cutting back and forth between the funeral scenes and the operations of government. For a few moments, we would be viewing the casket and the grieving widow and the children, and then the networks would cut back to an image of yet another leader coming in to meet with President Johnson at the

White House. Mayer suggests that it was a conscious effort on the part of network news administrators to convey to the public that despite this horrible event, it was business as usual and that there would be continuity in our government.

WC: Well, I'm not aware of any conscious effort to do that, but it would seem to me a perfectly reasonable thing to do. It's very definitely part of the story. I think that's the way they should have handled it. I'm sure the next day, the *New York Times* had the lead story of the funeral, and the second story was that the government goes on. That seems to me good journalism.

DC: Les Midgley later participated in a seminar where he was asked if that was a conscious decision by the networks to keep people from panicking over the assassination—sort of an attempt at social control.

WC: Oh, that's ridiculous. I don't think anybody was thinking about keeping people from panicking. I think it's just a journalistic function to show that the government's continuing to function.

DC: Midgley answered the question at the seminar by saying he was just doing his job.

WC: I don't know why it would be an issue.

DC: Well, I think it's just simply people who are interested in the question of how much the networks attempt to control people's behavior. I think they're using this as an example.

WC: I think they assume that these things that happen on the network are far more sophisticated than they are.

DC: You and Dan Rather did a special report on the Warren Commission report on the assassination early in 1965. Television critic Jack Gould wrote in the *New York Times* that the program was one of the more remarkable documentaries in television history up until that time.

WC: It was terrific. Les Midgley and I really conceived the documentary. There was so much doubt cast on the Warren Commission report that we also doubted it. So we decided to examine the Warren Commission and see if it could be proved. We spent over a million dollars, which was an immense amount of money in those days for a documentary. We reconstructed the ballistics tests and the audio tests. We looked at all the available films, including the Zapruder film. We reconstructed the entire thing. We talked to a lot of the witnesses. We concluded that nothing else could be proved beyond what the Warren Commission was able to establish. In other words, we endorsed the Warren Commission report that it was carried out by a single assassin and there was no conspiracy. It was perfectly possible to fire those three shots in that amount of time. It was perfectly possible with that particular rifle to get that kind of accuracy. Now, what we didn't have to go on was the same material that the Warren Commission did not have, and that was the fact that there had been a CIA plot against Castro, which alters the entire picture when considering the conspiracy issue. And obviously, to my mind, the fact that there's not been another investigation with the same kind of cachet that the Warren Commission had is, to me, a function of the CIA convincing the powers that be that it would not be in the nation's best interest to have one.

DC: So you are of a mind today that that real story is still not known?

WC: Oh, I don't think we know the truth at all today. I'm confused now about it. Lyndon Johnson may have thought there was a conspiracy and that it was the result of Castro knowing that we were out to get him and he got our man first. That's not an exact quote, but something like that. And I kind of have a feeling that that may be the story. I have some concern that there may have been a conspiracy.

DC: Do you recall CBS or yourself or any of the other people involved having any kind of pressure put on them while you were reconstructing this Warren Commission report?

WC: No, no, I don't think there was any. I think we were free to do everything we wanted to do.

DC: Do I understand you to say that you think there is a possibility that Oswald and Ruby, or one of them, may have been involved with other people that we just don't know about?

WC: I don't know all the theories that have been brought out, but I don't believe it came from within the U.S. government. But the possibility that Oswald was not acting alone has occurred to me ever since the revelation about the CIA plot against Castro.

importance of Vietnam, and to commit major resources to
the conflict. She writes that, quote: "The CBS team basically
felt it was their story. They were beating everybody and they
... proud of it."

...atization of the situation. But
that is pretty ... ...ned to keep it
...e didn't know ...
...ated when I w ... ...gnition that it
...r corresponde ...
...dn't know abo ... people out
...mplete as he ... ...ence, and all
and so forth ... generally
...r instance. I ... ...am from my
...ar II. I quest ... II was an
...s, in the air ... and the brief...
before it be ... the daily
...right thing whe ... ...rrespondents
...amese. We were ... ...l sometimes th...
...lopment of demo ... officers' part...
...took over that ... ...rrespondents,
...basic rationale ... ...e briefing
...ating rather ra ... ...d integrity.
...forces and we m ...
...I was opposed
...view partly ch ...
...e in 1965. I ha ...
...vast port facili ...
...eed for what at ... ...lot, of cour...
...ur commitment. I ... ...lked.
...ing to have 53,0 ...
...ere. And then I g ...
...alking 53,000, t ...

...rst trip

...t about his

...an excellent book. I think Morley's take on the Vietnam
situation is just right. I would give anything to write that
well. My gosh, I would be satisfied just to think as well as he

CHAPTER SEVENTEEN

Vietnam

DC: The war in Vietnam was probably the major ongoing story that the *CBS Evening News* covered from the mid-1960s through the early 1970s. Let's talk about Vietnam in the period that followed Kennedy's death. You interviewed Premier Ky of South Vietnam on July 18, 1965. I emphasize the exact date because it was very early in the war.

WC: Yeah. At first, I was very much impressed with Ky. He seemed more vibrant, personable, and likable than any of the Vietnamese leaders that I had met up to that time. I was impressed with him until he told me he admired Adolf Hitler. Then I kind of lost the thread, there, I think. But I thought he showed more potential for bringing the country together and that he had a more realistic approach to the war than any of the others.

DC: He made a favorable statement about Adolf Hitler?

WC: Yeah. He said he admired him very much. He thought he was a very effective leader. Hitler understood the use of air power, and that was important to him. Ky was a fighter pilot, of course, himself. He had a lot of gusto about him that I liked.

DC: Was this interview in Vietnam?

WC: Yeah, it was in Vietnam. I believe that was my first trip there.

DC: I just read Morley Safer's recently published book about his return to Vietnam.

WC: That's a fine book by the way. Just beautifully written. It is an excellent book. I think Morley's take on the Vietnam situation is just right. I would give anything to write

Cronkite reporting from Hue, South Vietnam, following the Tet offensive during the Vietnam War, 1968 (DI_05982).

that well. My gosh, I would be satisfied just to think as well as he does. Morley's one of the best. [*Safer's book is* Flashbacks: On Returning to Vietnam, *1990.*]

DC: I'll quote Safer here in talking about your trip to Vietnam, quote: "Walter was too skeptical, too savvy, and had too sensitive a shit detector to be taken in, but Walter can be diverted by machinery, by things with wheels and wings, and especially by things that float, and the military saw to it that he had a chance to see and use everything, go on air strikes, be made to feel an insider. His itinerary was designed to keep him away from correspondents and others permanently based in Vietnam who were considered to be naysayers. It did not entirely work." Safer says that he managed to arrange at least two meetings to counter, quote, "the lies and bogus optimism that had been so carefully orchestrated for Cronkite. One was with an army officer . . . who . . . catalogued the disaster to come. 'With a million men here, we still would not win.'" You had mentioned to me earlier that you were of the World War II generation, and that the people who were running the Vietnam War were some of the people who won World War II. As a result, you were inclined to believe and trust them.

WC: Yeah, that is pretty much true. I think Safer had it pretty close. He didn't know about all my contacts, however. I was not isolated when I was out with the brass. I was not isolated from other correspondents and other things. I worked in Saigon, but he didn't know about it, so I don't think that my isolation was as complete as he would indicate there. But basically, the attitudes and so forth, he's right about. Take General Creighton Abrams, for instance. I'd known him as a lieutenant colonel in World War II. I questioned Abrams quite directly. And there were others, in the air force particularly. In the early stages of the war, before it became our war, I was convinced we were doing the right thing when we provided military advisors to the South Vietnamese. We were trying to preserve the ground for the future development of democracy there. I believed that if the communists took over, that opportunity would be lost forever. That was my basic rationale for being there. That rationale began dissipating rather rapidly with each incremental buildup of American forces and we moved closer and closer to taking over the war. Then I was opposed to what we were doing out there. I think that my view partly changed after coming back from this trip out there in 1965. I had seen the preparations at Cam Ranh Bay for vast port facilities, far more than anybody could conceivably need for what, at that point, Johnson was saying was the limit of our commitment. I thought, why go do all this if you're only going to have 53,000 people—or something around that number—there. And then I got back home to find that, gee, they're still talking 53,000, they're not talking about going to 100,000. I realized that the statements that the American people were being told about the size of our potential commitment out there were untrue. That the military and the White House were planning for a much bigger operation than the American people were ever told. This was, I thought, a terribly unfortunate circumstance.

DC: Barbara Matusow says that CBS was the first news organization except for the *New York Times* to sense the importance of Vietnam and to commit major resources to covering the conflict. She writes that, quote: "The CBS team basically felt it was their story. They were beating everybody and they were proud of it."

WC: That was a slight overdramatization of the situation. But we were proud of our coverage, and we were determined to keep it going.

DC: Do you think you beat NBC and ABC to the recognition that it was a very important story?

WC: Oh, I think there's no doubt about it. We had people out there who were superb. Morley Safer and Jack Laurence and all our guys out there were just great. But, you know, generally, one of the differences that I recognized in Vietnam from my experience as a combat correspondent in World War II was an antagonistic attitude between the correspondents and the briefing officers at the so-called Five o'clock Follies, the daily briefing for the correspondents in Saigon. The correspondents were almost insulting to the briefing officers. And sometimes this brought almost insulting behavior on the briefing officers' part back to the correspondents. But I thought the correspondents, many of them, vastly overdid it. They needled the briefing officers, questioned their good faith, honesty, and integrity. Now, there was good reason to question the information the military was releasing, a great deal of the time, in Vietnam. But on the other hand, it was done like a group of jackals attacking a deer or something. I noticed it especially among the youngest correspondents. It's quite proper for newspeople to always be skeptical. Never be cynical, but always be skeptical. But there was some of this badgering that went on, and I realized that it wasn't done to get information. It wasn't even done for the purpose of impressing the briefing officers. It was done to impress the older correspondents, to try to stake out their ground as knowledgeable war correspondents. I thought there was an awful lot of that in Vietnam. There was some of that in World War II. The more knowledgeable correspondents usually were pretty calm, cool, and collected about it. The questions were loaded, with dynamite in them, but they were on a railroad track straight for the target. These kids were flailing around, trying to uncover something with their lack of knowledge, in many cases. In the early stages, I probably was guilty of that myself during World War II.

DC: After you made that first trip to Vietnam, in 1965, you returned with an upbeat report on the U.S. effort. In her book, Matusow thinks it was noteworthy that as early as 1965, despite your support of the Vietnam effort, you "allowed" Safer, Laurence, Peter Kalischer, and others to file very negative reports about the aspects of the war night after night on the *Evening News*. "Allowed" is her word. She also makes the point that the reporting from Vietnam marked a turning point in television's relationship to the government.

WC: I think that the latter part about the relationship between television and the government is true. Saying that I allowed it, that's pretty ridiculous. I didn't allow or deny anything to the news coverage of the Vietnam War. I had the authority to keep a report off of the air, but I wouldn't have stopped anybody from reporting what they wanted to report. That part is ridiculous. But it certainly was true that I didn't quarrel with their reporting. I took it at face value that they were reporting what they were seeing and what was happening. There were negative reports, certainly, in many ways, but some of them were not. Some of them were stories of heroism and courage and great difficulty. I supported the general principle of being there, at that point. But let me make it perfectly clear, when I talk about supporting the war, this was not an expressed support. This was simply my gut feeling about it. I never said anything on the air about my view of the war.

DC: Bill Moyers has said that he believes that if you had criticized the buildup in 1965, that Johnson could not have gotten away with the buildup in the first place.

WC: Well, I'd be very, very, surprised if that were true. I've never heard that, and I just don't believe it. No, Johnson was riding high, wide, and handsome in 1965. I would have been a mosquito bite on Johnson's rear end; he would have flicked me off like an insect. I'm surprised that Moyers said that. I'll be darned if I had that kind of power in 1965.

"IF I'VE LOST CRONKITE, I'VE LOST THE COUNTRY"

DC: Gates claims that by 1967 you were beginning to change your personal views about the war.

WC: By 1967? Oh yeah, certainly.

DC: Okay, so 1968 rolled around, and, of course, the North Vietnamese launched the Tet offensive in February. Why did you go to Vietnam, Walter, after the Tet offensive?

WC: I wanted to see the situation for myself. But in discussing it with Salant, I suggested that I ought to do a personal report on just what it seemed to me. We had all these conflicting reports coming in on one side and then the other. The American public was utterly confused now because of the Tet offensive. The Vietcong had risen. The North Vietnamese had gotten all the way down into Saigon. Villages we claimed were pacified immediately went back to the Vietcong. We lost them. We hadn't won any hearts and minds at all, apparently. I told Salant that it would be a good idea if I did first-person reports: "Why don't I go out there and just try to bring perspective through one person's eyes rather than try to be so unprejudiced and so unbiased?" We were being so objective we were not giving any guidance really. And it was with that intention that I went to Vietnam.

DC: Who went out with you?

WC: Since we had all the correspondents in place, I went by myself. I took the route through the Soviet Union and then down to Bangkok and on into the war.

DC: According to my notes, you interviewed South Vietnam president Thieu; Nguyen Xuan Oanh, who was one of the loyal opposition leaders; and Lieutenant General R. E. Cushman Jr. You also went to Hue.

WC: The battle was still on in Hue when I went up there. The main part of the battle was over, but the shelling, mortaring, and patrolling was still going on.

DC: Had you expected to find a battle at Hue?

WC: I knew the fight was still going on. Yeah, I went in with a military unit in a truck. We had to wear helmets.

DC: Did the military try to discourage you from going?

WC: No, no, you could go anywhere then. All you do is hitch a ride and go. That's the way correspondents ought to operate. Of course, in Vietnam they operated without any censorship. I don't believe in that. I think there ought to be censorship after you get there, but you ought to get the chance to see things with your own eyes. Then you can argue with the censor about what you put out. So anyway, that's what I did. I got into Hue without any trouble, but we were heavily shelled that night. I went out with a marine patrol led by a Major Clavell, and we took the little perimeter roads. We got a little firing, but nothing substantial. The shelling that night was the worst. There were several members of the press around there, including an Italian, three Americans, and a Canadian. They put us in a little private house right by the marine compound. It was a press camp, sort of, and the area was heavily shelled that night.

DC: Midgley discusses your trip to Hue in his book. He says that General William Westmoreland told you that Hue was under control, but that when you arrived there, you found that the marines were engaged in "a ferocious battle to recapture the city." He says that, quote: "Cronkite's CBS colleagues were impressed and more than a little alarmed by the way he went charging headlong into the street by them."

WC: Well, I joined that patrol, but I wasn't charging headlong into the battle. I was doing what everybody else would do, covering the story.

DC: Do you remember any difference between what Westmoreland told you about Hue and what you found?

WC: I don't really remember that, but I would not be surprised if that were so, because that was the story Westmoreland was giving about everything, about all these towns. I didn't believe it at the time, because I was hearing reports from other people. I don't think I went to Hue because I thought it was secure. I think I went there because I thought fighting was still going on there despite what he said, and I wanted to prove it for myself.

DC: Did you see any damage?

WC: Oh yeah. Hue was a beautiful old medieval city that was destroyed almost totally.

DC: Now, I understand that on your last night in Saigon, you had dinner with a group of correspondents at the Caravelle Hotel. According to Midgley, at this dinner you were "clearly distressed," and you asked over and over again, "How could it have happened?" You supposedly meant the mess in Vietnam. And the correspondents told you the whole thing had been wrong from the first, and a cover-up had been employed from the very beginning. Gates has written that, quote, "Ernie Leiser sensed that a slow, hard anger was building up inside [Cronkite]. Years later Leiser would recall 'I think Walter must have felt that he had been had, and he got mad, because he felt that this was an inexcusable and maybe a criminal deceit by the federal government.'"

WC: He's got it right. I was angry about it.

DC: After you returned from Vietnam, you broadcast a prime-time special at the end of which you made your famous statement on the air that, quote, "it seems now more certain than ever that the bloody experience of Vietnam is to end in a stalemate.... To say that we are closer to victory today is to believe, in the face of the evidence, the optimists who have been wrong in the past. To suggest we are on the edge of defeat is to yield to unreasonable pessimism.... It is increasingly clear to this reporter that the only rational way out then will be to negotiate, not as victors, but as an honorable people who lived up to their pledge to defend democracy, and did the best they could." You have stated elsewhere that this was the only time in your career that you had spoken out so personally on a controversial subject. Was this a hard thing for you to do?

WC: No, it wasn't at all. I'd made up my mind. As I say, I went out there with some idea of what I was going to do, and after I returned, my personal opinion about the state of the war would be expressed. No, I was rather proud of CBS and their willingness publicly to do it, and was delighted to do it.

DC: According to all accounts, CBS management was catching hell from the Johnson administration because of CBS News's coverage of Vietnam.

WC: That sort of pressure never got down to us on the news desk. Salant protected us to the very end from it. We never felt any daily pressure about putting these reports on or not putting them on. But we got constant pressure from the affiliates. Some stations threatened to pull out entirely. We got all kinds of terrible threats. I went out and met with the affiliates every time they had a convention, and spoke to them. I used to get comments such as "I know you really don't mean it, Walter. I know they put those words in your mouth." That used to make me absolutely furious. I got that all the time from social friends. People would grab me by the arm and say, "I know you don't really want to say those things." It was terrible. There was an awful lot of pressure, but, as I say, it never came down to Salant ever walking into the newsroom and meeting with us and saying we can't do these pieces. If that ever happened, everybody participated in the conspiracy of silence to keep me from knowing. As a matter of fact, the proof is the fact that they let me do those broadcasts on the war.

DC: To quote Gary Gates: "Walter Cronkite's criticism of the war was cautious and quite mild. He did not align himself with the militant anti-war groups. Instead, he reached out to his natural constituency, the moderates. Walter Cronkite sensed that the mood across the country was shifting, and that, in speaking out the way he did, he was reflecting that shift, even as he was helping to guide it." David Halberstam says, "It was the first time in American history that a war had been declared over by a commentator."

WC: Yeah, that's a great quote. I like that.

DC: After you made your statement about the futility of the Vietnam War, that's when LBJ supposedly told George Christian, his press spokesman, that if he had lost Walter Cronkite, he had lost the country. You told *Rolling Stone* a few years later in an interview that you would "hate to think that a popular newscaster could turn around American public opinion on anything. Nothing could be more dangerous than that for democracy." [*In his memoir,* A Reporter's Life, *Cronkite incorrectly quoted LBJ as saying he had lost "middle America" rather than "the country." In addition, he incorrectly cited Bill Moyers as the source for the quote. In a letter to me shortly after the publication of Cronkite's memoir in 1996, the late George Christian, who is the actual source for LBJ's quote, verified that the correct version is "If I've lost Cronkite, I've lost the country."*]

WC: I believe that to be true. You see, I don't think I turned around public opinion on the war at all. I think what Gates says is true. I was reflecting it, probably, more than directing it. But I didn't turn Lyndon Johnson around either, but this probably pushed him over. He was beginning to feel misled and misused by the military. I think particularly the Tet offensive had disturbed and alarmed him because, first of all, he later told me that the military said it couldn't happen. And when it did happen, the military claimed it as a great victory for us. As Westmoreland told me," If they could give me 200,000 more men, I can finish this thing off." I think that Johnson felt just like most of the American people did at that point on: let's just get out of this. But the president couldn't get out himself. He was too deeply committed. So the thing to do was to get out of the job.

1968 DEMOCRATIC CONVENTION

DC: Since we are talking about the Vietnam War, let's discuss the 1968 Democratic convention in Chicago, because that convention was all about the war. Did you anticipate trouble at the convention?

WC: We anticipated trouble. Before we ever got there, the Grant Park encampment was taking place there at Lake Michigan, right outside the Hilton Hotel, which was the Democratic headquarters. That's where the Weathermen and the SDS and the hippie, anti–Vietnam War people camped out. They were permitted to camp there by the police. Senator Eugene McCarthy and Hubert Humphrey were in the same hotel. But anyway, we anticipated trouble. We were geared for it. There had already been some police raids in Grant Park, some ugliness. So it began right on schedule.

DC: So you began your coverage, and then things really started getting hot. At one point during the coverage, Dan Rather was roughed up on the convention floor while on camera.

WC: Yeah. I said something like, "Dan, I think we've got a bunch of thugs out there." Something like that.

DC: Gates says that it was "the first and only time in his long career that Walter Cronkite displayed such undisguised wrath on the air."

WC: I think that's probably right. Yeah, that was the same convention that NBC's John Chancellor was hustled out of the hall, and he said, "I'm broadcasting from somewhere in custody."

DC: Who was roughing people up?

WC: Mayor Richard Daley's people were. It was very interesting. Daley had two or three motives for trying to keep tight control on that convention. One was purely crowd control, with all these demonstrators around. He didn't like them in the first place, you know. These "unpatriotic, dirty, unwashed people" just weren't his kind of people. And so there was a natural antagonism on the part of Daley that was easy to transmit to the police, who had exactly the same viewpoint. Another was civic pride. He didn't like the idea of this all being seen on the air from his city of Chicago.

    The third thing was, though, strictly political. I'm not sure about this, but I think that Daley had the impression that Lyndon was hoping for a draft from that convention. Daley was doing everything he could to manipulate the convention. He packed the galleries with his sympathizers, who he could order to do anything he wanted. By doing so, he hoped to perhaps control the convention by public demonstrations in the gallery. He could either silence people on the floor or he could support them, by packing the gallery. That required controlling tickets and a lot of other things. But it also required keeping the floor running the way he wanted it to run. So when there were little demonstrations here and there on the floor, he could either break them up or support them. That was where our reporters started getting in trouble. They were trying to find out what these demonstrations were about. Why were these people on the floor? Who were they? This was when the thugs ushered our correspondents out and tried to keep them away. And as a matter of fact, at one point, I believe it was Abe Ribicoff who attacked Daley from the podium. Daley was sitting out about six rows in front of him. And we caught Daley on camera, mouthing ugly words to him. That was all going on. Of course, the demonstrators outside the convention were also getting beaten up and very badly manhandled by the police. The Kerner Commission later called it a police riot. And, frankly, that's what it was. The Chicago police just went wild. They were just wild men, beating on these people for no reason. It was a terrible scene.

DC: And that's how Rather got into trouble with Daley's men down there?

WC: Yeah, he was trying to report on their little organized demonstrations.

DC: Didn't you have an exclusive interview with Daley while all of this was going on?

WC: Yeah. That was the worst tactical error I ever made in my career, I suppose. It misfired. I kept after Daley's office for an interview. He didn't give any interviews. One of his aides said, "We'll keep after him. I know that Mrs. Daley loves you. He'll give you an interview if you just keep after him." He agreed to come on the broadcast, but not until just before we went on the air for the *Evening News*. I got notice a couple of hours beforehand that he would be there. Daley was a very smooth politician when answering questions. He just didn't answer any questions he didn't want to answer. He was a great diverter of attention to something else. He always had a pea under the three pods. I thought, "They're not going to give me enough time here to eventually get a story out of him. He's going to divert the story." Now, I thought that they would have him in the outer room, which is the way we normally did interviews. They would tell me he was there, and when I got the moment for it, I would invite him in. So I decided that before Daley came in, I was going to make a statement to the viewing audience that the mayor had complained that the press had been biased against him and the Chicago police during the convention and that we wanted him to give us an explanation for that accusation. And then I would say, "Mayor Daley's here. Please come in." I would then tell him, "Mayor Daley, I'm not going to ask you any questions. Please go ahead and tell us how you can explain this police brutality."

I never had that chance. When he arrived, he just walked right into the booth and up to my desk! I had to make my introduction with him sitting there, which, I guess I weaseled on that a little bit, you know. I could not help myself from asking a couple of questions that destroyed my entire plan. As soon as I did that, I was back in the questioning mode of an interviewer, and I should have been asking different questions.

And so it was an absolute disaster. Which got me an awful lot of well-deserved criticism. It was a low point.

DC: Gary Gates quotes you as saying about the Daley interview: "I was deeply involved emotionally and I was seeking desperately to maintain my objectivity." Gates says, "Yet in its overall tone, the Daley encounter did not differ significantly from other interviews Cronkite had conducted over the years. In truth, Cronkite had no real instinct for the jugular. The evidence suggests that this quality . . . was also a large part of Cronkite's appeal."

WC: Well, yes, I know what he's talking about, and I think he missed the point by a wide margin. My interview technique is not to have the blood spurt from the open vein, but to have it drain slowly from the body until you see the white corpse sitting there. I'd like to think it's an intellectual, thinking man's interview. You've got to understand the subtleties in one of my interviews. You've got to have some sense of what's there before the interview takes place. It's not as cold as putting two men in a ring with gloves on and leading them out to the center and telling them to fight. It's a much different approach than that. And I do think that there's no question it lacks showmanship and that it's not in the best style of present-day television, probably. It's much more the Bill Moyers approach. I'd love to have programs like Bill does. That kind of thing could only be on the Public Broadcasting System. Really, that's my kind of interview, to spend an hour developing the personality. As I said earlier, I never did think I was very good at the fast interview. You know, the "you've got five minutes to talk to this guy" type of interview. I think in the other interviews, I've developed a lot of very important information from people, as Gary Gates would say, without ever appearing to strike the jugular.

DC: Maintaining the sense of fair play.

WC: Yes. That wasn't precisely the intent with Daley, though. I knew we only had a few minutes for Daley. I just didn't want to get involved in a dialogue with him. The intent there was fair play in the sense of giving Daley airtime, but let him hang himself if he was going to. Or that was what I figured. It just misfired.

THE HANOI HILTON

DC: Much later on, you traveled to North Vietnam for the release of American prisoners of war. How did that come about?

WC: I suppose we had some information that something was about to break in this regard. I decided to try to get into Vietnam for the occasion, if possible. I had a promise from the North Vietnamese, who we had dealt with at the UN, that if I went to Laos, they could get me into Hanoi for this prisoner exchange. We didn't know how it was going to take place, didn't know whether any press were going to be invited or what. But I was trying to make my own arrangements. The North Vietnamese said if you can get to Laos, we can get you into Hanoi. They said that when I got to Laos, I should stand by and they would get word to me about when and how to get into Hanoi. So I went to Laos and was there alone a couple of days. I contacted the North Vietnamese there in Laos, and they hadn't heard anything about it, of course. They said they'd check on it and get back to me at the hotel. Well, I'm there a day or so, and then suddenly David Kennerly, a photographer from *Time*, shows up, and then another newsperson from NBC. All of a sudden, everybody's piling in on my exclusive story. We realized that the North Vietnamese had told them all the same thing. So here we are, all assembling there, and that's the way it all worked out.

DC: Do you remember much about entering North Vietnam and Hanoi?

WC: Oh yeah, they sent out a broken-down old airplane for us, and we flew up there. The trip into Hanoi was not shocking from the standpoint of bomb damage to that degree, although it was quite a lot. The bridges into Hanoi were all down. There was some damage along the streets, but it wasn't a destroyed city by any means. The people looked downtrodden and terribly poor. The economy clearly was seriously disrupted, we could tell that. There was some motor traffic on the street, but an awful lot of foot traffic too. The motor traffic was pretty well broken-down old vehicles. The bicycles were all broken down themselves. It was clearly a destitute economy.

DC: David Kennerly told me that you were all taken to the Hotel Metropole for a lunch of beer and bananas.

WC: Yes, oh God, it was incredible. There was no food at all.

DC: After that wonderful feast, they then took you to the prisoner camp, which the Americans called the Hanoi Hilton.

WC: Oh, I remember that quite well. It was right in the center of town. They took us to a reception room, where we stood around while the commandant gave us a briefing about how well the prisoners had been treated, which, of course, was not true. Then he invited us to go see them in their cells. The doors were open to the cells, and there was a guard in each cell. We were permitted to go to the doors and look in and to photograph if we wished, and that was all. We could not to talk to them. They were not permitted to talk to us, and we couldn't talk to them. But I found a way to communicate with them. The prisoners didn't know what was happening. They had not been told they were being released. When I attempted to talk to them, we were shut up. The guards brandished their bayonets and guns. So I found a way to talk to them. I conversed with my cameraman. We talked about the shots. I would hold up my hand, framing the shot, and talk to him, but instead of talking about the shot, I would say to the cameraman that I understood that we had to be at the airport at ten thirty the next morning because they're all going to be put aboard a plane and flown out of Vietnam. These guys' eyes lit up, and when they did, the guard got suspicious and then shut us up. But I got the information across cell by cell as we went down the line. That was the first they knew they were actually being released. Of course, they suspected it when they saw us come in, but the information about timing and so forth they got for the first time that day.

DC: Did you think the prison had been cleaned up for your inspection?

WC: Well, I think so to a degree. Although we did later go back with John McCain, who was a former POW, and he had seen these pictures too and said that they were fairly representative.

DC: Well, let's talk about that trip you made back to Hanoi with John McCain, who, I should point out, later became a senator from Arizona. What were the circumstances for that?

WC: Well, some time after the war was over—I don't know, I think maybe it was the fifth anniversary—but we decided to take a former prisoner back and look at Hanoi today through the eyes of one who had been a prisoner there. We took John McCain back to the Hanoi Hilton and showed him a cell, which he looked at from the outside but would not take a step into. We were taken into the headquarters and given the inevitable tea while we were briefed by the commandant. The place was now an army photograph center, so there were no prisoners there. Or at least I don't think so, unless they were covering up. But the commandant knew the history of the place, but not from personal experience, so he wasn't a lot of help. But McCain met a couple of his former captors. They talked about McCain sort of reluctantly. There wasn't much real byplay.

DC: Do you believe that there are American POWs still in Vietnam?

WC: Oh, I find that very hard to believe. If there are, my inclination is to believe that they are defectors. I think there may be defectors who are around, and they confuse the issue by being seen. It's very possible. But that there are people being held against their will, I just doubt it. I don't know why they would do it in the first place. But I think some of these people, in various organizations, are preying upon the hopes of people who have loved ones missing out there.

Texas in 1969?) had with Eisenhower. These "Interviews under the Oak Trees" were conducted on his ranch. CBS eventually broadcast four interviews, conducted over a period from 1970 to 1973. Were those interviews difficult to do? He must not have been the easiest person to interview.

...n't remember them being particularly

...had an understanding that these interviews could ...ently reveal highly sensitive information. We had an ...: that we would record the interview on audiotape ...ously with the videotape. We turned that tape over to ...hen we finished. He had had a certain amount of time ...that tape. Anything he wanted deleted on ...

he wanted to do?

...series, after much negotiation ...Krim I think was the principal on ...his televised biography.

...al security wou...
...he lost
...een don...
...n we got
...t we co...
...ssassin...
...s expire...
...on the
...the grou...
...issue,
...used, s...
...er this,
...rview.

...Johnson t...
...u in any ...

...sn't at all. It seems to me this was a vastly ...rprise. This was not a current news interview, ...should not be purchased under any circumstances.

...e. You
...tate
...atch."
...it.
...And
...ading
...ex
...to.
...ng

...to embarrass the president by saying I couldn't accept the ...tch in front of them. So I thought, well, I'll accept it then
...personal presentation." Well, I didn't

CHAPTER EIGHTEEN

LBJ

DC: After Lyndon Johnson left the presidency and returned to Texas in 1969, you conducted his television memoir like you had with Eisenhower. These *Interviews under the Oak Trees* were conducted on his ranch. CBS eventually broadcast four interviews, conducted over a period from 1970 to 1973. Were those interviews difficult to do? He must not have been the easiest person to interview.

WC: No, he wasn't, but I don't remember them being particularly difficult.

DC: Were they interviews that he wanted to do?

WC: Oh, this was a contracted series, after much negotiation with Arthur Krim and others. Krim, I think, was the principal on his side. We contracted for his televised biography.

DC: So he was paid to do them?

WC: Yes, which made it much easier than a regular interview, obviously, although we had some problems. He was flanked by aides at all times during the interviews. Who was that LBJ administration guy who the University of Texas hired as a professor? He was the former national security advisor.

DC: Walt Rostow.

WC: Rostow was there, and others. They sat right off camera with files between their legs, and they'd go through files and slip him papers as he was doing the interview. It was completely different from Eisenhower, who had no notes or help during our interviews. This was mostly Vietnam-era stuff. He was very careful with that. He never yielded anything. It was always other people's fault, mostly. There was only one place

Cronkite interviewing President Lyndon B. Johnson at the White House, January 9, 1969 (LBJ Library Photograph by Yoichi Okamoto, A7515-5).

where we got in serious difficulty with him, and it ended the series a little prematurely. The problem was that he had not dismissed the idea of a conspiracy in the death of Kennedy. I forget what the quote was, but that was the thrust of it. I asked him whom else he suspected was involved in the assassination, and he said he wouldn't know that. I didn't get anywhere in pressing the question.

Now, we had an understanding that these interviews could inadvertently reveal highly sensitive information. We had an agreement that we would record the interview on audiotape simultaneously with the videotape. We turned that tape over to Johnson when we finished. He had had a certain amount of time to review that tape. Anything he wanted deleted on the grounds of national security would be deleted. But beyond that time allotment, he lost that right. We had full rights to everything that had been done. We were well beyond the time limit, weeks later, when we got a phone call from Krim, saying the president decided that we could not use that part of the interview about Kennedy's assassination. So we said, "We're terribly sorry. The time has expired." This led into a major fight that was carried out on the highest levels of CBS. Finally, CBS was forced to yield on the grounds of national security. I couldn't see the security issue, frankly, but they convinced us that this shouldn't be used, so we excised it. But in the bitterness that developed over this, we just never picked up the option to do another interview.

DC: CBS paid Johnson to do these interviews. Does that seem similar to you in any way to the practice of journalism by paycheck?

WC: No, it doesn't at all. It seems to me this was a vastly different enterprise. This was not a current news interview, which certainly should not be purchased under any circumstances. These were the man's memoirs. That's something he owns. It's his property, if you please, and it seems perfectly proper for him to sell those, even as he would write a book and sell a book. It is the televised book. But that does not apply to Richard Nixon. Nixon never permitted an interview, and he didn't write about his experience in Watergate. He ducked any explanation to the American people about Watergate. He never went on trial, and he never testified. He owed that explanation to the American people simply in his capacity as a public servant. He didn't own that. He owed us that. Therefore, he could not, in my mind, ethically sell that, as he did to David Frost. That was a completely different situation to me.

DC: You interviewed Johnson at his ranch. What was that experience like?

WC: I had great times down there at the ranch. I enjoyed it. There were several funny incidents. I remember one was about my Rolex watch. I had been presented a watch by the Rolex people. Dick Salant reacted to this with some considerable distaste, as did I. I'd never received gifts for anything, and this came absolutely out of the blue. The Swiss president of Rolex, the American president of Rolex, and a photographer just appeared in the newsroom one afternoon and said they wanted to see me. My secretary presented their cards, and I said, "Gee, I'm busy, but go ahead. They can come in for a minute." They came in and launched right into it, with the guy taking pictures of the president of Rolex giving me a fancy gold Rolex watch. And I said, "Why are you giving me this?" He said, "You are known around the world. You are honored as a great American. This watch has never been given to anybody except heads of state. You are being honored as the only person other than heads of state to ever receive this watch. It is a special presentation watch." And I said, "What about these pictures you're taking here?" And he said, "That's to have one picture to hang in the hall leading to my office. I have all the heads of state we've given them to. There will be no publicity, Mr. Cronkite, absolutely none about this at all. This is a personal presentation." Well, I didn't want to embarrass the president by saying I couldn't accept the watch in front of them. So I thought, well, I'll accept it, then worry about it later.

I went right in to Salant's office and told him exactly what happened. I had figured out by then why it happened, I think. Former astronaut Wally Schirra was working on the air with me to provide his expertise on the manned space program. Wally is an unconscious or otherwise—and I suspect conscious—plug artist. He would get plugs in for products on the air. He was constantly throwing something in. For example, our clock in our studio got out of sync with the countdown clock at one point, so Wally and I got into a big discussion on timekeeping and timepieces. This led Wally into saying, "What you need, Walter, is a Rolex, like the astronauts. We have these special Rolex watches." So it occurred to me that, by God, I was getting paid off for Wally's Rolex plug. I didn't tell Dick that part of the story. I just told him about my accepting the watch. He said, "What do you think the watch is worth?" Well, I don't know watches. I never cared about watches. I said, "I don't know Dick. Maybe 350 dollars?" And Salant said, "Oh, well, damn it, you've done it. I think I'd return it, but I won't embarrass you if you want to keep it." So I kept it. I wore it around for quite a while.

Shortly thereafter, I was doing one of the memoir interviews with Johnson, and we were talking about space. He'd been in charge of the space program, and he was very much involved in it. On that occasion, we were sitting under the oak trees, indeed, on the banks of the Pedernales River. I was wearing this Rolex when I was doing the interview. Suddenly, Johnson was staring at my crotch. I figured my fly is undone and reached down, surreptitiously checking. But he kept staring, and I realize finally he was staring at my wrist. He interrupted the interview and said, "Where did you get that watch?" I said, "Well, the president of Rolex gave it to me." He said, "That son of a bitch gave me one just like it, and he told me he only gave them to heads of state. How do you happen to have one of those?" We had a confrontation right there on my watch. I think he thought maybe I'd stolen it from his dresser or something.

Just as an aside here, I should add that I wore that watch around until I took it to a Rolex dealer downtown to have the band tightened. They said, "Where did you get this? I've never seen a watch like that. God, that's a beautiful Rolex." I told him the story. He said, "My God, you know what this is, don't you? That watchband is platinum." He said the watch was worth $12,000. I goddamned near fainted. I went home and put it right in the safe deposit, where it's been ever since. I've never had it out. At one time it was worth $60,000.

DC: That was a nice thank-you from Rolex. Well, going back to the LBJ interviews, did you stay at the LBJ Ranch or did you have to commute back and forth?

WC: I actually stayed at the ranch. We had the CBS crewmen down there, but they commuted from a town nearby. We worked early in the morning, at six o'clock or seven or something, for a couple of hours, and then he took a nap and then went to lunch. We were invited to all share lunch one day, including the whole crew. We had a pretty assistant producer there, and Johnson insisted she sit on one side of him, and I sat at the other side of the table. Mrs. Johnson, of course, was at her end of the table. The rest of the crew, the producer, and the cameraman, everybody was there for lunch. Now, normally the producer and I ate with the Johnsons, and the rest of the staff ate separately. And incidentally, they charged us for the meals. They later sent a bill to CBS. That's all right, you know, eight or ten people eating. But we thought it was so nice they were giving us sandwiches and were always saying, "Please, won't you have some more?" Then we had a bill come in. But all the presidents that I have known have been like that, not just Johnson. You have to be a tightwad to get elected president, apparently.

At any rate, Johnson came to lunch wearing his underwear and a robe. As he got exercised talking, the robe would fall open, showing his hairy chest, navel, and big fat stomach. Mrs. Johnson would give him this look, and he would disgustedly pull the robe around him. A moment later, it would fall open again. She would give him another look, and he would pull the robe tight again. Then he kept complaining about his diet. "They make me eat this gruel, and you people have that nice lunch." Then they brought dessert. He said, "I'm not allowed to have that." It was chocolate ice cream or something. So they brought him a bread pudding. Then he looked at me and said, "I can't have ice cream. Lady Bird won't let me have anything I like anymore." And then he said, "How is it?" He took a big scoop out of the girl's dish, and into his mouth it went. "Ah, it's not bad, but I can't have it. I've got to have this bread pudding. Is yours all right?" Then he took another scoop out. [laughs] Lyndon Johnson was certainly bigger than life, I tell you. Did I tell you about the night that Allan Shivers and I had dinner with him up in the White House?

DC: You mean former Texas governor Shivers? I don't think so.

WC: The same man. Well, there was some kind of a bill signing at the White House, a reception-type thing that I attended. And of all people, Allan Shivers was there. You know, he and Johnson didn't get along. I was about to leave, and I told the president good-bye, and he said, "Stay and have dinner with us. It'll just be with Lady Bird and me." I said, "Sure. What the hell, yeah, you bet." After he had my acceptance, he said, "Allan Shivers is also going to stay and have dinner." Well, I realized now I'm probably going to be the moderator of whatever was going to transpire between him and Shivers, or perhaps I was going to be the witness. We went upstairs to the private quarters, and of course Johnson showed off to Shivers, naturally. We sat on the Truman porch overlooking the south lawn and the Washington Mall. It was a nice evening. We had a couple of drinks, and then we went in to dinner. Somewhat to my relief, there was never any problem through the whole evening between him and Shivers. Shivers sat on one side and I on the other, and LBJ at the head and Lady Bird at the foot of the family table. And the only thing that was notable about the evening at all was how appalled I was with his talk about the Vietnam War. This was possibly inspired by his need to show off to Shivers, but also possibly the way he looked at things. He started talking just like Dr. Strangelove: "I'm going to send in MY planes. I'm going to send in MY ships. MY ships are going to lie offshore, and they're going to shell those little bastards. I'm going to send in MY troops. MY troops are going to move in here, and MY troops are going over there." It was mad, really mad. It was this imperial-presidency thing—pretty shocking, as a matter of fact. I never felt quite the same about him after that, frankly.

DC: Did Shivers seem uncomfortable by it?

WC: No, not necessarily, but he was hard to read. Actually, I was so fascinated by Johnson, I didn't pay much attention to how Shivers was reacting.

DC: Do you think Johnson was an emotionally tortured person?

WC: Yes, I do. I think that Vietnam was more than he could take, really. You know, he did so many domestic programs that were good. And to go out knowing he was going down in history as the president of an unpopular war, and fearing what history's judgment would be. I think he began to believe that there were things about that war that he didn't know. But that evening with him in the White House fed some information to me that led me to some of the right questions later on.

DC: There was a lot of talk about CBS's relationship with Lyndon Johnson over the years. Frank Stanton, in particular, was known to be a good friend of Lyndon Johnson's. Did you ever see any evidence that that relationship affected CBS in anyway?

WC: No. None of that was ever passed down. Of course, Johnson bypassed Stanton. He telephoned me two or three times directly. He watched all the newscasts. He would call me right after my newscast and say, "You got that one wrong. I want you to fix that on your next broadcast." He didn't do that very often personally, two or three times at the most, but his staff would do that. I became familiar with a phrase then that other presidential staffs use occasionally. A Bill Moyers or a George Christian or somebody would call me up saying, "Some of us around here feel that . . ." Well, you knew exactly, of course, who felt that. This went on in the Nixon administration and in Jimmy Carter's, too. "Some of us feel that . . ."

LBJ'S DEATH

DC: Your last interview with Lyndon Johnson was just shortly before his death. Was there anything memorable about the last interview that you did, just a few weeks before his death? Did he seem to be in ill health to you?

WC: No, no more than he had been for some time. But it wasn't really ill health. He just wasn't as vigorous as he'd been before. But I didn't have any sense of a sick man. You know, I was on the air live when Lyndon Johnson died. Tom Johnson, who was running the Johnsons' television station in Austin at the time, called me in the studio while I was on the air doing an *Evening News* program. My staff held him on the phone until the next commercial, which was shortly after the opening of the show. During the commercial, Tom said "I've got bad news for you. President Johnson passed away about fifteen minutes ago. This is my first call. I wanted you to know." And the camera came back on air with me on the telephone. I had to tell the television audience, "Just stay there a moment. This is a terribly important phone call. I've just been advised from Austin, Texas, that President Johnson died a few moments ago. Go ahead. What are the details?" We got, I suppose, a few minutes' beat on the other networks. We made one serious mistake, however. It was a very dramatic moment, and it happened during our 6:30 p.m. feed. When we repeated the show at seven, my gosh if we didn't tidy it all up, and we didn't show that dramatic episode. We should have. It was a terrible mistake not to have. What we should have done is start out with "A few moments ago, we announced the death of President Lyndon Johnson. It came to us like this," and go back and show the tape. That's one time when we outfoxed ourselves by cleaning up and perfecting our act, you know.

DC: Do you remember that was the broadcast that you opened with the news of the Supreme Court's announcement of the *Roe v. Wade* decision? It was on January 22, 1973.

WC: Oh, gosh, is that right? I had forgotten that. It's strange that I wouldn't recall that, because in the overall picture of things, the *Roe v. Wade* case was much more significant an event than the natural death of a former president. It had huge ramifications that continue today. But the way the message about Johnson was delivered has kind of obscured in my memory what else had happened that day.

DC: You told the *New York Times* in November 1983 that you felt that Robert Caro, in his biography of Johnson, went, and this is a quote, "a little heavy on him. Johnson was a complex figure, and certainly bigger than life in everything. My objection to the Caro book is that it's all one-sided, that he was an evil man. I don't really believe that he was all evil. He had an ugly side. Many of us do, I suppose."

WC: Yeah. I don't have much to add to that. Of course, that was before Caro's second book, making Texas governor Coke Stevenson out to be such a hero, which was equally inaccurate.

determining the ~~cause~~

understand the importance of the story?

WC: Everybody saw the story. They were eager to climb aboard.
The people who didn't see the story of course were the air
force, who had the original program before NASA was born. When
~~the~~ rocketry program started, the air force banned us from Cape
~~... the~~ operation as a military exercise,
~~... y~~. In those early days we had
~~... m~~ off-base, from a breakwater
~~... ~~ up into Cape Canaveral. Our poor
~~... ~~ breakwater and those rocks all
~~... ~~ed to their viewfinders, because
~~... ~~d, which was a signal that a rocket
~~... w~~ould give us no information ahead o~~f~~

~~..., ~~ memories of the space program are enough to keep us
~~... ~~months. Yes, I think she's got it pretty well right,
~~... ~~as I have said before I don't agree with everything in
~~... ~~, by a long shot. I don't know that Chet Huntley was
~~... ~~h the story. Huntley was out of that picture pretty
~~... ~~David Brinkley on the other hand went do~~wn~~

~~...~~didn't keep me from ~~... ~~lk ~~...~~ . But ~~... ~~ and
~~...~~ited about this achievement of man escaping his ~~... be~~
earth. My gosh, I mean here we had these highly

~~...~~ide simulators and visit with experts. Space was a perfect
~~...~~tory for television as well: Great visuals, human drama,

CHAPTER NINETEEN

Man on the Moon

DC: A very significant aspect of your career was your coverage of the American effort to put a man on the moon. Gary Gates says in *Air Time* that *Sputnik* convinced you that space exploration was certain to become a major story on television in the coming years. He states that you went to work immediately, studying astrophysics and rocketry to prepare for that story.

WC: Gates gives me a lot more credit for planned career moves than I ever thought of. I don't recall ever thinking, hey, I better get ready for the space program. I had an interest in rocketry and in jet propulsion dating back to World War II. The Germans built the first jet fighter, the Me 262, that made appearances toward the end of the war, and I was interested in that. Hitler's V-1 and V-2 rocket program at Peenemünde intrigued me. So it just didn't all come to me as a sudden shock. I knew about the Germans working here and in the Soviet Union, and I had been following what they were doing. *Sputnik* and then Yuri Gagarin's flight shocked all of us, of course. But starting with *Sputnik*, I did suggest that I would like to be involved in the coverage of it.

DC: Let me read you a quote from Barbara Matusow: "The space story was a natural for Walter Cronkite. To him, Cape Canaveral was like a giant toy store. He was so interested that he would go down to the cape on his own time before a space shot and ride simulators and visit with experts. Space was a perfect story for television as well: Great visuals, human drama, ingenuity, everything on a fixed schedule. It was one of the few positive stories of the 1960s." She believes that your close identification with this positive story boosted your image even more with the public and that you were called the "Eighth Astronaut," obviously referring to the Mercury program and the

Cronkite making one of his many newscasts on the U.S. space program, ca. 1960s. He believed that the exploration of space was the most important achievement of the twentieth century (DI_02343).

original seven astronauts. Matusow also says that Huntley and Brinkley were bored by space and didn't like the story at all.

WC: Well, memories of the space program are enough to keep us here for months. Yes, I think she's got it pretty well right, although, as I have said before, I don't agree with everything in that book, by a long shot. I don't know that Chet Huntley was bored with the story. Huntley was out of that picture pretty early on. David Brinkley, on the other hand, went down to the cape and was involved, and whether he was bored with the story or whether that was the typical Brinkley attitude, I think that's to be questioned. But the comments that I heard were that Brinkley was his usual somewhat acerbic and detached self at a time when there was high excitement on the part of everybody else during the launches. I do think that it probably didn't do him any good at the time. The national excitement over the launches was natural. I deny, however, the allegation that has been made from time to time, that I was some kind of toady for the space program, which is absolutely not so, as the people in the space program would certainly tell you. I was highly critical of a lot of aspects of the program and the management of it. I think the proof of that is that there are no letters or decorations to indicate that NASA thought particularly highly of my coverage. They weren't congratulating me or decorating me for being a member of the NASA team, by any means. I'm very friendly with most of those people, and still am today, but they have their critiques of my coverage even as I critiqued their administration of the program. But that didn't keep me from being very excited about this achievement of man escaping his environment on Earth. My gosh, I mean, here we had these highly trained astronauts taking these terribly dangerous machines out into space, to pioneer this new horizon for man. It was a tremendous, heroic story.

DC: Did you play any kind of role within CBS itself in determining the extent of space coverage, or did everybody understand the importance of the story?

WC: Everybody saw the story. They were eager to climb aboard. The people who didn't see the story, of course, were the air force, who had the original program before NASA was born. When the rocketry program started, the air force banned us from Cape Canaveral because they saw the operation as a military exercise, with all the associated secrecy. In those early days, we had to cover the space program from off base, from a breakwater in the little canal that goes up into Cape Canaveral. Our poor cameramen stayed on that cold breakwater and those rocks all night long with their eyes fixed to their viewfinders, because the lights were on at the pad, which was a signal that a rocket might go up. The air force would give us no information ahead of time. Fortunately, we became friends with someone who was close to the space program. That was Henri Landwirth, the manager of the motel where most of the astronauts and the press stayed in the Cocoa Beach area. He knew that when the engineers came back from the base, that they had scrubbed a mission. We all knew when a mission was about to go, because we were in the motel and these guys would go out, they would leave, they'd be gone from the bar, and then the lights would go on, and we knew something was about to happen. Then we'd all race out to the breakwater and sit there in the cold all night with campfires and heavy coats, trying to keep warm. Even in the summer, it got cold at night; in the winter, it was terrible. There were a lot of times that nothing happened at all. But our problem was knowing when they had cancelled a launch. They didn't turn off the launch-pad lights right away. But as soon as the first engineer came back to the bar, Henri would send a runner out and let us know that there was a stand-down and save us hours of unnecessary viewing.

But when they created NASA, the government realized that it had to get the public behind this vast expenditure. This was when Kennedy pledged that we would go to the moon before the end of the 1960s. That made this effort a big public program, and that changed things completely. A highly organized press operation was established.

DC: You got to know the original seven astronauts very well, obviously. Who did you get to know the best?

WC: Well, I got to know Wally Schirra best, but that came a little later, after the Mercury program. I guess maybe I knew Al Shepard the best, although I knew them all well. Scott Carpenter was an easy guy to know, as was Gordo Cooper. Gus Grissom was the fun-loving guy of the group, but very shy in the outside world. He didn't like publicity. He didn't like the hero-worship business. He was a very well trained and good test pilot and engineer, as they all were, obviously. He thought they ought to be left alone because they had to work, and, therefore, he wasn't friendly with the press. John Glenn was the oldest member of the group and something of a Boy Scout. The other astronauts kind of made fun of John because he was so much spit and polish and old Marine Corps regulations. He didn't participate in the high jinks and that sort of thing.

DC: He wasn't one of the guys, then.

WC: No, really in a sense he wasn't.

DC: Who was the leader in the group, do you think?

WC: It was kind of hard to tell. Possibly Wally Schirra. He and Cooper were the Katzenjammer Kids.

DC: Have you ever read Tom Wolfe's *The Right Stuff*?

WC: I thought that Wolfe's book was quite good. I think it captured the spirit of the great adventure very nicely, and it was critical on the right points. I thought the movie was terrible because it burlesques too many people, including the astronauts themselves. It depicted a fraternity-house atmosphere in the program that really wasn't so. They were high-spirited young people, but not to the degree made out in the movie. The book was much better about that. What that movie did to Lyndon Johnson was absolutely sinful. They made the press out to be a bunch of hyenas, and they depicted these brilliant German scientists in a stereotypical manner. It really had very little relation to reality.

DC: Was the Nazi past of Wernher von Braun and the other German scientists a taboo subject for the press?

WC: Oh, I don't think so. I'm sure that you'd find in the press coverage frequent references to it. I wasn't conscious of anybody staying away from it. I only remember one or two times where I sat around with Wernher von Braun in a conversation that could possibly have led to that subject. It was usually a kind of cocktail party or something, and I think the reason I didn't ask him was because it had probably been printed so many times, that there wasn't any point.

DC: Because this was scientific and technical news, as opposed to political, how did you prepare for your television coverage of these manned launches?

WC: I had to start from scratch because I am not mechanically trained in any way, certainly not scientifically. The whole business of rocket propulsion, of computerized guidance, the heat-shield problems, and the question of reentry and atmosphere, the G-forces and blackouts—all of that I had to learn from books. There wasn't much literature on it, however. I got most of my information from NASA's bulletins and papers. That's one of the reasons I went down to the cape as often as I did. I also did as much as I could with the astronauts. It was not a chore, because I wanted to learn. And I didn't do this on my own time because that wasn't necessary. CBS was glad for me to go down, and usually I filed stories when I went down. We almost always got a piece out of it—a story on riding a simulator of one kind or another, for example. One of the spin-offs was that I became absolutely fascinated with simulators. My ability to drive machinery is really remarkable, quite honestly. I catch on and can drive almost anything and fly anything, in the simulator sense. I landed an SST [supersonic transport] my first time on a simulator, and I landed an LEM [lunar excursion model] on the moon on my second try. I realized that I have a feel for that kind of thing. I would have loved to have been a test engineer or test pilot. So riding these simulators was heaven to me. But I took NASA's manuals and books, and I did my homework. I studied like fury on that.

DC: So you went down and got in these simulators, and you also did the weightlessness thing, didn't you?

WC: Yeah, well, such as you could, but there isn't any way to simulate weightlessness except in parabolic flight in an aircraft. They tried to do it in water tanks, which gives you some sense of the problem, but not really. And then they devised a wild thing in which you walked on a vertical plane, a huge wall, and they suspended you down on the wall with wires like a Peter Pan rig, and you walked on the side of the wall, and that was supposed to simulate one-eighth gravity. But it didn't really amount to much. I did that. I also did the parabolic flight.

DC: And there is some real weightlessness in that?

WC: There is; it's just that it's so temporary. My flight was one of their fairly early ones, but they did learn to stay in that height of the parabola for a considerable length of time.

DC: You covered Alan Shepard's flight on May 5, 1961. This was our first attempt to launch a man into space, although it was suborbital. Were there a lot of concerns?

WC: Oh, yeah, a lot of us had great trepidations about that launch. We didn't really think that we were ready to go. We had been watching Redstone rockets blow up on the pad or blow up in flight. The guidance system was not working. The Russians had put up Yuri Gagarin, and there was great pressure in the United States to get a man into space. I think I broadcast some criticism of it at the time, I believe. I just was worried that we were rushing that flight, so that day, watching it, I had great concern whether it was going to be successful or not. We were all delighted with the results, however.

DC: So you do still think that it was rushed?

WC: Yeah, I do. I assumed that they knew what they were doing, and, what the devil, it seemed to work. We didn't lose anybody.

DC: Do you think that the political pressure that's always been on NASA was one of the problems with the *Challenger* disaster?

WC: I think it very possibly was. I think that they had set themselves a program of launches with the space shuttle, and they were very anxious to hold to that schedule as near as they could. But there really was no excuse for having flown in that weather.

DC: So this political pressure that you perceived early on finally caught up with them?

WC: Yeah. It was almost bound to at some time. For one thing, there was bound to be some complacency as you go on, year after year, successful flight after successful flight. I do think that the *Challenger* was a result of pressure to hurry. But as the astronauts themselves said, this is so much safer than testing airplanes because we've built in all this redundancy to be sure that nothing did happen. The space flights were monitored far more closely than the experimental jets they had tested. And therefore, the astronauts didn't look on it as dangerous a mission, as the public undoubtedly did. You know, there was a lot of criticism about their bravado and that of their families, and their wives, and so forth. This was made much of in Tom Wolfe's book. Even at the time, there was a lot of cynical finger-pointing at that "Oh, this is a piece of cake" kind of attitude, but they really felt that way. I'm sure some of the wives were nervous, but for the rest of them, it was an accepted fact that this was probably safer than the other test operations they'd been doing.

DC: Do you think that everything that we did in space could have been done without a man on board?

WC: I think that's possibly so, technically. I believe it would be rather poor science to have done it that way. I think that man as an observer should be along because impressions can be gained that you're not ever going to gain through a television picture. I have a strong feeling that space is very much like the mountain—you climb it because it's there. If you can go, I think you're obligated to go. We could probably learn a lot about the depths of the ocean from a manned vehicle. We're doing more of that now, but that's no reason man shouldn't go down there and have a look himself.

DC: So it was after the Shepard flight when CBS built sort of a semipermanent broadcast studio at the cape for launch coverage.

WC: Yes. In the early days, we operated from the back of a station wagon. I sat crouched in the back, and that was my anchor position. And, gosh, we were out there in the rattlesnakes and water moccasins and mosquitoes out on the cape. It was really very primitive. But then as we moved into the Gemini program, they built us a very fancy two-story structure with a big picture window overlooking the pad. Basically, the control room was down on the first floor, and we were up on the second floor.

DC: Were you far enough away to be safe if a huge Saturn rocket had blown up?

WC: Well, I don't know. Nobody really knew what would happen if that thing really went. But, obviously, they hoped that this was a safe distance. It would have wiped out the press corps if they had a serious accident. The mission control was in a building that was the same distance, but it was kind of semiburied, like a bunker.

DC: What did you think of NASA's press relations?

WC: The guy who was the voice of Mercury control during those early space flights became so cocky that he designated himself as the eighth astronaut. He got to be something of a butt of a lot of jokes and the laughingstock, in a sense, around the space program, even among the astronauts themselves. He was responsible for an entirely unnecessary scare during the second orbital flight, which was Scott Carpenter's. There was a communication blackout during reentry, which is the most dangerous part of the flight. For a period of more than forty minutes, we didn't know whether the spacecraft had gotten through that dangerous moment safely or not. As far as we knew, Carpenter had either failed to reenter and had burned up, or the spacecraft was missing and did not land where it was supposed to land. But we stalled for forty-one darned minutes while Mercury control didn't tell us anything. Well, damn it, they had communication the entire time on the biomedical sensors; they just did not have voice. He did not land where he was supposed to—it was quite a number of miles off—but they did locate him in forty-one minutes. But this public relations guy didn't report that to us. That was really a major failing, for which he was never properly chastised.

LANDING ON THE MOON

DC: Probably one of your two most famous broadcasts was the first moon landing in July 1969. The other perhaps, was the announcement of President Kennedy's death. The lunar landing was the broadcast when you really earned your unofficial title of "Old Iron Pants." You were on the air for about thirty straight hours. That's remarkable.

WC: I think the program was on thirty hours. I think I was out for a little while.

DC: My notes here indicate that at one point you were on for an uninterrupted stretch of eighteen hours, followed by six hours for a nap, and then back on the air for another nine-hour stretch. That's twenty-seven hours. You wrapped up the coverage at 6 p.m. and then returned at 6:30 to anchor the news. And then you returned at 11:30 that night for a special report on the astronauts leaving lunar orbit. You certainly were a constant presence on the television those two or three days.

WC: I sure was. For God's sake, that's too much. But the strange thing is that I had all this time to prepare for the landing, and when it actually happened, I was speechless. I didn't have anything to say. All I could say was, "Oh, boy."

DC: Let's talk about Wally Schirra. How did he become the "CBS astronaut"?

WC: That was probably Bob Wussler's idea. Bob was a very brilliant producer. When some of the Mercury astronauts began retiring, it was decided that maybe we could get one of them to be on the air with us as the expert. I was all for that, of course, and then it was a question of who. It may have been obvious. Wally and I had always gotten along fine, and it was obvious that he would be a good personality on the air. He was a very loquacious and smart and bright and funny guy. He had a lot of enthusiasm. He was just right for the job. I think it worked very well.

DC: How was his relationship with the other astronauts after he went on television?

WC: Oh, I think it was fine. I think that if they'd ever sat down and said who's the guy most likely to go on television, they probably would have nominated Wally. He was just that kind of guy. He was a superb pilot, a flyboy type, which, despite *The Right Stuff*, they all weren't. Most of them were pretty serious guys. Wally was too, of course, about getting the job done, but Wally had a lot more of the "scarf around the neck" kind of macho-flyer thing than the others did.

DC: Anything stand out about the moon landing other than your being caught speechless when they actually made the landing safely?

WC: Oh, gosh, all of it. Most of it is pretty bright in my memory. The whole thing was just such a miracle. Of course, Apollo 8 had already gone around the moon. Everything had been tested except the actual landing on the moon. But still, it had only been tested once or twice, and here we were really doing it. I especially recall the tension that built before the release of that lunar lander, twelve miles above the moon, and then its descent. The sense that we all had that it might be coming down a little fast, which, it turned out, it was. The extreme tension as it approached the moon's surface and then landing. My God. The dust and the settling on the moon and then "Houston, this is Tranquility Base. The Eagle has landed." And of course, then we had to worry about what would happen when they opened up the vehicle and stood comparatively naked in the lunar atmosphere. How Armstrong would maneuver on the ground and whether he'd be able to walk.

And then, of course, there was the ultimate unknown, the lift off from the moon. It was so exciting. Nobody had ever tried to lift off of a surface in one-sixth gravity. We had no way to test that on earth. We didn't know if we could get off or not. They might just go into the sky and be totally uncontrollable. And they had to link up. Well, we were pretty sure of that one. That seemed to be fairly safe, but it still had to be done. And then they had to get out of lunar orbit. In order to do that, the rockets were fired on the dark side of the moon, where we had no communication. Rocket firing is inherently dangerous. You're touching off a lot of explosives and hoping that they'll be controlled. You're riding a firecracker. And they were doing that behind the moon, no communication at all, and we had to wait until they came around to be sure that they had fired off successfully. The whole thing was just heart stopping.

DC: Did you and Schirra work out any system in terms of when he could comment?

WC: Well, you know, it just works or it doesn't. A good guest commentator or color man just senses when to come in. Now, a lot of the time, you throw him a question, bring him in, but if he's got something to say, either he takes a nice opportunity when I take a breath and can come in with something like "Walter, something occurs to me about that . . ." Or he can lift a finger, indicating he's got something he'd like to talk about. It comes naturally. Now, I had a lot of prepared film and taped pieces I would have to lead into. I would say, "Well, Wally, at some point we'd like to have you tell us how astronauts train for this." He had some kind of advanced notice of doing a little prepared piece, but they weren't written for him. We call that a rundown. We used to get rundowns for, I think, almost every half hour, but they didn't mean anything. We might throw them out the window in the next piece. It was just they wanted to guarantee they had things to fill with if we all ran dry, so we had a run down.

DC: Wasn't Arthur C. Clarke a consultant for the moon landing?

WC: Yes. He was there with us for the moon landing. And so was Kurt Vonnegut. But Vonnegut was terrible. Oh, he just set the wrong mood, a big downer. To Vonnegut, the landing didn't mean anything. Why weren't we spending this money on schools? He was real sour.

DC: Had you anticipated this?

WC: Yeah. He'd written a piece about it before, and we got him in for that purpose, so I guess it was proper to do it. It represented a certain viewpoint, but, God, everybody was exulting over this thing, and here he is, a curmudgeon.

DC: How did Arthur C. Clarke do?

WC: He was wonderful, although a little too voluble. He'd go on really longer than we wanted. Give Clarke the air, and he'd stay there all day. But he was good. It was a great coup getting him with us. That's the sort of thing that makes a difference when you are a leader. If you're the leading broadcasting company, if you're the "Tiffany Network," if you've got everything going your way, people want to be on your broadcast.

DC: You told Italian journalist Oriana Fallaci, in the interview published in *Look* magazine in 1970, that the moon program was very important, but that you had decided that it was not as important as support for education, cleaning up pollution, drug control, rebuilding the cities, and so forth. Did this reflect a change in your views?

WC: I wasn't questioning the value of the original moon landing. What I was questioning was continuing the moon program after the first two or three landings. I was questioning whether we should go on with more moon landings. They were so expensive, and I thought we'd found out what was there, which was nothing. We'd gotten a lot of rocks by that time that were going to take years and years to take a look at. I thought it was kind of silly to continue the program at that point.

DC: Fallaci had quite a controversial reputation as an interviewer at that time.

WC: Oriana Fallaci was a great journalist. She is a very tough, tough girl. She was in the Italian resistance in World War II. I had met her down at the space program at Cape Canaveral. Boy, she asked tough questions at the news conferences. I admired her journalism. She's very big in the Middle East. She got in very strong with the Palestinians. For all I know, she's running a sabotage course or something now. She called and asked for an interview for *Look* magazine. I said, "No, Oriana, I can't do that right now." Honestly, I didn't want to do it, because she's a real tough interviewer and writes tough pieces. The next thing I know, I got a call from Gardner Cowles, the owner of *Look* magazine. He said, "Hey, we want Oriana Fallaci to do an interview with you for *Look*. She says you're turning her down." And I said, "Of course I'm turning her down. I'm afraid of Oriana Fallaci, scared to death of her." Cowles said, "Oh, come on." I said, "All right, if you insist, I'll do it." When she walked into the office and put down her tape recorder, she said, "I understand you're afraid of me." That's the way the interview started. I think Oriana Fallaci was the first person I told I was a widower, because I didn't want her interviewing Betsy. There is no telling what Betsy would have said to her. But she did a good interview. [*Fallaci died in 2006.*]

DC: You told another interviewer in 1987 that the walk on the moon was the most important event that you ever covered in terms of lasting historical importance. You compared it to the landings of Christopher Columbus.

WC: I don't think there's any doubt about that. A lot of important things happened in the fifteenth century, but can you quickly recall any dates other than 1492? It's the same thing with the twentieth century. The technological and scientific developments of our century just boggle the mind. And yet, I think that the one incident, the one episode that will be remembered, is when man escaped his environment on Earth and went to the moon.

DC: Did you ask NASA to consider you as a candidate for space flight?

WC: You're damn right. I really anticipated being selected to do that. Most of the people in the space program kind of indicated that the fix was in for me. Maybe it wasn't, but they said I had a good chance of making it. There were fifteen thousand applications or something, and they winnowed them down in regional interviews to about fifteen. We were going to Houston for further examination and interviews, and then five of us were going to be selected to be given physical exams, and out of that, two would be selected. One would be prime and the other would be a backup to go through the training. The journalist was supposed to go on the mission after the *Challenger* flight. The original thought was we were going to go on that *Challenger* mission that exploded after launch. But that was changed because of President Reagan paying off the teachers for supporting him in the election, by selecting poor Christa McAuliffe. Thank goodness the journalists didn't support him during the election.

anchor of the ...

covered Nixon when he was vice president and when he ran again
Kennedy for president. We've talked about your interactions with
Nixon in the 1960 campaign. Let's talk about his presidency and
Watergate but let's begin with the 1968 presidential campaign.
There was a great difference between the Republican convention
... the Democrat convention that year.

publican convention was in Miami
d to the tumultuous Democratic
eal question prior to the
ther or not New York Gov. Nelson
ixon. Spiro Agnew, who was the
time, was for Rockefeller, and he

or so later, Rockefeller scheduled a Saturday news
re in Albany at which he was going to announce his
s. It had leaked that he was almost certainly going to
for the presidency. Agnew held an informal lunch at his
s office in Baltimore and he got all the correspond
of his political colle
of sai
r's ann
ng to b
erence a
ng can
as not l
ingstock
is part
rd Nixon
ixon nam
was in
Republic

ockefelle

d gone aft
er experie
him in l
people who mentioned any kind of support were kind
people like Agnew. Rockefeller wasn't familiar
on't think Rockfeller probably had much of a

... heart for the battle ...ful.
                                        him,
                                        rld?"

                                boys
                                id,
                                ting

ide open. "I don't remember asking him for anything." I said,
Well, did you ask your parents for anything?" "No." It was

...what did you ask him for?" That blew it ...said, "I ... and

CHAPTER TWENTY

Richard Nixon

DC: Richard Nixon was the third president you covered while anchor of the *Evening News*. You had, of course, previously covered Nixon when he was vice president and when he ran against Kennedy for president. We've talked about your interactions with Nixon in the 1960 campaign. Let's talk about his presidency and Watergate, but let's begin with the 1968 presidential campaign. There was a great difference between the Republican convention and the Democrat convention that year.

WC: I'll say there was. The Republican convention was in Miami, and it was a tea party compared to the tumultuous Democratic affair in Chicago. The only real question prior to the Republican convention was whether or not New York governor Nelson Rockefeller would challenge Nixon. Spiro Agnew, who was the governor of Maryland at the time, was for Rockefeller, and he was the only one who would go out and speak out publicly for Rockefeller when, at that point, the conservatives were in control of the party. Despite their huge loss with Goldwater in 1964, the conservatives still ran the party. Agnew endangered his career by speaking out for Rockefeller when Rockefeller wouldn't speak out for himself. But Agnew kept insisting Rockefeller had to run; if Rockefeller wouldn't run, he'd be drafted. He argued that the liberal Republican governors had to stand firm. Rockefeller hadn't made up his mind yet whether he was going to run in 1968; and he was playing hard to get. Agnew came to the 1968 Republican Governors' Conference in Palm Beach on a mission to push Rockefeller. I went to Palm Beach and interviewed Agnew about what he was going to do for Rockefeller. Agnew was his suite with a terrible case of laryngitis. He could hardly talk, but he was adamant. There was a constituency out there for liberal Republicanism, and they needed Rockefeller! "We have to convince this man to run," Agnew told me. "I'm

Cronkite interviewing President Richard M. Nixon, ca. 1970s (DI_05797).

going to put together a caucus of Rockefeller Republican governors. We're going to put him up for president."

A month or so later, Rockefeller scheduled a Saturday news conference in Albany at which he was going to announce his intentions. It had leaked that he was almost certainly going to announce for the presidency. Agnew held an informal lunch at his governor's office in Baltimore, and he got all the correspondents and a lot of his political colleagues around. They had a big spread of sandwiches and beer and liquor to celebrate Rockefeller's announcement for president. Agnew was thrilled. He was going to be the kingmaker. But Rockefeller went to the press conference and said, "I'm not going to run." [laughs] Well, nothing can be more embarrassing to a politician than to be exposed as not being on the inside. My God, I mean, Agnew was a laughingstock with the press. He was so bitter that he, I gather—this part is surmised—that he picked up the phone and called Richard Nixon and said "I'm working for you. What can I do?" And Nixon named him as his running mate in payment for that. But it was in bitter anger that Agnew went over to the conservative Republicans. Up to then, he was a liberal.

DC: Why was Rockefeller so indecisive about the presidency?

WC: Well, he'd gone after it in 1964, and that had been a terribly bitter experience. My guess is that a lot of those who had stood with him in 1964 didn't have the heart for the battle in 1968. The people who mentioned any kind of support were kind of newcomers, people like Agnew. Rockefeller wasn't familiar with them. I don't think Rockfeller probably had much of a stomach for it, really. The pieces didn't seem to fall in place for him.

DC: How did you get to know Rockefeller? What were the circumstances?

WC: I got to know him as a politician and as the governor of New York. He was a very easy guy to know. He had no pretensions of economic grandeur at all. He was very much a kind of man of the people. All the Rockefellers are. I know most of them pretty well. David and Laurance Rockefeller are wonderful people. Nelson was too. I have great admiration for them. Because of my friendship with the Rockefellers, we were able to do a television special on the family. They'd never done anything like that before as a family group. In fact, Laurance and Dave had never done anything like that. The sister, Abby, was the hardest to convince to participate. Nelson was a politician, so he was anxious to do it. But the interviews were fine. David and Laurance did very nicely by us, and Nelson was wonderful. We sat there at his house, doing the interview, and I asked him, "What's it like to grow up in the richest family in the world?" Nelson said, "I don't know. Just like anybody else." And I said, "Did you all do any chores?" He said, "Of course, we boys always had chores to do." I asked, "Well, like what?" He said, "Well, sometimes I'd help the gardener." I was just not getting anywhere. I finally asked a brilliant question, I thought. I said, "Did you believe in Santa Claus?"

He paused and said, "I think I did." I said, "What did you ask him for?" That blew it wide open. "I don't remember asking him for anything." I said, "Well, did you ask your parents for anything?" "No." It was all there. He didn't have to ask for anything; he always had whatever he wanted anyway.

Laurance Rockefeller was also interesting in those interviews. We interviewed him on St. John's Island in the Virgin Islands. He owned half of that island and turned it into a national park. He's got a resort on one corner of it. But we went down there with a film crew and did the interview the next day. We checked in, and they gave us a couple of beach villas. We were sitting there, and it was evening, and the beach was deserted. We were sitting there out on the porch of our little villa, screened from the beach by some bush-like things. The beach was left in the usual condition that people leave beaches in. A couple of the umbrellas were turned over, and beach chairs were scattered around out there, and so forth. I looked up, and here comes down the beach a tall, lanky figure straightening up the chairs, folding the folding chairs, and stacking them. He straightened the tables in a nice line, and then he put the umbrellas back where they belonged. It was Laurance Rockefeller. I told the crew to get the camera out and shoot it. We got a wonderful picture of Laurance Rockefeller straightening up the beach, which we used in the special, of course. We told him the next morning that we'd done it, and he was pleased.

DC: As a longtime resident of New York, did you think Rockefeller made a good governor?

WC: I think he was a good governor, and I think he would have made a marvelous president. He was a very liberal Republican, and he had a social conscience. He supported education and all of the things that are so important.

DC: Nixon received the nomination in 1968. Did you talk to him during the campaign?

WC: Yeah, on two or three occasions. Frank Shakespeare, a former CBS man, was running the radio-television part of his campaign. Nixon would later reward Frank with the USIA [United States Information Agency] job and, later on, an ambassadorship. But Frank was trying to make Nixon more lovable and human or something, and he would occasionally invite just a single newsman up to Nixon's suite. I was one of the first to be invited to Nixon's suite in some city on the road show. I found a vastly different Nixon than I had known before. I assume this was the work of Frank Shakespeare, who told him to let his hair down for the press and be a regular fellow.

DC: You saw a different Nixon?

WC: Yeah, he loosened his tie, took his shoes off, put his feet up on the coffee table, and used some curse words, which I thought were purely planted. They seemed artificial to me when he said them. We later learned that he used a lot of profanity, but it seemed to me a struggle for him to do it. I must have had it entirely wrong, or else you learn very fast how to use profanity. It just seemed that he was trying to make a point of being a regular fellow. I don't remember anything particularly that was said, because he was very careful, but I remember the atmosphere.

THE NIXON PRESIDENCY

DC: Let's talk about the Nixon administration and your problematical relationship with Nixon and his staff. Of course, the story of Nixon's relationship with the press is tangled, and we don't need to get into all the details. There is a library of literature about that. But Gary Gates, in his book *Air Time*, says, quote: "The Nixon-Agnew years brought out the best in Walter Cronkite. Of all the major television correspondents, Cronkite was the most vigorous in his denunciations of the White House assault on the network news divisions." In his memoir, John Ehrlichman said that Nixon and the people around him were very aware of you and your influence on public opinion. He wrote: "I have watched Nixon spend a morning designing Walter Cronkite's lead story for that evening, then send it to Ron Ziegler, Kissinger or me, to send out to a press briefing to deliver it in such a way that Walter Cronkite simply could not ignore it." Now, here is a key member of the Nixon administration stating in his memoirs that these guys were sitting around thinking specifically about you. He doesn't say "the news media," he says "Walter Cronkite." I think that the implication is that you personified certain things to the Nixon people. Why did Nixon have a thing about you?

WC: I don't really believe that it was so much me. I do think I was more a point man as far as he was concerned. Probably the symbol of the so-called network broadcast power. Actually, on a one-on-one basis, Nixon and I got along pretty well, although I didn't like him. I didn't like what he stood for, and I didn't like this conspiracy against the press at all.

DC: You made public warnings about government management of the news as early as 1966, during the Johnson presidency. One of your warnings was featured in an article in *Nation* magazine, titled "Cronkite's Alarm." Following that, you gave a speech at Johns Hopkins that complained about the Johnson administration's handling of the Vietnam buildup and the secrecy about the extent of its military commitment. Was it during the Johnson administration that you first became concerned about news management by the government?

WC: Well, no, it began earlier than that. As a journalist, I have always been wary of governmental interference with a free press, and that dates back to Franklin Roosevelt's presidency. But the problem became acute with the Johnson administration because we were committing men to battle and the public was not being given the truth about the nature of the commitment and the size of the commitment. And this became illustrative of the dangers of a lack of candor with the American people on the part of any administration.

DC: In November 1969, Spiro Agnew gave his controversial speech at Des Moines during which he criticized the press. That was followed a week later by another speech in which he charged the national news media with political bias and eastern elitism. He claimed that "a small and unelected elite" determined the content of the news. Were you aware that Nixon aides Haldeman, William Safire, and Patrick Buchanan were orchestrating these attacks and that Agnew was just a mouthpiece?

WC: Well, that became known as the campaign continued. I don't think we were aware of that at first. I think we went out to try to find out who wrote that Des Moines speech. It was Bill Safire, I believe. But as I said earlier, people have forgotten the Agnew story. Agnew, for goodness' sake, was a flaming liberal when he was governor of Maryland, and he was getting in all kinds of political trouble in his party for his liberalism. But after Rockefeller publicly humiliated him, he was the laughingstock of the press. He was so antiliberal and antipress after that, that he would have done anything.

DC: Did you ever interview Agnew when he was vice president?

WC: I did a brief interview with him, but it wasn't productive. I mean, most vice presidents don't have anything to say. Vice presidents know they can't strike out on their own; they are just echoes of the president. But I had kind of liked him when he was governor of Maryland. He stood for some things that were very solid. This is terribly ironic in the light of what happened later, but he appeared to be less venal than most Maryland politicians. He seemed to be trying to straighten out statehouse corruption.

DC: The Nixon administration seemed to back off of its press attacks somewhat in January of 1970. But there were some episodes that occurred over the next couple of years that brought it back. The first was the CBS story on the Bau Me murder. That was the stabbing of a Vietcong prisoner of war by a South Vietnamese soldier. A CBS News crew apparently filmed the actual stabbing in a prisoner of war camp, where he was supposed to be protected by the Geneva conventions.

WC: Yeah, right. The administration claimed that we faked it.

DC: After the Nixon administration charged that it was faked, you showed it again on the *Evening News*, but this time in slow motion. You have said elsewhere that you showed this on the air to give the American public an idea about the very nature of this war. You won a George Polk Award for distinguished achievement in journalism for that broadcast.

WC: I remember the episode clearly. I think the clincher was that we brought forth the

South Vietnamese soldiers who had actually done it. We got our crew back up there and talked to them. As I remember, I think that's what ended the dispute.

DC: Another incident that caused distress in the Nixon White House was the *Selling of the Pentagon* broadcast in February 1971. That documentary led to an investigation of CBS by a congressional subcommittee. Frank Stanton was subpoenaed to testify and to bring outtakes of the show that weren't shown on the air, and he refused. The committee voted to cite him for contempt, which the House subsequently rejected. You were also asked to testify at the subcommittee hearing. You told the subcommittee that the government had too much power over the press.

WC: Well, too much power over broadcast news. That was one of our principal points, that broadcasting was treated differently than the print press. I wasn't deeply involved in the *Selling of the Pentagon* broadcast. That was a *CBS Reports* program. But I'm not a great defender of some of the editorial techniques used in *The Selling of the Pentagon*. I thought the focus on the use of federal money to pay for promotional films for the military was a bum rap on the Pentagon, actually. I had ambivalent feelings about it because I feel that people ought to know how the government is spending their tax money, and these government films in some ways did that.

DC: I know that you had some other problems with *The Selling of the Pentagon*, but we will talk about that later. In May 1971, you publicly scolded the Nixon administration, quote, "for committing a crime against the people by trying to prevent television from doing its job as the people's observer of the performance of their elected representatives." That was from the speech that you gave when you accepted the broadcaster of the year award. You also "lashed out" at what you called a grand conspiracy to destroy the credibility of the press. Now, that turned things up a notch. Gary Gates has written that your friend Joe Wershba, a longtime CBS producer, challenged you on the use of the word "conspiracy."

WC: Yeah, well, several people did. Now, it wasn't the case with Wershba, but I think in some cases it was jealousy that they weren't themselves out in front on the issue. They didn't like the publicity I was getting. But I had far more support within our organization than criticism. My critics were proved to be wrong when the Watergate tapes came out. It was indeed a conspiracy, an organized plan by the Nixon White House. Joe and others said I had no proof of a conspiracy and that I had overstated the case. But I was convinced that there was. I was not timid about any possible overstatement. I mean that quite honestly. I felt that it was necessary to make the case as strong as I possibly could make it. We had to wake up the American people to what was going on. We had to wake up the press to a great degree to what was going on. There was a very sympathetic press out there for Nixon, in many aspects, and I felt it was necessary to try to rally the troops, if we possibly could, to point out the nature of the attacks against us. To my mind, it was very clearly a conspiracy.

DC: But your charge was based strictly on the rhetoric that was coming out of the Nixon administration and some of their actions?

WC: Yes. The fact that the drumbeat of attacks, the cadence, was such that it had to be orchestrated. It wasn't just reactive, individually, by those who were offended at one story or another. It was a far too clear-cut operation. There were a lot of aspects to it other than the specific attacks against us. Somebody in the Office of Communications at the White House was going around to the local television stations, suggesting they didn't need the network news. The local stations were chicken, most of them. There was not much courage on the part of the owners. They weren't in the same tradition as newspaper publishers, who aren't known for their courage either, particularly. But the local broadcasters are in the entertainment business. They don't understand news or any part of it. And when the affiliates came under attack from local politicians and then the White House, for heaven's sake, they trembled and ran. The White House saw a great opportunity to go to these guys and say, "You don't need the network news. Why do you take it at all? You take the AP, you can buy those films, you can do the program locally." They made direct overtures to the local owners. All of this was part of this whole "conspiracy." I didn't have any doubts about it. I repeated that charge about a conspiracy in a speech at Yale. It got that same kind of reaction: "Well, how in the hell do you know it's a conspiracy? How can you make that charge?"

DC: The FCC chairman asked for transcripts of news analysis from the networks, because the Nixon administration was very upset about instant analysis of news conferences and presidential speeches by television news correspondents.

WC: You know, that pressure caused Paley at one point to suggest that we no longer do instant analysis. The ridiculous thing about that was that our analysis of presidential speeches was far less instant than the editorials that appeared in the next day's newspaper, because we had more time to think about it than they did. The editorials in the newspapers were written from the advance speech copy that was given out hours in advance. The deadline for the next day's paper was earlier than our deadline that night, when the speech was made. Eric Sevareid, for example, had a longer time to analyze the event than the editorial writers at newspapers. But that was the popular view of it.

DC: Did you discuss the conspiracy speech with Salant before you gave it?

WC: No. I never discussed my speeches beforehand. Well, except the time when Stanton was being threatened with contempt of Congress. The CBS lawyers called and asked what I was going to be saying and so forth. I took some offense at the fact that they were getting involved in it, but they just made a couple of points about the legal aspects of defending against a contempt charge.

DANIEL ELLSBERG AND THE PENTAGON PAPERS

DC: Another episode in this chain of events with the Nixon administration does directly involve you, and that's the interview with Daniel Ellsberg that you conducted on June 23, 1971, about the so-called Pentagon Papers that revealed secret government deliberations about the Vietnam War. Ellsberg, who had taken the papers illegally from the Pentagon when he was an employee of the Department of Defense, was in hiding from the federal authorities at that point.

WC: I remember that darn well. The Pentagon Papers had come out, and we'd done what we could with them on the air. We wanted to interview Daniel Ellsberg, but he was on the lam from the FBI. It was real cloak-and-dagger stuff. Gordon Manning, vice president of CBS, and I were directly involved. It was just unbelievably complicated. After a series of phone calls, it was agreed that we would take a film crew and go secretly to Boston. I had to go to the Commander Hotel in Cambridge. I was told to go to the lobby and I'd get a call on the pay phone, telling me where to go for the Ellsberg interview.

I got to the lobby, and I asked where was the pay phone. The guy said, "Oh, Mr. Cronkite. You don't have to use the pay phone! Use the hotel phone!" I said, "Well, thank you very much, but I'd like to use a pay phone." He said, "Well, it's downstairs. It's right by the men's room in the basement. It's very awkward, Mr. Cronkite. It's not a very comfortable place; it's very dark down there." So I went down to the basement. Now, there's no excuse in the world for hanging around the men's room to go down to that pay phone. You know, you can really not make that excuse unless you're looking for a homosexual pickup or something. Jesus Christ, it was impossible. So I went down and pretended to use the pay phone. I held the receiver switch down, and I pretended I was engaged in a call. I did that for an interminable length of time.

Eventually, the hotel manager came down, and he said, "Mr. Cronkite, you really can't be down here. Please come up to my office. You can close the door, absolute privacy." I thought, "Oh shit. What the hell do I do?" So I said, "Well, thank you very much." Geez! The whole game was lost, as near as I could tell. When I got upstairs, there were two student-type guys in the lobby. They said, "Where have you been?" I said, "I've been waiting for a goddamned phone call." They said, "No, no, no. We're supposed to meet you in the lobby." Anyway, we went out to a broken-down old car, and we drove out to a little bungalow house where Ellsberg was. When we got to the cottage, Manning and producer Stanhope Gould and the film crew were already there. They had to go through a separate procedure. We did the interview and got it on the air.

DC: I understand that Ellsberg presented a stack of documents two feet high to you and Manning that he wanted read on the air.

WC: Yeah. We kept having the argument with Ellsberg throughout that he'd wanted this to be an hour program in which he would read from the documents. We had a hell of a time because I think that Manning left it, when he negotiated with the go-betweens, that he would talk about that when he saw Ellsberg. He never promised it. He told him we would discuss that when we get together. And so we were forced to discuss it with Ellsberg interminably, and finally ended up convincing him that there was no way to do it on the television and have anybody watch it.

DC: The interview ran for eight minutes on the *Evening News*. Do you remember what kind of interview you were trying to get out of Ellsberg at that time?

WC: Just trying to get why he did it. Why he would risk his career, what he expected to do next, where did the thing go, was he going to remain a fugitive from justice, give himself up? What was his plan? How are you going to propagandize this thing further now that it was released? Nobody had gotten to Ellsberg. Nobody had seen him, nobody knew what he looked like, and nobody had any explanation of his side of the story. All we'd had was story in the *New York Times*. We knew that Ellsberg had worked at the Pentagon and that the FBI was looking for him. But nobody knew why he'd done it.

DC: You were quoted in your *Playboy* interview that you admired tremendously Ellsberg's courage and bravery and his fortitude in doing what he did. Do you still feel that way?

WC: Oh yeah. We had some concern with the Ellsberg interview, of course, as to whether we were aiding and harboring a fugitive. We were concerned about that. Salant, I guess, took it to the CBS lawyers, and we decided to risk it.

DC: Is there anything that you regret about that fight with the Nixon administration in their attempt, as you say, to control the news?

WC: Not that I can think of. I was very proud, as a matter of fact, of CBS's actions throughout. We took the lead in challenging Nixon's people. In fact, the others really didn't do that much. They were very weak, I thought. You know we went to St. Joseph, Missouri, and answered Agnew's Des Moines speech. CBS agreed that Agnew's speech ought to be answered. We thought, "Why not answer it right out in the same heartland where he made the speech?" I'd been asked to speak to the St. Joseph Chamber of Commerce several times, where I was born. So we decided to answer Agnew there. The people in St. Joe agreed to let us do a national broadcast and let the people there ask questions and let me answer them. It was a very effective program. We got the same type of midwesterners who were in the Des Moines audience for Agnew and let them throw the questions at me.

DC: During the Watergate affair, it came out that Nixon had an "enemies list." Your name wasn't on it. How come?

WC: I was always offended by the fact that he put out an enemies list midway in his administration and that somehow or other I wasn't on it. It was kind of a source of embarrassment among my colleagues. I didn't make it. But then he later described me to somebody as the best of a bad lot, so I guess we weren't the enemies that I thought I was with him.

DC: Well, it wasn't exactly high praise to be the best of a bad lot.

WC: Yeah! [*laughs*] Right.

NIXON IN CHINA

DC: I think the biggest story in 1972 was Nixon's trip to China. You were a member of the press delegation that accompanied him. I want to talk about that, but first, I understand that you got a scoop on China a few months prior to Nixon's trip. In November 1971, you, Gordon Manning, and Bernard Kalb arranged an interview with the first Chinese delegation to the United Nations on their transatlantic flight from Paris. This was when China was finally admitted to the UN.

WC: Well, what happened was, we flew to France to get an interview with the Chinese delegation in Paris. Kalb found out what plane they were going to take to New York. I think it was an Air France flight. So we just booked the rest of the first-class seats on that plane, smuggled our cameras aboard, and hid them under the seats. We got aboard early with a little connivance of Air France and slipped the cameras and tripods and stuff under the seats. We were the other passengers in first class. After we got underway, I got up and introduced myself. They were very cordial.

DC: Little did they know they had booked seats in a television studio.

WC: That's right. But they were very cordial. We just chatted for a while. I finally said, "You know, this discussion is terribly interesting. We happen to have a camera right over here. Would you mind telling the same thing to me for the camera?" They considered this among themselves and finally agreed, and we had an interview.

DC: So they obviously spoke English.

WC: Yeah, Huang Hua, the new UN ambassador, was the principal one. The deputy foreign minister, Chiao Kuan-hua, was also in the group. They talked about their hopes for the United Nations, the fact that China had been denied its place too long, and that it finally was about to play its proper role in world affairs. It marked an emergence of China into the world at large.

DC: I suppose when you landed in New York, there were television cameras and correspondents from the other networks?

WC: Oh, that was a marvelous scene. We got off the airplane, walking arm in arm, virtually, with the Chinese delegation. [*laughs*] Those are the really great moments of journalism.

DC: Okay, so in February 1972, you went to China in Nixon's press delegation. At that time, of course, an American going to China was like saying he was going to the dark side of the moon. Dan Rather and Eric Sevareid also went on that trip. What are you memories of that trip, Walter?

WC: Of course, the official ceremonies and meetings between Nixon and the Chinese officials were tightly controlled. So we were only able to show what every other network showed for those events. But we had some wonderful moments having nothing directly to do with Nixon and the Chinese. One wonderful moment was when Barbara Walters, who was fairly new in the business and was still with the *Today* show, decided to accompany Mrs. Nixon out to see the pandas or some darn thing. It was a sidebar, certainly, on the important story, so we did not send a correspondent, but we did send a camera crew. Interestingly, NBC decided not to send a camera crew, even though Barbara was going there. At one point, Barbara was able to stand next to Mrs. Nixon, which gave her an opportunity to do an interview with Mrs. Nixon. So she said, "Hand me that microphone!" And the CBS crew said, "Sure," and handed her the microphone. She did this interview with Mrs. Nixon and handed the microphone back to the CBS crew rather peremptorily. A little bit later that afternoon, the crew came in laughing to our little office there and said, "Hey, a funny thing happened. Barbara Walters insisted that we give her our microphone, and she did a little interview with Mrs. Nixon on our tape." The editors looked at it and said, "Well, it's not worth a damn. She didn't get anything out of it. Let's wait and see if we hear from NBC." An hour or two later, we got a call. Our guys decided to play a joke. They said, "Nope, we didn't have any mike there." NBC said, "Well, somebody's got to have had a crew there." "Nope, not us. Maybe it's the Chinese!" There was a Chinese crew there, but the Chinese didn't have it. We toyed with them all afternoon until satellite time was just about to come up. At the last minute, we said, "Oh, gosh, we found it." We sent it over to NBC and let them have to worry about trying to get it on the satellite at that late hour. That was a real highlight.

The trip, of course, was very dramatic and one of the great assignments of all time. It was very much like man landing on the moon. Westerners hadn't been there for years. We were a source of wonderment for the Chinese. They had these incredible state banquets that went on for hours and hours, night after night. We were able to see the Great Wall for the first time. And we saw Shanghai and the vastly different nature of people in Shanghai and Beijing. There was a much greater openness of the people in Shanghai than in Beijing. They were more willing to talk to you, more Westernized. The media performance of the Chinese themselves: the generals in their limousines with the shades drawn in the back of the car, with nearly everybody else on bicycles and walking. And you got the feeling that they were all in exactly the same clothes.

DC: Did you have access to any Chinese officials?

WC: There weren't any interviews given. We had spent time with the entire central committee after they posed for photographs at one point. They were quite open to us as far as permitting us into the various ceremonies, but no private interviews were given.

DC: Did you try to do any "man on the street" interviews?

WC: Yes, we did do some of that. The people on the street were cautious. But we did several stories. We went out to a collective farm, a hospital, a housing development, and a school. We also went to a military museum, and they showed us all the weapons that they proudly announced had been so successful against the Americans in Korea. Probably to demonstrate, you know, that the Chinese could crush the American people.

DC: You were over there with Sevareid and Rather and other correspondents. Would you all stay together, or would you just fan out and cover different areas?

WC: We fanned out. We did different assignments each day. Of course, I was anchoring, so I'd go on the morning assignment and get back in time to do the *Evening News*, which we did from China.

DC: What surprised you the most about China?

WC: I think the biggest surprise, quite frankly, was the air pollution. I had just not expected anything like the hairy winter air of coal smoke and dust. There was dust from the desert mixed with the coal smoke. It made the sky a deep grey. It surprised me a little that it was so similar to the Soviet Union at precisely the same point of time in its development. They were at about the same point that the Russian Revolution was when I was in Moscow. I was amazed how similar the whole bureaucratic organization and the attitude of the people were to the Soviet Union.

THE 1972 PRESIDENTIAL CAMPAIGN

DC: In 1972, of course, Nixon ran for a second term as president, and his Democratic opponent was South Dakota senator George McGovern. What did you think of McGovern?

WC: Oh, I thought he was an exceedingly well-meaning and very bright fellow who was trying to pursue honest liberalism. But he wasn't too skilled a politician, unfortunately. He was and he is, I suppose, a great democrat, but I mean a small *d* democrat. He believes definitely in the power of the people, and he is an optimist in that sense. I think that he ruined presidential politics in this country by the reforms that he put through in 1972, which were all hailed mightily at the time.

DC: You mean the reforms in the Democratic Party made by the McGovern Commission?

WC: That's right. At the time, we thought they were absolutely essential to the continuation of democracy. It took the selection of presidential candidates away from backroom dealing. Little did we know that it was a mistake to give the people the right to vote on the president. [*laughs*] That's facetious, of course. But taking the professional politicians out of the selection process was a serious mistake. As you know, those reforms ended automatic delegate status for officeholders in the state and federal government. Congressmen and governors didn't automatically get to be delegates. They had to submit themselves to the delegate-selection process of their state, whether it was a convention or a vote or what. I think that was the beginning of a lot of our problems.

I'm sort of jumping ahead a little bit, but take this thing where the press is blamed for delving into a candidate's personal life, such as in the case of Senator Gary Hart, for instance, in 1988. That really is a result of the fact that politicians don't screen the candidates any longer. In the old days, when the politicians met in the back room to decide on a candidate, or even on three candidates who were acceptable, they weighed candidates' background and capabilities. For instance, they would get together to select someone for a congressional race. Someone would declare that they wanted old Ike Thomas. Then somebody else would say, "Ike Thomas? He's a drunk! We can't run Ike Thomas." So someone else might like Scofield. "Scofield! He's slept with every woman in the district. You know, somebody's going to shoot him some day." And they would go through these lists, and they'd come up with acceptable candidates. Well, there isn't any screening process like that today. Jimmy Carter took advantage of the McGovern rule four years later. Carter is a terribly smart man. He took those 1972 rules, and he said, "Wait a minute. The game's changed. All you've got to do to run for the presidency is to go out and run. You don't have to have anybody's approval. Nobody clears you. You just enter the primaries." And that's what he did, and he got nominated and elected president. That's changed everything. Those McGovern reforms of 1972 got us in a lot of trouble. As far as McGovern himself goes, of course, his populist campaign wore out, that's all, just running against an incumbent president. That's hard to do.

DC: There was an assassination attempt on Alabama governor George Wallace in May 1972. Wallace was running for president. You and your colleagues at CBS won an award for the coverage of that event.

WC: That was my colleagues. I didn't have anything to do with it. The cameraman was the guy who should have been honored. He was tremendous. He was right there, followed Wallace down to the ground, held absolutely steady, and then he went back and got the tussle with the shooter. That was truly calm under fire. I visited Wallace at the hospital. I thought he was a very interesting character. I interviewed him two or three times, once in Montgomery in the governor's office. And I interviewed him on the campaign trail. Then I visited him in the hospital. I just thought it was the right thing to do.

DC: Why did you think he was an interesting person?

WC: Well, for one thing, which should have made me dislike him more, perhaps, was that I think he was a lot smarter than the image he portrayed of this kind of redneck. I think he was pretty bright. And I think he was an absolute, total liberal, a populist in the old southern tradition. And except for the race business, which is a very big "except for," he would probably have made a pretty good president, actually. And when you got him away from the racial issues, he was interesting and good. I'm not sure what he really felt about segregation. I don't know whether he really believed what he was preaching or whether he figured that taking that line was the only way he could become a leader in the South.

DC: You know, he later claimed that he never really believed in racial segregation, that it was just a political pose.

WC: Of course, that makes it all the more frightful, I should think. I mean, to do something that you know is wrong but still do it for personal gain.

DC: Talking about that 1972 presidential campaign. Of course, that's the year the Democrats had that crazy convention in Miami.

WC: Oh, yeah. My God, McGovern's acceptance speech didn't get on the air until three o'clock in the morning.

DC: Did that play havoc with your coverage?

WC: Well, no, except that nobody was watching. I mean, we were on gavel-to-gavel anyway. It didn't matter to us particularly, although we didn't care much for the late-night sessions. You know, they should have done something like put him on the next day—or anything rather than put him on at three o'clock in the morning to talk to no one. That was the year that apparently my name was thrown out as a vice presidential possibility.

DC: Frank Mankiewicz, who was with the McGovern campaign, says that he wanted you on the final list of five choices and that you made the first cut. Mankiewicz has been quoted as saying they were deadly serious about you as a vice presidential nominee.

WC: Well, I never heard any details about it. I always assumed that they were sitting around, just noodling, and somebody said, "Well, you know, if you're talking about popularity and you want a ready-made man, how about Walter Cronkite?" Somebody said, "Yeah, how about Walter Cronkite?" Somebody else said, "Yeah, well, it's a great idea. Well, let's see. Let's think of someone else." [*laughs*] I kind of had the feeling that's the way that was.

DC: Did anyone approach you about the possibility?

WC: I heard about it weeks later. I guess somebody wrote the inside story about the McGovern camp or something, and it came out at that point.

DC: Has anyone ever asked you to consider being a vice presidential nominee in a serious way?

WC: The nearest that I've come to that was in 1980 when liberal Republican congressman John Anderson ran as the third-party candidate in the presidential election. Morton Kondracke, who was writing for the *New Republic*, called and asked me if I was considering accepting John Anderson's bid to run for vice president on his ticket. I told him I didn't know what he was talking about. No one had approached me. Kondracke asked me what I would do if Anderson asked me. I told him that I'd be honored to be invited to be on the ticket with John Anderson. I would always consider it an honor to be asked to consider something that important, or something like that. I was just getting rid of him with that finish, meaning that it would be nice to be asked, but I have no intention of doing it.

Right after that, I sailed my boat from Miami to the Chesapeake, and I was gone for a week or ten days. After about a week, we docked in North Carolina, and I called my office. My producer came on the line and said, "What is this about your running for vice president? The story's out that you're John Anderson's selection for vice president and you've accepted." I said, "No, no no. This guy with *New Republic* called me, and I said I'd be honored to be asked but I couldn't accept it." He said, "Well, it has come out in the press that you're running." So I dictated a denial for CBS public relations to release. I learned a wonderful lesson about the best way to deny something such as that. Just deny it; don't worry about thinking of a diplomatic way of saying no. I later found out that Anderson had seriously thought about asking me.

WATERGATE

DC: Now, June 17, 1972, is when the break-in occurred in the offices of the Democratic Party's national committee headquarters at the Watergate in Washington. As I said earlier, that whole series of events that we call Watergate is a tangle of complicated circumstances, and I don't think we need to get into the details of that. But let's talk about some highlights as they relate to you and CBS specifically.

WC: The Watergate affair was very difficult to follow because there was a new development every three or four days, and it was very hard to associate that with what you had read three or four days earlier. The other problem was that the story came out in the *Times* and the *Post* in such dribs and drabs the rest of the press around the country didn't pick it up. Even the AP was keeping the story to two or three paragraphs for each new development. It was absolutely impossible to follow. I said to my producer, Sandy Socolow, that we hadn't been successful in producing anything new in the story. But I felt we could do a real public service by taking this story from the very beginning, tie it all together in two big pieces and identify all the players, explain their participation and what happened, and point out what we don't know and so forth. And that's what we did. We gathered these two extraordinarily vivid stories of Watergate. We went on the air just a couple of weeks before the election in November 1972. Those two programs didn't prove to be effective in changing the course of the election, but they were very important in terms of educating the public about the affair. Kay Graham, the publisher of the *Post*, gave us credit in many speeches for really saving the whole story. She said they realized their stories weren't making any impact. The pressures from the Nixon administration were getting really severe on the *Post* in many ways. They were to the point of giving up when we brought the whole thing to some kind of a focus.

DC: You brought new life to the Watergate story in a sense. That first program was on October 27, 1972.

WC: That's right. Don't forget that Watergate was a very traumatic experience for the *Washington Post*. It barely came out of that one alive. It also caused considerable turmoil at CBS. The first piece we did on Watergate ran for more than fourteen minutes. It was the longest piece we'd ever done on the *Evening News*, and it was on a Friday, I believe. The special counsel to Nixon, Charles Colson, called Paley and complained vehemently. He made all kinds of threats, I gathered, because of this piece. Paley called Salant and raised hell. Paley said, "Surely there must have been some other news this week. How can they possibly take the whole broadcast?" Salant said, "Well, I can agree with you on that." Salant very cleverly seized upon Paley's complaint about devoting the entire news program on Watergate as the focal point of what was wrong, and that saved the day.

DC: You mean that Salant got Paley to focus on the length of the program rather than the content?

WC: Exactly, and that saved the day. So Salant called us in and demanded that we shorten the next day's piece by half, to seven minutes or something like that. That's all. Content was never mentioned. Just shorten the piece. I went along with that, believing it was Salant's decision and it was only about length. So we shortened it. It didn't hurt the piece that much; it possibly even helped it. But Stanhope Gould, the producer, and the staff that worked on it were terribly indignant about having to cut the tape. Gould said, "There's politics in this," and I said, "Well, I don't think so. I think that Dick Salant was telling us the truth. It's just the length." I later asked Salant, and he denied that Paley dictated his decision. Salant knew that if I knew it was Paley who forced the decision, I would have blown my top. If there'd been top-level interference, it would have been very messy. So he protected all of us. We got the second piece on, and it worked out well. I went ahead for years telling people that Paley had never interfered with any story we'd ever done. Until I learned this story much later, then I had to change and say except once.

DC: The Watergate story was the first time that I'm aware of when you got up from behind the desk to talk. That practically threw the country into turmoil.

WC: And of course, the newspaper columnists wrote that "he does have legs and he does wear pants," you know. [*laughs*] But I got on my feet to emphasize the importance of the story. We decided to make it a chalk talk, which is something I always liked to do. That let me point out "this is John Ehrlichman, and this is how he is involved, and this is Bob Haldeman," and so on.

DC: Whose idea was it for you to give the chalk talk?

WC: It was mine. My fame with chalk talks started during the Korean War, as we have discussed. I believe it's a very effective way of presenting material. Teachers have been doing it, for heaven's sake, for a hundred years.

DC: There's some difference of opinion about who had the original idea at CBS to cover Watergate a little bit more extensively. According to Daniel Schorr, you were in Washington at a dinner at the International Club with CBS correspondents, and you asked the group for suggestions on enterprisers for the program. Schorr says that Ed Fouhy proposed Watergate and that Schorr backed him up. And then that's when the decision was made to do Watergate.

WC: I remember the correspondents meeting, and I wouldn't doubt at all that I would ask for enterprisers. I also wouldn't doubt that perhaps it was suggested, but that it led immediately to the kind of broadcast we did, I doubt considerably. It wouldn't really matter whose idea it was. It came from the fact that we were having great trouble with the Watergate story.

DC: Well, as you said, the point is that the story was done. Ben Bradlee, editor of the *Washington Post*, has been quoted as saying that when you did the story, "It was as if the story had been blessed by the great white father." [*Cronkite chuckles*] You told *Rolling Stone* that your coverage, quote, "wasn't meant to be an editorial saying don't vote for Nixon. It was meant to lay the facts out. This was the only time in my entire years on the *Evening News* that there was interference from either political or commercial interests," which is what we just talked about.

WC: But, you know, talking about Ben Bradlee and the *Washington Post*, the work that Bob Woodward and Carl Bernstein did for the *Post* in the Watergate affair is really what started all of these investigative teams and the investigative whistle-blowing reporter and this business of relying on unnamed sources. I am so offended by the idea of investigative teams and references to "our investigative reporter." All reporters are supposed to be investigative reporters. It's a terrible redundancy to call them "investigative reporters." I object to it, and I think it's vastly overdone in television particularly, and I think for a while it was overdone in newspapers. But as far as the Watergate story was concerned, I admired the work that the *Post* did. I do believe that there was a certain fiction created, in the sense that I don't think there was a "Deep Throat." I think that Deep Throat was several sources and that the way to protect the sources was to create this character known as Deep Throat. Now, I could be absolutely wrong about that. The *Post* went all out on the Watergate case, to its great credit at the time, but I think that in retrospect it went with a lot of highly undocumented material. I mean, that whole business of putting so much on Deep Throat without ever substantiating who Deep Throat was. [*On May 31, 2005, former FBI agent W. Mark Felt admitted that he was the Deep Throat informant for Woodward and Bernstein. Felt died in 2008.*]

DC: Looking back after a few years now, does the Watergate affair still seem as important as it seemed at the time?

WC: Absolutely. I feel that Watergate was a very definite threat to our democracy. This was why it was an important story. It was a story the importance of which was hard to convince people overseas, who didn't quite understand what had happened, and still didn't understand. It was a serious threat to a democratic society. The seriousness was, obviously, that a presidential administration was going to illegal lengths to keep itself in power, which meant stealing an election. It was a terrible thing for the top people in government to do. And they deserved everything that came to them, and more.

DC: You talk about Europeans not being able to understand it. Do you think many Americans understand it?

WC: Oh, absolutely not. A lot of Americans didn't understand it at the time, and they don't to this day. A lot of people think that wonderful and innocent man, Richard Nixon, was done in by the press. He didn't do anything wrong—just the press did that to him. I don't know how they could be so blind.

DC: In the middle of the Watergate affair, Agnew had to resign as vice president when allegations were made that he took bribes as governor of Maryland. In October 1973, you anchored a special called *The Vice President Resigns*, which covered the event. That was followed by the "Saturday night massacre," when Nixon fired Archibald Cox as special prosecutor on October 20. You did an exclusive interview with Cox shortly after the firing.

WC: Those programs were not ones of great personal achievement. They were a news team effort. That's why my memory of them is blurred. The things that I remember distinctly, of course, are the ones that I really initiated and worked on personally. The Washington bureau developed the Cox and Leon Jaworski interviews. That Saturday night massacre, by the way, was interesting. I was speaking at some kind of news award dinner, and the place was filled with all of my friends, of course, and one by one they kept being handed notes and disappearing from the table. I'm speaking away, making a hell of a speech, and people are leaving. I had no idea what was going on. I kept thinking, Jesus, this speech is really laying an egg; they're all going back to work. Finally, somebody slipped me a note and told me what was happening.

DC: On October 26, 1973, Richard Nixon held the first press conference that he had had in months. He attacked the network news programs as almost being a threat to national security. He ended the press conference by declaring, quote: "Cronkite's not going to like this tonight, I hope." And then he walked off. A couple of weeks later, Nixon, in his next press conference, denounced the "outrageous, vicious, distorted reporting on his administration." He declared that, quote, "the real villain is CBS in general and Walter Cronkite in particular."

WC: Really? That's pretty specific.

DC: Nixon got personal, and sort of obsessed with you in particular. This was right after the Saturday night massacre. He attacked you twice in a matter of two weeks during national press conferences. At the time, you told *Newsweek*, "I suppose that a man under attack as Mr. Nixon is would look for anyone to lash out at."

WC: Well. That's damn interesting. Those things must have just rolled off my back. You know, after Nixon resigned so ignobly, I think I must have pushed those memories out of mind. I was more focused on the ongoing story of the new Ford presidency, and I just haven't looked back until now.

BEBE REBOZO

DC: You also interviewed Nixon's close friend, businessman Bebe Rebozo, during this period. I think it interesting that Rebozo agreed to do it, since Nixon was so angry at you and CBS. He didn't usually grant interviews, I understand.

WC: That's right. We all went through hell to get that interview. That was a serendipitous sort of thing. Everybody would like to have had Bebe. I was down in Florida, at Key Biscayne. A friend of mine had recently moved down there, and we were visiting him. He said, "By the way, Bebe Rebozo's mother and sister live next door to me. His mother is a great fan of yours. The old lady watches you every night. I bet she'd just be thrilled to see you." I said, "I'd love to meet her. Let's go right over there." So Madame Rebozo and her daughter became very dear friends of mine. I dropped in on her frequently, and I worked it into finally getting her son to sit down for an interview. That's how we got the Bebe Rebozo interview. But that was one of those interviews also that needed a lot of interpretation. There were a lot of hidden things in there that just weren't immediately apparent to the viewing public, I thought.

DC: For example?

WC: Well, it was kind of strange. One thing about Bebe, of course, which everybody had trouble with, was why was Bebe Rebozo such a close friend of the president of the United States? He was a small-time real estate operator, really small time. He was a nice enough guy, but why did Nixon go spend all this time with him? They went off to an island alone, and they went off in his boat alone. Jesus, what the hell was going on? I still don't know that anybody knows, but all kinds of things were suggested. I was pressing him. I said, "Well, why did Nixon like you?" I told him virtually what I've said to you. Why? "You're not acquainted with world affairs. You've never been involved in national politics. Why you?" And Rebozo said, "Well, we enjoy each other's company." I said, "Well, why? What do you do together that is so much fun that he couldn't do with his secretary of state or someone in the administration?" He said, "Well, he's just able to let down his hair. You know, we just talk, and I imagine every important man needs somebody like me to have around." That was probably the most astute thing he said. It was probably because Nixon had said that to him at some time. At any rate, he said, "We joke a lot." I said, "What do you joke about? What kind of jokes?" He said, "Oh, we play little pranks and jokes on other people." I said, "Well, give me an example." He said, "I remember one time he and I got one of those mannequins of a woman out of a store window and dressed her up with a wig and the whole thing. We put her in the bed of one of our friends. We were all out that night, and when we came in, he discovered this woman in his bed. It was a big laugh for all of us, a big laugh."

So, you know, you're saying to yourself, wait a minute, what the hell is so funny about that? Why is that a big laugh? Maybe it was because there wouldn't ever be a woman in this guy's bed? Nearly everything Rebozo said had that effect, to make you say to yourself, wait a minute, what'd he say? It was that kind of interview. I kept pressing. I said, "Well, can you think of any other pranks?" He couldn't think of any. Now, I understand that when people ask you what's the funniest thing that ever happened to you, you can't think of one funny thing that ever happened. It takes a few beers and a cigar or two to break those things loose. I understand that, but I thought it was a revealing interview. Here you had Bebe Rebozo, a pleasant guy, apparently willing to answer any questions, with absolutely nothing to say. It just emphasized the point: Bebe Rebozo is nothing. Why does the president of the United States take time off to go out boating and spending a weekend alone with Bebe Rebozo? That was the interesting fact, that he was so dull.

DC: Well, during that spring and summer of 1974, Nixon's decline was sharp and quick as the impeachment hearings continued in Congress. It was in March 1974 when Nixon held a press conference in Houston, and he asked Dan Rather if he was running for something, and Rather said, "No, Mr. President, are you?" What was your reaction to that incident?

WC: I applauded it. I think that it's probably not a good idea for a correspondent to step out of the role and to debate the president or anybody else in an interview situation; that's not what you're trying to do. But on the other hand, the Nixon remark itself was snide and probably deserved some kind of an answer rather than just take that kind of thing lying down. You know, there's no requirement that a newsman turn the other cheek to that kind of remark. I thought Dan's remark was perhaps not the best advised thing, but it was certainly nothing that I would severely criticize. The fact that Nixon made a snide remark to a correspondent seemed to me to entitle that correspondent to make a response.

DC: Were you shocked or surprised that Rather did it?

WC: Well, I don't think I was shocked, necessarily, but I was surprised. We were immediately concerned about repercussions at the shop. And complaints did come, you know, from the usual source in those days, the local affiliates. "What kind of correspondent have you got there that is answering back to the president? "You're not supposed to do that." Well, again, the affiliates didn't understand the role of the press in a free society. We're nobody's toy.

NIXON RESIGNS

DC: In August, when Nixon announced that he would make a statement to the American people about his future, you were in Martha's Vineyard on vacation.

WC: I was on vacation, but I kept in touch with the office, even when I was out sailing. It was clear that Nixon was going to make an announcement that night, I guess, and the local harbormaster came out and got me, said it was urgent that I call CBS. I was on a boat just outside the harbor. I called the office from the boat and came in and dashed for the airport. That was the afternoon when the White House said there'd be an announcement that evening. I went to Washington for that night.

DC: A controversy arose later over the way Nixon's resignation speech was analyzed by you and your colleagues Dan Rather, Eric Sevareid, and Roger Mudd.

WC: Well, Roger was entirely wrong; he made an accusation that was totally unfounded.

DC: Roger Mudd?

WC: Yeah. He was down South somewhere. I think we brought him in by remote from somewhere. I don't think he was in the studio. It was another case of Roger not putting himself out for a story, not getting into Washington, but persisting on his vacation. But Roger alleged that Sevareid, Rather, and I had agreed ahead of time to go easy on Nixon in our comments during the resignation special. And that was absolutely false. There had been no such agreement. Sevareid and I have put our heads together on this a couple of times, and Sevareid seemed to remember that Bill Small, who was head of our Washington bureau, said something like "let's not kick the guy when he's down," or something of that kind. I don't remember that, but Sevareid remembered it.

At any rate, Rather, in a pattern that we have seen much of in his anchor role, and most recently in the Persian Gulf War, was suddenly waving the flag. There's something compulsive about that in Rather. And he did it that night. My gosh, he talked about how Nixon was the president of the United States and how you've got to respect the office of the presidency, etc., etc. It surprised both Sevareid and me, I must say. Rather was getting practically teary-eyed about it. It really shocked Sevareid and me. But I don't think it affected our coverage at all, except maybe, possibly, to make it a little stronger just to counterbalance this strange raving of Dan's. As I say, we've learned since then that that's the way Dan responds to crises like this. I think he's got some feeling that he's got some personal responsibility to rally America in its times of crises, or something of that kind.

DC: Well, it wasn't just Mudd who made that charge. Daniel Schorr gave a speech at Duke University, implying that the news team of Rather, Sevareid, and Cronkite had sold out the night Nixon resigned. He claimed that CBS management asked you and your colleagues to go easy on Nixon in your discussion immediately following Nixon's resignation speech that night. What was your reaction to Schorr's charge?

WC: Oh, that the son of a bitch had done it again. That was one of the early episodes of Schorr's kind of appointing himself a one-man ombudsman or something of CBS news coverage. I don't know what had gotten into Schorr. He'd always been kind of a troublemaker, in a sense. I don't know—he was always trying to elevate himself with his internal criticism of CBS News. It was unfortunate, because he was a darn good reporter, an excellent reporter, a good writer, and a good broadcaster. I liked Dan Schorr. He and I had been friends, and I really liked the guy. But doggone, he's sure gotten off on some strange wickets from time to time. And he really was persona non grata around the CBS News department because everybody felt that their comments could be the target for one of Schorr's crusades.

DC: I understand that Sevareid in particular was outraged, because he had defended Schorr when he had gotten in trouble with CBS in 1964 because of an incident involving Schorr during the Goldwater campaign. Did Sevareid feel betrayed?

WC: Yes, he did. We were all very unhappy about it.

DC: Schorr accused you of giving out misinformation on the *Evening News* about his resignation in September 1976. Schorr's position was that he was free to return to CBS but chose not to. He claims that you reported that he had been encouraged not to come back.

WC: I haven't seen his memoir. That doesn't surprise me a bit, but I don't recall a complaint at the time. But, you see, Schorr always put his own spin on everything that happened. Dan interpreted everything differently from anybody else. There was always a Schorr version and everybody else's version on almost everything that transpired.

DC: Returning to Nixon's resignation. Do you recall how you felt about it? Did you feel that CBS had played a major role in bringing it about?

WC: Well, we didn't really feel a sense of success in that we'd driven him from office or anything like that. I was very much impressed by the human tragedy of the event. Here was a man who had risen to the presidency of the United States and who, in many ways, had served the office well being forced from office because of his own actions and those of his colleagues and his employees at his direction. I felt sad about it. I felt very sad for his family. And I felt sad for the country and the fact that we had to endure this tragedy and this debacle. I did feel that justice had prevailed, however, and that this was the way it had to be. It was very unfortunate, but probably well, that he was sparing us the long, drawn-out impeachment procedures that would have ensued on Capitol Hill. I felt a relief that we weren't going to go through that. I think those were my basic emotions that night. I think that was pretty much what we all expressed.

DC: You didn't feel like you needed to take it easy on Nixon, though.

WC: Well, I didn't see it as a matter of taking it easy on Nixon or not taking it easy on Nixon. There wasn't any point in even thinking of it on those terms. We had a story to report, and you report it as it appears to you. Sevareid was doing more commentary, of course, and I was anchoring and doing the news aspects of the show. But my attitude was certainly not one of taking it easy on the man deliberately. But I think the circumstances required a sort of decency at that moment.

DC: Decency?

WC: Not piling on. I mean, you clearly recite the events that led to his decision to resign. That was the story. We showed film clips of his presidency and so forth. But you don't go out, it seems to me, and say, "And there was an opinion among certain people that he was a little nutty," or something or other. I don't think you have to pile on that kind of speculative material.

DC: What was your view of Nixon's presidency otherwise?

WC: Well, I think that it was not a bad presidency. It would have been a rather good presidency, perhaps, over the long run. Certainly in foreign policy, he was the most attentive and probably the best student that we'd had for a long time. He was terribly innovative in opening up China and trying to make overtures to the Soviet Union. He went further in that direction than anybody had. Nixon came up with some very interesting plans. He was going to push Moynihan's plan to save Social Security. And then the political pressures got simply too great; he just couldn't handle it. But that he would go that far with a very innovative plan on Social Security, which has never been popular with the more conservative Republicans, was very encouraging to me. There were other aspects of his presidency that I thought were carried on quite well.

But there was an arrogance about Nixon. Whether that's the word or not, I don't know, but he conveyed the feeling of the imperial presidency. The ridiculous dressing of the presidential guard with the high hats, Napoleonic uniforms, and the brass horns was symbolic of his arrogance. I believe Nixon had a psychological problem of some kind. Many times, he looked a little odd to me, his eyes looked strange. I remember one night at a state dinner at the White House. I was watching him, and his eyes were following the molding around the room, all the way around as if he were watching a mouse up there on that molding or something. He got several of us looking up to see what was going on. There was just a real wild look on his face, a strange appearance. And there were other moments when he obviously seemed to be a little bit out of it.

had been explaining Scott's fuel problem as he entered the
atmosphere. Then Cronkite's voice began to take on more and
more concern. They didn't know where Scott was. All at once
rs came into his eyes. 'I'm afraid
a catch in his voice. His eyes
y have lost an astronaut.' What

s another
dependent y
while on th
at Fred Fr
e 1964 Repu
s happened
during the
ng that mana
o change the
air, and he
threw it dow
tions. Final
ew York wante
is hand and s
."

think I may
ened more than
kind of a thi
ention, with a
ention floor a
of the candid
word "eroding
't use "erodes
this stuff goi
rodes" too ofte
overage to a co

gent, coming
live with no
ional reaction

ate stage,
trust Wolfe's
it weren't so.
tion about
e. I feel the
ly, I guess.
ly there was
of fact, I
perhaps, not
I choked up,
able to go c
far simpler
example, th
rehearsed the

Ernie Leiser's use of so-
he six- to seven-minute film reports on
jor events, as opposed to news headlines. He says that

CHAPTER TWENTY-ONE

Broadcasting the News

DC: I think it would be interesting to talk about Walter Cronkite the working news broad-caster who had his own way of doing his job. We've already discussed some of those points as they related to such areas as covering the political conventions and the space race, for example. But there are some odds and ends about broadcasting that I want to talk about that we've missed.

Let me read a quote from Tom Wolfe's *The Right Stuff*. He's talking about Scott Carpenter's orbital flight: "Cronkite had been explaining Scott's fuel problem as he entered the atmosphere. Then Cronkite's voice began to take on more and more concern. They didn't know where Scott was. . . . All at once Cronkite's voice broke. Tears came into his eyes. 'I'm afraid that . . .' There was then a catch in his voice. His eyes glistened. . . . 'I'm afraid . . . we may have . . . *lost an astronaut . . .*' What instincts the man had! There was . . . the Genteel Gent, coming up with the appropriate emotion . . . *live* . . . with no prompting whatsoever!" Let's talk about your emotional reaction to some news situations while you were on the air.

WC: Well, first of all, I don't remember at this late stage, having gotten to that point of say-ing that. But I trust Wolfe's reporting. I'm sure he wouldn't be quoting it if it weren't so. Certainly, it was my reaction at the time, no question about that. But I do tear easily. I'm a softy, I suppose. I feel the emotion of an event very deeply and very obviously, I guess. So I have no apology for that at all. But, certainly, there was nothing calculated or phony about it. As a matter of fact, I think it would be more effective and more proper, perhaps, not to show such emotion. At Kennedy's assassination, I choked up, and I questioned myself whether I was going to be able to go on, for a moment. And there have been other stories, far simpler stories, some stories about helpless animals, for example, that caught me almost unawares. I wrote them myself, rehearsed them, and went on the air, and suddenly the enormity of it kind of struck me. I've had that happen far more than I like to count. I don't think it's an admirable character in an anchor. I don't mind it about human beings—that's fine—but in anchoring, I think you ought to keep your cool.

DC: But then, Walter, anchors are human beings, too.

WC: Well, that's correct. Sometimes.

"I QUIT"

DC: There is another story that's floated around about how fiercely independent you could be from any kind of management direction while on the air. You've already talked about your annoyance at Fred Friendly's attempt to direct you closely during the 1964 Republican convention. But the story that I want to discuss happened during the space coverage. Allegedly, Sandy Socolow, during the John Glenn flight, passed you a note on the air saying that management in New York had sent word that they wanted to change the coverage in a certain way. You were talking on the air, and he passed you this note, and you crumpled it up and threw it down and just kept on talking. You ignored the instructions. Finally, when he handed you another note saying that New York wanted something different, you reached over and took his hand and squeezed it hard to let him know "that's enough."

WC: I think I may have slapped his hand. Oh, I think that happened more than once. The story that's gotten out about this kind of a thing was in Chicago at the 1968 Democratic convention, with all the horror going on all around the convention floor and outside on the streets. I was talking about one of the candidate's strength eroding, and I must have used the word "eroding" a few times. They passed me a note that said: "Don't use 'erodes' so often." And, gee, there we were with all of this stuff going on, and they were worrying about my saying "erodes" too often. I finished speaking, and then I threw the coverage to a correspondent on another camera. Maybe it was a commercial—I don't know. But I looked at this note, and I crumpled it up, took my earphones off, and I said to no one in particular, "I quit." I got up. I was furious that they were niggling about that. Now that I'm retired and listening to other broadcasters, I realize that it does get annoying if somebody keeps using a word over and over and over again. They were right, and I was wrong to take that attitude. At the time, it seemed like such a terribly minor point when you're involved with these earthshaking events.

DC: How long did you quit?

WC: Oh, for about twenty seconds. I didn't leave. It was just my temperamental reaction, and then I calmly sat down and put the headset on and continued as though nothing had happened.

DC: I'm sure there were a large number of heart attacks at CBS when that happened.

WC: I remember Sandy Socolow being on his phone right away, declaring, "I don't know anything; I don't know what he's doing."

DC: But you clearly insisted, for your own good reasons, that you were in charge when you got on the air.

WC: Well, certainly as nearly as possible. You can't really be in charge, but you've got to be a major member of the decision-making team. I think back in the control room, they'd love to be able to control it completely, almost put the words in your mouth if they could. And I think perhaps they do, to a probably greater degree today than they did in my day.

HEADLINES VS. ENTERPRISERS

DC: Gary Gates discusses your producer Ernie Leiser's use of so-called enterprisers, the six- to seven-minute film reports on recent major events, as opposed to news headlines. He says that there was a lot of tension about that because you opposed the enterprisers.

WC: I didn't oppose the enterprisers. I opposed the time being given to them. I thought they were too long and were cutting into the headlines. I've always had a conflict with nearly all the producers because I considered very seriously the responsibility we had to deliver news to the increasing number of people who claimed they were getting all of their news from television. I said if we had that monkey on our back, we had the responsibility to at least give them a guide to their world that day, a headline service. I never pretended that we could do anything more than be a headline service. I felt that the headlines, and by that I mean the fifteen or twenty seconds of information on the leading news of the day, were more important than only covering some of the news of the day and then an in-depth look at one or another of the stories of the day. My feelings about that did create tension. That dialogue went on constantly.

PUTTING THE SHOW TOGETHER

DC: A lot has been written about how your news broadcast was put together. Matusow's book provides quite a detailed description of that process. She claims that the more successful the *Evening News* became, the less directly involved you became. She said that you no longer participated much in the day-to-day decision making, sometimes even not coming in until five o'clock. She also says that you had always remained aloof from the overall management of the news division, preferring not to get involved in hiring, firing, or assignments.

WC: She's right in all aspects. However, it requires an explanation about my not being there and not being as involved. That was a result not of my lack of interest, but of my prominence and leadership, in a public relations sense, at CBS. It demanded so much of my time. I never waited until five o'clock to come in unless I had been out of town on some assignment or something and flew back. No, I was there at nine o'clock or nine thirty every morning. I always checked in immediately on what the day held, what the planning was, what they were thinking of doing. I made a suggestion or two, but I was not actively involved at that point. I was involved in so many aspects of CBS's public relations. That kept me busy all day. I was also doing other things like documentaries, specials, and elections that took me away from the desk.

If you ask me now in retrospect would I change that, the answer is yes. I would simply tell CBS, "I'm sorry, my job is to put out the evening news, and all the rest of this is peripheral, and I'm not interested in it, and you must protect me from it." But I didn't. I got involved in the presentation of the news department to the outside world. It was also true, as she says, that I had wanted nothing to do with internal politics at CBS and the matter of hiring, firing, and making assignments. I thought that was the surest way to get into trouble. I think that shouldn't be the role of the anchorperson in any way. In my head, I was quite wise to eschew that.

DC: I think in one way she was also questioning your title as managing editor.

WC: Well, managing editor, I think, was a perfectly justified title. What goes into the broadcast and how it's played, that was my job, and that's the job of the managing editor of a newspaper. But hiring and firing was not my job. There were some complaints occasionally because it was thought that I didn't fight hard enough to either get people on our staff or protect people when they were being removed for management reasons. I think there's some justice in that. It was part of my standing at arm's length from personnel situations that I didn't want to get involved in. There was a phrase I used frequently, "It's their candy store," and I used it about myself and about other people. It is their candy store—let them do what they want with that. When it got down to my daily job of putting the news on the air, then I would exert whatever powers I had. Up to that, I didn't want to get involved. I thought it would water down my authority for the news.

DC: Les Midgley replaced Leiser as the executive producer in September 1967. In his book, Midgley has written that you could be "difficult," especially with writers with whom you worked directly and correspondents whose work you found wanting. Midgley writes that you were, quote, "willing to work all hours of the day and night to do the job" and that you "had little use for people who were not willing to do the same." He writes that you were "the most competitive person" he had ever met. "If NBC covered something that CBS did not have . . . he complained bitterly that our organization was falling completely apart. . . . Cronkite thrived on deadline pressure. Sometimes he seemed to deliberately . . . read copy until it was so late that changing anything could become a crisis. He visibly enjoyed making changes live on the air, adding a new story, or cutting to make the thing come out exactly on the second. We had differences . . . but our news backgrounds were similar, and almost always our judgments were the same." Reaction?

WC: I'd say he's dead on target. We fed our broadcasts to the network affiliates at 6:30 in the evening, New York time. And then the broadcast was turned around and repeated on tape for that portion of the affiliates who wanted a later feed. The normal routine was that we did the show 6:30 to 7:00, and then I would retreat out of the studio, which we called the fishbowl, to my office, and the production staff would retreat to Midgley's office. Both of us had glass offices right on the newsroom floor. Midgley watched the other networks, switching back and forth from NBC to ABC. I'd do the same in my office. I'd see something on one of the other networks I thought we ought to have. I wasn't discreet or diplomatic a goddamn bit. I'd go storming into the fishbowl, usually madder than hell. You could see their expression: "Here he comes." I was pretty damn mean about it. "Why in the hell? Did you see that piece on NBC? What in the hell goes on around here that we can't have pieces like that?" And it always shook up everybody. I don't think I was the most popular character in the world at that moment. It was meant to shake them up, but it wasn't calculated.

A far more diplomatic approach would have been better. I know that. I probably should have waited until everybody had gone and then conferred with Midgley or Leiser about my criticisms. Leiser always took more umbrage to that than Midgley did. Les was very calm. You couldn't disturb Les. Leiser was more visibly disturbed by my attacks. I think what Midgley says is perfectly true. I didn't spare the writers' feelings any. I would rewrite liberally from their material. I did push them to go deeper into what they were trying to do, getting new angles on the story. I never succeeded, really, although I tried to hire wire-press-service-experienced writers because they're all fast and they understand time cycles better than other people who work for one deadline a day. With a wire press service, you can find a new angle buried down in the twentieth paragraph somewhere. Maybe you make a phone call and update that angle, and you've got a new lead for the story. I kept insisting on the fact that we shouldn't think of ourselves as an afternoon newspaper. We were the next morning's newspaper. And we ought to be operating one time cycle ahead.

I NEVER succeeded in getting anybody to do that. One of the great problems with newspaper and wire-press-service people who come to radio and television broadcasting is that they atrophy. If they're doing daily news, the job is too easy by comparison to what they've been doing at the wire service. I'm not talking about those who are doing documentaries, but those who do the daily news broadcasts. Writing those shows is something a wire-press-service person can do blindfolded with their right hand tied behind their back and chained to the chair. You're writing a minute or fifteen seconds of copy or twenty seconds of copy on a story. That's two paragraphs. You read the news service wires, and you read the first two paragraphs of the news service wires, and you rewrite them a little bit, and you've done your job. Well, not done your job. You've done a job. If you write it rather cleverly, you've done a fine job. But there's no depth in the thinking, reporting, or writing at all. It's very difficult to keep people alert and bright doing that job. The same problem afflicts the editors of news broadcasts. They also atrophy. Having to edit things in these one- or two-paragraph forms provides very little challenge to them. If they do know better, and many of them don't, they just get lazy. It doesn't seem worth the fight to change two paragraphs. But it should. I mean, those people need to keep their interest high despite the nature of the broadcast and demand more on every item, even if it's a fifteen-second item. The producer needs to say, "That's the same thing I read in the afternoon newspaper. I don't want that. Find me another angle."

DC: Were those blowups your way of dealing with the problem you're describing right now?

WC: Oh, it was. It was consciously done. I had the same sort of problem that the presidents of the United States complain about, the momentum of bureaucracy. You can't change its direction. There was a thing in film that just used to drive me crazy. We had interviews of people who were involved in the news, and you saw them in the living room of their house, and the interview took place. In and out and that was it. I told them I wanted to know where they live. I want to know how they live. The living room doesn't tell me anything. I want to see a wide shot of the street where they live. It will tell me a lot about those people. Then I want to see a medium close-up of the front of the house and then into the living room. Won't take you four seconds to set that up like that. But get it for me. Get it! I went out of there after twenty years never having gotten those shots. I just couldn't convince people that's what we ought to have.

DC: According to Midgley, you seemed to think that everyone you worked with should also share your exhilaration about reporting the news and they should also thrive under pressure. Gates claims that John Merriman and your other writers often "deeply resented" your attitude. He also says that the writers felt that you should have been involved earlier in the editorial process.

WC: I think they're right. As I've said, what I should have rejected is the pressure I got from CBS to do a lot of things other than put the show on the air every day. There was a lot of that, you know. I mean, just the promotional stuff. The local affiliates' anchorpeople would come to town, and I would have to take off a half an hour to go to another studio and do promos with them. And I had to do interviews with local-newspaper television critics. God, they kept me busy twenty hours a day just doing that. It got to where they were bothering me so much just dribbling into town that we finally started setting aside two entire days every year just for me to meet with them. They'd come in, sit down, do them, and they'd go out, and someone would shout "next." If I were doing it again, I'd simply tell those people to bug off. I've only got one job, and that's to put the *Evening News* on the air. I would cut down on those promotional efforts and CBS public relations things. Salant insisted that I answer all of my mail, for instance. That was perfectly ridiculous, of course.

DC: I can only imagine how much mail you must have received at the height of your popularity on the *Evening News*.

WC: Oh, God, it was immense. I'm not complaining about that, because it was an indication of our success, but I could not be expected to answer every letter, for Pete's sake. Also, I tried to be kind to people, preserving my image, I guess, in a way, but also my contacts. I'd talk to anybody who called me and wanted to talk to me. That was a terrible time consumer. And I let it happen.

But there was another aspect that is not as easily explained away and I can't apologize for. Whenever we had special broadcasts to do—the election was coming up, space shots, or whatever—I had a lot of studying to do. I had to get my notebooks together, which the guys out there on that desk may have appreciated, but didn't appreciate the priorities I was putting on that. And they were right. I would come in at five in the afternoon, and I'd rewrite their copy very quickly. Well, they didn't like me to rewrite their copy, and they would prefer that I had conferred with them before I tossed it in the bucket. And if I had conferred with them, they could have rewritten it themselves. And I understand that. I would take that same attitude if I had been a writer on the rim. But I am a fast editor and a very fast writer, and I put things together the way I want them to be. I'd slash at their copy, and occasionally, I would throw it back to them and say, "I want to check that fact. I don't believe that." Or, "Why can't we get a statement out of this guy? Do we have to go with what we've got here?" And I'd do that an hour before the broadcast, and the pressure was on. I can see the resentment.

DC: So here you have the most widely watched news program in the United States. Millions of people were waiting to hear what you had to say about something, delivering the news of the day, and you're asking people to get copy back to you a couple of minutes before you go on the air. Did that make you nervous?

WC: No, it didn't. I would get nervous sometimes on special broadcasts or maybe on the news if I thought there was a big hole in our coverage or that we were really delinquent in something. Then I got nervous for the broadcast, but not for my presentation of it. It wasn't stage-fright nervousness. Maybe I had more of an anxiety that we get it right on the air. But, no, I never had stage fright. I've had much more stage fright talking to a hundred people in a room than talking to eighteen million. When I was doing the telecast, in my mind I was speaking to only one person out there, not eighteen million. But it was different when I spoke to a hundred people sitting out in a room. For one thing, I usually knew who those people were, and they often were colleagues or experts of some kind. You get kind of nervous about appearing before them. But in the broadcast, my mindset was that I was usually speaking to one person. Very frequently, I tried to imagine I was speaking to a person who might be taking an opposite view. If it was a moral issue, for example, I very frequently thought of my mother, what she would think of my broadcasting that on the air.

By the way, do you realize that when Gary Gates wrote his book, he was a writer on the show? So he was writing from the viewpoint of one who was offended by being rewritten.

DC: Well, that's a good point to make.

WC: It is, and an important point to make, because he had that personal resentment. I don't think that Merriman objected to that nearly as much as Gates makes it sound that he did. I think the other writers did, yes. I do think Merriman thought that I ought to be out there earlier, and would make it easier if I was out there, but I don't think he resented it as such.

DC: In his book, Gates cites an incident after the Southern California earthquake in 1971, when NBC's coverage was allegedly better than CBS's. He states that you "stormed into Midgley's office and opened with 'I think someone should be fired.'" Gates says, quote: "Shortly thereafter the LA bureau chief was removed."

WC: I don't remember the bureau chief being fired. Bureau chiefs in Los Angeles didn't have great longevity during that period anyway, but I don't remember cause and effect there. I'll tell you, I admit that I was much too free with the "somebody needs to be fired" business. This is also part of my persona that I would not recommend to anybody. I was very free with "That son of a bitch ought to be fired." You know, "Get rid of that guy! Fire him!" I didn't really mean it, and I didn't expect anybody to carry it out. If I did, I would have pursued it in a different fashion. The evening Cronkite overreaction was not to be taken seriously. But I doubt that it was my words that caused that guy's removal as bureau chief. He might have been fired because of the poor coverage.

DC: Did you feel close to your staff?

WC: No. I wasn't nearly as close as I'd like to have been. I felt very connected to them, of course, because we were all comrades in arms fighting the daily news battle. I always felt that was close enough. You know, I loved the newspaper business. When I had the time, I enjoyed the after-hours barroom drinking. But by the time I was on CBS,

I'd gone beyond that. Those were kind of the wonderful freshman and sophomore years, but I was up to a senior level now. I had a home life, and that was an important focus. I didn't get away from the office for lunch. I didn't go out to dinner much in the evening either. Betsy and I had an annual Christmas party at our place in Manhattan that was considered a big event of the year at which we had everybody, all the staff. And while I felt a friendliness, as I say, it wasn't an arm-around-the-shoulder buddy system with me.

DC: There is a little anecdote from 1968 that I picked up in a couple of different places. It was the night of the Nixon-Humphrey presidential election returns. The election was so close that it was apparent that a winner would not be known until the next day, so many of the CBS crew drifted off the set. At one point, you supposedly noticed that people were getting rather scarce around the studio. All of a sudden, you exclaimed, "Goddamn it! Where is everybody? This election isn't over yet." The story is that phone calls were made and everybody returned and stuck it out with you for the rest of the night. Is that a reasonably accurate version of what happened?

WC: I don't remember the incident, but it sounds perfectly probable. Yeah, I'm sure it happened. But you know, I had it easy. It's easy to work for that length of time if you're on top of things. The adrenaline is flowing, and you've got to be thinking and working. What is really terrible is the role that the correspondents and analysts have. They might appear for five minutes once an hour, and probably not even that much. There are assistants who have very little to do. Boy, that'll drive you really mad. Mine was the easy job of staying on the air. I was just as up seventeen hours later as I was when I started. It never occurred to me that there was any problem to it. I'd get off the air, and I wasn't ready to go to bed. I wanted to go out somewhere and get a drink and a hamburger and talk about it for a while.

SETTING THE AGENDA

DC: Les Brown is quoted in *Making News* that it was the *New York Times* that set the agenda for each *Evening News* broadcast, and he is critical of that.

WC: That was certainly true for a very long time. I think that during my days, we got away from that. I suspect that in some ways that approach is back today. But I did find it terribly offensive that we had no mind of our own at CBS when I came there. That continues among many of the journalists, and I think probably among television journalists today, generally. They criticize the newspapers roundly, but on the other hand, they let the newspapers set the agenda. "If it's in the *Times*, it must be a worthy story": that's the way they approach news judgment. "What's in the *Times* today? That must be the big story of the day."

DC: Martin Mayer claims that's the reason why so many of the news broadcasts on the three networks have the same stories night after night.

WC: Well, you see, I contradict myself now a little bit. I think by the 1960s, we had graduated from that to a very sizable extent. I think the other networks had not totally abandoned that. I don't think that we let the *Times* set our agenda probably anymore than the *Des Moines Register* let the *Times* set its agenda. And in this case, I don't think the *Des Moines Register* lets the *Times* set its agenda that much. But news judgments are likely to be the same across the country on local stations. Well, maybe not on local stations; some of those are pretty flaky. But most newspapers and network television are almost always going to play the same story. When Agnew was leading Nixon's conspiracy charges against the press, using "nabobs of negativism" and all those William Safire lines, he was criticizing us for setting the agenda on the television news. But, of course, the truth was that all the way across the country, these editors at these Republican newspapers in the Middle West and in Orange County were playing the same story. But the question is always "What interests the most people?" That sets the news agenda. That's what you learn in Journalism 1 and 2 at the University of Texas. And that question is nearly always going to be answered the same way at every news outlet.

DC: But you do say that there was a problem.

WC: Oh, there was a very big problem, particularly in the early days of television news.

DC: Well, that raises another question: how much social activity or communication goes on between the personnel of the three networks?

WC: I think that there is a fair amount. I don't believe that it's quite to the degree that it once was in the newspaper business, where every town had a newspaper bar or two or three where the guys verbalized at the bar. Interestingly, those bars were never the formal press clubs, like the Headliners Club in Austin and similar clubs in other cities. The formal-press-club-idea never worked out in most cities. They weren't a good place for working journalists. They were always filled with public relations agents, politicians, business leaders, and the news media brass and their buddies. But there were favorite bars frequented by the working press. New York had several, and each newspaper had its own one or two bars. Guys would cross over to the other part of town, and they knew the bar where a particular newspaper gang went. That kind of barhopping doesn't exist anymore, I don't think, what with the profession making a little more money. These days, a fair amount of fraternization goes on between journalists in New York and in Washington because of the active social scene in those cities. Instead of bars, shoptalk goes on at cocktail receptions. Now there is a club in New York where quite a few of us belong. It's the Century Club. That's a club of intellectuals, primarily, from all walks of life. There are quite a few of us who belong and see each other there a lot.

DC: So there wasn't really any kind of detective work going on at these bars or at cocktail parties to find out what the other network news organizations were up to?

WC: No. I was always closemouthed about anything that I didn't want the other networks to know about, but it's hard to keep a secret in our business. For one thing, you've got to order up lines and satellites, and that stuff becomes very quickly known. You order up a satellite somewhere for a special broadcast you want to do, and the next thing you know, the technicians at the satellite switching point will call the technicians at NBC or ABC and ask if they were planning to order up anything from Buenos Aires. And those guys at the other networks would say, "Why no, we're not." "Oh, well, CBS ordered something up from Argentina, and we just wanted to know if you were going to do it as well." That kind of thing. And, of course, the technicians at NBC tell their newspeople that something must be going on in Buenos Aires. So the word gets out quickly.

CBS RADIO COMMENTARY

DC: Let's talk about your broadcasts on CBS Radio. I listened to them on KRLD radio in Dallas. They weren't news broadcasts. They were commentaries, which surprised me the first time I heard one because they were so different from your television news broadcasts.

WC: Those radio commentaries were Fred Friendly's idea. When Friendly took charge of CBS News, he almost immediately asked me to do a two-minute commentary every day on the *Evening News* broadcast. He had in mind the old news-and-commentary radio programs that Ed Murrow and Eric Sevareid had done, where they did ten minutes of news and five minutes of commentary. Friendly told me that I ought to do a commentary every day on television. I convinced him that it was a bad idea. I didn't think that our viewers were sophisticated enough to understand how a newsperson works and what our ethics are and how it's perfectly possible for us to wear two hats. If I went out there every day and did an editorial commentary at the end of my regular broadcast, people would have tagged me right away. They would believe that the entire newscast reflected my beliefs. But Friendly did persuade me to do those brief commentaries on CBS Radio. I had my doubts about it, but I also was intrigued by the idea of my taking a completely separate role in a totally different forum.

DC: Why did you think that those who listened to you on the radio would not then carry that over to your television role?

WC: To be frank, I never was convinced that it wasn't going to catch up with me. I thought that some day the roof was going to fall in. Somebody was going to write a big piece in the newspaper or something. I don't know why to this day I got by with it! We just got deeper and deeper and went further and further testing the water, and I never got called on it.

DC: But you were willing to take the chance on the radio.

WC: Yeah, that was the fun part of it. You know, to say what I wanted to say and getting away with it. The commentary was cautious. I would say things like "people feel that," or "it is believed by some people," but it certainly was commentary. They were supposed to be analysis, but they really were commentary.

DC: What was the time length of those radio broadcasts?

WC: I think they were five minutes long. I'm surprised that none of the affiliates ever rose up in arms about them. It was the weirdest thing. It was just like those radio broadcasts were going out into a vacuum somewhere and disappearing. It was strange.

DC: Did you write them yourself?

WC: No, I had a writer always for it. I only had two writers in the whole period I did them. I selected the writers carefully. I met with them every morning, and we talked about the commentary, and they took notes, and they sketched in what I wanted to say. I practically dictated the piece, or many times I did. Sometimes the writers brought ideas and just said they'd like to do a piece on it, and I said "Good, let's try it." They had it ready about an hour before the broadcast so I could rewrite it or turn it down if I didn't like it and still have time to turn out something else. I very seldom did that. On occasion, I wrote them myself, but it was on a rare occasion that I sat down and actually typed out the thing. But they were very much reflective of my thinking. I think we did them live at about two in the afternoon. We taped it some days, when I couldn't be there, but it was usually live.

DC: There's a quote attributed to President Johnson to the effect that if Walter Cronkite said on his television broadcast what he says on his radio program, there would be revolution in the streets. That's not a verbatim quote. The implication is that your commentary was very liberal, maybe even somewhat radical to a man like Johnson.

WC: They weren't radical, but they were certainly liberal, no question about it. I'm surprised that he knew about the radio broadcasts. I guess he probably got transcripts or something. As I said, I was always amazed at what I got by with on the radio and why it never caught up with me, because I lashed out on the radio. I hit Johnson pretty hard in those radio broadcasts. Those things were fun to do, but I kept waiting for the shoe to drop, something to happen. But it just went out into a great void. Apparently, nobody but Lyndon Johnson ever heard them. [*laughs*]

DECIDING WHAT IS NEWSWORTHY

DC: You told *Rolling Stone* magazine in an interview in 1987 that, quote: "Unfortunately, you've got to throw a brick through a window to get any attention. What puzzles me is the placidity of the people in the inner cities in the last few years. TV has let us down, to an extent, by not staying with these hard-to-depict problems. At the cost of the more interesting broadcast, they should be addressing the issues." Do you want to elaborate just a little bit about that? That's a pretty strong statement.

WC: Because of the time limitation of twenty-three minutes or twenty-four minutes you have every day, the *Evening News* is almost totally reactive to the day's breaking stories. If somebody throws a brick through a window or sets off a bomb somewhere, we'll cover it. But it is almost impossible for us to stay with those problems day in and day out, elaborating on a problem here and a solution there. Television isn't equipped to do that. I think, actually, Don, that this may be what the networks are coming to now. They're all making moves, and the statements from their executives indicate they are planning to get out of the daily news business totally. Turn that over to CNN, if you please, and abdicate that responsibility. Perhaps replace the *Evening News* with kind of a daily *60 Minutes*–type thing. It's a little more tabloid than I would like, but on the other hand, it might allow in-depth stories that don't require a huge staff. I find it very hard to argue against that.

DC: Speaking about having to throw a brick through a window to get attention, some have claimed that network coverage of the civil rights movement initiated what is now a standard tactic of staging a protest just simply to get the coverage and publicity.

WC: I think that's probably so. But you know, I always found reason to argue against that point regarding people staging protests for television. People have always staged protests, long before television. The purpose is to get public attention, to get in the paper, to get people to notice. They've always done that. The Civil War draft riots weren't staged for television. The racial riots in New Orleans weren't staged for television. It's got the same relationship to television as anything today has to television. It's a high-impact medium, and things that have always been done appear stronger, more vigorous on television than they do in print. And it has nothing to do with the fact that television is there as opposed to the fact the press is there.

DC: How do you handle a situation in which someone or some group is obviously trying to stage a news event and therefore needs the news media to be there for it to "happen"?

WC: Well, that's a very, very tough decision to make. I don't think you can make a rule about it. I think it's something that has to be decided on at the moment as to the nature of the protest and the nature of the demonstration. You certainly can't make the judgment on the basis of whether you approve of the demonstration or not. That's the first thing you eliminate as a consideration. You've got to decide: is it newsworthy or not? I think that when you get down to deciding would they demonstrate if our cameras were not there, then you've got a serious problem facing you. I don't know what the real answer to that is. If you thought that the demonstration was likely to lead to bloodshed if cameras were there, you would have to say you wouldn't go. On the other hand, if it's going to take place anyway, then how do you know that? We did learn one thing, of course. It's essential that we be as invisible as we can be. Lights attract demonstrators like moths to the flame. You can't use lights. We learned that during the Watts riots. It's preferred not to take a big truck with "Eyewitness News" written all over it. In other words, try to bury yourselves in the woodwork as much as possible. Which is all part of the business of not inciting to riot. It's a tough news judgment.

COVERING THE CIVIL RIGHTS MOVEMENT

DC: While we are on the subject, it's clear that the civil rights movement in the United States was a pivotal moment in the history of TV journalism. For the first time, television had the technical and financial resources to compete with the newspapers on a daily basis, and the civil rights movement was the first important and sustaining story over time to come under the new microscope of television network news.

WC: Well, I guess that's right, as a continuing story.

DC: Network coverage educated the public about the issues involved in the civil rights movement. Many viewers in the early sixties were appalled at what they saw. It was television exposing the masses to a great moral issue. Because of its civil-rights-protest coverage, in the South CBS was called the "Colored Broadcasting System."

WC: Oh, yeah, but that didn't make any difference to us. We did get some pressure from the southern affiliates. They were unhappy about the coverage. Not all of them, by any means. Some of them were quite enlightened. But we never felt that pressure on the news desk itself. I've got to constantly emphasize that. I've made the point before, but we had a marvelous management that kept it off our backs on the *Evening News.*

DC: I understand that the night of the Martin Luther King assassination in 1968, you were in Washington, D.C. Frank Stanton supposedly called CBS News that night and said, "Stay on the air," because he feared that Martin Luther King's death was going to result in nationwide reprisals and riots. Does that sound familiar to you? That Stanton was concerned in that way and asked CBS News to stay on the air that night?

WC: I wouldn't be surprised if Frank expressed that concern. Frank was very close to the Urban League and that group of people. But this was the reaction of nearly all of us. I remember the news of the assassination came just before we were leaving the air on the 6:30 feed. We turned around, obviously, and went on the air live for the 7:00 feed. We got off the air at 7:30. I remember my saying, "I'd hate to be up on U Street tonight [in Washington, D.C.]." I remember specifically saying that. And so it was in all of our minds.

DC: So you were broadcasting out of Washington that night.

WC: Yes. I don't remember that we stayed on the air. I think I left to come to New York. I think the decision was that I'd better get up to New York, that we were in for trouble.

AFTRA AND LABOR STRIKES

DC: In the mid-1960s, Walter Cronkite went on a labor strike. What was that about?

WC: Well, back in 1951, I would guess, CBS put its newspeople into AFTRA, the American Federation of Radio and Television Artists, without any vote from us at all. I wasn't opposed to trade unionism, but I didn't like the way we had been put into this union without being consulted first. But at any rate, nothing happened during all those years until a strike developed in the spring of 1967. To be honest, I wasn't paying any attention, except I knew the company was having trouble with the Hollywood types and it looked like they might go on strike. About that time, all of us in the news division realized that it would also involve us. They must have had a mail ballot, but I'm sure I voted against the strike because I didn't think we had anything to do with that. So as the strike was voted, this mood welled up inside the news department: let's get out of this darn union. We don't belong in a union with jugglers. That was a quote from Chet Huntley, who was quoted saying that we don't belong in the same union with tap dancers and jugglers and singers and acrobats. And he was right. That's what we were all complaining about. But my point at that time was, "We can't get out now. This isn't the time. You can't have gone on here for fifteen years, and then when the chips are down and you've taken some benefits and you've got an AFTRA pension and maybe they protected your job and now that they're calling a strike, you can't say, 'Oh, I quit.'" So I said that we couldn't quit at that point. I said, "Look, I don't want to strike. We don't belong in this strike. It's not for our benefit, but we're obligated now because we didn't complain before. And therefore there's nothing we can do but observe the strike." So I observed the strike. I did not go to work. And CBS pulled in this guy, Adolf Hitler, or whatever his name was, [*laughing*] Adolf Zinger or something . . .

DC: His name was Arnold Zenker.

WC: Oh, yeah. He was in the accounting department at CBS.

DC: This was his one day in the sun!

WC: Well, he went on to parlay a business out of it! He actually went around trying to be an anchorman for a while. A station hired him in Baltimore. He was there for maybe a year or two, and I think then he went somewhere else for a while, and then he started a consulting business in Boston, teaching business executives how to appear on television.

DC: Talk about starting at the top!

WC: Yeah, right! [*laughs*] But I told my colleagues, "Now, when this is over, let's talk about getting out of this union and forming a union of our own." And we worked on that very hard. We hired a labor attorney, who contributed his service, and he worked with us. We examined our NLRB [National Labor Relations Board] rights. But our membership split on whether it was good to get out or not. Some thought we ought to stay in AFTRA and have a unit of our own. Others thought that our union should be the Writers Guild, which was appropriate. We have like interests, and furthermore, it would have increased our strength as a union because we could have shut down the news departments. So anyway, it didn't work. There were too many opposing ideas for us to unify behind anything. But network newspeople are not the sort to get together to protect their group interest. We all had good salaries and were independent, and there was no great imperative to get out of the union.

DC: And you're still in AFTRA.

WC: We are still there. Later on, our technical union went on a strike, and I took a rather active role in that one. They were trying to get AFTRA to observe their picket line. I went to the AFTRA meetings at that point, and I spoke up for a point of view that earned me a lot of enmity among some of the engineers. By that time, they had interfered with the broadcast of some sporting event out at Shea Stadium. I forget if it was football, baseball, or what it was, but somebody had cut the cable, and at the broadcast center, somebody put some sand or something in several tape machines. I went to the meeting and said, "Unless the head of that union will come before us and apologize for that action, renounce violence and sabotage, promise to find the perpetrators, and pledge before us that this sort of thing will not happen again, I could not possibly support a strike." They wouldn't do it, of course. But my viewpoint and some other viewpoints prevailed, and we didn't honor the strike.

THE ANCHOR AND HIS AUDIENCE

DC: Walter, one of the things that I find interesting is how some viewers pay such close attention to the personal appearance of some televison broadcasters. By that, I mean the broadcaster's style of clothing and how he or she combs or does their hair and whether they have a new tan. It seems that the slightest little change in how you combed your hair, for example, set off a flurry of comments in the newspapers.

WC: Oh, the attention given to anchorpeople and television personalities is just awful. I think it's one of the reasons that Dan Rather performs the way he does. I think he's terribly self-conscious about that, and it shows. Dan's worried about public reaction to everything that he does. My attitude was that I couldn't care less. I wanted the public to like me, quite clearly. I wanted approval, but I was never going to let my private life be governed by that. I went to burlesque shows, you know, when I visited New Orleans. I dropped in on every nudie show I could, and probably still would, except that I kind of lost interest. But I never posed with girls on my lap, or whatever. I don't worry about that kind of thing. Now, people who run for office who have to go to the public and ask for their approval every two years; I think that's a whole differ-ent ball game. If I had to live like that, I probably wouldn't have stayed in television. I regret the loss of privacy that did occur. But there again, it doesn't weigh on me. There are times when I wish it didn't exist, but it's all part of the game; it's really no big deal. I don't know if I ever told you the story about the woman who thought I was wearing a wig.

DC: No. [*laughs*]

WC: Betsy and I went off on the longest vacation I ever took up to that time. We went to the South Pacific. I was in the sun a great deal, and at that time my hair bleached out very quickly into a blond color. I also didn't have a haircut for a while. It was when long hair was beginning to come in, along with the natural look. We got rid of that "greasy kid stuff" look, you know. So I came back, and I said, "Well, the heck with it. This seems to be the way everybody is wearing their hair today." So I went on the air, and, my gosh, the switchboards lit up all over America. I mean, the switchboards in many towns were just overwhelmed. "What has Walter Cronkite done to his hair? Is that a wig?"

The CBS publicity department called me at home after the broadcast. "We've got these calls coming from all over America. We need a statement. What is it that you're wearing on your head?" I said, "I'm not going to dignify that shit with an answer. You can't reach me." And I hung up on them. I always was offended by all the attention paid to cosmetics in our business. It bothered me a lot. For a couple of weeks, the press department went crazy. It was in newspaper columns and everything. Then I got a letter, with this very embossed letterhead, from Bronxville, New York. It was in this very lovely, cultured hand, and a very well written letter: "Dear Mr. Cronkite: How could you possibly do this? Don't you understand what you've done? You are the bridge between the generations in this terrible time we're having with communica-tions between people. Both the older and the younger generation trust you, and you may be the only person in the country that fits that description. But how in the world can we trust you when you've found it necessary to duck behind the subterfuge of a wig?" She had me in tears. It was so plaintive a call for the honesty and integrity that I had lost by wearing this terrible wig. By this time, I'm thinking, I've got to make a statement; this is terrible. She ended the letter with: "And so you see, Mr. Cronkite, it's no more important for an older man to have a full head of hair than it is for an older woman to have a good pair of boobs. Sincerely yours, Isadora Katz." [*laughs*]

DC: [*laughing*] That's great.

WC: I went on the air the next night, and I did a little Andy Rooney piece on my hair. My punch line was, "It's my own hair, and besides, you've got to admit that no self-respecting wig maker would make a head of hair that looked like this."

DC: It had to be terribly frustrating to have to deal with that kind of thing.

WC: Oh, golly. Yeah. Sure. You know, you'd think that people would be looking beyond that sort of thing. And the trouble is, the publicity people take it so seriously, you know.

DC: Aren't there people in your business who encourage that?

WC: That's right. They do. Well, I used to be annoyed because my mother, of all people, would say, "Oh, I just love to listen to Walter on the radio. He has such a nice voice." Here I struggled over my words and what I was going to say, and it was, "You have a nice voice."

ANCHORING WHILE ILL

DC: You talked earlier about Sandy Socolow's observation that you got laryngitis prior to big events that you were anchoring and that the laryngitis would clear up as the broadcast began. Were there any occasions when you did a broadcast while you were really ill?

WC: I think I did some shows when I had colds and such, but nothing serious. Oh, I nearly forgot one incident. In April 1975, when South Vietnam fell to the North Vietnamese, I anchored a two-and-one-half hour retrospective look at news coverage of the Vietnam War. I had a very painful lower-back problem, and I had to be put in traction at home. It was a typical thing, a deteriorated disk or something of the kind. It had just suddenly popped, though. It was one of those times when I was leaning over to literally put on my shoes, and, you know, suddenly I couldn't straighten up. But I was at home when the war ended, and I was not about to let that war end without me. So a doctor came and shot me full of stuff. They took me down to the studio and literally propped me up in the anchor chair with pillows at my back and a platform under my feet to get my feet up to the right angle. CBS had a nurse and doctor standing by as I did the broadcast in considerable pain.

RELATIONS WITHIN CBS

DC: Let's talk about a couple of controversies within CBS that you felt unfairly raised questions about your integrity. One was caused by the CBS Special Report *The Selling of the Pentagon*, and another was related to the CIA. I'm especially interested in how both controversies illustrate how the *Evening News* operated when you were the anchor. Let's first talk about *The Selling of the Pentagon*, which was broadcast in February 1971 and was narrated by Roger Mudd. We touched on that program earlier in reference to the Nixon administration's attack on the press. The program examined the Pentagon's expenditure of millions of federal tax dollars to persuade the public to favor huge increases in its congressional appropriations. There was a controversy over the editing of an interview with marine colonel John McNeil. It was alleged, and I think maybe proven, that McNeil's answers to several questions were all edited out of sync to make it seem that he was answering only one particular question. Colonel McNeil sued CBS. The producer included in the program clips of some Pentagon promotional films that you narrated, which showed that you had been one of the persons hired by the government to do these government films that CBS was now criticizing. Bill Leonard later said that he and you had an argument about using a clip of you selling Pentagon stuff.

WC: I can't remember the specifics of it. But I know that I felt that I was being singled out. In fact, a lot of people had done those films. It was a popular thing to do in Washington. They made it appear as if I was the only one that did it, and I didn't think that was fair. I said if they were going to do that, they ought to show a lot of other people doing those films. That was the major nature of the argument. I wasn't very proud of those Pentagon films. In one of them, a recruitment film, I wore the uniform of a marine colonel. In the other—I don't know that I appeared on camera—I narrated a "Red threat" story.

DC: How did you get involved in making those films?

WC: Because they asked me to and, I guess, paid me something, but not much. You know, I was just a voice around Washington. This was years before I anchored the *Evening News*. In fact, I was doing the local news in Washington and the talk show on Sunday. I was beginning to do our major public events, but I didn't see any problem with doing those films at the time. As a matter of fact, in those days, during the Korean War, it seemed a patriotic kind of thing to do.

DC: How do you feel about it now, in retrospect?

WC: Oh, I think it was a mistake. If I were running a news operation, as indeed is the rule today, I wouldn't do those sorts of things. We did all sorts of things, such as industrial films, that we would not do today. In those days, there was no appreciation that there was a conflict of interest. But it is a very definite conflict of interest. I think this matter of purity, however, in the press, as far as conflict of interest goes, is a very delicate and difficult subject. If you eliminated every possible conflict of interest, you would have to require newspeople to join a monastic order and take a pledge of poverty. There'd be no other way to do it. It becomes a conflict of interest right away as soon as you own any property. Own an automobile and you have a conflict of interest with automobile laws, licenses, taxing, and gasoline prices. Perhaps that's a bit ridiculous, but it is a complex subject.

Where you must draw the line is with speech making. If you make a speech for an industrial society, a trade union, or an individual company, and you're paid a very handsome fee, people can allege conceivably that you have some interest in that organization. If you only do it once, I can't really see that you're going to be corrupted by that, but who knows? You accept a ride in a corporate jet, accept a ride with the military to a distant place, and you're being corrupted, presumably. So it's a judgment call. But there was a day when that just wasn't the case and we didn't think about that at all.

DC: The other controversy related to the CIA. According to Daniel Schorr's memoir, you attended a luncheon at CBS on February 4, 1976, given by Bill Paley for George Bush, who was then director of the CIA. Schorr says that an argument erupted at this luncheon over the issue of CIA agents posing as reporters. Schorr alleges that you started the argument because you were angry over an accusation by ABC correspondent Sam Jaffe that your name had appeared on a list as having actually worked as a CIA agent. According to Schorr, you demanded that Bush disclose the names of those agents who had posed as reporters so that you could clear your own name. Bush was sympathetic, according to this account, but said it couldn't be done because the agents had been promised "eternal secrecy." Bill Paley agreed with Bush. Schorr goes on to claim that this was because Paley himself had been a CIA agent.

WC: I think Schorr's version is approximately correct. I remember that I was very hot about this issue. I may have had something to do with that luncheon taking place. I think that I had expressed my objections to Paley, and I told him that I would like CBS's help in clearing my name. I wouldn't want to swear on that, but I kind of recall that there was a preliminary conversation that probably inspired the meeting.

DC: Had you known George Bush before this?

WC: No, just by reputation. I knew his father, Prescott Bush, when he was a U.S. senator from Connecticut. I thought Prescott Bush was a fine man. I don't know, but I may have met George in the company of his father. I met George Bush the first time in China, when he was ambassador to China.

DC: So you don't remember much about that incident with Bush?

WC: No, I don't. But Paley was acting as a peacemaker there because I was so aggressive about it. I think my aggressiveness sort of embarrassed Paley. He didn't expect it would be quite that strong. I was not the best company man in meetings of that kind. I remember another time, when Arthur Taylor was the president of CBS. He'd wanted to prove to the Pentagon and the Defense Department that CBS was really in America's corner, and all that kind of thing. So he asked if I would have lunch with him and James Schlesinger, who was then secretary of defense, in his office. Of course, I was glad to. I always had trouble with Schlesinger, who was so pedantically arrogant, you know. Please don't take offense, Don, but Schlesinger was so full of his college-professor-type thing. You shouldn't take offense, because I've never seen any academic arrogance in you. We certainly wouldn't be spending all this time in close quarters if you did suffer from that.

DC: I take that as quite a compliment. Thank you. But, unfortunately, I do know what you mean.

WC: I'm sure you see a lot of that. But anyway, during lunch, Schlesinger said something about "Well, of course we know that all of you newsmen are patriotic." And I just went right through the ceiling. I said, "Patriotic we're not; don't you believe that for one minute. We have no obligation to be patriotic. That is the worst thing we could do is to be patriotic, because just whose version of patriotism would we have to follow? I happen to believe that those people out there on the streets marching against the war in Vietnam are just as patriotic as you people conducting the war. They're patriotic because they believe that the best way for Americans to be patriotic and to be proud of that flag is that we get the hell out of Vietnam. And patriotism is no part of it. Let's leave that word out of this discussion." Poor Taylor, I thought he was going to jump out the thirty-fifth-floor window. He thought the whole goddamn thing had gone absolutely haywire from what he had planned. The whole reason for the luncheon had been shot to hell. It was much the same way with Bush and the CIA thing.

DC: I know how from reading some of the biographies of Paley how incredibly uncomfortable and displeased he was that the Nixon administration was so upset with CBS, and they were specifically critical of Walter Cronkite. Here is the president of the United States referring to you in a negative way at a press conference on two separate occasions. Paley had played up to every president since he had been head of CBS.

WC: Well, that's the nature of our business. Television is show business. People in show business want to be invited to the White House. It's as simple as that. To them, the greatest thing is to be invited to a state dinner at the White House. They want the president to call them by first name and be buddies with them; that's what they want out of life, and it's important for them to have those contacts, too, since the broadcast industry is controlled by the government in a sense, through the FCC.

DC: Barbara Matusow discusses Murrow's falling out with Paley and the negative consequences on Murrow's career. Matusow says that, quote, "this was a strong lesson that Walter Cronkite learned. He found out that no one was irreplaceable as far as the company was concerned, and this encouraged Cronkite to play everything safe from then on. Cronkite avoided confrontations with management, and he never spoke out against the sins of television, like Murrow. Cronkite also stayed out of office politics and avoided getting embroiled in other personnel problems, including those of his friends." She charges, for instance, that "Gordon Manning's firing is an example of one of Cronkite's friends getting the axe and Cronkite remaining totally silent. Cronkite's specialties were purposely non-controversial, like space and the environment."

WC: She seems to forget politics, which I suppose is noncontroversial. For heaven's sake, I object very strenuously to the Matusow book on nearly all scores. And I attribute a lot of it to the fact that I didn't give her an interview. I would not sit down and spend the time with her she wanted. She wanted to spend a day with me, and all that. And I turned her down because I just didn't have time to do it. She's dead wrong.

Taking those issues one by one. Murrow going over to the USIA shocked me. [*President Kennedy appointed Murrow the director of the United States Information Agency in January 1961.*] I mean, his going into politics, as it were, and taking a government job, I was very sorry about. I knew something of the fact that he and Paley were estranged to a degree, although I didn't know to what degree or how important it was, and it certainly had no influence on me whatsoever. Now, as for my playing it safe, as far as the company goes, I think two things about that: one, in a sense, I did, in that I didn't play politics. I simply wouldn't get involved in that sort of thing, and I didn't think it was my duty or my job. I wasn't going to throw any weight around at all. I didn't believe it was my role to do so, not even for my own benefit in many cases. Nearly every job that came to me I didn't ask for.

As for Gordon Manning's firing, that was Jack Schneider's doing. And that was because Manning was a very highly principled man who was perfectly willing to carry the brunt of arguments to management that other officials at CBS were not willing to do. He would go right up to Schneider and argue for things. I think Schneider thought he was too argumentative. It was also a promotion matter, you know. Fred Friendly had quit, and Gordon should have been in line, and Gordon wasn't appointed. That started the whole discussion that ended up in Gordon leaving for NBC. He wasn't appointed to head the news instead of Friendly, because he had been so argumentative. He carried a lot of the arguments that Friendly would not carry up to top management, and top management didn't like that.

DC: Did you ever have any desire to be head of CBS News?

WC: No. I never wanted to be an executive in business at all. Many times, I would speculate on what I'd do if I were president of CBS News. I did that almost daily. But I never wanted the job. I think many producers do; they're already in the executive area. They definitely think that way. And one of the great tragedies in the news department is that they not only think of getting ahead in the news department, but a few, unfortunately, thought about getting ahead in the network. They looked forward to the day that they would be moved over from news into programming or something of the kind in the network. That was Howard Stringer's problem. He was ambitious. Van Gordon Sauter was the most ambitious ever to get over into the big leagues of the network, and then Stringer inherited that trait. And that's very bad. It shouldn't happen, because once they do, they're representing their own career rather than representing the news department. They are not willing to fight for the news department with the same degree of aggressiveness that they would if they did not have personal ambitions to please the top management. I also wasn't much of a water-fountain-gossip type. I was in my office or on the desk constantly. I never wandered around the building as other people did, constantly exchanging rumor and gossip, nor did I spend much time with them in the evening. I wasn't very collegial in that respect. I had my own set of friends and my own set of social priorities, and that did not include hanging around the CBS staff. I think I was probably thought of as a pretty cool and distant figure for that reason.

DC: Well, that raises a question. What kind of person did you include in your social circle?

WC: They were writers, theatrical producers, business leaders, and political leaders. There were very few television people. A few comedians were friends of ours, and actors and actresses.

DC: But you didn't bring the shop into your social life, in other words?

WC: No, I didn't. I had done that when I was with United Press. I lived United Press and lived the news business twenty-four hours a day, seven days a week. But in New York, Betsy and I kind of got sidetracked from that. To tell you the truth, I found the newspaper and press service business very interesting. Everybody involved in it was always talking about the news and how we got a scoop and so forth. I found in radio and television a much more dispersed sort of thinking. They weren't my kind of newspeople. They kind of did their jobs, and then they gossiped about the office, but they didn't seem to have that same intense interest in the news itself. I'm not talking about my fellow reporters and correspondents as much as I'm thinking about the office staff. You know, in the newspaper, you've got all those rewrite men and all those wire filers in the press service. They're all intensely interested in their job. In the broadcast environment, the people on the desk don't seem to have that kind of interest. The writers don't seem to be that deeply involved. I don't know what it is. It may have been me. It may have been I just didn't develop that with them.

UNHAPPINESS WITH TELEVISION NEWS IN THE 1970S

DC: Despite Barbara Matusow's charge that you weren't willing to "speak out against the sins of television," I note that in 1976 you took a strong public stand against what you considered to be formula news broadcasting taking over the television news industry. I think the event that brought you out, and at least where you got an awful lot of attention in the press, was when Barbara Walters was hired as the coanchor at ABC and given a million-dollar contract. That stunned the television world, in a sense. During an address at the CBS-TV network affiliates convention in Los Angeles on May 5, 1976, you were quoted as saying that "Barbara Walters' contract did shake me up. At first, there was a first wave of nausea, the sickening sensation that perhaps we were all going under, that all of our efforts to hold network television news aloof from show business had failed." In that same speech, you also criticized the razzle-dazzle presentations of the local eyewitness-news formats and the pretty-boy anchors. I know you've talked about this before, but I'd like to get your summation again about how you were feeling then and why this all came out and what you were trying to do.

WC: I think as we look back on the Barbara Walters hiring, it is clear that her contract was a watershed. It did move—unfortunately, as it turns out—the news departments into show-business salaries and into show-business attitudes to a great degree. The local stations simply sold out to the consultants and ratings. Most of them, not all by any means, but most ceased to be worthy competitors of the newspapers in the sense of being responsible news gatherers and disseminators. Instead, they became a broadcast version of the tabloid newspapers, in a sense. The consultants were advising them that they had to have action in the first twenty-five seconds, and any old barn burning or jackknifed trailer truck would do, but just get action up there. And they told them that nobody should appear on the air more than ten seconds at a time, and, you know, all these terrible things. You had to have two anchors so there could be happy-talk banter between them. It was just ghastly, and once it started, it spread like wildfire across the country. It started at WABC in New York. Anyway, all of this was coming together at this time. The point was that television news had become so big and so important that the local stations wanted to get their hands on it and make it as profitable as possible. The profit motive became all important at that point. Up to that time, news had always been a loss leader. It was something that you did in order to establish credibility in the marketplace and as a public service. Local stations had news programs because the FCC licenses required it. News service was looked at as one of the criteria for renewing their licenses. They had to be fair and honest and upright, all the ethical things that any news program should be. This was written in the communications law. But the local stations found a way around it with this show business approach. So yes, I was very upset at that time. The stations began hiring these vacuous pretty boys and pretty girls instead of journalism people, instead of people that had newspaper experience or good radio news experience or television news experience. They were hiring pretty boys whose hairdo was more important than their news sense or knowledge. We got into the era of the news reader instead of the news manager, news writer, and news reporter.

DC: And I take it you think that it's gotten worse rather than getting better?

WC: Yes, I do.

DC: At that time, you were also saying that you were urging local stations to quit using these fly-by-night on-the-air personnel. I think 50 percent of these local newspeople changed jobs every two years. You offered an interesting alternative, I think. Do you recall that?

WC: I always believed that we ought to hire off the local newspaper, if that's what you're talking about. Those are the people who understand their community and the people and history of the community. These are the people that ought to be controlling the news broadcasts. I believe that if you put them on the air, they would exude such authority that they didn't have to be pretty people. I have a plan that I would put into effect if I ran CBS News today. I would go around the country to the best newspaper people I could find and bring them to CBS. I would pay them five times what they are being paid at the newspaper. I would give them a ten-year contract. And I would say that I can't tell you what the hell you're going to be doing. You may be working in the library, or you may be the anchor of the *Evening News*. You're going to get the same salary right on through; no matter what that job is you're doing, you're going to get paid on this contractual basis. But you're going to do whatever we ask you to do, just like you do on a newspaper. You don't come to a newspaper and say I'm only going to write police news or write theater criticism, or I'm going to do that and do this. You come and work on the desk, you work on the paper, or work where you're needed. And that's what we would do at CBS. We would end up paying far less than we have to pay today for one of the greatest news organizations the world has ever put together.

DC: How would that improve the news?

WC: Well, first of all, you would have good news writing and editing. You would have superior news sense in the organization. You'd have a corps of people who could fit in any place. You could send them overseas or keep them at home or send them to Washington or put them on the air. Primarily, you'd have news authority, the sense that the people at CBS News know what news is and know how to get it to you and put it in front of you as honestly and straightforward as it can be done.

DC: Well, of course, some critics charge that the newspapers themselves—the *USA Today* syndrome—are becoming more and more like the eyewitness-news programs on television.

WC: Well, there's some truth to that too, of course. The newspapers, in attempting to compete for the public's attention, have come into television's backyard and have tried to compete on the basis of entertaining the public instead of informing them. I made this pitch to the AP managing editors thirty-five years ago. I was already concerned that newspapers were beginning to be more entertaining rather than informing. Television is going to beat them at the entertainment game, beat them every time. So now the newspapers are printing the news in these one-line, one-sentence reports, especially international news. Well, that's what television does. The newspapers need to give us more news and information in-depth, not in one-liners.

CONFIDENTIALITY OF SOURCES

DC: You testified on May 20, 1974, in Los Angeles, at a special hearing on the confidentiality of a reporter's sources. William Farr of the *Los Angeles Times* was hauled to court because he refused to disclose his sources about stories that he had written on the 1969 Charles Manson trial. How did you get brought into that?

WC: Farr and his attorneys asked me to come out as an expert witness, in a sense, on press responsibilities and duties and privileges.

DC: You said at that trial that the gag-rule enforcement "is a problem for the courts, not the reporters. Any journalist worth his salt would hold on to his confidants. I think you are going to get much fairer justice in this country by protecting the freedom of the press." You said that if Farr were forced to reveal his sources, "it would be another nail in the coffin of freedom of speech and the press. It's that serious." And then you said that withholding sources by a reporter is highly ethical. Is there anything you want to add to that as far as your view?

WC: No. I've said this many times, in many forms, in many places. It seems to me that the protection of sources is fundamental to the ability to report adequately. But I am somewhat disturbed over the tendency today to protect sources apparently when it isn't necessary to protect sources. I think the anonymous source is too frequently used today. The *New York Times* has made almost a whole technique out of reporting by not quoting sources. I think that they've gone much too far. Maybe we ought to get back to some aspects of the old Associated Press rule. Fifty years ago, before World War II, the AP had a rule that a source had to come first in every story, and it led to ridiculous things like "Sheriff Clint B. Jones of Muskogee County said that in a head-on accident today, three people were killed on Route 61." And then from there on out, everything was quoting the sheriff. That obviously was unnecessary. But I do think that in a lot of Washington reporting, there is too much anonymity. But once it is clearly established that a source must be protected, such as in the case of a whistle-blower, and there is no other way to get the story, then that source must be protected.

DC: Walter, during these conversations, I have made many references to Gary Gates's history of CBS News, which has provided a basic chronology for some of our discussion. His book, *Air Time*, was published in 1978. Did you help Gates with the book?

WC: No, I don't recall his ever even interviewing me for it. He must have, in the course of the thing. But there were no long sessions, certainly. And I haven't read it. Frankly, I've read very few of those books you've mentioned. I try to read them, and they just bore me. I find them fairly inaccurate for the most part. The parts that interest me most are other newsmen's alleged versions of things that took place, but even there, I'm not so sure the reporting is accurate. I guess it's a little like psychiatry. I can't imagine lying on a couch, looking at my navel, for God's sake—well, that's kind of hard to do lying on a couch—but this navel examination, wondering who am I? Trying to discover myself. These books are the same sort of thing—just a lot of navel-gazing. Reading books about yourself is just too damned self-indulgent. I've got better things to do.

1,2,3,4,5,6,

HARRY REASONER AND ROGER MUDD man the CBS News Presidential Desk. Assignment: Complete, perceptive coverage of every aspect of the Presidential race, throughout the 50 states and the District of Columbia.

ERIC SEVAREID'S penetrating comments come from the CBS News Analysis Desk. Assignment: A continuing analysis of the election trends. What has happened—and why.

MIKE WALLACE is the man to watch at the CBS News Gubernatorial Desk. Assignment: All the developments and results in the 25 states electing governors.

ROBERT TROUT will be at the CBS News Congressional Desk. Assignment: Comprehensive reports on the 35 Senate and 435 House elections.

WALTER CRONKITE'S command post is the CBS News National Desk. Assignment: Coordinate all reports for an informed, authoritative survey of the entire election scene.

and VPA for Good Measure

VPA—Vote Profile Analysis—is a revolutionary, scientific measure of the vote, developed by CBS News. With VPA, the six astute CBS News correspondents above can tell you more about an election—sooner—than you've ever known before.

VPA is a fast, extremely accurate way to indicate winning candidates early in the evening. It is also much more than that. This remarkable technique for election night reporting digs deep into exactly *how* a candidate has been elected. It provides a fast analysis of voting trends in different geographic areas, among various religious, ethnic and economic groups—tells you *whom* they voted for and *why*. VPA adds a whole new dimension to television coverage of an election.

Nearly two years of intensive research from coast to coast have gone into setting up VPA. This research has been gathered from 1,960 VPA sample precincts and stored in a multimillion dollar IBM computer complex at CBS News Studio 41 (the newest, most advanced television studio in the world). On election night, a special corps of reporters in these 1,960 precincts will begin calling actual returns into CBS News Election Head-quarters as soon as the polls close. These returns, when evaluated against the original research from these precincts, will give an accurate early picture of each state's political behavior.

CBS News has already used VPA in covering 21 elections and primaries since 1962. It's been right every time. (VPA's amazing accuracy has led The New York Times, The Washington Post, the Los Angeles Times and Newsweek magazine to subscribe to this CBS News service.)

See how VPA works Tuesday night.

It's a CBS News exclusive.

CBS NEWS

for the most unique election night coverage

CHAPTER TWENTY-TWO

Colleagues and Associates

DC: We've talked about many of your colleagues and associates at different points in your career. I'd like to add some brief additional comments and anecdotes about some of those individuals. Let's begin with Sig Mickelson, who was head of CBS News and was the person who selected you to be the anchor of CBS's coverage of the 1952 political conventions. He was fired in February 1961 and replaced by Richard Salant. Mickelson was obviously an important figure in the development of television news.

WC: Well, Sig was particularly important to me, of course. Sig had the job of organizing television news for CBS. It was a discovery process for him, throughout. Sig had an integrity that was absolutely unassailable in his efforts to put television news on the right path at its very beginning. He was a student. He came from academia. So he was terribly thoughtful about the impact television was going to have on our society. Of course, I don't think even Sig could have foreseen the ubiquitous, all-pervasive form it became, but he tried to set us on the right path in all of his decisions. Partly because no one knew what was required at that time, he made some rather strange choices in hiring his deputies. I don't think they worked out terribly well in a lot of cases. I'm not so sure that was any failing of Mickelson's in personnel management, as much as not knowing what the requirements of television were going to be. Nobody knew what kind of people were going to be needed. But the consequence was that the leadership of the Mickelson team wasn't as strong, probably, as it should have been in that particular period. I don't know anything about his dealings with the hierarchy at CBS. As I've said before, I really paid no attention to the politics at 45 Madison or later at Black Rock, the name we gave the CBS corporate building. But Sig and I worked very well together. He was a very good friend. I admire Mickelson immensely for the journalistic principles upon which he

A *CBS News* poster of the 1964 presidential election news team: left to right, Harry Reasoner, Roger Mudd, Eric Sevareid, Mike Wallace, Robert Trout, and Walter Cronkite. *CBS poster reproduced from an ad in the October 30, 1964, edition of the* New York Times, *copy in Cronkite Papers (DI-05813).*

stood at the time. I saw no evidence at my level of any compromises he made. Whether they were required or not, I don't know, but his biggest problem was that he was the victim of a rivalry with the old-guard radio people, the Murrow group, primarily.

DC: Would Fred Friendly be one of those?

WC: No, I don't think so. I think that Friendly probably always thought that he could run the division better than anyone else, but I think at the time, he was getting along with Mickelson in the production of the *CBS Reports* series.

DC: Is there anything that you would attribute to Mickelson in particular about his contribution to the development of CBS News?

WC: I believe it was Sig who began to establish the standards on which television news— CBS and, therefore, the others—was built. We were the leader and remained so until recent years, so that influence has been industry wide. I think Mickelson was the first to establish those high principles of noninterference in the news department by top management. As the head of CBS News, Sig was the buffer. He was adamant about keeping the pressure from advertisers or politicians or whoever from the newsroom. It wasn't a new concept, but it was new to apply it to the growing forces of television, where more money was being spent and greater commitments were being made, and advertisers and politicians alike who wanted to control the medium in those early stages. They weren't permitted to do that, and I think Sig deserves a lot of the credit for that. [*Mickelson died in March 2000.*]

CHARLES COLLINGWOOD AND ERIC SEVAREID

DC: According to some sources, your promotion to the *Evening News* was a disappointment to Eric Sevareid and Charles Collingwood because they both thought that they were in line behind Doug Edwards. Did you ever pick up on that?

WC: I never had any problem at all with Eric or Charlie. I always thought they were friends and never ceased to be, particularly Collingwood. Both are absolutely exquisite gentlemen, and I wouldn't have expected to hear anything personally from either of them. I never heard any rumors that they might feel that way. I always thought that they both felt somewhat to superior to me and my focus on breaking news. But it was never expressed in any personal way or in any lack of cooperation in broadcasts that we were assigned to do together. The suggestion that has been made that there was a kind of camaraderie of elegance among the Murrow people, I think, is true. I was fairly close to both men. Certainly, I felt quite close to Collingwood, although I think many people did. He was the kind of person who had the capacity for close friendship. I felt Collingwood was very badly mistreated by CBS, and by Dick Salant in particular, in the later days of his career. Charles operated in kind of a strange way. He was a very passive man. "Elegant" is the word that describes him best. He was a superb reporter and thoughtful writer, but he had a streak of laziness about him, a certain uncaring attitude about whether he got an assignment or didn't get an assignment. He drank a bit and gambled a lot and led a very fast kind of social existence. I think that Salant got down on him, but I don't know why. Salant basically passed the word around that Collingwood shouldn't be given any important assignments. They gave Collingwood the dregs of documentaries and so forth. But he never complained, as far as I know, and he never quit. He kept on doing whatever he was assigned to do, and he always did it very well. He was a helpful mentor to some of our young correspondents. Charlie died a few years ago [1985]. Collingwood was always terribly good, I thought. Frankly, I thought he should have been the anchor after Doug Edwards. Now, I wasn't thinking that at the time. I wasn't thinking, "Oh, gosh, I thought it was going to go to Collingwood." But I thought many times while I was doing the show over those years that Collingwood would be a better anchor than me. He was definitely a better broadcaster. I always admired his appearance, looks, and personality. He was called "the duke" by his friends, which was appropriate.

DON HEWITT

DC: Don Hewitt is widely acknowledged to be one of the most important pioneers of television news. You worked with Hewitt from the beginning of your CBS career, beginning with the 1952 political conventions. We've already talked some about Hewitt. Is there anything else about your work with him that comes to mind?

WC: Well, I've always thought there was a very mercurial aspect to Don Hewitt. He certainly has a vivid imagination and great innovative talents that have made *60 Minutes* the great success that it is today. But it seemed to me and to Salant that under Hewitt, the *Evening News* was out of control in a way. I was always concerned that Don was maybe stretching too far to get a story. I always worried that he would promise something to a news source that perhaps shouldn't be promised and that couldn't be delivered. I've already mentioned a few examples. But Don was an exciting guy to work with, and he produced an exciting broadcast. But Dick Salant and I felt that the *Evening News* should be based on a more solid journalistic foundation. Don's style is more of a tabloid style, and we wanted more of a *New York Times* style.

DC: Sounds like Don Hewitt got you into a couple of tight spots with the Kennedys in particular.

WC: Yeah, but the absolutely worst one was with Frank Sinatra. Oh, gee. Hewitt used his good connections to get us the first exclusive interview with Frank Sinatra, who wouldn't do interviews. But he agreed to this one. He said that he admired my work on the air. So we went out to his house in Palm Springs. On the way, talking about Sinatra, Don asked me, "How are you going to handle the Mafia issue? He's real fierce about not talking about the Mafia." I said, "I thought I'd handle it by waiting until the very end of the interview, and then just put it to him, you know, 'You've been accused of having Mafia connections. What's your answer to that?' And then when he dodges it, I'll throw out some of the facts and I'll show him the picture." Well, the picture was one that showed him posing backstage with several guys known to have Mafia connections. The photo was taken at a nightclub known to be a Mafia-owned business. And Don said, "That's the way to do it, that's the way." Then Don said, "Now, what about the marriage? I understand that he refused to talk about his marriage to Mia Farrow." I said, "Well, I didn't know that." Don said, "Well, I know he had refused in the past." And I said, "Well, in that case, I'll save that for just before the Mafia question!" Don said, "That's a good way to go."

Well, we were doing the interview, and I slipped in the question about his marriage. Sinatra said something innocuous, and we got through it without any problem. We got to the Mafia, and—whammo!—Sinatra walked out of the room, retreated into his bedroom, and didn't say a word to me. His lawyer, who had been listening to this, said, "Well, that's all for you guys! Get the hell out of here! You're going to get sued for this one." Hewitt went running after Sinatra. Don had promised him we weren't going to ask that question.

DC: What happened? Did you just pack up and leave?

WC: No. Don actually talked him into coming back. Not only talked him into coming back, he persuaded him to talk about the Mafia! Sinatra came back, and I showed him the photograph of him with these mobsters. He said, "Look, I'm a nightclub entertainer. The Mafia may have an investment in this place. Who knows? The owner of this place is a friend of mine. What am I supposed to do? Not like him? Hate him? Welch on him? These people employ me. I work for them. The picture in the nightclub: all those fellows came backstage. What am I going to do? Tell them I didn't want my picture taken with them?" That was his answer, which, as far as that goes, is pretty straight. Of course, it doesn't go far enough, but it was a good answer.

DC: So when you were going into an interview that Hewitt had arranged, you must have worried about what he had promised that you didn't know about?

WC: Oh, my God. All the time! But Hewitt was good at it. He did get the interviews, you know, and we had a lot of wonderful stuff. [*Hewitt died in 2009.*]

MIKE WALLACE

DC: Mike Wallace is another longtime colleague. We were talking about Hewitt and how interviews are done these days. How do you feel about Mike Wallace's interview style?

WC: I both admire and abhor it. I admire Mike's pure ability to do the adversarial kind of interview as well as he does it. I could never do it. I don't believe that it's the best way to get information. My technique is absolutely the opposite from Mike's. For that reason, I'm not terribly good on a live interview, because I like to develop an issue, chew around it, let a person ponder on it. I think you get more that way of real, lasting value. But it takes a while, and it takes a lot of editing. It may not be quite as honest in some ways as what Mike does, because it is all in the editing, and you've got to be very careful with that. Then it is really up to the ethics of the editor whether you do an honest picture or not. Don Hewitt and Mike do that too. I mean, they edit their interviews very tightly. A live interview is something else again.

DC: In March 1974, Mike Wallace did a story on *60 Minutes* about press junkets and conflicts of interest. At the end of the broadcast, Wallace announced that "even Walter Cronkite took these junkets." [Robert] Metz, who wrote a history of CBS, says, and I'm quoting right out of the book: "Walter was pissed off. He told the press that his trips were of a personal nature, made with friends and they had nothing to do with his assignments with CBS. Cronkite apparently seethed for an awful long time." *New York Magazine* claimed that you and Wallace "have not always gotten along, but these days, they are not getting along better than ever." Mike Wallace vigorously denied that this was the case. Is all of that accurate?

WC: That's true. As a matter of fact, I was very sore at Wallace. I thought he was building a career on my ashes. I still think that was what was motivating him at the time. He selected me because I was very visible at that time as the anchor of the *Evening News*. It makes the reporter look very big to be able to take after a very important figure in his own company. It makes him look courageous and brave. I felt that was nine-tenths the reason Wallace did it. Wallace's piece featured a rather inconsequential trip that I'd made with Pan Am Airways, involving the novelist James Michener.

But I was particularly pissed off at Don Hewitt, who was a notorious junket taker. As a matter of fact, Hewitt took all kinds of emoluments and privileges from anybody on anything at all times. Most of the time, it was to get a story or to get in places. He found ways to justify it, I'm sure, most of the time, but his style was always a problem and a considerable worry and concern for CBS management. It was one of the reasons why we dropped him as the producer of *CBS Evening News*. We couldn't trust his judgment on things like that.

SANDY SOCOLOW

DC: I want to ask you about Sandy Socolow, a person with whom you've had a long professional relationship. When you were anchoring the midday TV news show in the mid-1950s, Sig Mickelson hired Socolow to work with you as a writer.

WC: Oh, yeah. Sandy was great. He was an old International News Service [INS] reporter. He is a very savvy New Yorker, a City College graduate. He had edited the City College newspaper, and after college, he got in the Korean War. He went to Japan and Korea in the army information department and ended up in Tokyo. He made contacts there that he used to get a job with INS in Tokyo after the war. He covered much of the Far East on various assignments for INS. From there, he came back to New York—I guess with INS, I'm not sure. But during that period, he got a job with CBS. He was with me throughout my tenure as anchor of the *Evening News*.

DC: Why do you think you two have been able to work so well together all these years?

WC: Sandy is a very savvy guy about working with people. He can work with anybody. He is very good at his job, and it didn't take any adjustment on my part to work with him, which is the secret of success, since I was the boss. But he is a good, fast writer and a fast thinker, with excellent journalistic instincts. He has all the right attributes for that kind of work. There were an awful lot of people in television news in those days who were from radio, and they weren't very good newspeople. But Soc was fresh. He hadn't acquired that radio syndrome. Sandy and I are still very close after all of these years.

HUGHES RUDD

DC: Hughes Rudd was a CBS correspondent when you were news anchor. I understand he was one of the only correspondents that you had a hand in hiring.

WC: Yes, that's right. Hughes worked on the *Kansas City Times*, and he did some writing for the Calvin Company, which was a major industrial film producer in Kansas City. Bill Vaughn, who was a friend of mine when we lived out there, was a humor columnist for the *Kansas City Star*. He and Hughes Rudd did some writing for the Calvin Company. I was doing some of those industrial films in those days. I flew out to Kansas City and did some work for the Calvin Company. That's how I met Hughes. We got to be good friends. I was a great admirer of his writing. I got him the job at CBS as a writer and correspondent. Hughes had a rough kind of style on the air, and I don't think some of the bosses thought too highly of his broadcast capabilities. But others thought very highly of it. His style was sardonic. Hughes was one of our correspondents in Europe for a period. He was in Berlin and Moscow. Actually, Hughes was a bit of a controversial figure. The biggest problem was Hughes drank heavily at night. He never drank on the job deliberately, but sometimes a job would slop over into his drinking hours, which was unfortunate. But when he had a few drinks, he became somewhat belligerent, and wherever he was in the world, he would call up Bill Paley in the middle of the night and bawl him out for some entertainment show he'd seen that night that he didn't like very much, or something or other. This obviously created something of a crisis.

DC: Yes, I would think so.

WC: But Hughes was very good. I think the morning show he hosted in the 1970s was the best one CBS ever had. It had real character to it. He left CBS in 1979 and lives in France now. [*Rudd died in October 1992.*]

HARRY REASONER

DC: Harry Reasoner was not only a CBS correspondent when you were the anchor, but he also was one of the substitute anchors, along with Roger Mudd, whenever you were on vacation or out for some reason. According to Gary Gates: "Occasionally, Walter Cronkite betrayed a certain resentment toward Harry Reasoner's constant socializing with his editorial staff. He liked and respected Reasoner well enough, but his competitive antennae were so sensitive that he could not help but view him as a tough rival. One day in 1969 Walter Cronkite complained to Les Midgley about the frequency with which his staff had lunch with Reasoner. Midgley replied, 'Look, Walter, I'm sure if you ask them, those guys would be delighted to have lunch with you, too.' Cronkite's only reply was to frown and walk away. That was not what he had in mind." When Reasoner left for ABC in 1970, Gates says that he was deeply touched by your farewell to him on the *Evening News* broadcast until Reasoner learned later that the "entire bit had been written by his good friend Charlie West."

WC: I don't recall this resentment business. I can't imagine complaining to Les Midgley about it. What would I complain about? That strikes me as very odd. I think I may have been envious, even jealous to a degree, perhaps inwardly, of Reasoner's relationship with the guys. I can see that because I didn't have it. I didn't have it because I didn't see that as one of the important things to be doing. You know, it was a shame, because Reasoner was a very gifted broadcaster. He was one of Sig Mickelson's recruits. But Reasoner didn't have much else to do. He wasn't exactly a hard worker. He had all day to go to lunch and enjoy life. I think I made a great mistake in not doing that kind of thing. I think I'd have been much better off doing that. I would reorganize my days and my life completely if I could do that over. I would devote my entire time to doing the *Evening News* except going out to lunch for two hours every day and having fun. But I didn't. I never went with anybody except when lunch was forced upon me in some important aspect of something. I envied the camaraderie that Harry enjoyed with the staff, but I didn't try to participate in it. I thought that we were friends, all of us, but I didn't make an effort to show that friendship. As for my complaining about Harry to Midgley, I don't know. Les and I were very dear friends. I'm trying to imagine a situation in which we're sitting there with our feet on the desk and talking about Reasoner. I possibly could have said something that could have been interpreted that way.

DC: What about this bit about when Reasoner left for ABC and he found out somebody else wrote your farewell?

WC: I don't know that happened, but it may have. You know, things like that get exaggerated in the retelling. Somebody says something about some aspect like that, and then the next person tells that story, and it gets bigger and bigger. I don't recognize any of that, except I recognize the fact that I wasn't that friendly with the staff. Charlie West and I frequently had lunch together. I played tennis every morning with another one of them. So it wasn't that I was really ignoring them exactly. [*Reasoner died in August 1991.*]

CHARLES KURALT

DC: In the fall of 1967, Charles Kuralt premiered his "On The Road" feature as a regular segment on the *Evening News*. It became an enormously popular segment of your program. Let's talk about Kuralt and his "On the Road" segment.

WC: I like Kuralt a lot, and I like his work immensely, but I was very opposed to making "On the Road" a regular feature. I thought it was bent a little toward entertainment, for one thing, and for the other thing, it locked us in time-wise. If we promised Kuralt these three or four minutes, it meant that we didn't have enough of a hard-news hole. The news time was considerably reduced, and we didn't have the flexibility we needed for headlines. I felt the same way about the enterpriser pieces. That was not entertainment at all, but if we promised three of those a week or something, it really affected our ability to cover the rest of the news.

I would oppose any kind of regular feature on broadcast. Indeed, if I remember properly, we kind of accepted a compromise on the Kuralt tapes, that they would not be slated on given days or even a given number a week. Kuralt was in favor of that himself too, so we had no problem selling that. His pieces, of course, were wonderful—you know that. They were originated, if I remember, by Salant, who felt that we needed to relieve the intensity of the broadcast as a result of the war. We needed something to emphasize that things are normal in this country, things are going on that always have, and that we're not all out there in the foxholes of Vietnam.

DC: It has been claimed that Kuralt's "On The Road" feature and your persona played a role in calming people down a little bit during a terribly divisive era. But you are saying that was a conscious thing as far as Kuralt's segment was concerned?

WC: Yes, it was very definitely part of it.

DC: Was that Kuralt's idea to go on the road?

WC: I think it might have been his idea to do it. I think it might have been more of Salant's idea that it would be done to balance the war coverage.

DC: Is Charlie Kuralt off camera like he is on camera?

WC: Oh, very much so. He is very calm and easygoing and very friendly. He is a very nice man. Charles Kuralt has never said anything ill about anybody that I know of. I think his CBS News *Sunday Morning* program is outstanding. [*Kuralt died in July 1997.*]

BERNARD SHAW

DC: In an interview with *Parade* magazine, Bernard Shaw of Cable News Network said that when he was in the military in the early 1960s, you played a key role in his decision to go into journalism after he left the service.

WC: I was in Hawaii filming a *Twentieth Century* program on the man who spied on Pearl Harbor. Every time I returned to my hotel the three or four days we were there, I had a message to call Corporal Bernard Shaw at such and such telephone number. I got several of these messages, which always happened when I got into a town. There would be a piece in the paper that I was in town, and a lot of people would call for one reason or another. You usually got so busy you just couldn't call them back. I didn't get a chance to call this Corporal Shaw. This went on for a couple of days. I came in one afternoon, and the desk clerk handed me my messages. The desk clerk said that there was a young gentleman waiting to see me in the lobby. And it was Corporal Shaw. He said, "I just wanted a few minutes of your time, Mr. Cronkite. I want to be a newsman, and I want to get your advice on how to do it." And I said, "Well, anybody as persistent as you are has already got it made as far as being a newsman goes; you'll be very successful. But I'll buy you a drink and talk to you." So we chatted for twenty minutes or so, and I found him to be an interesting, bright young guy. He was very serious and dedicated to the idea of being a television or radio newsman. He was in the army [*Shaw served in the Marine Corps.*] and was in a public relations role of some kind. I said that was the best way to do it. I told him that he should try local television somewhere when he got out of the army. I asked him where he was from, and he said Chicago. I said, "Well, go back to Chicago and let me know when you get there, and I'll at least get you an interview at our station there. And by golly, a couple years later, he called me. He was in Chicago. I got him an interview, and he got a job. It started him in the business, and that's something I'm very proud of. He later worked in the 1970s at the CBS Washington bureau. We lost him to ABC, and then he became the anchor of CNN. Bernie is a terrific journalist and news anchor. [*Shaw was CNN anchor from 1980 until his retirement in 2000.*]

Meir.

WC: Golda Meir was fascinating to me. She was really almost more interesting for what she said off the record than what she said on. I guess you could say that about almost any leader. But she was much more candid off record. She was willing to talk about ... 1973 war. She readily admitted that Israel started the 1973 ... ... version. She told me that off- ... l. She said at one point, "You ... us are always praising Moses, for ... My God. Just look at Moses. If he ... of left we'd have all that oil."

move to Anwar Sadat of Egypt, who you interviewed
once. The first time was in the fall of 1970, and
...ssed the issue of Israeli withdrawal from Egyptian
... seized four years before in the Six Day war in 1967.
...uote from the interview transcript that is ...
...orical importance ...

...ews organization
We did that interview under a spreading banyan
...s estate, out on the river. And quite honestly,
... couple of hours, but it was probably one of the
...ews I think I had done up to that time with

...ght for it, but he was willing to do so. Stalin wisely chose
...t to fight, but it was a very dangerous period.

CHAPTER TWENTY-THREE

Interviews with World Leaders

DC: We've discussed the in-depth presidential television memoirs that you did with Presidents Eisenhower and Johnson. But you have done a number of significant television interviews, if not memoirs, with the leaders of other countries. You've pointed out that some aren't worth talking about, such as your noninterview with Francisco Franco of Spain, and you have said that other interviews, such as those with French president Pompidou, West German chancellor Willy Brandt, and UN secretary-general Kurt Waldheim, for example, weren't that memorable to you. But there are few others that we should discuss.

WC: Well, I should point out that my interviewing of these people increased during the 1970s because of Barbara Walters. She gets credit for intensifying the effort to get exclusive interviews with world leaders. She did it to a degree that it became really a challenge, but also, in a way, a damn nuisance. I guess I wasn't terribly aggressive in those days. But Barbara was so aggressive, and it was such a personal thing with her. She was trying to prove herself as a journalist, and that was about the only way she knew to do it. She worked so hard at it that she forced all of us to play the same game she was playing.

GOLDA MEIR

DC: Let's begin with your interview of Israel's Golda Meir.

WC: Golda Meir was fascinating to me. She was really almost more interesting for what

---

Cronkite with Cuban president Fidel Castro in Havana, ca. 1982. CBS Photo Division, copy in Cronkite Papers (DI_05795).

she said off the record than what she said on. I guess you could say that about almost any leader. But she was much more candid off record. She was willing to talk about the 1973 war. She readily admitted that Israel started the 1973 war, which was not the official version. She told me that off camera. Meir was quite wonderful. She said at one point, "You know, I don't know why all of us are always praising Moses, for heaven's sake. Moses! Moses! My God, just look at Moses. If he had just turned right instead of left, we'd have all that oil." [laughs]

There is a wonderful story about Golda Meir's first visit to Washington as Israeli prime minister. Meir had lived in Wisconsin as a young woman, but she was returning to America as the premier of Israel. She went to the White House for a reception, and President Nixon, who was totally lost with small talk, just couldn't manufacture a conversation at all. He'd just named Henry Kissinger as secretary of state, and Abba Eban was the Israeli foreign secretary. Eban, of course, spoke the eloquent English of Oxford University. Golda Meir entered the foyer of the White House; the president privately spoke to her and said, "You know, we are both blessed by having Jewish foreign ministers." And Meir said, "Oh, Mr. President, I'm doubly blessed. Mine speaks perfect English."

When Sadat finally made his trip to Israel, and they landed at Tel Aviv airport, and they had all the current officials and the former officials in the government standing out on the tarmac, she was there as the former prime minister. And when Sadat got to her, he gave her a very big greeting, and she shook her finger in his face, just like an old schoolteacher, and she said, "Why didn't you tell me you wanted to come to Israel?" [laughs]

ANWAR SADAT

DC: Let's move to Anwar Sadat of Egypt, who you interviewed more than once. The first time was in the fall of 1970, and you discussed the issue of Israeli withdrawal from Egyptian territory seized four years before in the Six-Day War in 1967. I have a quote from the interview transcript that is of no great historical importance, but as a Texan, I thought it made an interesting anecdote. At one point, Sadat wondered if he could ask you a question. You replied that you hadn't intended the interview to go that way, but you said, "I'm ready for the question." Sadat said, "Well, Walter, let us say that part of . . . Texas is occupied by foreign troops, and then you were asked to make peace with those who occupied this territory in Texas, in spite of the fact that most of Texas is desert, as much as I know. Well, are you going to sit and discuss everything while these areas are occupied?" And then you said, "I understand your point sir. But I think you might get a little argument from Texans about the fact that most of Texas is a desert." Sadat: "Please, sir. Are you a Texan?" Cronkite: "Well, as a matter of fact, partially. I was educated there." Sadat: "Good. Good." I don't know if you remembered that or not. [*Cronkite chuckles*]

WC: Well, Sadat had just been made president. He'd never done a television interview for a Western television news organization prior to that. We did that interview under a spreading banyan tree out on his estate, out on the river. And quite honestly, it went for a couple of hours, but it was probably one of the dullest interviews I think I had done up to that time with almost anybody. He was a very nice man, but he'd only been president a very short while, and he was the sixth and least of the vice presidents, by all accounts. He was the one least expected to be selected by Nasser as his eventual successor, and yet Nasser's political will named him. When I interviewed him, right after Nasser's death, most of the experts thought he would a temporary president. By the time I went back in January 1971 to do the next interview, it looked like he was going to last. In fact, that's why I did the interview. But he didn't have very deep thoughts on anything, or if he did, they were so obscured by rhetoric that they were hard to extricate from the mass of verbiage. So it was just dull. But at one point, I suddenly was shaken awake when he said, "Then I shall go to Jerusalem." And I said, "You're going to Jerusalem? My gracious. When are you going to Jerusalem?" He said, "Oh, when we have peace. When the Israelis withdraw from the Golan Heights, when they withdraw from the Sinai," etc., etc., etc., "and then I'll go to Jerusalem." And clearly, it was merely rhetoric. What he was saying was a metaphor for "there will be peace in my time." I couldn't imagine that he would actually do that within a few years.

MARSHAL TITO

DC: We will talk later about your most important interview with Sadat when we discuss the Carter presidency. But another important interview that you did in 1971 was with Marshal Tito of Yugoslavia.

WC: Oh, that whole thing was quite memorable. We went out to something that, as I recall it, they called the Yugoslavian White House. It is a summer residence outside of Belgrade on a river. It is a beautiful place. We did an interview in the study of the building. Tito was really up for the interview, and very humorous. There were a lot of jokes exchanged back and forth. We hit it off exceedingly well. We asked if he would walk in the garden afterward for picture purposes—one of those transition things you do for television. He asked if we would like for his wife to come along, and we said of course. My wife was also there, so we invited her down. Tito, his wife, and I walked around in the garden on camera. She was quite an impressive woman. At that time, we seemed to be getting along just famously. It was all very friendly. I was much impressed with Tito, as much as I was with Sadat. I admired his personal courage, which, of course, he'd shown throughout World War II as the leader of the guerrilla forces fighting the German army and the right-wing guerrillas. And then, of course, his standing up to Stalin. Yugoslavia was the only Soviet satellite that was able to break away successfully from Moscow. He anticipated he might have to fight for it, but he was willing to do so. Stalin wisely chose not to fight, but it was a very dangerous period.

I had been in Moscow at the time of Tito's visit to that city, so I covered the story from that end. I was at his embassy. The Yugoslavs, of course, had a party for Tito. There were so few foreign correspondents in Moscow in those days that we were given the status of ambassadors, so we were invited to all the parties. Thank God the Russians extended that to us, because it was really the only place we got to see any Russians. I was fascinated with Tito for his independence from Stalin and also then for his leadership of the Third World, which played a major role in the history of the twentieth century. The Non-Aligned Movement was a very sensible thing on his part. I thought it was brilliant, to keep the world from being divided into only two camps. It certainly had a major impact on world politics. As a result, Tito was not looked upon with favor by American foreign-policy makers, nor by the Russians. But he carried it off exceedingly well. The great mistake he made was this crazy presidential-succession thing that has caused the breakup of Yugoslavia today. It was certainly not the way he planned it.

ALEXANDER SOLZHENITSYN

DC: You interviewed the Russian novelist and dissident Alexander Solzhenitsyn in June 1974 in Zurich after he had just been expelled from the Soviet Union.

WC: That was a great interview. It was negotiated through Solzhenitsyn's attorney in Berlin, and we finally worked it out. We had a person who translated both sides of the discussion and translated rapidly. Solzhenitsyn spoke very rapidly, and the translator apparently kept up quite well, and it was a good discussion. I don't remember the specifics of the actual interview very much. I do remember coming to a very interesting conclusion, which I think was borne out later on to the degree that we don't hear much of Solzhenitsyn anymore, really, in this country. Solzhenitsyn found democracy as practiced in the United States totally unacceptable. He later gave a speech at Harvard where he declared openly what I sensed very much in our interview. He considered democracy chaotic, very near to being anarchy. He felt that the American people had too much freedom and no discipline. He believed that people needed to have discipline imposed on them to make them work properly. Now, here was this man who'd suffered the ultimate in discipline, and he thought the freedoms that we enjoy in the Western world were too great. It was very interesting. He was very firm on that point about how messy and undisciplined democracy was.

DC: Some people have accused Solzhenitsyn of being mentally unbalanced.

WC: I wouldn't suggest he's unbalanced at all. He was just very firm about his beliefs. Of course, he hadn't been out of the Soviet Union very long at that point, and he hadn't seen America yet. He was talking about what he had seen of democracy in Germany and in Switzerland and what he was reading about democracy in the United States. He was finding it hard to absorb. The shock was obviously very great for him.

FIDEL CASTRO

DC: One other interview I want to talk about is the one you did with Cuba's Fidel Castro in Havana. I know that you did that interview in 1982, which was a year after you left the *Evening News*.

WC: I had a long talk with Castro, but it wasn't on camera. He wasn't going to sit still for an interview at that time, but I wanted to talk to him. Bud Benjamin, my producer, and I went to Havana. We went over to his living quarters—I think they were his living quarters—about nine o'clock at night. We expected, because of the hour, that he was going to serve us something to eat, snacks or something. We were there until two o'clock in the morning, and he never served a damn thing. We could hardly hear him in the end because our stomachs were growling so loudly. Bud and I both smoked cigars at that time, and he passed the cigar box at the beginning of the interview, and we each took a cigar. From there on out, he chain-smoked cigars for five hours and never offered us another cigar. He had one of the best translators I've ever had in my life. He was so good that you forgot completely the conversation was being translated. And we had a fascinating conversation. Castro asked me about as many questions as I asked him. He asked me about my personal life, not about politics in the United States.

DC: He was asking you questions?

WC: He was fascinated about my war experience. Fascinated about the landings in Normandy. A real war buff. But we had a very candid discussion. At one point, I said, "Tell me something. I've traveled the world now, been in a lot of communist countries, including living two years in Moscow. I have yet to see a communist country that understood the necessity of maintenance of machinery or buildings or anything else." Castro threw up his hands and said, "Oh, boy, I know that problem." He said, "It's absolutely terrible." I said, "Well, why is it? And Castro said, "First of all, it's inherent in the idea of Communism. People don't own things, so they don't take care of them. That's the answer you capitalists give, but it's true. That's one problem. Another problem is the budget." He said, "Let's consider housing, where the bad maintenance is particularly noticeable. We believe that everybody is entitled to adequate housing, and so we are constantly building more housing to try to keep up, instead of maintaining the housing we've already got. We just keep falling further and further behind. As far as machinery goes," he said, "we're teaching a whole new generation of peasants, urban peasants as well as rural peasants, to use machinery, and they don't understand it." He said, "We just don't have the people to teach them they've got to be oiled and cleaned." Well, for his first answer to be that because people don't own it, they don't take care of it . . . [*laughs*]

DC: Did he say anything about his relationship with the Soviets?

WC: Yeah, but at that time the relations were good. He said, "We're not a Soviet satellite. They don't tell us how to run our government. We're brothers. They help us because we're brothers and we need help. We send things to them because they need it. We sent troops to Angola because we believe in that cause. That's not a satellite arrangement of any kind." He tossed that off.

DC: Were there a lot of other people present?

WC: No, just us. He talked a lot about "what you North Americans think of as Cuban infiltration in Central and South America. We've got a program, and we're going to continue it. The people in South America and Central America love us for it. We're probably making inroads for Communism, but that's not our intention. We are sending our teachers and our doctors to these countries that so badly need it. You've been sitting there for a hundred years and haven't done anything for these people. We're doing a lot for them. At great expense for ourselves." He said, "We're training doctors as fast as we can, and teachers as fast as we can, to go out to these countries and help them. They need help desperately." Frankly, I admired most of what he had to say. I thought it was candid. I believe him about the teachers and the doctors and what they're doing in Central and South America. I don't doubt at all that they have an ideological purpose as far as proselytizing Communism, but still, they're doing some good.

DC: Did his charisma come across in that setting?

WC: Oh, yeah. He's very warm. We sat next to each other on the couch. He'd frequently reach over and pat me on the knee, making a point. He was getting a little heavy physically, but this was before he began turning noticeably gray. I said, "Why don't you open up your harbors to American sailors? It would be a good source of revenue. People would sail over here." Castro said, " Why can't they sail over here now?" I said, "Well, there's an awful lot of reasons. Your naval patrols pick them up at sea, and that's one reason. But you get into harbor, and you get harassed and put under guard." Castro said, "Well, we ought to see about that. If you came over, I wouldn't arrest you." I said, "I tell you what. How about my coming over and taking you sailing?" We talked about it, and I was thinking of doing it. My boat was in Miami. I thought, boy, that would be great. Then I thought, wait a minute. If it became known that my boat had gone over there and taken Castro sailing, I couldn't bring that boat back to Miami. Those Cubans in Miami would have burned it the first night home. I wouldn't blame a lot of them, though, if they wanted to do that.

WC: I've always thought that was a mistake. I don't know where
I've made any decisions. The suggestion has always been that
... set the news agenda and that I decided what went into a
... is certainly some truth to that, in
... oned by either the newspapers or
... don't exist to the larger public.
... people set the news agenda or that
... ing that agenda is fallacious. The
... involved there were three major
... lusion
... hen
... also
... the
... st, the
... These
... else wha
... cluded
... apers
... b be sur
... out of
... go-roun
... per

a good example often cited, Walter, about your
... was when you interviewed Henry Kissinger from
... hours before the Carter-Ford presidential debate
... ber 1976. He had just met with Ian Smith about the
... of majority rule in Rhod...
... cast t
... he ha
... was qu
... you thi
... ecomes.
... rtant on
... articula
... than if
... man; he
... at certi
... oints he
... when he
... ell the p
... er.

t says a
... Mankiewi
... ree there
a preside
... uld hope t
... New York ... mes, and any other newsman. We're not
... presidency, we don't have any axes to grind or
... hes
... iasm
... only
... them
... reporting
... an that I agree with you at all. But people got that idea. So
... l over America people assumed that I agreed with them. That's

CHAPTER TWENTY-FOUR

Gerald Ford, Jimmy Carter, and Ronald Reagan

DC: Gerald R. Ford became president upon Nixon's resignation in August 1974. Several months later, in April 1975, you had an interview with President Ford in the White House. What stands out in your mind about Ford?

WC: Well, Ford was probably the most personable, as far as just being a regular fellow, of any of the presidents. He was an old-shoe fellow, no presumption and no pretense. I don't think he was terribly bright in the presidential sense, but on the other hand, he didn't take on airs of being an intellectual either. He and his family were delightful to be around. They were just good old neighborhood folk. He didn't have much to say about the presidency. The interview wasn't very revealing about policy. But as a caretaker, you probably couldn't have picked a better man.

DC: So you think Nixon made a wise choice?

WC: Well, yes. Of course, I still don't guess we know the truth about Nixon's pardon. We don't know for certain if Ford made a promise to Nixon to pardon him. I don't know, but that suspicion is certainly very high.

DC: Have you ever run into any close sources that would imply that?

WC: No, I haven't. It is just a general assumption I live with along with everybody else.

Cronkite enjoying a laugh with President Reagan and his staff following his interview with Reagan days before Cronkite retired as anchor and managing editor of CBS Evening News, *1981. Photograph by Diana Walker, Walker (Diana H.) Photographic Archive, Dolph Briscoe Center for American History (DI_05812).*

THE MOST TRUSTED MAN IN AMERICA

DC: In 1975, during the Ford presidency, *U.S. News and World Report* magazine listed you among the ten most influential decision makers in America. This was based on a leadership poll in which the people polled were leaders themselves.

WC: I've always thought that was a mistake. I don't know where I've made any decisions. The suggestion has always been that we set the news agenda and that I decided what went into a broadcast. I suppose there is certainly some truth to that, in that if things don't get mentioned by either the newspapers or the television, they, in a sense, don't exist to the larger public. But the idea that only a few people set the news agenda or that some are all-powerful in setting that agenda is fallacious. The point being that when I was involved, there were three major networks, all operating independently. There was no collusion of any kind. And we have the Associated Press, and we then had a strong United Press International, and Reuters was also in the act, all operating independently. Then you have the major newspapers, the *New York Times*, the *Washington Post*, the *Baltimore Sun*, and the *Boston Globe* on the East Coast. These were all operating independently. Nobody tells anybody else what the lead story should be that day or what should be included in the newspaper or what should not. As far as the newspapers go, they all read each other's newspapers, you know, to be sure they're not being beaten on a story. Nothing is frozen out of a newspaper simply because it had been ignored the first go-round. If it appears in another newspaper and the first newspaper is made aware of it, they'll catch up with the story. The same thing is true on television. So I don't see where this power really lies to set the agenda. Certainly, if you had a monopoly, then it would be a terribly powerful thing, and that's one of the things we object to in foreign governments, where the press is under government control. The government sets the agenda in some countries, and that's dangerous. But we don't set the agenda here. Now, there are influential people. I think it would have been better to say that television is very influential, and perhaps among those, at this moment, Walter Cronkite is the most influential of the three. But that's as far as they would be entitled to go.

DC: Well, a good example often cited, Walter, about your influence was when you interviewed Henry Kissinger from London two hours before the Carter–Ford presidential debate in September 1976. He had just met with Ian Smith about the question of majority rule in Rhodesia. Kissinger announced on your broadcast that Smith had accepted the American plan. This was before he had time to tell President Ford. Later, Frank Mankiewicz was quoted in the *Washington Post* magazine, *Potomac*: "The more you think about it, the more extraordinary the interview becomes. If there is a message for Americans, and it is an important one, get Cronkite to deliver it and it will be believed. Particularly in an election year, it is more likely to be believed than if a president tells it to us. Cronkite is more than a newsman; he is more than a television celebrity. He is in fact the great certifier of American fact and opinion." I think one of the points here is that Kissinger chose to make this announcement when he was being interviewed by you rather than waiting to tell the president first. That may also tell us more about Kissinger.

WC: Yeah, that says a lot more about Kissinger than about me. But I see what Mankiewicz was getting to, and I think he had a point, to a degree, there. Sure, why shouldn't the people believe me instead of a president, particularly one running for reelection? I would hope that they would believe me, and anyone writing for the *New York Times*, and any other newsman. We're not running for the presidency; we don't have any axes to grind or any irons in this fire at all.

DC: Walter, did you find being labeled "the most trusted man in America" to be a burden?

WC: I have a pat answer to that, but it is the truth. No, not at all. I was greatly honored that the polls should show that, because that's what I assume every journalist would like to be, and that's to be trusted. That is the goal every day, every minute, every hour that you're working. So what could I do, simply because they said I'm the most trusted? It didn't put any additional burden on me that any serious journalist carries at all times. There's no way to add to that.

DC: It didn't make you second-guess more about what you were going to say?

WC: I hardly think so. No, it never was a conscious thing with me. I probably didn't pay attention to it at any time except when I was being introduced before a speech and somebody quoted it again.

DC: Do you think it had an impact on your off-the-air public statements?

WC: Well, off the air, the only place it could possibly have affected me might have been at a social performance. I might not have gone into quite as tacky a bar as I would have before. But I don't think that was a function of being declared the most trustworthy. I think that was just a function of being a public figure, so that probably would have happened anyway. In fact, I think I'm making a mistake even raising that, because I don't think they're the same thing. And now you say my off-the-air comments and speeches and so forth. I never pulled any punches in the off-the-air speeches. I probably surprised a lot of people in my speech making. I would address a group that had only seen me on television, and they thought that I agreed with them because of my strict insistence on being objective in reporting the news. Now, the fact that I don't disagree with you does not mean that I agree with you at all. But people got that idea. So all over America, people assumed that I agreed with them. That's probably why I was trusted and lovable and all that, because I didn't cross them by what I had to say on my newscasts. But when I made these speeches—and I was saying things that they violently disagreed with in many cases—it was a real shock to them. I saw people going out of auditoriums and ballrooms in which I spoke, literally shaking their heads. You know, "I can't believe I heard him say that!" But that did not deter me, and it shouldn't have deterred me.

THE BICENTENNIAL: JULY 4, 1976

DC: Now, getting back to events during the Ford presidency, obviously one of the biggest was the bicentennial of the signing of the American Declaration of Independence. CBS coverage of that day was called *In Celebration of Us.* You anchored, of course, from six in the morning until midnight. You were on the air a long time. Let's talk about that. Did you have anything to do with the planning?

WC: Oh, quite a lot. Perhaps the greatest thing that Nixon did for us was to ignore the bicentennial. He flubbed it completely. And as a consequence, the federal government didn't do a damn thing, basically, which was absolutely wonderful. It saved the bicentennial. As a consequence, all over America, every little crossroads town planned its own bicentennial, and that's what made it great. And New York did it in the big way, with the tall ships, fireworks, and all. That kind of led the way in our coverage, but we cut away from the activities in New York to see what was happening in towns all over America. I can't remember what we did if we went to Washington. I can remember all the other little, tiny town celebrations, but I can't remember anything about Washington. I think we went down and looked at the Constitution in the archives in the National Archives. I guess we had a camera in there. I can't remember anything else. But it was just a glorious, spontaneous upwelling of enthusiasm for that day in American history.

As we realized that activities were going on all over the country, we decided that we had to get out there. So we decided to do a lot of remotes to these small towns. We put as many cameras out around America as we could.

DC: The logistics must have been really difficult.

WC: They were. It was more of an engineering feat than it was a textual feat. It was very simple to write the show, but doing the remote pieces was difficult.

DC: Where were you located?

WC: We were set up in Madison Square Garden. Part of the reason we were in Madison Square Garden was because the Democratic convention was going to be there, and that's where all the equipment already had been moved. CBS built a whole huge control room. Our studio was really not much of a studio, just a desk, and I was right in the control room with the people concerned with the remotes. We made up a rather elaborate schedule, but everybody knew that it wasn't going to work that way. We even wrote a script for my initial remarks, but I threw it away without telling our executive producer, Ernie Leiser. He was absolutely horrified before the broadcast because we kept telling him that we would have to go off the schedule eventually and the rest of the day would be ad-libbed. Well, I was just inspired when we came on the air. Instead of "Good morning from CBS News" and so forth, my first words were "Up, up, up, everybody. It's your birthday!" Leiser goddamn near fainted. "Shit! The whole thing's gone. Cronkite's not using the script. Oh, God. Where are we going next?" But we knew we had a great show. It was the most exciting day. Every piece that came in, we said, "Wow, boy, wasn't that great?" Sometimes, of course, they were less great than we wanted them to be. The greatest failures probably were some of the interview guests that we brought into the studio to fill time. That was the wrong idea. Wrong, wrong, wrong. We didn't need to fill time. But we'd already lined up the guests, so in came a bunch of entertainers.

DC: I remember one scene was with the tall ships in New York and the bagpipes playing "Amazing Grace." It was a beautiful scene. You didn't get outside of the studio, did you?

WC: No, I never looked outside. I couldn't look out. There wasn't any place to look out of that set. When we signed off the air at midnight, I had a limousine waiting for me. The driver was a young would-be actor who was moonlighting. I said, "Come on, let's see the town." Everybody back at the studio had said, "You must be going right home and go to bed." "Hell, no," I said. "I'm going out and see New York." We didn't get back home until four o'clock in the morning or something like that. We went to P. J. Clark's and sat around and talked.

DC: So you did a twenty-four-hour day.

WC: Well, yeah, it was about twenty-four hours. I was on the air eighteen of those. But I wasn't tired at all. The adrenaline was flowing. I remember the driver's name was something funny like Cary Brant. He said, "My name's Cary Brant. I'm an actor. Do you think I should change my name?" I said, "Well, I don't know. You look kind of like him too." [*laughs*]

DC: So, obviously, you think that was a very successful broadcast.

WC: I thought it was one of the great broadcasts of all time. I enjoyed it as much or more than any broadcast I ever did. I should mention it when people ask about my biggest moments. It never would have occurred to me until you brought it up, but it was.

DC: Do you remember any major problems that you had at that time?

WC: Oh, we had the usual failed remotes. Things that we were going to do that were supposed to happen but didn't happen. I don't really remember anything distinct. I mostly remember those interviews that were duds. I had two or three of those. I tried to drag something out of people, and they had nothing to say. I could only get, "Isn't it a wonderful day?" No historical perspective at all. That was the only thing that was wrong about our coverage.

THE 1976 POLITICAL CONVENTIONS

DC: You mentioned that you did the bicentennial broadcast from Madison Square Garden because the national Democratic convention would be held there that same month. Do you recall much about that convention, which nominated Jimmy Carter for president?

WC: That was the convention where John Glenn did the keynote. That was the most impressive thing about that convention to me. It was how John fell on his face. It was sad. Everybody thought he was presidential timber, and he made just one of the world's worst speeches. It was just ghastly. I am a good friend of John's from the space program, and I committed myself to go up to his room after his speech. We were all expecting to go up to a big congratulatory and happy party. Instead, it was like going to the party when the reviews come in for a very bad Broadway show. A lot of people didn't show up. So there were just a few old friends gathered around telling John what a great speech it was. But everybody knew it wasn't. It was a very difficult moment. The rest of the convention, I don't remember too much about. By 1976, the convention programs had become scripted, routine, and dull. The primary race had determined the course of the events, and this fellow, the governor of Georgia, James Earl Carter, who nobody had heard of a year before, is suddenly standing up there accepting the nomination of his party.

DC: According to a story in *US* magazine about the 1976 political conventions, quote: "Walter Cronkite threw a temper tantrum and ripped his microphone off of its holder because it was faulty, and stormed off the set, saying that he would return whenever it was repaired." Then the magazine claims you stormed off the set and then locked yourself in the Port-O-Can for ten minutes. It didn't say which convention.

WC: Oh. [*chuckles*] No, no, no. I'm saying no because I don't remember any such thing. I'm sure as hell I would remember it. I've never locked myself in a Port-O-Can, for Pete's sake. I couldn't stand ten minutes in one of those things in the first place. That is wrong. You couldn't be mad enough at anybody in the world to spend ten minutes in one of those places. Geez, no. I don't recall ever hearing that before. I was perfectly capable of being annoyed about failing equipment. That was one of my great problems, that I was intolerant of other people's mistakes and intolerant of my own. I would blame other people for my own mistakes, which I must apologize for now, but I don't remember that.

DC: Carter won the election in 1976. A few months after he took office, you anchored a broadcast that was unusual in the history of the presidency. You and Carter did a two-hour telephone call-in radio show from the White House. The public called in and asked Carter questions. Whose idea was that?

WC: I don't really know who originated the idea. Whether it came out of the White House or came out of our shop, I'm not sure. But everybody thought it was great. Carter was very anxious to do it, and we were anxious to do it. It was meant to be the first of a long series, which would have really made American history. The problem was that AT&T's telephone lines couldn't handle the load, so we decided not to make it a regular program.

DC: Oh, so there was a technical problem.

WC: Yeah, but the program was superb. Carter was brilliant. I don't know that other presidents could have done as well. Carter has a fantastic memory for detail. Everything is clearly filed in a very orderly fashion in his mind. He can recall situations and call up the information that he has placed there, as the rest of us only can do with a computer. The only problem was that he was so full of information—rather arcane, some of it—that he went into greater detail in his answers than necessary. For instance, a woman called from Wisconsin. She asked, "When is the government going to do something about stabilizing milk price supports?" or something like that. Carter said, "Well, you must recall, I'm sure, the history of the milk price support program. It came about immediately after World War I, with the shortages in Europe and elsewhere, and we asked our farmers to produce a lot more milk than our domestic needs could possibly take care of. When the war was over, we were overproducing to the degree of something like 230,000 pounds of milk and milk products every year, and therefore, for the first time, the milk price supports were the first of our agricultural crop supports, and we put in a support of three cents a pound at that time." I'm just making the details up, of course, but that was the kind of answer Carter gave. It was incredible. He went through every increase and every argument for every price support. I could imagine that poor little lady in Wisconsin, her eyes are going bleary, mouth gaping.

DC: Not to mention everyone else listening to the program.

WC: Oh, my God. Radios were being turned off around the country. The really extraordinary thing about that program was that for two hours I was sitting on the edge of my chair, ready to cut off a long-winded question from the public, because anybody could make a phone call. We had a dozen people screening these calls as they came in—not in any way editing them for content, but just for the seriousness of the question and whether the person spoke English so you could understand it. We were running a three-second delay in case they became abusive or profane. I had little notes to myself about which lines to use to cut people off. We were worried about the long-winded ones who wanted to make a speech. We were sure we were going to get those. We got none. If you'd rehearsed these questions, it couldn't have been better.

We had only one small problem, and that was from a narcotics addict who wanted to argue about the narcotics laws, and even he wasn't unreasonable. It was just that he wanted to keep carrying on. I had to cut him off. The person I needed help with was the president of the United States. I wasn't prepared for that. Carter went on and on about milk price supports. I think I finally did cut him off on that one. I said, "I believe you've answered the question, Mr. President. Let's move on." But the program went very well. The president was pleased with it, and CBS was very pleased with it. We were ready to go with one every month or two, and it would have been great. But AT&T couldn't handle it.

DC: How did the other networks react to this? Were there any protests?

WC: They had to quote from us, you know. It made news, and they didn't like it. I mean, they didn't like it in the sense that they wished they had it.

DC: But that wasn't the reason why you didn't do another one.

WC: No. That would be all the more reason for doing another one.

DC: How was Carter personally? I mean, off camera?

WC: Oh, I always thought Carter was great. I still think he's great. I think because of that brain power I'm talking about, that kind of brain power made him the smartest president we've had in my time. His failing was as a politician. He did not know how to organize the White House and how to get along with Congress. Carter promised he was not going to work with the bureaucracy in Washington. He would be a people's president. Well, he tried to do that. In fact, he did it. And it doesn't work. He proved that. Now, I thought Carter did some very fine things. I thought his human rights program really was the first time since World War II that people overseas looked up to America. He was pooh-poohed by the professional politicians, but I believe he may have had a great following among the common people of the world. Another good thing he did was to appoint a lot of blacks to high positions.

DC: He was criticized for not being able to see the big picture. He was such a detail man that he was unable to see the forest for the trees.

WC: I don't think it was a question of seeing it. I think it was a question of being able to react to it. In reacting to the big picture, he focused on the little minutiae, and that was what threw him off track. That was a staff problem, because he brought in the Georgia mafia instead of finding the best experts in the country. He brought in those he could trust personally. He had a deep suspicion of political infighting in Washington, which he had every right to be suspicious of, certainly. At the same time, that restricted him to this little coterie of people instead of going out and finding the best brains to run his White House.

DC: Carter was unusually candid, which is good, but unfortunately, the American people sometimes don't appreciate candor. I'm thinking particularly about his famous speech about there being a malaise in American society. Although I don't believe he actually used the word "malaise."

WC: Carter was absolutely right, of course, about it, and, you know, if he had been more of a politician and could have put together the machinery to fight that malaise, then we wouldn't be in nearly the problems we're in today.

SADAT-BEGIN INTERVIEW, NOVEMBER 1977

DC: One of the most important events of the Carter presidency was the Camp David Accords between Egypt and Israel in September 1978. That was preceded by Anwar Sadat's stunning trip to Israel in November 1977. He was the first Arab head of state to visit Israel. Menachem Begin was the Israeli prime minister at the time. Let's talk about the role you played in this surprising development.

WC: We talked earlier about my interviews with Sadat and his comment about going to Jerusalem and how I realized that was just a metaphor, just rhetoric. There were several little flurries of excitement because he told others that he was going to Jerusalem and they didn't understand that it was a metaphor. But in 1977, a Canadian parliamentary delegation visited Cairo and went to the Egyptian parliament to hear Sadat make a speech. In this speech, Sadat said, "And I shall go to Jerusalem." The Canadians left immediately after that. They flew to Cyprus or somewhere before going on to Israel. They saw Begin for a private interview. During the course of that meeting, one of the Canadians said, "We heard Sadat say he will be coming to Jerusalem. Do you have any plans for him to come to Jerusalem?" Begin said, "No, not that I know of, but tell him he's invited."

That story started circulating around the world over the weekend. I said to my producer, Bud Benjamin, "You know, somebody is always asking Sadat about going to Jerusalem, and he always says he's going to go when there's peace, and it doesn't mean anything. It's a figure of speech he's using." Bud said, "Well, if nobody asks him over the weekend, maybe we ought to interview him on Monday and knock this darn story down if it's still kicking around." I said, "Let's do that." We set up a satellite interview with Sadat on the following Monday. I said to Sadat, "Well, there is speculation about this comment you made about going to Jerusalem. Would you go to Jerusalem?" Sadat said, "Oh, yes, Walter, yes. I'd like to go to Jerusalem." I said, "Well, do you have any conditions for going to Jerusalem?" He said, "Well, we certainly should talk about peace." And I said, "Well, meaning the return of the Golan Heights?" "Oh, yes, and the Sinai." I said, "And those are your conditions before you would go to Jerusalem?" That was going to be the last question. Sadat said, "Oh, no, no, Walter. I have no conditions for going to Jerusalem. No conditions at all." I said, "Then you'd go to Jerusalem now?" He said, "Yes, yes, Walter." I said, "What do you need to go to Jerusalem." "An invitation. If Mr. Begin would invite me, I would go." I said, "That's all it takes?" He said, "That's all it takes." I said, "When will you be prepared to go?" He said, " I can go anytime." I was still trying to pin him down. I said, "Could you go this week?" Sadat said, "Sure, certainly, Walter. I'd go this week." By this time, Bud, who is in the control room, is going ape. So his guys get on the phone to Jerusalem to get Begin. That's the way our team worked. The CBS Tel Aviv bureau came right back and said Begin was on the way from Jerusalem to Tel Aviv. They said that he was giving a speech, at the Hilton that night. Our guys in Tel Aviv arranged a room next door to the speech and they were able to get Begin to agree to go on the air with me after the speech, which was in the afternoon New York time.

So sure enough, we got Begin on. I said, "Mr. Prime Minister, we've just been talking to President Sadat, and he says he's ready to come to Jerusalem for a visit." Begin said, "Tell him he can come." I said, "I think he needs something more than that. He needs an invitation." "Tell him he's got an invitation." I said, "Well, I think that he wants a formal invitation." "All right. I'll send him a formal invitation." I said, "Well, President Sadat says he could come this week." Begin said, "Well, I was going to London, but forget it! Tell him to come!" So that was it. Sadat went, and I flew there with him.

DC: It was November 14, 1977, when those two interviews were taped. The *Evening News* broadcast it as though they were appearing live on screen together, or that is at least the impression that some viewers got. Tom Shales at the *Washington Post* charged that your broadcast was a manipulation of the newsmakers by TV diplomacy.

WC: I know there was a lot of talk about TV diplomacy. Ridiculous. My intention, quite clearly, was just the opposite. I was knocking down the story, not building it up. It was purely journalistic enterprise. ABC had a distorted version of this event that they have promulgated ever since. Leonard Goldenson's book quotes Peter Jennings on how they knew about Sadat's plan all the time and just didn't bother to put it on the air. That was a very weak excuse. I think Jennings was hurt because, I think, he did have some knowledge of this but didn't act on it and, therefore, kind of blamed himself. I think very highly of Peter Jennings's reporting. He was very good on the Middle East, and I think that he might indeed have had some inkling that it was an important story, but didn't follow through. [*Jennings died in 2005.*]

DC: Roone Arledge complained that ABC actually had the news first but didn't put the leaders on camera because it was too "showbizzy."

WC: Oh, my goodness! [*laughs*] Well, that's really good for the laugh of the week.

DC: In her book, Barbara Matusow says that you were very uncomfortable with this role in diplomacy. But in an interview that you did with *Rolling Stone*, you stated that "I'm perfectly comfortable with that, because that's a fallout of reportorial practice and nothing more than that."

WC: I don't know where Matusow would get that impression, because I never was uncomfortable. I was uncomfortable with the TV diplomacy charge. I hated having to answer some newspaper critics who suggested we were indulging in television diplomacy. I felt that the answer was straightforward, honest, true, factual, and I never had any deep concern about it. The Sadat-Begin episode was a matter of journalistic enterprise in which I take great pride.

DC: When Sadat flew from Egypt to Tel Aviv, you, Barbara Walters, NBC's John Chancellor, and the *Time* correspondent traveled with Sadat on the flight from the Egyptian air force base to Tel Aviv on November 19, 1977. I understand that you and your colleagues sat with Sadat in his private cabin on the way over there.

WC: He invited us in one by one. We never sat together as a group with Sadat. It's not a very long flight, but I was fortunate enough to be with him when the Israeli air force escort came up. I think Barbara and John died because of that. I was with him as he looked out of the window, and here, flying right alongside so that you could see every pore in his face, was the Israeli pilot looking right into the cabin. You know, he and Sadat waving to each other. Hell of a moment. They brought a camera in for that.

DC: So did you do an on-camera interview?

WC: No, we didn't do it on camera. We were just having a friendly conversation. He probably would have had us all there except it wasn't that big a cabin. The interesting part of that trip was that CBS outfoxed NBC and ABC again. We made arrangements with Sadat to fly with him from Cairo to Tel Aviv. Nobody else did this. So we made our flight arrangements to go to Cairo, not to Tel Aviv. We went out to JFK airport, and we all happened to meet at the airport. We hadn't expected to run into everybody at the VIP lounge, waiting to board the plane to Athens. So here was John Chancellor and Barbara Walters. We realized they were all going to Athens and then transfer to a Tel Aviv flight. I asked them if they were going to Greece and then to Tel Aviv, and they said yes. We said, "Well, how about that. I guess we're all in the same plane." So they made the boarding announcement for the plane to Athens. Our plane to Cairo was scheduled to leave a little later. We gathered our stuff and pretended that we were boarding the plane with them. We kind of hung back, and everybody else rushed ahead and got on the plane to Athens. When they closed the door to the plane, the ABC and NBC guys realized we weren't there. We left for Cairo a few minutes later. Jesus, Barbara Walters had a terrible night flying to Athens. After they arrived in Athens, they knew we were going straight to Cairo. So they had to cancel their flight to

Tel Aviv and chartered a plane to Egypt. Then they had to get to the military airport outside of Cairo to catch Sadat's plane. They got there just as we were loading up the plane. I was very disappointed to see them, [*laughs*] but I already knew they were coming, because when Sadat saw me, he said, "And where's Bah-bah-rah?" I said, "I don't know where BARBARA is. She went to Athens or something." Sadat said, "Well, Barbara called us early this morning and said she was on her way to Cairo and to hold the plane. I'm looking for Barbara."

DC: I'm sure that made your day. How was Sadat during the trip?

WC: Oh, his adrenaline was pumping. He was very excited. He knew that history was being made. He also knew of the threats that had come from the Arab world. The Arab states were all breaking relations with him. He was well aware of the complications, but also terribly excited about the possibilities.

DC: Was his wife with him on that trip?

WC: You know, that's very funny. I can't remember her being there. It's kind of strange he would have left her home, for two reasons. First of all, she was so much a part of his life, and Begin was never without his wife at his side for any kind of official function. I think she must have gone. She is a very intelligent, very lovely woman. I may be terribly wrong, but I have a theory that her influence on him may have played a role in his assassination. She was very much for women's rights and for birth control, and she was constantly on him about that, particularly birth control. When I did the interviews with him for a program, *Sadat's Egypt*, which came along later, he said, "I am very shortly going to announce a population control program. I've been delayed in doing it for various political reasons, but I'm going to do it very shortly now." Well, he never did it. He was assassinated that spring. It was public knowledge that he was going to start a birth control program. I think that outraged the fundamentalists. When I told him that the fundamentalists say that the Koran forbids birth control, he said, "I know the Koran better than they know the Koran."

DC: I understand that Barbara Walters beat you in the competition to interview Begin and Sadat.

WC: Yeah, she got to them an hour or so before I did. It wasn't much of a beating, because by the time the programs went on the air, they were in the same time frame.

DC: Apparently, Sadat told someone that he got a great big kick out of the fact that after you interviewed them, you asked if there was anything that they told Barbara that they hadn't told you.

WC: [*laughs*] Yeah. I'm sure I did that. That was not unusual, not during the interview, but when the interview's over. I very frequently would check like that with somebody, when it was a competitive situation. Just so I wouldn't be blindsided.

DC: In September 1978, you anchored coverage of the Camp David meeting and the official signing of the Camp David Accords.

WC: The most extraordinary thing about that was that within minutes of the signing, I was over at both of their embassies, doing interviews with them separately about the agreement. Begin already was disagreeing with what I thought was pretty clear about the terms of the accord. He was reinterpreting the agreement almost instantly. Sadat confirmed my understanding of what I read in the agreement. I think there were different interpretations about the timetable for withdrawal from the Sinai.

DC: We haven't discussed Begin. What were your impressions of him?

WC: Well, they aren't as favorable as Sadat, by any means. I did not find in Begin any breadth of imagination as to what could be done in the Middle East. He was a doctrinaire conservative Israeli, in my mind, and there was no real vision there. He was forced all the way into these associations with Sadat. I think he was clearly uncomfortable with them. That was possibly because his was a more democratic government and he was going to have more problems politically. But I also think he was a man of fairly limited vision.

DC: You went to Cairo in December 1979 to interview Sadat for the CBS special on Egypt that you mentioned earlier. This is the trip that you went with Sadat to a mosque and to the Aswan Dam and to his birthplace at Mit Abul Kom. You and Sadat had a very interesting discussion about the Nile River.

WC: Sadat's birthplace was wonderful, and so was the mosque. He took me to the mosque, and he sat against the wall. I don't know whether this was for safety reasons, for comfort reasons, or what. It was terribly hard on the back. We sat cross-legged for an hour or so in the mosque. I was beginning to rise when the Muslims were rising during prayers, but Sadat put his hand on my shoulder. I remember his leading me through this thing by holding his hand on my shoulder when I wasn't supposed to rise. Later, we went to his family's farm, and he showed us how, as a boy, he stood in the cold water, turning an Archimedean screw to raise water to irrigate. He showed us a young guy doing it just as he'd done it when he was a boy to irrigate this same spot of land. As we were there, a neighboring farmer came up to argue with him about the sale of the land. The farmer wanted to buy Sadat's land. They had quite a little discussion about it. As the man went away, Sadat shook his head and said, "I'm not interested in selling the land." But it was all very friendly and so personable. The Aswan Dam was very interesting. He showed me through one of the temples at Aswan, and we discussed it.

DC: Did Sadat seem any more conscious of security than what you'd expect?

WC: No. Far less than an American president.

DC: During one of those interviews, Sadat urged the United States to intervene militarily in Iran and rescue the American hostages.

WC:　Yeah. He was very, very adamant about that.

THE IRANIAN HOSTAGE CRISIS

DC:　Let's talk about the Iranian hostage story, which occurred while Carter was president. On November 4, 1979, Iranian revolutionaries stormed the U.S. embassy in Tehran and took fifty-three American hostages. They were held hostage for 444 days. Barbara Matusow says in her book that you made the decision to end your news program each evening with a reminder of how many days it had been since the hostages had been taken. She also says that political scientists have since concluded that your "constant reminder . . . played no small part in the voters' eventual rejection of Jimmy Carter."

WC:　Well, that's a political scientist's view of it, and I guess the writer's view of it. And it's highly possible. I would not argue against it having had that effect. It was not the intended effect, however. Actually, it's very interesting that the point was never made during the course of that year. The political scientists never made the point. The administration, as far as I know, never made that point. Other writers didn't make that point. It is all hindsight.

DC:　You mean after Carter's defeat?

WC:　Yeah. The reason I did it was that I saw the story disappearing from the front page and going to the classifieds and leaving the newspaper entirely. It hadn't happened yet, but I could see that happening. And I wondered if we were going to not have it on the *Evening News.* I mean there wasn't anything to report. I thought, that's exactly what these Iranians want. We couldn't do that. We had to remember that the story was alive and those people were still there. And the way to do that was to have some kind of a reminder every day that they were still there. We didn't have anything to report, because they had shut down information from Tehran. We couldn't let them shut us down like that. We had to keep this reminder in front of the American people that these people were still locked up there. That was why I did it. It had nothing to do with politics, and there was no reason why I should have believed at the beginning that they were going to be there that long. Hell, we all assumed they'd be out in a month or sometime soon.

DC:　You said that it would be playing into the hands of the Iranians just to drop it. Couldn't it be argued to the contrary? Didn't the Iranians want someone to be reminding the American people every day that they still had their hostages? Isn't that the whole point of having hostages?

WC:　Well, they apparently were doing everything to keep us from covering the hostages. We couldn't get anything out; we couldn't report. We couldn't get to any Iranian contacts. We couldn't talk to the hostages. I don't know what the Iranians wanted. Nobody knows to this day what they wanted with those hostages. It seemed to me that it was important to remind the American people that they were there.

RONALD REAGAN

DC: Ronald Reagan won the Republican nomination for president in 1980. The Republican convention was in Kansas City that year, and that was the last Republican convention you anchored for CBS. Although there was no drama about who was going to be the presidential nominee, there were some interesting things going on about the vice presidential nomination. You played a bit of role in that.

WC: Well, that was fascinating. On the convention floor, the story was breaking that Ford and Reagan had made a deal and that Ford was very possibly going to be the vice presidential candidate. We'd already arranged to get Ford as an interview before the evening session began. So I had my pigeon right there, and I adroitly, I think, led him into a discussion about what it would take for him to be vice president. He spelled out his terms, which were much harsher that Reagan had been led to believe they were. Kissinger was the one trying to negotiate this thing, primarily, and Kissinger apparently wasn't really telling Reagan what Ford was telling him. Or Kissinger wasn't absorbing completely what Ford was telling him. At any rate, Ford made clear on the air that he expected to be kind of a copresident. My God, that just blew the thing sky high. The Reagan people were listening to this in their hotel room, and with that, they said that deal is off. And that was the end of that deal, and then they turned to George Bush.

DC: Teddy White, in his book on the 1980 campaign, said it was one of the best interviews of your career. One of the reasons he says that is because, as you said adroitly, you pressed him on the air. In fact, what happened is that Ford dodged your questions, but you asked him, "Is it something like a copresidency?" And then he said yes, that's something Governor Reagan ought to really consider.

WC: The most delightful thing about that interview was that when Barbara Walters found out that I was interviewing Gerald Ford, she ran up to our studio and started pounding on the window, demanding admittance. She said, "I'm supposed to have an interview with him! I'm supposed to be getting this interview!" She went hysterical. The security people tried to quiet her down. She lost her cool completely. Finally, the staff asked security to get rid of her. She was standing outside when Ford left our studio, and she practically physically carried him into the ABC booth.

DC: Let's talk about Ronald Reagan. I understand that you first met him in 1964 when he campaigned for Barry Goldwater for president.

WC: I was at the first speech he ever made for Goldwater. It was at Knott's Berry Farm in California. We were all down there waiting for Goldwater to appear to make a speech during the California primary. There was a large crowd of the conservative Orange County types. Reagan suddenly came on stage to warm up the crowd. I don't remember a damned thing he said. We never paid any attention to what those warm-up people said. We all talked through it. I gather he made a few jokes, because there was some laughter from the immediate circle who could hear him. Then Goldwater arrived, and we were all standing there in the front area, and Reagan came and stood right by me. Goldwater made his speech. And I said to my news companions on my left—Reagan was on the right—I said, "You know, this isn't Knott's Berry Farm. It's Barry's Nut Farm." And Reagan said, "I don't think that's very funny." And I said, "I wasn't talking to you." Or something like that. That was our exchange. That was my first meeting with Ronald Reagan.

DC: After he was elected governor of California in 1966, I believe you interviewed him in Sacramento.

WC: I went to Sacramento to see how he was doing as governor. I guess this was in 1968, about the time that he was first being mentioned as a possible presidential candidate. I had a very pleasant visit there with him. I was rather impressed with the way he seemed to be taking over as governor. I was not overwhelmed, but he seemed to be making a go of it. I doubted very seriously he could be a serious presidential candidate. He seemed too lightweight for that. Later in 1968, I saw him at the Republican convention in Miami when there was a brief, little campaign to nominate him for president. But Nixon had it all locked up. I didn't see much of him again until 1976, when he challenged Ford for the Republican nomination. And then, during the 1980 campaign, I saw him in New Hampshire and around, and we got along fine.

And then when Reagan was elected president, he did a very nice thing. It was my retirement week at CBS, so I asked him for a one-on-one interview in the Oval Office. Of course, he'd only been president for two months, and the interview didn't develop into very much. But I did have an exclusive interview with the president of the United States, the first he'd given since he'd come into office. The nice thing was that when the interview was over, Reagan asked me to come into his private office for a moment. That's the little room off the Oval Office. When we went in, George Bush, James Brady, James Baker, David Gergen, and Ed Meese were waiting for us. My producer, Bud Bejamin, was with me. They had a cake and champagne, and they gave me a little farewell party. We stood around and told some pretty dirty jokes. We must have been there at least an hour. We had a wonderful time. Diana Walker, a photojournalist who covered the White House for *Time* magazine, happened to come by after I told an especially dirty joke that Reagan really liked. Thankfully, she didn't hear it. She snapped a great picture of us all doubled over with laughter, holding champagne glasses. I have it framed on a wall at home.

DC: What kind of impression did you get of that group in that setting while they were off the record?

WC: Oh, they were the hail-fellows-well-met of all time, all party boys. It was wonderful. You know, the Reagans gave wonderful parties. They were a wonderful host and hostess. If you wanted somebody to come over to your house and have a good time and tell stories, you couldn't beat them. And they were good dancers.

DC: How did George Bush seem to be fitting in with this group at this time?

WC: Oh, as a vice president would. It was clear that the others were more important figures to the president than Bush was.

DC: I understand Reagan had a keen interest in some incidents early in your career.

WC: Well, I accused him of stealing all my stories, I swear to goodness. I'm not sure it was deliberate. He was a great storyteller. He would hear a story somewhere, and boy, he'd embroider it. He would tell it in a news conference or on a broadcast. In my early broadcast days, I did play-by-play sports announcing using telegraph reports for KCMO in Kansas City. I told Reagan a story about when the wire went down in the Southern Cal–Notre Dame game and I had to keep the game going with my imagination until the wire came back up. The next thing I know, Reagan is at a White House dinner telling about the time the wire went down on a baseball game and he had to keep the baseball game going. I don't know whether it ever happened, or whether he picked it up from my experience, or what. But I had told him the story when we talked. He didn't tell me his baseball story at the same time, which makes me think there wasn't one. I also told him my hearing was affected by a gunshot in the war; next thing I knew, he was telling people his hearing was affected by a training camp gunshot. I don't know whether they're true or not; it's just very odd that they suddenly came up later, not at the time.

DC: What's your evaluation of Reagan as president?

WC: Oh, my evaluation of Reagan is that he was a lightweight, totally unfit to be president of the United States, and he performed accordingly.

DC: How did he get elected president?

WC: Because he didn't have much competition that particular year and people were ready for a change. He had this great upbeat message, you know: the "Let's all cheer for America" business. Morning in America. People wanted to hear that. He promised to get rid of regulations and to lower taxes, all the things people wanted to hear. Mostly, the voters were ready for a change. The Carter administration had just, you know, been a disaster in most people's minds.

giving up the anchor post. According to Bill Leonard, wh...
succeeded Dick Salant as head of CBS News, you came to him in
the late summer of 1978 and said that the weight of the progra...
day afte...   ...etting to you. You wanted to sail your boat
                           a damn fool not to quit while I'm ahead,"
                                ...s saying...   ...t you off. He

finally c   ...nd Salant wave...
he quest: ...es that every

that you   ...times to
e.   ...told him
u favor F   ...fore then
                                                                            ...ngs were
as solely   ...anted with
he had nev   ...bout a
ch was som   ...and the
ey had a da   ...ubling me
it. They t   ...ilt on
ause he di   ...ators
ple over t   ...ind of
n anchor un   ...s were
y summer wh   ...t teeth
oreign stor   ...do
to do Wash: ...e early
and qualifie

sounds as tho
e sense, beca

t's not so.
He was a good

expec
negoti...
forced out. That was just completely totally wrong. I can
...highly erroneous to say that I was being
...or me even to contemplate   ...at I hadn't

CHAPTER TWENTY-FIVE

Leaving the *Evening News*

DC: You left the *CBS Evening News* in March 1981. There are conflicting reports about how and when you started thinking about giving up the anchor post. According to Bill Leonard, who succeeded Dick Salant as head of CBS News, you came to him in the late summer of 1978 and said that the weight of the program day after day was getting to you. You wanted to sail your boat and relax. "I'd be a damn fool not to quit while I'm ahead," Leonard quotes you as saying. Leonard says he put you off. He ran to Salant in a panic and told him about it, and Salant waved his hands and said, "Oh, hell, forget it. Walter does that every hour on the hour."

WC: [*laughs*] That's true. I had mentioned several times to Salant that I intended to step down at sixty-five. I told him that was the absolute latest and that I might go before then if things got tough. I was unhappy about the way things were progressing. I was beginning to get a little disenchanted with television news at that point. This thing we talked about a little earlier, about the Barbara Walters phenomenon and the way local news was becoming tabloid journalism, was troubling me deeply. I was feeling that the structure was sort of built on sand. I can't really tell you now what all of the indicators were that played on me, but I think it was mostly the kind of people who were doing television news. The local stations were bringing in the pretty boys and pretty girls with perfect teeth and empty brains, and the networks were also beginning to do that. It was getting out of hand and reminding me of those early days of radio that I didn't like. I was just beginning to feel that the professional and ethical front wasn't going to hold and that maybe it was time to get out. I thought if I got out early enough, I could still do some writing and reporting and do some work for CBS. I'd always thought I'd

Cronkite working in his CBS office, surrounded by books and mementos, ca. 1970s (DI_05799).

stay with CBS and do documentaries and special coverage. That was my plan right up to the time that I left the *CBS Evening News* in 1981.

DC: Leonard says that you raised the issue again in 1979. He claims in his memoir that you said that you couldn't take it much longer. That you wanted to stay with CBS News and do documentaries, but just not be tied down to the day-to-day grind. Leonard said that they agreed to let you go, but contingent on three conditions. One was that you would do a one-year transition. The second was that you would cooperate with the transition. And the third was that you would remain at CBS and not work with anyone else. Matusow injects another point. She claims that Betsy feared that you were ruining your health and that she thought it was time to give it up.

WC: My back problem was really bothering me. I also was having serious bouts of indigestion, and my doctor kept telling me that I had to slow down. I didn't pay any attention, but I think he got to Betsy and told her she needed to put the pressure on. But nobody ever really tried to tell me what to do, you know. Betsy never did. There was just a lot of things kind of coming together. But the real issue was my disenchantment with what we were doing. I just couldn't see that I was making much of a contribution any longer with the *Evening News*. I don't remember those three conditions Leonard mentions. I think those were more in the mind of CBS than they were in communicating to me. And I don't think it happened quite like that.

DAN RATHER

DC: When it was finally decided that you would retire from the *Evening News*, the question came up about your successor. Bill Leonard claims that you favored Dan Rather over Roger Mudd.

WC: That's true.

DC: Why did you favor Rather over Mudd?

WC: Oh, it was solely for one reason. Roger had no overseas experience. He had never been overseas. He'd refused to go to Vietnam, which was something of a scandal among his colleagues. In fact, they had a dartboard at our Saigon bureau with his picture on it. They threw darts at it. He disliked overseas stories because he didn't understand them. I think he thought all the people over there were Hottentots or something. You can't be an anchor under those circumstances. It just couldn't work. Every summer when he substituted for me, they had trouble getting foreign stories on the air because he didn't like them. He wanted to do Washington. He was a hell of a good political reporter and qualified in every way except that one significant thing.

DC: It sounds as though your endorsement of Rather was in a negative sense, because it was either Rather or Mudd.

WC: That's not so. I thought Rather's qualifications were ace high. He was a good reporter and a good on-the-air man. No, he was well qualified.

DC: Matusow writes, quote: "Walter Cronkite did not have much use for Roger Mudd. They disagreed on many matters."

WC: Roger has a peculiar personality that didn't mesh with mine. He's kind of a bully type. You know, he was a southerner, and he reminds me of that sneering, evil brother of the hero of the southern novel. [*laughs*]

DC: You felt a little arrogance there maybe?

WC: Yes, "arrogance" is the word.

DC: I have heard that when the announcement was made that Rather would be your successor, the news division split into factions that caused a rift.

WC: That's true. There were a lot of staff members who were very much for Mudd, and a lot of them didn't like Rather, but Rather had his supporters.

DC: The point is that Bill Leonard claims that this rift created pressure to get Rather in your chair sooner than the agreed-upon date of November 1981.

WC: That's right. The original plan was for me to go through until November, until my sixty-fifth birthday. But CBS couldn't put up with the squabbling. They feared the news division would fall apart unless Rather got in there as soon as possible.

DC: Bill Leonard claims that as a result CBS pushed you to leave a little early.

WC: That's true.

DC: In his memoir, Leonard says that, quote, "there would be no pushing Cronkite aside . . . any sooner than he had planned. Walter was never one to relinquish any microphone or camera willingly." [*Cronkite chuckles*] Peter McCabe, in his book, *Bad News at Black Rock*, says that you confided to friends that you were being forced out, quote: "He seemed more and more determined to demonstrate his authority. One day he burst into the newsroom objecting furiously to changes that were being planned for the program, *his* program. The proposed changes were quickly quashed and to assuage Cronkite it was decided that no changes would be made, either to the set of the *Evening News* or to the way the news was being presented."

WC: I don't remember that episode, but we did agree that some changes would be made after Rather came, and not before. One problem was that Rather was holding meetings with my producers after hours to talk about the broadcast and the changes to be made. That upset me a very great deal. I think that's when I confided to friends that I was being forced out, but I meant that I was being forced out of consideration about how we run the broadcast. I don't remember the business of my trying to hold on. As I kind of remember my psyche at the moment, it was that I was anxious to get out, and the lame-duck thing didn't suit me very well either. I found the idea of suddenly being free that spring and having the whole summer ahead of me very attractive.

I knew it was very awkward for CBS because I had the three months off. I was going to work until June, and Rather would be there until September as my vacation substitute. I'd be back from September to November, and then Rather would take over again. It didn't make any sense. So we decided that I would leave in June and not come back in the fall. But then this Rather-Mudd factional squabbling began. Also, I wasn't going to be happy working on the transition arrangements. That's never a good idea. When you make a major change, it's always best to just do it all at once. There was no point in my hanging around. But then CBS came to me and made an offer that I hadn't expected. Their offer was too grand for me even to contemplate negotiating. But it is highly erroneous to say that I was being forced out. That was just completely, totally wrong. I can understand how people would think it. But it just did not happen that way.

DC: Matusow says, quote: "The closer retirement time came, the more ambivalent Walter became. . . . He went around CBS glowering, letting it be known that he felt left out and unappreciated."

WC: Well, I can tell you that's just not so. I was looking forward to it. And I was being massaged totally by management, for heaven's sake. I was given a golden arrangement that I had not anticipated. So I had no reason to be unhappy. I think the funk was more over the logistics of my getting out, of closing up the office, and the pressure on me to do interviews with the press. My God, the pressure was enormous. Everybody in the world wanted an interview. It was just unbelievable.

REGRETS AND FRUSTRATION

DC: Walter, do you regret leaving the *Evening News* when you did?

WC: I very much regretted it because it didn't work out as it was planned. Dan Rather and company shut me out from doing anything else. I wasn't called in to do any programming or documentaries. I had my own program, which was *Walter Cronkite's Universe*. It was a thirteen-week replacement program in the summer that did exceedingly well the first year, did very well the second year, and the third year they deliberately killed it by preempting it with specials. That annoyed the hell out of me. But that first year after I stepped down, I gallivanted around the world, getting interviews with people and doing things. Bud Benjamin and I produced several pieces for the *Evening News*, and they were all very well received and quite impressive pieces, I think. I got the first interview with Polish Solidarity leader Lech Walesa. We did several interesting things that year that got on the air. When I came back from Poland, the Solidarity movement was very much in the news with its labor strikes against the Polish communist government. CBS News did a special on the situation in Poland, and they asked me to appear on it. I could see Rather gritting his teeth as he asked me questions about Poland.

About that time, the ratings were slipping on the *Evening News*, as was anticipated. People who had been loyal Cronkite followers wanted to see what was on the other networks. That was understandable. That fall of 1981, our ratings did slip a little bit, around World Series time, which NBC had. That shouldn't have surprised anyone. The *Washington Post* asked my dear friend Sandy Socolow, who still was the producer of the *Evening News*, what they were going to do about the slipping ratings. Sandy said that he expected to see more of Walter Cronkite on the broadcast, or something like that. Well, that cut it with Rather and Gordon Van Sauter, who had taken over as president of CBS News. They both admitted later on that they agreed that they had to cut me out of the broadcast. Apparently, they feared that whenever I was on the broadcast, there would be unfavorable comparisons with Rather. They needed Rather to establish himself as his own man. Well, I can understand their coming to that. And I can understand how the *Washington Post* interview with Socolow would have triggered it. I think if I had been in the same place I would have had the same feeling about it.

But they have kept me off the air for ten years. It goes on to this day [1991]. That's unconscionable and unreasonable. They scuttled my *Universe* program. We did twenty-two and twenty-three shares in the ratings. It was a damn good program, and it was a real winner. The third year that we were on the air, we got no publicity, no buildup, not even on-air promos. Then they did these preemptions every three or four weeks, which killed us. They announced that because of the low ratings, *Universe* would not be back. It was a deliberate maneuver. It had been done to other programs, and it was done to us. By that time, 1984, Van Sauter was in charge, and they brought Howard Stringer in as the producer. They'd fired Socolow, and they'd changed the format of the *Evening News*. They put all this feature junk in there, absolute junk. They did a pictorial lasting two and a half minutes on eagles in Alaska. Well, this was so sickening that I began to criticize it publicly. A couple of my critical comments came out during one of my University of Texas seminars in Austin. One of them was after Dan Rather did his seven-minute walk-off in Miami because of the delay caused by the tennis match CBS was broadcasting. I told students that I would have fired him for that, and, of course, that got out.

My criticisms were getting so much public attention that Van Sauter decided he had to do something about it. He tried to bribe me with a program of my own. It was at a lunch, with Van Sauter and Howard Stringer. That's where I got the admission from Van Sauter that keeping me off the air was deliberate. I probably made a great mistake by not invoking my contract, which guaranteed me some airtime, and then walking out on them. Quite frankly, I was venal. They just bought me with a million dollars a year. I thought, well, the hell with them. If Van Sauter and Stringer want to pay me a million dollars a year not to work, that's all I ever need. But it was a mistake. I should have fought for some airtime as promised in the contract. And then when I didn't get it, I should have quit with dignity. But I didn't. I didn't want a daily program. I just wanted to do documentaries and occasional special events, such as political conventions and that sort of thing. But they wouldn't even do that except for token appearances that were utterly meaningless.

DC: Could you have gone to NBC or ABC if CBS failed to carry out its contract with you?

WC: I wouldn't have gone to NBC if they had asked me. ABC practically did, and I said no. I didn't want to go back to a daily program. I'd gotten off of that. I wanted to do documentaries.

DC: Do you think it was Rather who kept you off the air?

WC: Yes, I'm sure it's Rather, because after all, Van Sauter's been gone for years. And every one of those news division presidents that came in had meetings with me and said, "Now, we want to use you. We have some plans. What can we do?" And then nothing would happen. I gathered that Rather heard about it and he said that's not going to happen. Rather really ran the news division.

DC: Did you ever talk to Rather about this?

WC: I did. It was very interesting. When Laurence Tisch took control of CBS in 1986, I was on the board of directors. Tisch was making public statements about how he expected to return the news department to the great days of Murrow and Cronkite. Rather panicked. He came to see me, and we had a very interesting hour of his pleading that none of this was his fault, that he hadn't had anything to do with keeping me off the air. I felt that he was trying to get right with me because he thought I had Tisch's ear. This was before Tisch had named a head of the news department. He'd fired Van Sauter right away and put Howard Stringer in, presumably as a temporary appointment, because he was acting president of the division. Dan really was in a dither. He pleaded what a great friend he'd always been of mine, what a great admirer he was of mine, and how he looked forward, now that the air was being cleared, of our working closely together. It was the biggest bunch of crap I ever heard. Dan did admit, however, that Van Sauter had told him that perhaps it would be better if I weren't appearing on the air and that Rather had agreed. But he claimed that he was thinking that I would be off for just a few months. I just listened to him. I didn't question him.

DC: How did you become a member of the CBS board of directors?

WC: When my resignation was announced, Paley called me and said, "What in the hell is going on? Why doesn't anybody tell me these things? I'd never let you resign. How can this thing happen?" He was really upset. He said, "Why didn't you come to me? We could have worked something out." When I told him that I was leaving the *Evening News* by choice, Paley calmed down and said, "I want you to come on the CBS board right now."

DC: Did that make anybody uneasy at CBS News?

WC: Oh, they must have gone ape. But even though it was Paley who brought me on the board, Tom Wyman was the president of the company. Wyman was a Van Sauter man, probably more than Van Sauter was Wyman's man, actually. The whole cabal was Wyman and Van Sauter, basically. As soon as they saw that my being named to the board didn't mean I'd be named Paley's successor or something, they went back and breathed easier. I'm certain that Tom Wyman assured Van Sauter and Rather that my being on the board of directors didn't mean anything. Which it didn't.

DC: You don't think it gave you some clout?

WC: Well, possibly, but there was no tradition of the board or board members interfering in the operations of the company, which was good.

OLD ANCHORMEN DON'T FADE AWAY

DC: Ed Joyce, who was president of CBS News, has written in his memoir that, quote, "election night 1982 proved to be a challenge because CBS didn't know what to do with Walter Cronkite. Rather made it clear that he did not want Walter Cronkite sitting with him where he felt the public would be contrasting their performances. He would be perceived as the junior partner. He was having problems adjusting to his new role and didn't need Cronkite sitting there. Cronkite, however, made frequent phone calls asking for the details of his role in the 1982 election." Joyce says that the problem of "handling Cronkite had been made infinitely more complex by Paley" because he had made you a CBS board member. Joyce says they finally came up with the idea of putting you in Washington, where you could interview experts about the meaning of the election results.

WC: The reason I was on their tail about what the assignment was going to be was so I could do my homework. That was not because I wanted to freeze them into an assignment or that I was particularly anxious about it. I didn't know what to study because they wouldn't tell me what they wanted me to do. That election night assignment in 1982 didn't work well, because I was in the position of any correspondent trying to get on the air. We'd get these experts lined up and get them into the studio, and then I'd sit there with them for hours, waiting for Dan to go to me. I understand that has always been the problem for anybody other than the anchorman. There is a whole legion of CBS correspondents out there who think I'm a mike hog because I took a long time getting to them when they were ready. It's an inevitable conflict.

DC: Did you feel that Rather snubbed you?

WC: No. I might have felt it, but I wasn't justified in feeling it. A lot of the Cronkite supporters thought that I was treated very poorly that night. Bud Benjamin, our producer, who was with me down in the studio in Washington, was highly indignant the rest of his life about it. He thought that we were really given the short end of the stick. And I guess I felt that way too at the time, but I partly understand.

DC: Let's talk about the 1984 political conventions. You asked Ed Joyce to give you an assignment in the New York studio. Joyce has written that you said, quote: "I'd like to follow the events during the early part of each evening, but later in the night when some patter is developing, Dan could turn to me and say something like 'Walter, you've seen a lot of conventions, what do you make of this?'" Joyce agreed to that.

WC: Actually, I thought it worked out pretty well. I think I had a lot more to say and things to report on than I had time to do on the air. But I suppose that's what all correspondents on television think at all times. I thought that Dan was gracious enough when we were on the air. A lot of people felt otherwise. They thought he seemed uncomfortable when I was invited to the desk to talk with him, but I didn't feel that way.

DC: Then, of course, in the 1984 election night coverage in November, Joyce says that Rather just absolutely cut you out of the broadcast.

WC: Yeah. I didn't do anything.

DC: And then at one of the conventions in 1988, when you were allowed to make some comments, Rather reached over and patted you on the hand and said, "So good to see you, Walter." How did you feel about that?

WC: It was all part of the act. I understood that. CBS was trying to bury the hatchet on the air and make us all one great wonderful team, that sort of thing. I think it's unfortunate that any person feels about another as I do about Dan. But to me, in his approach to me, some of which is based on known fact and some of which is purely my own suspicious nature, I guess, Dan just reeks of insincerity.

translated, ~~~~
awful. It was cut with a voice-over. Then we dashed back to
the airplane a few minutes late. As we drove up, the pilot was
calling out "Hurry up, hurry up. It's getting dark but we'll
go." We bounced off this field as it was getting dark, and we
were on the way. To get back to Warsaw he had to listen to a
~~~ station in Warsaw for navigation. Oh my God! He had a hell
~~~~ ~~ ~~~~ in Warsaw. When he finally did, the
~~~~ im it was hard to see anything,
~~~ g to Warsaw, the pilot said, "You
~~~'ve flown at night since 1944." Oh

I covered it, but not very well. I had lost my own
~eople, and I was depending on what was supplied me
~airo for spotters and so forth. I didn't have my own
~ The production team is terribly important in making
~ like that work well. You've ~~~~
~assign~~~

I went ~~~~ ~~~~ He was
~th me. ~~~~ ~ retina
~r. I wa~~~ ~he man,
~ a res~~~ ~ as to
~ a woma~~~ ~ying
~o appea~~~ ~ts.
I didn'~~~ ~. It
~isaster. ~~~~ ~e told
~levision ~~~~ ~cause h
~didn't w~~~ ~ion.
~ there w~~~
~ a very ~~~~

~e same tr~~~
~olidarity ~~~
~ty-fifth a~~~
~ in your ~~~~

~g airplan~~~
~e town in ~~~~ ~own to ~~~~ cal ~~~ and
~own was awful. We had a hell of a time finding ~~~~ ~omewhere to interview Walesa, to the
new
gs
~ was

C: In 1984 you also participated in the CBS special on the
~rtieth anniversary of D-Day, which was filmed in Europe.

CHAPTER TWENTY-SIX

The Post-Anchor Years

DC: You did get one very important news assignment after your retirement, and that was the funeral of Anwar Sadat in 1982.

WC: Yeah. I covered it, but not very well. I had lost my own team of people, and I was depending on what was supplied to me there in Cairo for spotters and so forth. I didn't have my own producer. The production team is terribly important in making something like that work well. You've got to mesh a dozen different assignments and jobs to put together a broadcast of that kind. I went out to Cairo on my own. I didn't have Bud Benjamin with me. I didn't have a writer with me. I didn't have a researcher. I was there just on my own, completely. So I had to depend on a researcher and on a spotter that the bureau found. I got a woman who's supposed to know all these women that were going to appear at the funeral. Well, that proved to be impossible. I didn't know anybody, and neither did my spotter. It was just a disaster. I was sitting there trying to describe this scene for television. I was at the burial with a monitor, but the monitor didn't work very well. It was a very bad broadcast. I don't think there were any reviews of it that faulted me, but I felt it was a very poor job.

DC: That's the same trip during which you traveled to Poland and interviewed Solidarity leader Lech Walesa and General Jaruzelski and did a twenty-fifth-anniversary show on the Hungarian revolt. What stands out in your memory about the Polish trip?

WC: A terrifying airplane trip. Bud Benjamin and I flew down to a tiny coal mine town in Silesia somewhere to interview Walesa, and the flight down was awful. We had a hell of a time finding an airplane to charter. They finally ended up chartering us a plane that belonged to an aerial sport club in Warsaw, with a pilot that they got from some-

---

Cronkite, a devoted sailor, aboard his beloved Wyntje, *undated (DI_05804).*

where who had been a pilot with the Free Poles in London during the war. When we flew down there, the weather was just frightful. My God, it was scary, being in this little, tiny single-engine plane. This pilot was a very nice fellow, and he spoke very good English. I liked him immensely, but in flying down there, he had no instruments, no damn two-way radio, nothing. We flew exactly like they flew barnstorms in the United States in the twenties, by flying low, getting down through the clouds, and following the railroad track, and then getting the identity of the town by flying so low I could read the name of the town off the railroad station platform. The weather was clearing up, thank God, by the time we got down there. We landed on a grass strip on the side of a hill. The pilot said that we had to leave by sundown. Well, Walesa was late, and the interview went longer than planned. By the way, Walesa and his whole retinue reminded me of Bobby Kennedy's 1968 campaign, with the young people surrounding him. He was constantly taking advice from them, conferring with them, deciding one thing one minute and then something the next. There seemed to be nobody in charge—it was a chaotic business. And they all adored him. It was a damn good interview; I'm very proud of it. Unfortunately, it had to be translated, which ruined it, really, because those things are awful. It was cut with a voice-over. Then we dashed back to the airplane a few minutes late. As we drove up, the pilot was calling out, "Hurry up, hurry up. It's getting dark, but we'll go." We bounced off this field as it was getting dark, and we were on the way. To get back to Warsaw, he had to listen to a radio station in Warsaw for navigation. Oh, my God! He had a hell of a time finding that airport in Warsaw. When he finally did, the lights at the airport were so dim it was hard to see anything, but we landed. As we were flying to Warsaw, the pilot said, "You know, this is the first time I've flown at night since 1944." Oh, boy.

DC: What about your interview with General Jaruzelski, who at that time was the president of communist Poland?

WC: I tell you, Jaruzelski was an insidious-looking man. He was unsmiling and wore dark glasses all the time because of a retina problem caused by snow blindness. There is no humor in the man, apparently. But I was rather impressed with his arguments as to why he had to stay in power. He stressed that he was staying in power but that he was listening to Walesa's complaints. Nevertheless, he said that Walesa couldn't come to power. It wouldn't work because the Russians wouldn't permit it. He told me that he was keeping a heavy hand on civil affairs because he wanted to protect Poland from a Soviet military occupation. At the time, I was skeptical, but rather impressed with his explanation. As things worked out, I believe that Jaruzelski did keep the Russians at bay. I believe that he kept the Soviets from invading when Solidarity went on strike. I think he prevented a bloodletting and that he was a real hero.

WALTER CRONKITE'S UNIVERSE

DC: Walter, let's talk a little bit about your *Universe* progam. What did you try to do with that program? What was its focus?

WC: The basic idea was to take subjects that could have a strong impact on our world, but were not getting attention from the evening news or the daily newspapers. The environment was a major area we were interested in—also, scientific exploration and the cutting edge of science. We also were interested in human rights. We were really aiming at not only exposing dangers to our existence, but also solutions. I wanted to emphasize solutions as much as possible. The format of the show was that I would do one rather exciting exploration of some kind, or story of some kind, each week on *Universe*, and then we had a couple of other reporters who worked on *Universe*, and they would do one or so, but not the lead story. We would put these stories together in a single package. I would be host as well as do the lead story. I went to Mount McKinley and did an interesting couple of stories there. I did one on the use of lasers in geographical surveys. I did an 8,700-foot dive off of Baja California to the faults and fissures in the ocean bottom, where we are finding new forms of life. It possibly proves that everything on earth isn't the result of photosynthesis, but actually some living things are chemosynthetic. Oh, I did the story of the gal who was trying to reintroduce chimpanzees to the wild. Bud Benjamin was my producer.

DC: In 1984, you also participated in the CBS special on the fortieth anniversary of D-Day, which was filmed in Europe.

WC: Yes, we taped in London before we went over to the fortieth anniversary of D-Day. It was a roundtable with all of the old CBS correspondents.

DC: Rather anchored that roundtable program. William Shirer says in his book that during the program, he noticed, quote, "some friction between Dan and Walter, who may have wanted to anchor the program himself. Dan started the broadcast with a question to Walter, who sat at his right, and Walter promptly put him down. 'Well,' he said, in his richly avuncular fashion, 'I think, Dan, I would put the question a little different.' Which he then proceeded to do." [*Cronkite chuckles*] Is that an accurate characterization?

WC: Oh, yeah. Shirer's accurate. It was ridiculous to have Dan on that program. I was very much offended, and so were nearly all of the other correspondents. Why the hell bring in this young man when you had all that talent who had been there, for God's sake? Charles Collingwood, Winston Burdett, Dick Hottelet, and Eric Sevareid, the whole war correspondent crowd was there. Rather simply didn't belong there. But I didn't mean to put him down on the air. That was not my intention, although it sort of sounded like that. I realized it did afterward. He phrased the question rather awkwardly. I forget what it was, but, you know, there was an assumption in the question that was ill founded.

THE CBS BOARD OF DIRECTORS

DC: You recently [1991] left the board at CBS after a stockholders' meeting in the middle of May. Why?

WC: I'd been on there ten years. Actually, they decided two years ago that they ought to relieve the board of the seventy-year-olds. There were three of us who were more than seventy. They took the oldest the first year, which was former secretary of the air force Roswell Gilpatric. He was eighty, but still a terribly vital man. And then this was my year. Next year, Marietta Tree will leave. I wonder who promulgated that? And my guess is that it was Laurence Tisch's idea. He got rid of two of his most severe critics, who were old Paley people. And Gilpatric wasn't too solid a Tisch supporter either.

DC: Was real business done on the CBS board, or was everything decided before the meetings?

WC: The board did real business all right, but it was financial business. What I found disappointing was the board did not discuss program policy at all. And the rare occasion when we would take up programming, it was only to see pilots of the next year's product. The board would sit and grimace and laugh and then turn back to finance and not do anything. Newton Minow and I both thought that the board ought not to discuss programming per program, but should discuss philosophy, such things as children's programming, violence in programming, sex in programming, and things of this kind. That was part of our business to do so. But we got nowhere. The board was not interested in doing that kind of thing, even on the news programming. Now, this is a very fine line, you understand. It would be a terrible thing, I think, if the board tried to second-guess every program. It'd be a sinful thing if it tried to second-guess the news department. I didn't want to get into that area. If you got into an entertainment philosophy, then you might find yourself getting into news philosophy, and that would be dangerous also.

DC: Ed Joyce, in his book, claims that you criticized Dan Rather and CBS News during some board meetings.

WC: Yes, I did, but I didn't get anywhere with it. I got a lot of nods of agreement in my years on the board, but then no action. I thought that maybe just airing these things in front of the board would cause the management to do so something about it. As far as I know, it had no effect.

DC: Was Paley playing much of a role in those days? This would be between 1981 and 1991.

WC: In the early days of my membership on the board, he was quite active. He would listen and ask questions and indicate his approval. He shared my position on most of these things, but then nothing ever got done.

DC: Joyce says that you were especially critical of the decision by CBS News to do fewer stand-ups from Washington.

WC: Ed Joyce was definitely against Washington news. He had a philosophy of "let's go out to where the people are and not worry about Washington and these inside-the-Beltway discussion things." That is not a bad idea, but you've got to balance that with the Washington news. We never did Washington news properly, really. We never got a cycle ahead on Washington news. We never got into reporting to the people legislation that was beginning the process through Congress, which is when those matters should have been brought up, at the time when the people could still mobilize against it or for it. We only began to pay attention when it was passed. By then, it was too late. For ten years, I worked on getting ahead of this cycle. The correspondents protested and said, "My God, all these bills that are introduced are not going to go anywhere." I said, "Well, you know the ones that are going to go somewhere. Come on. You know who's behind a bill, who the signatories are, and you know what committees it's being sent to." It just took a lot more work to do it, that's all. But I never got it done.

DC: In April 1985, Ted Turner tried to take over CBS. What was your response?

WC: Oh, I was dead set against it because Turner proposed to finance the takeover with junk bonds and then sell off everything in the company but the broadcasting operation. He would dismember the company. So all of us objected to that, and we finally found a way out of it by buying back several billion dollars worth of stock.

DC: When Turner made his bid, you were quoted in the *New York Times* as saying that you could not prejudge what Turner might do at CBS. You said, quote: "It might be very much like becoming president of the United States. Maybe the office makes the man. He has proved flexible in the past." I've got in my notes that your quote apparently angered CBS president Thomas Wyman, and he called you to complain.

WC: I remember that Wyman was upset about it, but I think by the time he got to me, he'd cooled down quite a bit. I think Wyman asked me on the phone, "Does this mean you're supporting Turner?" I said, "No, it doesn't mean I'm supporting Turner." He said, "Well, I think we ought to get our ducks in a row," or something like that. He wanted to present a solid front.

DC: In November 1985, the CBS board had its first meeting with Laurence Tisch as a member. He had just purchased 12 percent of the stock. According to several sources, Bill Paley and Tom Wyman were already at odds by then, but that Paley's only supporters on the board were you and Marietta Tree. One source claims at that board meeting you made a sweeping criticism of the state of things at CBS News, including Van Sauter's management of the *Evening News*. One source claims, quote: "Some members of the board viewed Cronkite's opinions as sour grapes. Nonetheless, the barrage was beautifully timed that morning to coincide with Tisch's arrival." Tom Wyman is alleged to have angrily protested your remarks. Is that version correct?

WC: It's approximately the way it happened. My relationship with Wyman had been a very tenuous kind of thing anyway. Early on in my service on the board, Wyman had, at one point, said, "We have finished all the other business. It's time for the directors to bring up anything they'd like to bring up." So I made the charge that the *Evening News* had gone soft under Van Sauter. I said, "This is not a way that we should discharge our responsibilities as broadcasters." I made my little speech about that. Wyman was sinking down in his chair, glaring at me and thumbing his pencil. He came out of his chair like a tiger and said, "In all my experience in business, I have never been charged with being irresponsible." He'd taken my comments personally. I hadn't meant it to be personal to Wyman at all in any way. I had nothing against him. In fact, I rather like Wyman. [*Wyman died in January 2003.*] The board, I think, also was somewhat shocked by my comments. But Wyman just launched this diatribe. That set the pattern for the future of my relationship with Wyman on all news matters.

At the next few board meetings, Wyman would bristle as soon as I began to speak. I appealed to Wyman on many occasions to get rid of Van Sauter and address the problems with the news division by getting some newspeople in there. It did no good. Wyman got in trouble with the board at the time we were trying to defend against Ted Turner and others who wanted to take us over. One of the more serious matters was that he suddenly revealed to the board that he had talked to Coca-Cola about selling the company to them. Well, I was indignant, as several other members of the board appeared to be, over the fact that he would have such conversations without conferring with the board first. That led to a kind of ad hoc board meeting to discuss Wyman's fate. At that point, I said that he probably should go because of his failure to confide in us about the Coca-Cola talks, but beyond that, he had let the prize possession of CBS Inc., the news division, go soft. I was right, as I look back ten years later. It was the beginning of the end of CBS's leadership in the news business. So I put in my two cents' worth, saying that was enough to convince me that he ought to be bounced from the chairmanship. Now I must say, I later learned that several members of the board were aware of the Coca-Cola deal. He had talked to them. Those people did not open their mouths at the time that it came up to the board, and let Wyman hang there and swing in the wind.

DC: Was the decision to get rid of Wyman made at that ad hoc meeting in September 1986?

WC: We decided pretty much that Wyman had to go.

DC: According to my sources, at the next board meeting, Paley and Tisch left the room, to allow the other board members to make a decision about Wyman. After several hours of discussion, Wyman resigned, and the rest of the meeting was devoted to handing over temporary control to the new team of Tisch and Paley.

WC: That's right.

THE PERSIAN GULF WAR

DC: Walter, I saw you on the air with Dan Rather the night the United States began bombing Baghdad last January [1991].

WC: It was interesting. Tom Johnson, the head of CNN, called me and said Pete Williams, the Pentagon press spokesman, and the White House itself had sent word that CNN ought to get its people out of Baghdad. Tom said he understood that all the news organizations had received this call. He asked my advice, as Tom does on occasion. He does that with a lot of people. He's that kind of an executive. And he said, "What should I do in this situation?" I said, "Well, I don't believe in doing anything that authority asks you to do in a circumstance like this. My inclination is if the government says get out, you should stay. That's just because I don't believe them on these things." I was very skeptical and cynical about it. But I said, "On the other hand, you've got to think about your people, and I suppose the thing you'd probably do is ask them to do what they want to do. Let them volunteer to stay or not to stay. Give them all the facts." Just at that moment, Tom said, "Please hold for a minute," and he took a message. When he came back on the line, he said, "Listen, Walter. They just told me that Baghdad's on the phone right now. Would you talk to Bernard Shaw and Peter Arnett? They're there right now. Would you have a word with them on our air." I said "Sure. Put them on."

So I had this little talk with Bernie and Peter. Well, now, that got a lot of people obviously kind of excited about this whole thing. It wasn't very long after that I got a call directly from Dan Rather, saying it looked like the balloons are going up this evening, and "I can't do this without you. [*Cronkite laughs*] I want you in here. Can you come in?" Very shortly after that, I got a call from the news director at CBS, who confirmed that they wanted me to come in and do what I could. So I did. I was delighted to go in. I was feeling terrible about being out of the mix and not having any of the briefing material at my disposal and all that. I really wanted to get where I could see the news wires and hear the reports. I was invited to take a position at the anchor desk to Dan's right, and there were three positions around the anchor desk for interviews and people to come in and do things. So I took this position, and eventually Dan turned to me, and I went on the air with a little piece, answering his questions and kind of throwing in some comments of my own from observations. And then I stayed there.

Dan seemed a little uneasy, and a little bit later he did throw it to me again. I think I suggested to him that I had something I'd like to say. He let me say it, eventually coming to me for it. And then he disappeared. We went to a commercial or something, and he left. Well, that's perfectly reasonable to go to the bathroom, for God's sake. But immediately after he came back to the desk, the news director came up and said, "Walter, would you mind stepping down now? We want to put Ed Bradley up here for a while." So Ed Bradley sat there for a couple of hours and never said a damn thing. They finally put him on for something. It was really an excuse to get me out of there. I sat around in the studio, but off camera, until one o'clock in the morning or so. At that point, they invited me back to do another piece. I did that, and I did one more, and then I left. The news director asked if I could come back at about five o'clock the next evening. I said, "Fine, five o'clock tomorrow I'll be in." Well, I finally got on the air at 10:40 in the evening, I think. And then they brought Ed Bradley back, and they got me off the desk a second night. I blew my top and said, "Come on. You know you don't really want me here. If you really need me some time, I'll be home. You can give me a call." The producer begged me to stay, so I went back and did a spot at 1:00 or 1:30 in the morning, and then I went home and waited, and they never called me again.

DC: What do you think about the way the military handled the press coverage of the Persian Gulf War?

WC: I think it was ghastly—totally undemocratic, totally unnecessary. There's no more delicate relationship between a government and its people than the commitment of those people to war and the performance in that war. In furthering that policy, it's absolutely essential that the people be fully informed. We sent our boys, and now our girls, into war. We darn well need to know what our troops are doing in our name. I made an analogy to Nazi Germany in a *Newsweek* piece and in my congressional testimony. When we uncovered the concentration camps, we saw German citizens shed copious tears and plead that they had no knowledge whatsoever about what was going on in those camps. They pleaded that the German people were innocent of that. It was Hitler's fault, and so forth. Well, I think it's possible that a great number of them were innocent of knowing what was happening in the camps. But they became responsible the minute they applauded, as most of them did, Hitler's clamping down on a free press and on free speech. When Hitler did that, they said, "We don't want to know. Go ahead." That should be a warning not to let government go out and do anything in your name without your knowing full well what it's doing.

So we should be, as a people, terribly indignant about what the Pentagon and the White House did to us in the Gulf War. What they did was send fifty thousand of our people and fifty thousand more of friendly nations' people into a war in which they deliberately excluded the press. They set ground rules that created pools and had the temerity to say, "Well, you guys all signed off on pools." The government knew that was a flat-out distortion. The pools were inadequate and did not cover the entire battlefront. They were too limited in size. Having said all that, I also will say, with tongue in cheek, that I applauded the military letting television cameras into the press briefings, thus exposing the ignorance of most of the press. I really mean that. I think that may have been deliberate. The military knew inexperienced war reporters would ask most of the questions. And then when that was shown to the public, the public was going to say, "Well, those people are stupid. We certainly shouldn't let them go to the front if they're that dumb."

The reason I think that there's something diabolical about that is that the briefing is actually the one thing I would not let be public. The briefing ought to be so frank with the reportorial corps covering the war that you would want to censor what those military officers said to them. They should not have any compulsion about telling just exactly what has happened. That said, you really can't permit free use of live television cameras at the front. The television companies, most of them, fight for live television coverage from the front. I don't think there's any way that can be permitted. If you've got a live camera in front of you, I don't know how you're going to control what that camera's going to see. There's almost no way, even if you have a military monitor there saying, "You can only point this to the left of our lines; you can't point it to the right." There are going to be occasions where you accidentally swing to the right or something, like the accidental pictures of a rape victim in Florida that occurred recently. Even at the very best of circumstances, the mere fact that the enemy can sit a mile behind the lines and watch CNN broadcast the approach of the Allied soldiers on the front should be an obvious security violation.

So I maintain that we actually *should* have a system of censorship. I wouldn't get worried about that word. The Pentagon is so concerned over using the word "censorship" that they call it a security review. Come on now, that's censorship. Let's call it censorship and not be worried about the word. We should have censorship; it worked in World War II perfectly well. You recruit a corps of good censors, and you have a review procedure, and you have an appeals procedure. You set it up so that it's about as rapid as any editorial process could be for a newspaper or a television network. Then you let the reporters go anywhere they want to go on the front. There should be certain restrictions on certain highly classified operations, but those should be very, very rare circumstances. The rest of the time, the camera should be there and record our history. Even if it has to be delayed weeks in getting out, or months or years, record it. We ought to have a right to see it eventually. I know you as a historian feel that particularly keenly. We don't have a full history of this Persian Gulf War, and we don't have a full history of Grenada. We don't really have a history, up close, of Panama. The military pictures, such as they might have been, are one-sided. They were taken by the military, for the military.

DC: David Hume Kennerly [*Pulitzer Prize–winning UPI photojournalist and former White House photographer*] told me the other day that the situation for news coverage in Vietnam was completely different than the one we have today. He pointed out that there were much fewer correspondents in the field covering that war. In Vietnam, there was this small band of newspeople, and the logistics weren't that difficult. He argued that the much larger number of people who now want to cover the action causes legitimate problems for the military.

WC: I hear that from some of my colleagues. That's the elitism showing through from the old-time war correspondents, which is justified. It's protecting standards, if you please. I think the Pentagon uses that as a subterfuge. David is using it for vastly other reasons. It's a hell of a lot easier if you get rid of all those little guys and do it on your own out there. For one thing, it's nice to have the war to yourself and be able to do an exclusive without competition. But that's no big deal. It's going to be a constant source of minor annoyance for the Pentagon people to have to handle it, and among the press itself because selections have to be made for pools. And there's no question about it, there have to be pools. It sounds like I'm contradicting myself when I say that there have to be pools. There have to be some pools at some places where you cannot get everybody to the scene because they can't get there on their own. In that, of course, you have to have pools. Freedom of the press doesn't mean that everybody who has a camera or a pencil and paper is entitled to be present for every event.

DC: But that's a very appealing argument to the public, to have an army general complain that all of those correspondents running around are putting his people in danger.

WC: That doesn't hold up. They say there were five hundred or so correspondents in Saudia Arabia. You can't tell me that it's so damn difficult to put one on a destroyer. One extra person on a destroyer isn't going to be critical. You can put two news correspondents on a cruiser, four or five on an aircraft carrier, every tank battalion can have one or two. That's not going to burden their logistical supply. You could darn near take care of five hundred people that way, and if you can't, that's too bad, but you still are sure that everything is covered. In World War II, very frequently, everybody couldn't go up to the one place where action was, simply because to get up there was dangerous. Not that the military would keep you from going, but the number of guys who were going to want to go out in the cold and face the danger of the point group that was trying to get into that little town was pretty damn limited. Now they all say they want to go, but you'll find out when the day comes that probably there are going to be six or seven really gung-ho guys who are going to get in the jeeps and go out there. But when you've got the war in its earliest stages, some pooling would probably be necessary, but it's got to be considered only a temporary measure, and it's got to be fair, and it's got to cover all areas of activity.

DC: John Corry, formerly with the *New York Times* and now on the faculty at Boston University, did op-ed pieces during the Persian Gulf War, saying essentially that the

American press should be cheerleaders for the American military. He may not have used the word "cheerleaders," but that was his meaning. And he's also been very critical of the press, particularly the television correspondents at CNN, who kept saying that they were neutral in the Gulf War.

WC: I think if the press can maintain neutrality and objectivity in wartime, that's where they ought to be—not only in wartime, but at all other times as well. The most patriotic thing the press can do is to remain neutral. If it joins in the cheerleading, it ceases to function in the fashion that the press is supposed to function in a democracy, and in ceasing to function, it actually becomes unpatriotic. The patriotic thing to do is to remain the source of free, unbiased information. It's a difficult role, though. I think that's very difficult to do when you're in a war situation, particularly if you're a correspondent with the troops. However, things should be quite different on the home front. I think that we've got to understand where neutrality begins and ends in a military conflict. You can't be neutral when you're up in the battle with the forces; that's not the place to be neutral. The place to be neutral and skeptical is back on the analytical home front. That's where it's necessary to question policy, tactics, strategy, morale, the health of the troops, and casualty figures. Those things ought to be put under the journalistic magnifying glass.

DC: Was the press skeptical in World War II?

WC: Truthfully, there wasn't a lot of skepticism, because the reasons for World War II seemed obvious to all of us. It was very clear that the risk was there. The Axis was an aggressive military machine that had already captured most of the free world; it was pretty clear what was at stake. We haven't had anything like that clarity in the last three encounters since then, except that Korea was an obvious case of aggression. It is true that in World War II, censorship did prevent some aspects of the story from being played up, at least at home. In the first couple of years, there was a ban against bodies being shown. That was lifted, I think, in 1943. I don't recall. I wasn't on the home front. But I think the public in World War II got a little more concerned about censorship because the war went on long enough for them to know there were unfortunate things happening. People began to ask questions: "Wasn't anyone killed in this battle?" The military itself, you see, realized that they had to tell us stories of heroism. They wanted to get the hero stories out, and you can't tell the hero stories without having some blood involved. So it got trapped by its own needs, in a sense. At any rate, there were restrictions that kept the home front from being informed.

DC: CNN portrays itself as a worldwide news service, and it argues that it therefore cannot afford to appear to be a voice of the United States. That caused much controversy here in this country during the Gulf War.

WC: Well, I think CNN is perfectly right, and they are a world news service. You know, this whole concept of an unpatriotic press in wartime is one that bothers me a very great deal. I think it's used by demagogues to create an entirely false impression of what a free press should be in a democratic nation. Every government, I suppose, would like to wrap itself in the flag and say, "To criticize us is to be unpatriotic." But that's the way of dictatorship. That's not democracy.

another fifteen years after we completed the formal
conversations upon which his autobiography and this book are
based. During that decade and a half, he was one of the most
active and energetic "senior citizens" in America. When he
wasn't sailing in his beloved Wyntjie in waters off Martha's
Vineyard . . .   ummer and in the British Virgin Islands in
                                    arly spring, he was busy making speeches,
                                    s, giving interviews, meeting with
                                    n active social life in Manhattan. He
experienced a media revolution since Walter and   meetings with students at the University
ersations in the early 1990s. At that point, the   h established the Walter Cronkite
iness seemed reasonably healthy. CNN was the only   cation, and at Arizona State University,
our television news service. The evening news   . Journalism and M   ion
BS, ABC, and NBC still dominated broadcast news.

serious   these
y, he w   ly
m, and   or
uld you
rogram?

t's dest
And he w
ich did
Although
, the In
nose disc
he intrus
, that we
e an inter

ronkite se
ethical s
his repu
conversations reveal, that didn't mean Walter was an
uncaring conduit for straight news delivery. He had
opinions of his own and was a thoughtful interpreter and
of political and cultural developments and events. As

                                                                                                   or
                                                                                                   ss

                                        on "permanent   made
                    y that can meet strict
        ity requirements. Walter designated the
ter as the agency to serve as the steward for "his"
Don rock. University of Texas President Bill Powers accepted

Epilogue

W ALTER AND I HAD NO FINAL, contemplative, "what was it all about" discussion. That wasn't Walter Cronkite's style, anyway. He lived another fifteen years after we completed the formal conversations upon which his autobiography and this book are based. During that decade and a half, he was one of the most active and energetic senior citizens in America. When he wasn't sailing in his beloved *Wyntje* in the waters off Martha's Vineyard during the summer and in the British Virgin Islands in the late winter and early spring, he was busy making speeches, narrating documentaries, giving interviews, meeting with students, and leading an active social life in Manhattan. He especially enjoyed his meetings with students at the University of Texas at Austin, which established the Walter Cronkite Regents Chair in Communication, and at Arizona State University, which named its School of Journalism and Mass Communication after Walter.

Despite his problematic relationship with CBS News during these years, Walter didn't disappear from the media. He frequently appeared for interviews on CNN and was a regular contributor to programs on PBS and NPR. He hosted and narrated special documentaries for cable networks, including the Discovery Channel, the History Channel, and the Arts and Entertainment Network. He was thrilled to serve as the anchor for CNN's coverage of his old friend John Glenn's historic return to space in the launch of the space shuttle *Discovery* in 1998. In 2005 and 2006, he wrote opinion columns for a national newspaper syndicate. He even played on Broadway as the voice of the book in the 1995 revival of *How to Succeed in Business Without Really Trying.* In 2002, he became known to an entirely new generation of children as the voice of Benjamin Franklin in the educational-television cartoon program *Liberty's Kids.* And in 2006, seeking to restore its link with Walter Cronkite's legacy, CBS News invited him to record the opening introduction to the *Evening News* broadcast, newly

---

University of Texas president William Powers accepting the moon rock that NASA gave Cronkite, 2006.

anchored by Katie Couric. Walter was delighted to accept the invitation. His distinctive voice opened the nightly broadcast until six months after his death.

The world has experienced a media revolution since Walter and I had our conversations in the early 1990s. At that point, the newspaper business seemed reasonably healthy. CNN was the only twenty-four-hour television news service. The evening news programs of CBS, ABC, and NBC still dominated broadcast news. Although the serious decline of the newspaper business troubled Walter deeply, he was not trapped in the past. The Internet intrigued him, and he was fascinated with its possibilities. What else would you expect from a man who was enthralled by the space program? Walter was greatly troubled, however, by the Internet's destructive impact on journalistic ethics and standards. And he was appalled by Rupert Murdoch's Fox News Channel, which did not exist until two years after we completed our work. Although we later had long discussions about the media revolution, the Internet, Fox News, and related developments and events, those discussions were casual chats between good friends without the intrusive presence of a tape recorder. I wish now, of course, that we had recorded those discussions. They would have made an interesting and informative addition to this book.

Walter Cronkite set the modern gold standard for objectivity and high ethical standards in journalism, and he was deservedly proud of his reputation as the most trusted man in America. But as our conversations reveal, that didn't mean Walter was an empty and uncaring conduit for straight news delivery. He had strong opinions of his own and was a thoughtful interpreter and analyst of political and cultural developments and events. As we discussed earlier in this book, Walter had given commentary on issues and events on his daily CBS radio program in the 1960s and 1970s, but it really took Walter's departure from the *Evening News* to give him the total freedom to make his personal views more widely known. He was a strong advocate for the United Nations and the concept of world order and justice, and he openly supported policy initiatives ranging from political campaign finance reform to national health insurance. He criticized right-wing television evangelists Pat Robertson and Jerry Falwell, declared that the war on drugs was a disastrous mistake, and opposed the U.S. invasion of Iraq.

At the height of the impeachment travail of President Bill Clinton in 1998, Walter and Betsy invited the Clintons to go sailing with them at Martha's Vineyard. Walter made certain that his sailboat took a very public slow pass by the docks of Edgartown in broad daylight, in full view of the White House press corps and television news crews. As President Clinton later joked, that was a time when he really needed to be photographed beside the most trusted man in America. After Walter's wife and partner of nearly sixty-five years died in March 2005, Senator Hillary Clinton delivered the eulogy at Betsy's funeral at Saint Bartholomew's Church in Manhattan.

From a personal perspective, I was delighted and honored that Walter continued over the years to be involved with the University of Texas at Austin and its Dolph Briscoe Center. Among his contributions was his service as the university's official voice for its "We're Texas" capital campaign and other public service announcements. Walter actively helped the Briscoe Center with its public programs and acquisition of media history collections. In 2006, NASA honored Walter with its prestigious Ambassador of Exploration Award, which included an actual moon rock or "lunar sample." By law, moon rocks remain the property of the federal government, so they can only be on "permanent loan" to a designated public agency that can meet strict preservation and security requirements. Walter designated the Briscoe Center as the agency to serve as the steward for "his" moon rock. University of Texas President Bill Powers accepted the moon rock from Walter in a memorable public ceremony at the university on February 28, 2006. It was Walter's final visit to the UT campus.

After Walter died on July 17, 2009, former president Clinton delivered a heartfelt and eloquent eulogy at CBS's official tribute to Walter at New York's Lincoln Center on September 9, 2009. President Barack Obama and former astronaut Buzz Aldrin also gave thoughtful eulogies in celebration of Walter's life. Attended by a virtual *Who's Who* of the news industry, the program also featured musical tributes from Wynton Marsalis, Mickey Hart, and Jimmy Buffett, all friends of Walter's.

Walter's will designated the Briscoe Center as the permanent home for the papers, books, and artifacts documenting his life and career. Although he transferred most of his professional papers to the Center back in 1989, his personal papers, along with many books and artifacts stored in his apartment in New York and at his place on Martha's Vineyard, joined the rest of his collection at the Center after his death.

In May 2010, the Briscoe Center opened a major exhibition at the Lyndon B. Johnson Presidential Library and Museum of Walter's papers and artifacts. I was deeply satisfied by the enthusiastic and warm popular reaction to our exhibit and by the opportunity that it provided us to share with the public some of the key documents and items illustrating Walter's life and legacy. For many generations to come, Walter's archive will be a priceless resource for scholarly research and teaching and for public appreciation of the significant contributions that Walter made to his profession and to the general public good.

Acknowledgments

I AM GRATEFUL TO A NUMBER OF PEOPLE who have helped me with this project, beginning with my original work in the early 1990s. The University of Texas at Austin granted me the time to conduct the original interviews as part of our project to establish the university's Walter Cronkite Collection and to document his legacy. The late Robert Jeffrey, dean of the university's College of Communication, and the late Mike Quinn, associate dean of the college, introduced me to Walter Cronkite in the late 1980s. My staff at the Center during that period, especially Kate Adams and Alison Beck, assumed additional administrative work while I was working with Walter on the original project. My sincere thanks to them both. For the recent *Conversations with Cronkite* phase of my work, Briscoe Center administrators Ramona Kelly, Brenda Gunn, Echo Uribe, Alison Beck, and Erin Purdy have been helpful in numerous ways, and I am deeply grateful to all. Independent researcher Diana Claitor helped find photographs, and Hal Richardson scanned them. Dr. Holly Taylor, who heads the Briscoe Center's publication program, has done a terrific job as my editor. The book's designer, Derek George, also did a great job, as did proofreader Kip Keller. The University of Texas Press is the distributor of *Conversations with Cronkite*. I appreciate the work they have invested in this project, especially Dave Hamrick, associate director of the press. I am indebted to CBS's Morley Safer, one of the most outstanding broadcast journalists of his generation, for his thoughtful foreword.

My partner of thirty-six years, Suzanne, has had a husband missing in action for about two months. I'll make it up, I promise.

As he has done so many times in the past, former Texas governor Dolph Briscoe has stepped forward to help me with this project. It was Dolph Briscoe's generosity that made it possible for *Conversations with Cronkite* to be published. There is truly no adequate way that I can express my thanks to him for all that he has done for me and for the Center.

And of course, I am especially grateful to Walter Cronkite, my dear friend, who paid me the highest compliment of my life by inviting me to work with him on such an intimate and personally significant project.

All proceeds earned from the sale of *Conversations with Cronkite* are dedicated to the support of the Briscoe Center's Walter Cronkite Papers and its News Media History Archive. Because of Walter's generous gift of his papers and his active involvement and support, the Briscoe Center's News Media History Archive is considered one of the nation's most important archives on the history of television and newspaper journalism.

DON CARLETON

Additional Sources

THE WALTER CRONKITE PAPERS

The Walter Cronkite Papers, measuring more than 300 linear feet, include research files, audio and video recordings, and clippings on news events of the 1960s and 1970s, with a special emphasis on space exploration and politics; mail from viewers, representing opinions about current events from the 1950s to the 1980s; personal correspondence with well-known figures, many in the news business; television and radio production materials from CBS programs such as *You Are There*, *The Twentieth Century*, *Eyewitness to History*, and *CBS Reports*; and Walter's files on his public appearances, narrations, speeches, business interests, awards, and personal life, especially his boats, travel, and organizations with which Walter was associated. Other materials include scripts and outlines, memos, and source materials for documentary productions by the Cronkite Ward Company and Cronkite Productions, Inc. The Cronkite Papers also include a large number of photographs that document Walter's early life and his reportage from World War II and Vietnam, as well as his interviews with U.S. presidents from Harry Truman to Ronald Reagan. The Cronkite Papers are available for research at the Briscoe Center for American History, the University of Texas at Austin (www.cah.utexas.edu).

ARCHIVE OF AMERICAN TELEVISION INTERVIEW

In 1998 and 1999, I conducted a total of four and a half hours of videotaped interviews with Walter for the Archive of American Television project, sponsored by the Academy of Television Arts and Sciences Foundation and produced by Michael Rosen. Those interviews covered many of the topics Walter and I discussed during our conversations a few years earlier.

The foundation recently placed those interviews on its Web site: http://www.emmytvlegends .org/interviews/people/walter-cronkite.

WORKS MENTIONED

Ambrose, Stephen. *Eisenhower: Soldier and President*. Simon & Schuster, 1991.

Caro, Robert. *The Years of Lyndon Johnson: The Path to Power*. Knopf, 1982.

———. *The Years of Lyndon Johnson: Means of Ascent*. Knopf, 1990.

Ehrlichman, John. *Witness to Power: The Nixon Years*. Simon & Schuster, 1982.

Friendly, Fred. *Due to Circumstances beyond Our Control*. Three Rivers Press, 1999.

Gates, Gary Paul. *Air Time: The Inside Story of CBS News*. HarperCollins, 1978.

Goldenson, Leonard, with Marvin J. Wolf. *Beating the Odds: The Untold Story behind the Rise of ABC*. Scribner, 1991.

Halberstam, David. *The Powers That Be*. Knopf, 1979.

Joyce, Ed. *Prime Times, Bad Times*. Anchor, 1989.

Leonard, Bill. *In the Storm of the Eye: A Lifetime at CBS*. G. P. Putnam's Sons, 1987.

Matusow, Barbara. *The Evening Stars: The Making of the Network News Anchor*. Houghton Mifflin, 1983.

Mayer, Martin. *Making News*. Doubleday, 1987.

McCabe, Peter. *Bad News at Black Rock: The Sell-out of CBS News*. Arbor House, 1987.

Metz, Robert. *CBS: Reflections in a Bloodshot Eye*. Signet, 1976.

Midgley, Leslie. *How Many Words Do You Want? An Insider's Story of Print and Television Journalism*. Birch Lane Press, 1989.

Safer, Morley. *Flashbacks: On Returning to Vietnam*. Random House, 1990.

Salinger, Pierre. *With Kennedy*. Doubleday, 1966.

Smith, Sally Bedell. *In All His Glory: The Life of William S. Paley; The Legendary Tycoon and His Brilliant Circle*. Simon & Schuster, 1990.

Sperber, A. M. *Murrow: His Life and Times*. Freudlich Books, 1986.

White, Theodore. *America in Search of Itself: The Making of the President, 1956–1980*. Harper & Row, 1982.

Wolfe, Tom. *The Right Stuff*. Farrar, Straus and Giroux, 1979.

Index